1/92

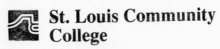

LINCOLN
DOUGLAS
and
SLAVERY

LINCOLN DOUGLAS

and

SLAVERY

In the Crucible of
Public Debate

DAVID ZAREFSKY

The University of Chicago Press
Chicago and London

David Zarefsky is dean of the School of Speech and professor of
communication studies, Northwestern University.

The University of Chicago Press, Chicago 60637
The University of Chicago Press, Ltd., London
© 1990 by The University of Chicago
All rights reserved. Published 1990
Printed in the United States of America
99 98 97 96 95 94 93 92 91 90   5 4 3 2 1

Library of Congress Cataloging-in-Publication Data

Zarefsky, David.
    Lincoln, Douglas, and slavery : in the crucible of public debate /
David Zarefsky.
        p.   cm.
    Includes bibliographical references.
    ISBN 0-226-97875-3 (alk. paper)
        1. Lincoln-Douglas debates, 1858.   2. Rhetoric—Political
aspects—United States—History—19th century.   I. Title
    E457.4.Z29   1990
    973.6′8′0922—dc20   90-30121
                                                                CIP

⊗ The paper used in this publication meets the minimum requirements of the American National Standard for Information Sciences—
Permanence of Paper for Printed Library Materials, ANSI Z39.48–1984.

For my son
MARC PHILIP ZAREFSKY

and the memory of my father
JOSEPH LEON ZAREFSKY

Contents

Preface

In the years since 1976, campaign debates have again become a regular feature of American politics. Not just in the general election campaign, but during the primary season as well, candidates for national office are expected to appear together on the same platform to discuss the issues of the day. The expectation that debates will be held has trickled down from national elections to state and local contests too, and it has been extended from two-person races to fields of multiple candidates. To refuse to debate is widely regarded as a sign of weakness; disputes turn on the number, format, and sponsorship of debates, but not about the basic question of whether debates are a good thing for the political system.

With predictable regularity, candidates and their advisers bemoan a decline in the quality of public debate and issue challenges to restore the level of the discussion to that of the Lincoln-Douglas debates. The seven encounters between Abraham Lincoln and Stephen A. Douglas in the summer and fall of 1858 have receded into folklore, into what Norman Corwin described as "a shadowy zone in the back of the head where one files away miscellaneous impressions based on knowledge, half-knowledge, and misinformation."[1] The details of the debates, the arguments, even the results, are not well remembered, but the debates are widely regarded both as a milestone in Lincoln's career and as the model for what political argument ought to be, the standard from which we somehow have fallen and the ideal that we should seek to restore. This view, however, is based on a stereotype of the debates and a failure to appreciate the real genius they displayed in the strategy and tactics of argument. In Reinhard Luthin's aphoristic phrase, the debates have been "vastly more admired than read."[2]

The debates have been treated often in historical and biographical writing, but they have been regarded as important historical events rather than as significant texts. The effects of the debates, not their content, has been the focus. There has been considerable disagreement among historians as to what the effects were. The early accounts exalted Lincoln and denigrated Douglas as little more than an apologist for slavery. Revisionists defended Douglas's theory of popular sovereignty as the middle ground between slavery and abolition and denounced Lincoln for so starkly drawing the issues that compromise was impossible and the nation lurched toward civil war. Recent writers have attempted a more balanced view that does credit to both candidates. But a dominant theme of historical studies is that the debates are important as milestones on Lincoln's road to the presidency or as steps in the demise of Douglas's national appeal.

To be sure, the debates *were* important historical events; they were even so regarded at the time. Because of Douglas's national prominence, and because they might offer a portent for 1860, the debates attracted national attention. The *Louisville Democrat* regarded the debate as "the ablest and the most important that has ever taken place in any of the States, on the great question which has so long agitated the country, elected and defeated Presidential candidates, built up and broken down parties." With allowance for local pride, the pro-Douglas *Chicago Times* proclaimed that the upcoming election, "in its consequences, present and remote, will be the most important to the people of this State and to the whole country that has ever been held."[3] (One must be careful not to overstate the importance attributed to the debates, though. The *American Almanac*, a reference work of the time, did not include them among the two hundred most important events of 1858, and Fehrenbacher notes that they hardly could be regarded as "the most memorable event of a year which also saw the bitter Lecompton controversy in congress, the continuation of a severe economic depression, the climax of the so-called 'Mormon War,' the laying of the Atlantic cable, a remarkable religious awakening, two gold rushes, and a knockdown brawl in the House of Representatives.")[4]

What is particularly important about the debates is that they were a sustained public discussion of the issue most troubling the nation. To focus on public discussion is to say that the speeches were not abstract philosophical theses. They were attempts to reach and persuade audiences, who brought to the discussion their own predispositions and concerns. The argumentation is pragmatic, as each candidate attempted both to make his views palatable to the audience and also to modify the audience's view of itself and of the issues. The Lincoln-Douglas debates, then, illustrate how the question of slavery was transformed in the crucible of public debate.

For all that, however, the substance of the debates has received little attention. The romantic and picturesque aspects of the seven contests have been emphasized more than the content of the argument or the relation between the arguments and the culture of the time.[5] Perhaps that is because it is difficult to read repetitive arguments that are not completely developed in any one place, perhaps because the discussion seems so indirect and diffuse, perhaps because the issues no longer trouble us. In any case, what is missing is a rhetorical perspective on the debates, focusing on how gifted advocates selected their arguments and appeals from the available means of persuasion and how they shaped and fashioned the arguments to meet the needs of the audience and situation.

This book is an attempt to provide such a perspective. It will examine the debates as public argument. Primary emphasis will be given to the reconstruction and assessment of appeals that were often presented in fragmentary fashion in any given debate but that cohere across the debates as a whole. The focus will be on the rhetorical dynamics within the text—the strategic and tactical choices that are evident, the means by which burdens of proof were discharged or transferred, the interactions among arguments, the nature of the political audiences, and the ability of particular argument patterns to reflect or modify the pre–Civil War political culture.

A rhetorical perspective on the debates helps to explain what happened during the twenty-one hours of argumentative interchange and how linguistic and strategic choices both reflected and affected the course of the deepening controversy over slavery. It explains how the competing positions of Lincoln and Douglas were grounded in the culture, language, and values of their time and what happens when two such competing positions are brought into direct conflict in the public forum. It shows how the advocates reconfigured the issues and ways of speaking about them, responding to the needs of their own situation but also looking backward and forward in time.

Achieving such objectives requires that public rhetoric be seen as dynamic as well as static, process as well as product. The text of the debates is not simply the words that Lincoln and Douglas spoke but the evolution of arguments and appeals over time and in the context of a close election campaign. Moreover, arguments affected one another, as each candidate sought to deal with the themes espoused by his opponent. The debates, in other words, shaped and reshaped the campaign even as they were constrained by it. Through the close analysis of such a classic set of texts, this book illustrates how public rhetoric can be conceived historically, as both agent and index of social and cultural change.

The thesis of the book is that the debates were marked by four general patterns of argument: conspiracy argument, legal argument, historical argument, and moral argument. Only the last engaged the issues of slavery and self-determination directly. These issues receive scant attention in the debates and are often addressed obliquely in the guise of conspiracy, legal, or historical arguments. The reasons for this indirection are to be found partly in the ambivalent position of Illinois audiences, who opposed both slavery and abolition, and partly in the incommensurable nature of the two moral positions. The Lincoln-Douglas debates illustrate how public argument can proceed in the face of these constraints—constraints that often reappear in our own time on issues other than slavery.

The discussion unfolds in three parts. The first two chapters set the stage for the debates by describing the issues and tracing their historical background and by chronicling the senatorial campaign of which the debates were a part. The next four chapters constitute the heart of the analysis. Each of the four argument patterns is explained, traced across the debates, and assessed. Throughout the project, the concern is for the relations between arguments and audiences, so the mode of analysis is rhetorical rather than literary. The last two chapters extract larger questions from the analysis. The penultimate chapter explores the resolution of the issues and the continuing life of the debates, and the final chapter relates the debates to general questions about public argument and culture.

In the pages that follow, the candidates and their political and rhetorical positions will be explained, but mastery of a few basic facts may be useful at the outset. Stephen A Douglas was the incumbent senator who was seeking a third term. Douglas at the time was the most prominent Democrat in the country, with the possible exception only of President James Buchanan. Abraham Lincoln was the candidate of the newly organized Republican party and, though a prominent Springfield lawyer, was much less well known at the time. Senators were elected by combined ballot of the two houses of the state legislature, so the real election was for the state senators and representatives who were pledged to support either Lincoln or Douglas. The debates took place between late August and early October in the course of this campaign. The popular vote for candidates pledged to Lincoln was slightly larger, but Douglas carried more of the legislative districts and was reelected to the Senate.

Any scholar assumes substantial debts in the course of a research project, and this book is no exception. My first debt is to Mr. and Mrs. Theodore W. Van Zelst. A generous gift from Ted and Louann endowed the Van Zelst Research Chair in Communication at Northwestern University. My appointment to this professorship during 1984–85 freed me from most normal academic responsibilities and enabled me to undertake the initial research on which the book is based. The Van Zelst Research Chair has nurtured several major communication research projects and was instrumental in my having the time needed at the outset of this work.

In addition to general library sources, research was undertaken in the Government Publications, Special Collections, and Newspaper and Microtext departments of the Northwestern University Library, in the Special Collections Department of the University of Chicago Library, and in the Illinois State Historical Library, the Chicago Historical Society Library, the Henry E. Huntington Library, and the Library of Congress. Librarians and archivists were uniformly helpful. Some of my travel and research expenses were generously supported by the Northwestern University School of Speech Alumni Fund during the administration of Roy V. Wood, my predecessor as dean. I also have benefited from the able research assistance of Frank E. Tutzauer, Carol Miller-Tutzauer, Stephen P. Depoe, and K. Michelle Howard.

An essay giving an overview of this project ("The Lincoln-Douglas Debates Revisited") appeared in the *Quarterly Journal of Speech* (72 [May 1986]: 162–84). This essay and the comments I received helped me sharpen my focus and envision the overall structure of this book. An early version of chapter 3 ("Conspiracy Arguments in the Lincoln-Douglas Debates") was published in the *Journal of the American Forensic Association* (21 [Fall 1984]: 63–75) and was similarly helpful.

I particularly appreciate the suggestions from seminar participants and lecture or conference audiences on whom I tried out my ideas for various parts of this book. They include people at Baylor University, the University of Wisconsin, the University of Texas, two programs of the Speech Communication Association, and two conferences sponsored jointly by that body and the American Forensic Association.

This manuscript has been reviewed by Frederick Antczak, Erwin Chemerinsky, Stephen P. Depoe, Thomas B. Farrell, Fred Kauffeld, Michael Leff, and Donald M. Scott, all of whom made helpful suggestions. Esther Langer, a wonderful secretary at the Northwestern University School of Speech, translated from my longhand to the word processor, where subsequent revisions and corrections were done. The interest of my brothers and my mother and the encouragement and support of my wife Nikki and my children were, as always, invaluable.

This book is dedicated to the two men whose lives I bridge and whose coming and going occurred at pivotal moments in its preparation. My son Marc was born as I was nearing the end of my initial research and was beginning to organize and write. His arrival undoubtedly delayed the appearance of this book, but, like his sister Beth, he has enriched my life beyond measure. My father died on the day I was to have had my first meeting with my editor from Chicago. An exceedingly modest man, he no doubt would have found it strange to be the honoree of a book. But his attitude toward work and his standards of judgment, clarity, and common sense have influenced this and other writing, probably even more than I know.

D.Z.

Evanston, Illinois
September 1989

1

The Issues and the Men

At the end of July, the two candidates met on the road to Bement, a small town in east-central Illinois. That they encountered each other was not a surprise since the Republican challenger had been trailing the better-known Democratic incumbent for most of the month, taking advantage of the crowds attracted by his rival. Democratic speakers and news-papers ridiculed this travel schedule, suggesting that the Republican could find larger crowds if he joined one of the "circuses and menag-eries" traveling around the state. As a way to overcome this problem, Republican advisers suggested, and the candidate proposed, a series of debates, so that both men might "divide time, and address the same au-diences during the present canvass." The incumbent, who had every-thing to lose from joint appearances, was not pleased, and yet to decline the challenge would have seemed unmanly in the West of the mid-nine-teenth century. So for a week the candidates and their aides dickered over details and struggled for advantage. How many debates, where they would be held, who would speak first and last, were all items to negotiate.

Finally, the challenger was ready to agree to his opponent's terms. They met outside Bement, one returning from a speaking engagement in Monticello and the other en route. He had his reply, Abraham Lincoln said, but he still needed to compare the copy with the original. Go on to Monticello and compare the copies, Stephen A. Douglas answered, and then send the reply back to me at Bement. Lincoln spoke at Monticello and then returned to Bement to deliver his reply. Douglas answered the next day with proposed dates and places, and, on July 31 Lincoln, though complaining that Douglas would have four opening and closing speeches

1

whereas he would have only three, wrote, "I accede, and thus close the arrangement." Even more in retrospect than at the time, the story of the 1858 Senate campaign is dominated by the Lincoln-Douglas debates.

I

The road to Bement stretched back in time—all the way, perhaps, to the founding of the country, back through what Jaffa called "a series of famous compromises, once familiar to every schoolboy": the Constitution, the Missouri Compromise, and the Compromise of 1850.[1] If the origins of the road were sometimes obscure, its path could clearly be traced to January 1854, when Douglas, as chairman of the Senate Committee on Territories, introduced a bill to organize the territories of Kansas and Nebraska. His motives were complex. In correspondence, he maintained that his objectives were "arresting the further progress of this savage barrier to the extension of our institutions," by which he meant extinguishing Indian titles and promoting resettlement, and "to authorize and encourage a continuous line of settlements to the Pacific Ocean."[2] The latter was probably Douglas's most basic motive, committed as he was to the transcendent value of national growth. He was a nationalist who believed in the Madisonian principle that a larger republic was more likely to contain factional divisions; any struggle between North and South would be less significant as the nation grew to encompass additional territory. As Jaffa characterizes Douglas, "He wished, through expansion, to submerge factionalism in the melting pot of Union."[3]

But the Little Giant, a sobriquet applied to Douglas since the 1830s, had other interests in organizing Kansas and Nebraska as well. He wanted to help Missouri senator David R. Atchison, who was in a tough election contest with Thomas Hart Benton. He wanted to increase the odds that a proposed transcontinental railroad would follow a northern route—an unlikely event if the railroad had to pass through unorganized territory without civil government. (Indeed, the railroad had figured in Douglas's efforts to organize the territory as long ago as 1845.)[4] He wanted an issue that would be a Democratic "litmus test" in order to prove that President Franklin Pierce would not dispense patronage positions to freesoilers.[5] Although successful leadership on the issue would enhance Douglas's presidential prospects in 1856, there is little evidence that he was motivated by the prospect of personal political gain.

Douglas had proposed a similar bill the year before, only to see it languish at the end of the congressional session. By the time that he reintroduced the bill, the political situation had changed. The Gadsden Purchase had been consummated, and momentum was building in favor of a southern railroad route. Southerners were less likely to support Douglas's plan, which would encourage a competing route, unless there was something in it for them. Yet Douglas needed to move quickly, even though Nebraska was virtually uninhabited, if he were to forestall the southern route. Atchison and the southerners suggested to Douglas that the price for their support was some concession that might allow slavery in the new territory.[6] By offering such a chance, Douglas would appease the South and convince the region that the Southern Unionists of 1850 were right in thinking that their section would receive its fair share of attention and opportunities. But the entire territory lay north of latitude thirty-six degrees, thirty minutes, so slavery was prohibited under the terms of the Missouri Compromise.

After considerable agonizing over how to appeal to the southerners, Douglas submitted revisions of the bill that first implicitly and then explicitly repealed the section of the Missouri Compromise that had outlawed slavery north of latitude thirty-six degrees, thirty minutes. In its place, he proposed that the decision on slavery would be made by the actual inhabitants of the territory. In this form, the bill passed Congress on a narrow vote and was signed into law by President Pierce.

Although he initially had sought the ambiguity of providing for "popular sovereignty" without explicitly repealing the Missouri Compromise, Douglas insisted afterward that its repeal was not a major concession since its principles had been "superseded" by those of the Compromise of 1850. This compromise related to a different geographic area, the region obtained from Mexico in 1848. It provided that states to be formed from these territories would be admitted with or without slavery as the inhabitants themselves chose. The difficulty with Douglas's argument, however, was that no record suggested that the Congress that passed the Compromise of 1850 had intended thereby to repeal the Missouri Compromise. Even as late as 1853, the Nebraska Bill before Congress did not propose to repeal the Missouri Compromise; its staunch supporters concluded that the 1820 measure had become a "sacred compact" and could not be repealed. Douglas had warmly supported the 1853 bill even though it did not call the Missouri Compromise into question.[7] Reportedly, he was reluctant to suggest repeal yet found it politically necessary to do so and then sought to make the shift as harmless as possible. For this reason, he contended that he was merely applying the principles of the 1850 Compromise and that the entire matter was a settled issue.

Like it or not, however, Douglas's tampering with the Missouri Compromise became a lightning rod. He was right that the legislative history of the 1820 act made clear that it was anything but sacred. Northerners had been hostile to the Compromise originally, but, as the settlement patterns of the 1840s turned the bargain in their favor, they increasingly regarded it as sacrosanct. By contrast, there was little Southern pressure for repeal prior to Douglas's action. Several factors, though, made the status of the Compromise a litmus test. First, in 1853 President Pierce engaged in the widespread removal of judges in the Minnesota, Oregon, Utah, and New Mexico territories, a move that some northerners saw as a means to assure proslavery decisions in the territories. In response, the *National Era* in April and again in October 1853 called on antislavery congressmen to reaffirm the Missouri Compromise explicitly in any bill that might be presented for the organization of Nebraska.[8] Second, during the course of his bitter campaign against Thomas Hart Benton, David R. Atchison pledged that, if elected to the Senate, he would secure a Nebraska Bill that permitted slavery or else he would not stand as a candidate for reelection.[9] Third, Senator Archibald Dixon, a Kentucky Whig, introduced explicit repeal of the Missouri Compromise, before Douglas took the cause of repeal and made it his own. Dixon was concerned that the Southern Whigs, whose numbers were dwindling, must stand up to the Democrats as advocates of Southern rights. There is some speculation that Dixon was encouraged by William Henry Seward, who wanted to split the Northern and Southern Whig forces.[10] Little serious credence was given to Douglas's assertion that the Missouri Compromise was a trifling matter. "The telling argument in 1854," Hamilton has written, "was that land solemnly guaranteed to freedom might be lost to slavery."[11]

In Douglas's view, the slavery provision of the Kansas-Nebraska Act was also a red herring. No matter what the ordinance said, slavery was not likely to establish a foothold in Nebraska. Climate and soil would prevent many slaves from going there. No real concessions were being made, therefore, so in the interest of national harmony it was better to remove the redundant *verbal* exclusion of slaves. Douglas denied that any congressional action, including the Northwest Ordinance, had affected the spread of slavery. The institution was either extended or contained on the basis of climate. Therefore, the South would gain an option that it could not really exercise, and that would break the logjam so that the territories could be organized and settled and new—presumably free—states admitted to the Union. From this perspective, the genius of the Kansas–Nebraska Act was that it removed a bitter, divisive issue from the halls of Congress and remanded it to those who would be most directly affected—with Douglas confident of what the outcome would be.

Many southerners shared the view that the Kansas-Nebraska Act involved the symbolism of regional equality rather than the expectation of tangible gains. The *Richmond Enquirer*, for example, editorialized, "All agree that slavery cannot exist in the territories of Kansas and Nebraska."[12] Only two of the more than fifty southerners who spoke in Congress entertained any hope that slavery might expand. To many northerners, however, to grant even the possibility that slavery might extend to Nebraska was to make a major concession. After all, slavery already existed in Missouri; why should it not spread westward into Kansas?[13]

Douglas's revised bill also proposed, for the first time, splitting Nebraska into two territories, the southern territory to be called Kansas. This split is of obscure origin but probably was not prompted by the desire to create one free and one slave state. Instead, it was a move to facilitate the railroad, by giving widely scattered settlements along the Kansas River and the Platte River the chance to develop without being dependent on the progress of the other (and, incidentally, freeing Douglas of the need publicly to choose between St. Louis and Chicago as the railroad's eastern terminus). Very soon after the bill was introduced, it was the subject of a blistering attack in a pamphlet titled *Appeal of the Independent Democrats*. The pamphlet viewed the Kansas-Nebraska Act as the thin entering wedge for a host of evils: opening all unorganized territory to slavery, slowing the rate of settlement in the territories, preventing the construction of the transcontinental railroad, and placing the country under the "yoke of a slaveholding despotism."[14] Such a series of evils could imply only that there was a conscious plot or conspiracy to produce the diabolical outcome.

Despite the organizational efforts of the congressional radicals, opposition to the bill was slow to develop, and Douglas's maneuvering was a major disincentive. Equivocating the terms *freedom* and *slavery*, and regarding freedom not as an individual right but as a community preference, he wrote the editor of the *Concord, N.H., State Capitol Reporter*, complaining that his opponents alleged "that this bill opens that whole country to slavery! Why do they not state the matter truly, and say that it opens the country to *freedom* by leaving the people *perfectly free* to do as they please?"[15] Douglas spoke in the Senate during the debate, concluding on March 3, 1854 with a speech that one biographer described as "the most powerful speech of his long oratorical career."[16] After disagreement between the two houses of Congress as to whether the franchise should be extended to aliens, the bill passed by a margin of two to one in the Senate but by only a 113 to 110 margin in the House. Pierce signed it into law on May 30, 1854.

One consequence of the Kansas-Nebraska Act was that it reawakened Abraham Lincoln's interest in politics. After serving a single term in Congress, Lincoln had returned in 1849 to private practice of law in Springfield. He saw the Kansas-Nebraska Act as the opening move along a road toward a slave society. That outcome would render impossible the achievement of economic integration for which he and other Whigs had striven. [17] Antislavery, therefore, soon displaced internal improvements in his array of values. He also regarded the Kansas-Nebraska Act as an impediment to American foreign policy because it deprived "our republican example of its just influence in the world." Regarding the charge that the 1854 act was merely carrying out the "popular sovereignty" positions of the Compromise of 1850, he had little patience. The popular sovereignty provision of the 1850 measure, he told a Peoria audience, "was made for Utah and New Mexico, and for no other place whatever. It had no more direct reference to Nebraska than it had to the territories of the moon." [18]

In Illinois, Douglas found himself vilified, and not just by Lincoln, for his role in the Kansas-Nebraska Act. Twenty-five Chicago clergymen wrote that his stance was immoral, whereupon he denied the prerogative of the clergy to comment authoritatively about civil matters. To his father-in-law, James Madison Cutts, Douglas reportedly said, "I passed the Kansas-Nebraska Act myself. I had the authority and power of a dictator throughout the whole controversy in both houses." But he seemed genuinely surprised by the mobs who attended his speeches on his trip back home; he could have traveled all the way from Washington to Chicago, he later said, by the lights of his own effigy. [19] In the fall 1854 midterm elections, Northern Democrats lost sixty-six of ninety-one House seats; only seven of the forty-two Northern Democrats who favored the Kansas-Nebraska Act were returned for the next session. [20]

Two clear effects can be traced to the Kansas-Nebraska controversy. First, it was the final blow to the existing party system. To be sure, both parties had undergone strains for some time. Nichols and Klein point out that, within the Democratic party, "Northwestern Democrats had never forgiven southern party leaders for giving up half of Oregon while taking all of the Mexican southwest, for defeating rivers and harbors bills, and for withholding support from Cass in 1848." Meanwhile, Northeastern Democrats objected to low tariffs, and former president Martin Van Buren had taken Democrats with him over the free-soil question. The Kansas question forced northern Democrats to choose between antislavery and popular sovereignty. Some indication of how the Kansas issue divided loyalties may be found in the vote of Northern Democrats in the House—forty-four to forty-four. [21] This designation, of course, destroyed party unity, which was necessary to support further territorial expansion.

As for the Whigs, they had been split into "conscience" and "cotton" Whigs for some time. Holt maintains that the party did not *have to* splinter and die. Northern Whigs could have attacked Democrats for even introducing the Kansas-Nebraska Act, and Southern Whigs could claim to be more proslavery than the Democrats. "Such Janus-faced campaigning," Holt observes, "had been used successfully by Whigs in the past."[22] But this strategy was not realistically available because of the second effect of the Kansas-Nebraska Act: it changed the terms of political discourse, making the slavery issue not an isolated local matter but an issue charged with emotion and symbolism. Berwanger writes that, from the time of the act, "the slavery extension question took precedence over every other problem in American political life."[23] It became the focal point for definitions of one's aims and values. Knowing where one stood would be crucial, so the potential for rhetorical ambiguity was limited indeed.

II

The Kansas-Nebraska Act was silent on one key question. At what point may the residents of a territory exercise their right of self-government? This was not a trivial matter since the outcome of the decision could be predicted from its timing. If new territories could exclude slavery only when they became states, they would be unlikely to do so. If slavery had been established during the territorial phase, voters would be unlikely to pass it over. Likewise, if the very first inhabitants made the choice, slavery would likely be approved, if only because the first residents of Kansas would come from neighboring, slaveholding, Missouri. From the antislavery standpoint, the ideal would be to have a decision made shortly after the area was open for settlement, but with enough of an interval that Northern emigrants might have time to arrive. In any event, the act was silent on that point—and intentionally so. The phrase "subject to the Constitution" was artfully ambiguous so that Northern Democrats could assure voters that the decision could be made at the territorial stage and Southern Democrats could argue that it must await statehood. It was finally agreed to defer this question to the Supreme Court, with all parties having pledged to abide by the decision.[24]

Meanwhile, of course, the uncertainty about timing created pressure from all sides for quick settlement of the new territories. The race was on. Missourians flocked to the new territory, not so much because they wanted to take their slaves there as because they wanted to be sure that no free-soil territory on their border would endanger their own property. Small but widely publicized groups of free-soil settlers came from New England, but most came from the Old Northwest. An 1855 territorial census revealed that 83 percent of the settlers in Kansas had come from the Old Northwest, Iowa, Kentucky, or Missouri. Most disapproved of slavery but were more interested in settling the land than in resolving the slavery question, and in any case they did not trust the more radical New Englanders' advocacy of equal rights and privileges.[25]

The combination of rapid settlement, disputed land claims, and the absence of civil government made for a level of civil disturbance not unlike that elsewhere on the frontier, but each such incident was quickly interpreted as part of a proslavery or antislavery plot, thereby intensifying the level of tension and the polarization of political loyalties. Slavery in the territories had become a symbolic issue, magnified in importance even as it was devoid of practical effect; after all, no territory remained unorganized after 1854. For southerners, the issue was a measure of their success or failure at seeking equality within the Union in the face of a growing northern majority. For northerners, the issue focused on a choice between free labor and slave labor as the model for a developing Western society since it was widely assumed that the two could not coexist.[26]

So long as the Kansas question was unsettled, the live symbolic issue furnished a basis for organizing opposition to the Buchanan administration. When Senator Toombs of Georgia proposed a bill in 1856 that provided orderly and fair procedures for admitting Kansas as a state, the anti-Nebraska forces defeated it. They were less interested in the quiet admission of Kansas, probably as a free state, than in a live issue that might garner more support.[27] It was a volatile situation, publicized most by the proslavery attack on Lawrence and the caning of Senator Charles Sumner, both occurring in May 1856.[28]

Meanwhile, the promised court case was proceeding along to the Supreme Court. The case involved a slave named Dred Scott, whose ownership had changed over the years. He had been taken by his former master, an army doctor, on trips from his home in Missouri to military posts in Illinois, a free state, and in Minnesota, part of the Wisconsin Territory from which slavery was excluded by the terms of the Missouri Compromise. The slave brought suit to obtain his freedom on the basis of his residence on free soil. Although the case was complicated, broadly speaking there were three questions. Did Dred Scott have the right to bring suit in the federal courts? Was he free by virtue of his temporary residence in Illinois? Was he free by virtue of his residence in Minnesota?[29]

The Court that heard the case was strongly pro-Southern, though not proslavery. None of the justices was a slaveholder; none sympathized with the peculiar institution.[30] But they were committed to states' rights and on the face of it found that the Missouri Compromise interfered with the sacred right of self-government. In 1855, President Pierce had intimated to Taney that the Missouri Compromise was unconstitutional,[31] and, by early 1857, word was in the air that the Court was about to deny the power of a territory to exclude slavery. In advance of his inauguration, President-elect James Buchanan conversed with one of the justices and reportedly obtained a preview of the decision, to which he pledged in his inaugural address to adhere, whatever it might be.

The decision, released on March 6, 1857, had three essential parts. First, Dred Scott as a black man could not be a citizen of the United States (although some states might choose to extend citizenship to blacks) and therefore had no standing to sue in federal court for his freedom. Second, his residence in Illinois did not make him a free man because once he returned to his home in Missouri he was subject to the laws of that state.[32] Finally, his residence in Minnesota did not make him free because the law under which slavery was excluded—the Missouri Compromise—was itself unconstitutional, infringing as it did on the right to property that was distinctly asserted in the Constitution.

In some respects, the decision had little practical effect. It invalidated a law that had already been repealed three years before; it denied freedom to slaves in an area without slaves. Scott himself was manumitted shortly after the decision was announced and died not long after, on the day before the fourth Lincoln-Douglas debate, as a free man. But as a symbol, and a source of public argument, the decision was both substantial and powerful.

Little controversy attended the first part of the decision, although it is the most overtly racist. Prior to the passage of the Fourteenth Amendment, state citizenship and federal citizenship were not identical, and there was no clamor for Negro citizenship during the mid-1850s. Indeed, those opposed to slavery in the new territories often wanted to exclude blacks altogether, whether free or slave. The only question was why, in the light of this part of the decision, anything else was necessary. If Dred Scott had no standing to sue, then the merits of the case were moot, and there was no need to proceed to the substantive issues. Lincoln and others would later exploit this anomaly, contending that the troublesome part of the decision was merely *dicta*, the opinion of the court, and that denial of Negro citizenship was the only binding rule.[33]

The decision regarding Scott's residence in Illinois was also fairly innocuous since the principle of interstate comity had long been articulated by the courts, even if often observed in the breach. But the third part of the decision, *post facto* outlawing the Missouri Compromise, spawned a firestorm. In part, this was because of the status of "sacred compact" with which the Compromise had lately been invested. As Jaffa explains, the Taney court "denied the validity of a law which had stood upon the statutes of the country for thirty-four years, a law which Douglas himself in 1849 had described as having an origin akin to that of the Constitution, canonized in the hearts of the American people, and as a sacred thing which no ruthless hand would ever be reckless enough to disturb."[34] The *Dred Scott* decision may have had this effect generally, but it created specific, seemingly intractable, political and rhetorical problems for virtually every Northern politician.

Douglas had based his theory of popular sovereignty on the belief that the decision for or against slavery could be made by the actual inhabitants of a territory, acting through their representatives in the territorial legislature. But territorial legislatures were not sovereign governments, like states; instead, they were creatures of Congress. On the face of it, a prohibition imposed against Congress would seem to apply to territorial legislatures as well. Douglas had said, in advance of the decision, that the issue was properly a matter for the court and that he would abide by the outcome. He could not now denounce the decision without repudiating himself, a Court composed predominantly of members of his own party, congressional Democrats from the South who quickly came to regard support for the decision as a political litmus test, and a president of his own choice. Yet he could not continue to defend popular sovereignty unless he could find some way to reconcile it with the *Dred Scott* decision persuasively.

Equally serious were the problems posed for the coalition of former Whigs and former Democrats who had opposed the Kansas-Nebraska Act and who by 1857 had coalesced as the Republican party. They had come impressively close to electing a president in 1856, and the key element of their platform had been opposition to the spread of slavery into new territories. That was an ideal touchstone since it stopped short of the extreme of abolitionism yet offered a practical program by which slavery might be restricted and since it also appealed to those who wanted to preserve the territories for white people and not for blacks, whether free or slave. Now this platform had, in effect, been declared unconstitutional. The party's alternatives were either to find some new issue or to oppose the *Dred Scott* decision. By and large, it took the latter course, although advocates also had to be careful not to impugn the legitimacy of the Court. But they had more options than did their Democratic colleagues. They could denounce the decision as unprincipled and politically motivated, and they could take advantage of its breadth, maintaining that only the denial of Negro citizenship (with which they did not quarrel) was a definitive ruling and that the rejection of the Missouri Compromise was only *dicta*.

The *Dred Scott* decision, in sum, has about it an air of unreality. It seems a purely symbolic verdict that directly affected no one. But as a symbol and a portent it was immensely influential, structuring the political and rhetorical situation, creating opportunities and constraints, and looming large in the public discourse that would culminate in the Lincoln-Douglas debates.

III

Much the same could be said of the last of three main precursors of the debates, the controversy over the Lecompton constitution. Even while the timing of popular sovereignty for the territories remained indeterminate, the proslavery settlers of Kansas, perhaps sensing that time was not their friend, petitioned for admission as a state—without having been invited to do so by Congress and long before the territory had the population then required for admission.[35] By the time the convention, which met in the town of Lecompton, had finished its work, it was clear that a majority of the residents were antislavery. Even had the proposed constitution been adopted, Kansas would not for long have remained a slave state. But Kansas voters decisively rejected it on August 2, 1858, less than three weeks before the first Lincoln-Douglas debate.

Nevertheless, the Lecompton constitution was of crucial symbolic importance and continued to influence political discourse. For the South, it was a question of abstract principle: whether any more slave states would be allowed into the Union after an antislavery majority had developed in the North. For the Buchanan administration, it was a question of administrative law: the proceedings at Lecompton had been legal and constitutional. For Douglas and his supporters, it was a question of political philosophy and morality: the constitution did not represent the will of the people, and the vote had been fraudulent; violating the cherished principle of popular sovereignty. For Republicans, it was a question of practical politics: after Douglas's break with Buchanan over Lecompton, they needed to protect themselves against being swallowed up in a fusion movement in which they would become the tail to the Douglas kite and the purity of their own principles would be lost.[36]

The facts of the Lecompton matter can be set out briefly. In his inaugural address as territorial governor of Kansas, Robert J. Walker pledged— with the support, he thought, of President Buchanan—that any document resulting from the Lecompton proceedings would be submitted to popular vote. His aim was to coax the free-state forces to abandon their rival organization and participate in the Lecompton process so that Kansas might enter the Union as a Democratic state. The president of the Lecompton convention, surveyor John Calhoun, likewise favored submission of the constitution to a referendum.[37] While the convention was sitting, however, an election was held for a new territorial legislature. The free-state forces participated in the election and gained control of the new legislature, thereby making it clear that public sentiment was against slavery in Kansas. Probably in response, the Lecompton convention—a proslavery body since free-state forces had boycotted the election of delegates—decided *not* to submit the entire document to referendum. Instead, they decided to hold a limited vote only on the slavery clause— the constitution with or without slavery. (A vote for the constitution "without slavery" would not have changed the status of slaves already in the territory.) After the convention adjourned, but before the limited referendum was held, the new legislature met and ordered a referendum on the entire document—although the results might not be binding.

Kansas faced two referenda barely a fortnight apart. On December 21, 1857, the limited referendum produced a vote of 6,143 to 569 for the constitution "with slavery." Most free-state advocates boycotted the vote. Then, on January 4, 1858, the entire constitution was rejected by a vote of 10,226, with 138 supporting it "with slavery" and twenty-four "without slavery." Needless to say, few proslavery citizens participated in this vote.[38]

Congress spent much of the spring of 1858 trying to determine which vote was legally valid. Buchanan's position was critical. He personally favored submission, yet he did not believe that the convention was obliged to submit the document to the people and neither confirmed nor denied Walker's promise of a referendum. Buchanan's biographer contends that Walker exceeded his instructions and read a mandate into the president's expression of hope.[39] Buchanan would not try to force the convention to change its mind, particularly since there was ample precedent of state constitutions not submitted for popular vote. As senators and congressmen noted, neither the federal Constitution, nor the constitutions of the original thirteen states, nor those of most of the states added since, required submission. Ohio, Kentucky, Tennessee, Illinois, Alabama, Missouri, Maine, Vermont, and Wisconsin were admitted without referendum.[40]

Besides, Buchanan was convinced that Lecompton was legal. The delegates had been duly elected, and, if free-state forces chose to boycott that election, the results were their own fault. "The people" of Kansas, as Florida senator Mallory said, are only those who bothered to vote, who, "under the shadow and by the power of law alone, have made their wishes and their wants known to us."[41] Buchanan agreed with those in Congress who insisted that there was no choice but to accept the work of a duly constituted convention. No restrictions on statehood could be imposed on new states that exceeded those imposed on any existing state, and the only restriction permitted by the U.S. Constitution was that the state's form of government must be republican.[42]

Buchanan recognized that there were defects in the Lecompton document, but he insisted that they could be fixed through amendment. In his February 2, 1858 message, he declared Kansas to be, "at this moment, as much a slave State as Georgia or South Carolina," insisted that only a constitutional change could exclude slavery, and stated that "in no other manner can this be obtained so promptly, if a majority of the people desire it, as by admitting it into the Union under its present constitution" and then moving immediately to amend. He put no stock in a clause prohibiting amendments before 1864, finding it "absurd to say that [the majority] can impose fetters upon their own power which they cannot afterwards remove."[43] The president thought that immediate admission would remove the Kansas question from the public forum, thereby denying Republicans a necessary platform. And he knew that he had the votes. According to his biographer, he could count on thirty-six of the thirty-nine Democratic senators and as many as 110 of the 130 Democratic congressmen.[44] Victory seemed so close, and the chance to be rid of the issue so attractive, that he decided to make Lecompton a party issue and to compel the votes of wayward Democrats.

But not Senator Douglas. After Buchanan's December message had not explicitly recommended adoption of the Lecompton constitution, Douglas leaped wishfully to the conclusion that the president *would not* do so. When it became evident that he had misread Buchanan, he met the president at the White House and dramatically announced his defiance. To a thinly veiled threat of retaliation, Douglas admonished the president to remember that "General Jackson is dead." He made his stand a matter of principle, although opponents were quick to assert that he was prompted only by the needs of political survival in Illinois. His actions were, as Fehrenbacher has noted, "so inconsistent with his previous line of conduct that they seemed almost out of character." The political realist had become a doctrinaire; the strong party man was waging an insurgent revolt; the champion of territorial self-government proposed to reject the action of the territorial legislature.[45]

For Douglas the question was simple. As he had written to John A. McClernand the previous November, "The only question is whether the constitution framed at Lecompton is the act & will of the people of Kansas, [or] whether it be the act and will of a small minority, who have attempted to cheat & defraud the majority by trickery & juggling." He added, "If it be the will of the people freely & fairly expressed it is all right, if not it must be rebuked." He took the same position in Senate debate, insisting that his vote was cast without respect to the slavery question but was "predicated on the great fact that a majority of the people are utterly opposed to this instrument as their fundamental law."[46]

Douglas denied that Congress was powerless to oppose the Lecompton constitution so long as it guaranteed a republican form of government. Rather, he insisted, despite its legalistic form, the document was "only a petition . . . which Congress could accept or reject, or dispose of as it saw proper."[47] He denied Buchanan's contention that immediate amendment was possible, not so much because of the prohibition in the text itself as because radical alterations in government can be achieved peaceably only when public sentiment is virtually unanimous, not when there is intense conflict as in the case at hand.[48] His major argument, however, was that, unless submitted to referendum, the constitution could not be known to reflect the will of the people. He dismissed the Lecompton convention as unrepresentative, reversing his stand from June 1857, when he had said that those who did not vote for delegates had only themselves to blame for the consequences.[49]

Referenda might not be explicitly required, but they clearly had become the norm. As Klein summarizes, only thirty of the sixty-three state constitutions adopted between 1776 and 1858 had been ratified by popular vote, but only nine states still lived under charters that had never been ratified by the people. Moreover, as Wells notes, "a popular referendum had been held in almost every instance where there had been deep and fundamental cleavages in the body politic like those that now existed in Kansas." Douglas used this same principle to reconcile his demand for a referendum in Kansas with his willingness to accept Minnesota without one. Submission was not always essential, but it was a good way to determine the popular will if there was any doubt.[50] To his Southern opponents, however, the referendum was not a neutral way to find out the will of the people but an active challenge to that will as already expressed by the Lecompton convention. It would be, as Congressman Atkins of Tennessee said in using Douglas's own phrase against him, "a palpable violation of the doctrine of non-intervention, and of the rights of the people of Kansas."[51]

Douglas had hit a sensitive nerve, as many Northern Democrats had misgivings about Lecompton. The principle of majority rule seemed to have been violated, Buchanan's apparent pledge to Walker had not been carried out, Kansas voters had not really had a chance to reject slavery, and the document could not be amended for seven years. In Holt's words, "Promised that popular sovereignty would produce free soil, [Northern voters] found that the majority will could not prevent a pro-slavery constitution from being rammed down the throats of Kansans with the aid of the Democratic president."[52] His break with Buchanan won Douglas the sympathy of these voters.

Republicans also opposed Buchanan over Lecompton, both because it lacked majority support and because it would result in the admission of a slave state. Senator William Pitt Fessenden of Maine denounced the proposed constitution as "an outrage, deliberately planned, followed up remorselessly," and Congressman Calvin C. Chaffee of Massachusetts ridiculed the president's assertion that approval was necessary to avert the dissolution of the Union. "This, sir," Chaffee said, "has been so often threatened that it has lost its terrors, even to the 'old ladies of both sexes.'" Senator Lyman Trumbull argued that the convention itself was illegal since the territorial legislature lacked authority to call for it; one of the precedents he cited was an 1848 ruling by Buchanan himself. Several Republicans in Congress developed a conspiracy claim, alleging that the Lecompton constitution was part of a long-standing plot to foist slavery on the people of Kansas against their will.[53]

The Lecompton controversy handed the Republicans a powerful issue—except that it was muddied by Douglas's defection. To preserve the purity of their own position, Republicans needed to castigate the Little Giant, and the easiest way to do that was to attack his conversion as short lived and not genuine or to suggest that his opposition to Lecompton was at odds with his support for the Kansas-Nebraska Act. A Christmas 1857 letter from Trumbull to Lincoln illustrates both approaches. He deemphasized Douglas's rift with the administration, calling it "temporary" and predicting that it "will be settled forever the moment Kansas is admitted as a state, no matter under what constitution she comes in." Trumbull also refuted Douglas's claim that Lecompton violated the principle of the Nebraska bill, arguing instead, "The Lecompton Constitution denies no right to the people of the proposed *state*, which the Nebraska bill did not deny to the people of the *territory*. Both alike deny the right of self government & popular sovereignty to the people upon all questions except that of slavery, & on that, since the Dred Scott decision which Douglas endorses, the people have no right while in a territorial condition to pass."[54] This letter illustrated what would become a standard Republican argument—that the Kansas-Nebraska Act, the *Dred Scott* decision, and the Lecompton constitution all fit together so neatly that they must be part of a concerted plan for the spread of slavery.

In early 1858, then, the Lecompton issue placed Douglas in what Beveridge has called a desperate situation: "On one hand he was assailed by the Administration forces and old line Democrats who could not forgive even Douglas for breaking with his party in Congress; on the other hand by the Republican party of Illinois, fresh, eager, bellicose, and led by their ablest man." Trumbull predicted that Douglas would retain the support of most Illinois Democrats but that, having broken with Buchanan, "Douglas' prospects for a nomination at Charleston are gone."[55] The feud with the president was real; one correspondent wrote Douglas of his belief that Buchanan "hates you in the most bitter and unrelenting manner" and "would sacrifice you [even] if it would sacrifice the Democratic party in doing so."[56] But many Republicans minimized the significance of the feud or dismissed it as motivated by expediency. A tentative agreement to patch up the quarrel followed a conciliatory Douglas speech in the Senate in June, and the terms of the reconciliation were telegraphed to the senator as he headed west to campaign.[57] But Illinois public opinion was more intensely opposed to Lecompton than Douglas thought, and, when he reached Chicago, he delivered a tirade against the administration and reopened the rift for good.

Republicans, too, were in disarray, partly because they could not respond to the Panic of 1857 by calling for higher tariffs or a national bank without antagonizing former Democrats among their supporters.[58] Prominent Eastern Republicans, including William Henry Seward, Anson Burlingame, Henry Wilson, Simon Cameron, and Horace Greeley, urged support for Douglas as the best instrument for achieving Republican objectives. Most influential was Greeley, whose *New York Tribune* had a circulation of nearly twenty thousand in Illinois alone.[59] There was even speculation that Douglas might become a Republican, but few Illinois Republicans considered that prospect seriously.

Meanwhile, the Lecompton controversy worked its way to a conclusion. Democrats controlled both houses of Congress, but their numbers included many defectors. After a ringing speech by Douglas concluding the debate, the Senate voted on March 23 to endorse the Lecompton constitution; the tally was thirty-three to twenty-five. The House, however, rejected the constitution and agreed even to a conference committee only after the speaker broke a 108 to 108 tie. In conference, Representative William English of Indiana proposed a face-saving compromise. As a kind of indirect resubmission, he altered the size of the land grant embodied in the constitution and then maintained that, because of this change, the entire document needed to be reconsidered by the voters. Those who opposed a referendum, so Hodder explained, could "cover their retreat by claiming that it was the land grant and not the constitution that was submitted," while those who had favored it could "show that they had, after all, gained their point."[60]

Douglas opposed the English bill, insisting that it was a bribe. If Lecompton passed, Kansas could enter the Union immediately; if not, she must wait until she had the requisite population. If she came in, she would receive a generous land grant (though no more so than was common at the time); if not, nothing was said about the size of land grant that she might expect under any alternative constitution. Douglas's opposition to the English Bill, which in any case was less energetic than his attack on Lecompton, may actually have helped the cause since it bolstered the idea that the bill was not really resubmission to a referendum.[61] Many Republicans also opposed the English plan, agreeing with Douglas that, if Kansas currently had population enough to come in as a slave state, it should also be able to come in immediately as a free state. Nevertheless, enough votes were mustered that the English bill was able to pass by the narrow margins of thirty-one to twenty-two in the Senate and 112 to 103 in the House. The bill provided for a final referendum on August 2, in which Kansans rejected the Lecompton constitution by lopsided margins, better than eight to one. Every county, even Johnson County bordering on Missouri, voted it down.[62]

The Lecompton struggle made plain the counterproductive effects of the Kansas-Nebraska Act. Not only had it not promoted local self-government, but it had also, in Rawley's words, "elicited the worst traits from the American people: fraud in voting, guerrilla fighting, sophistical logic, trickery, terrorism, passion, insult, extreme partisanship, murder, and — underpinning all else—a vicious racialism."[63] It also marked the practical end of the dispute over slavery in the territories. If the peculiar institution was not at home in Kansas, it was not likely to be better received in any other existing territory. Recognizing this fact, slaveholders began to remove their chattels. Reportedly, there had been fifty-five slaves in Kansas in 1856; by 1860 the number was down to two.[64] The politics of Lecompton and the rift between Douglas and Buchanan continued, however, leaving political allegiances in flux as Lincoln and Douglas prepared to campaign for the seat in the Senate.

IV

The controversies of the mid-1850s took place not in a vacuum but against a backdrop created by the rhetorical and political culture of the age, a set of values and practices that served as common knowledge and the premises for public appeals. The American Union was seen as a precious and unique experiment in governance, sanctioned by God and sustained by minimizing the scope of governmental action. The period was marked by faith in progress but also by a romanticism evident in the fact that people "espoused causes and went forth on crusades . . . . They were willing to accept simple explanations for complex social problems, easy 'cures' for pervasive ills."[65] The Union was not just a political but also a symbolic and mystical idea embodying a fundamental agreement on the goals of man in a society marked by political and technological change. As Forgie notes, "It was a convention of American public language between the 1790's and the Civil War to speak of the Union and the relationships among Americans in familial and domestic terms." This tendency reflected the assumption, he explains, "that the survival of the Union depended on offsetting the centrifugal and atomistic tendencies of an amorphous and rapidly expanding democracy by the cohesive force of emotion."[66] Like Union itself, the West was particularly important as a symbol, representing social and economic opportunities, Americans' sense of their freedom, a moral battleground, and the incarnation of the future.[67] When the issue of slavery was focused on the territories, then, both the cherished symbols of Union and West were rendered problematic.

Nineteenth-century America was also characterized by religiosity and familiarity with the Bible, which provided "a common stock of reading experiences and literary references" and which "served as the prime source for parable and citation, for quotation and allusion." The culture was marked both by revivalism and by an impulse for reform, prompted by the teaching of the Second Great Awakening that man could participate in his own salvation and that, being saved, one had a responsibility to others. Abolitionism, feminism, pacifism, temperance, and nativism were among the expressions of this strong wave of religious enthusiasm. More generally, it infused public discourse with a sense both of urgency and of personal responsibility for the improvement of conditions in the world. "Everyone," Bode related, "could perform good works if he wanted to, for he enjoyed the blessings of free will." As a result, through his soul man became "the master of his body. He could make it do what he wanted."[68] But this same sense of urgency also contributed to widespread anxiety and anger when things did not work out properly.

Politics played a prominent role in the culture of the mid-nineteenth century. Party differences were important, and much of one's identity was bound up with the statement that one was a Democrat or a Whig. Issues were important as well, and they were widely discussed. It was a period marked by what was later called the "civic culture." Baker describes it as "an informed citizenry who participate in public affairs, weigh the issues, and make responsible judgments on personnel and policy."[69] Yet politics also served as a source of communal entertainment, in which "the petty struggles of political jobbers over the spoils of office" were effectively transformed "into an epic encounter of chivalrous knights over lofty ideals."[70] Politicians were seen as "self-centered and corrupted wirepullers out of touch with the people" and parties as "unresponsive and beyond popular control."[71] Moreover, the lack of real and meaningful choice between the parties was seen as a threat to republicanism and something to be fought through the development of new organizations.

By the standards of the late twentieth century, America in the mid-nineteenth century must be classified as racist. Negroes were commonly regarded as biologically inferior, so even many who opposed slavery did not view the institution as a great moral evil. Slavery had been confined to the South, but race prejudice existed throughout the country. Few defenders of racial equality could be found, and, when abolitionists espoused that thesis, they made audiences even more convinced of their doubts. Even for those opposed to slavery, the question of what to do with the freed blacks seemed insurmountable. It was taken for granted, even by Lincoln, that the races could not coexist peacefully and that emancipation inevitably would lead to race mixing and miscegenation. By 1860, only five states, all in the Northeast, had provided for equal rights of suffrage.[72] Several of the Western states, including Illinois, had laws excluding free blacks not just from the polls but from the state. In Kansas, most free-soil settlers wanted no blacks among them, whether slave or free—a sentiment, Nevins reports, "which they shared with the great majority of Illinoisans, Indianans, and Ohioans."[73]

For those who thought that slavery could be ended, even though only gradually, the question of what to do with freed blacks was answered by the colonization movement. Colonization assumed that the races could not coexist in harmony and therefore proposed to "transplant blacks to regions where they could rule themselves and develop their own democratic institutions free of white interference." As Fredrickson explains, this sentiment was powerfully ambiguous: "The concept of a democratic world of distinct races enjoying perfect self-government on their 'own soil' repudiated internationalist racism while affirming the inevitability of domestic racism."[74] It was a valuable compromise, and that fact may help explain the appeal of the colonization movement to such influentials as James Madison, Andrew Jackson, Henry Clay, Daniel Webster, John Marshall, General Winfield Scott, William H. Seward, Edward Everett, and many others, including for a time, both Stephen A. Douglas and Abraham Lincoln.[75]

Southerners, meanwhile, sought to protect the institution of slavery, which was bound up with their entire way of life. For Southern society, the issue went beyond slavery itself to control of one's own destiny. When northerners presumed to tell the region how to regulate its own domestic affairs, Southern freedom and independence were threatened—a condition that led to slavery.[76] Regarding *slavery* as a devil term, as did their

Northern brethren, Southern slaveholders nevertheless defended the paradox that the evils of slavery could be avoided if chattel slavery were preserved!

In addition to the cultural values of Union, individualism, and reform, the prominence of politics, and the significance of race, mid-nineteenth-century America also had distinctive orientations toward oratory. This was the "golden age" of oratory, marked by the Senate speeches of Webster, Clay, and Calhoun, by the political campaign rally, and by the occasional address. Anderson notes that "every occasion demanded a speech, and every speech was a celebration of American destiny." The demand, he concludes, was "for public utterances which were creedal and prophetic."[77] Speakers tried to be informative and entertaining, but they were assured of attentive audiences who were able to follow complicated debates and to sustain interest through long presentations. Experience going back to the Puritan sermons led audiences to expect lengthy speeches; although cautioning that the role of stump speaking is sometimes overstated, Gienapp writes that audiences "were willing— and able—to sit through speeches lasting three hours or more without losing interest."[78] The length of the Lincoln-Douglas debates would not seem excessive to audiences of the day.

Particularly in the West, joint canvasses or debates were a staple of political campaigning. Capers describes them as "more gladiatorial combats than national debates," with a "premium on showmanship, not logic." They persisted, however, because they filled several needs. They were a source of both entertainment and education, and they reduced the costs of campaigning. Only later in the century, when incumbents enjoyed longer periods without interruption in office, did the tradition of debates weaken. Understandably, incumbents did not wish to advertise their challengers or make them appear equal by sharing the platform.[79] The media that reported these contests were primitive by today's standards. Only 5 percent of the newspapers called themselves independent; the vast majority were under the control of one or another political faction on which they were dependent for subscribers and sometimes operating expenses. Moreover, most papers had limited and local circulation; only Horace Greeley's *New York Tribune* had significant circulation outside the immediate area.[80] Journalistic objectivity was an unknown convention.

The principle of popular sovereignty was appropriate to, and in some ways constitutive of, the political culture of its time. It was articulated in the midst of congressional deadlock over the Wilmot Proviso. This statement, which would ban slavery in any territory to be acquired through the Mexican War, was repeatedly passed by the House and defeated by the Senate, with neither body willing to compromise. To break the log-jam, some entirely different approach would be needed. Coming up with one would be difficult since attitudes had hardened. Northerners supporting the Proviso regarded it as a response to the excessive expansionism of the Polk administration, while southerners opposing it regarded the conflict as a test of the equality among states within the Union. Even though they harbored little hope of carrying slavery to the lands won from Mexico, still they resented the stigma of an official prohibition that was "intolerably threatening to their honor and self-esteem." Consequently, from 1846 onward, they saw the key issues as "concepts of equality, rights, and honor."[81]

Popular sovereignty offered a way out. Its precise origins are uncertain since it was an idea "in the wind" in 1847, but it was popularized by Lewis Cass. In a letter written in December 1847 to A. O. P. Nicholson, a Tennessee lawyer, editor, and politician, Cass laid out the doctrine that Congress had no power to govern the territories, who themselves were the only appropriate judges of their local affairs.[82] The doctrine had the virtue of removing the slavery dispute from Congress, so that body could get on with its business, and transferring the decision to the more remote territorial legislature, where an adverse verdict would do far less damage. Moreover, Cass and others believed that in practice popular sovereignty would lead to freedom, the very result desired by the Wilmot Proviso supporters. The fundamental ambiguity surrounding popular sovereignty was already present. At what point in their territorial existence could the people manifest their will? This ambiguity, which perhaps was an intentional means of coalition building, would be left for the Supreme Court to settle when a case arose. The Democrats were thus able "to convert a political issue into a courtroom case," a valuable stratagem as long as the Court did not issue a ruling.[83]

Douglas originally had other ideas for settlement of the Mexican War disputes. He favored the immediate admission of the entire Mexican cession as a state, circumventing the issue of slavery altogether during the territorial period. Seeing that his preferred approach would not gain support, Douglas relented. In December 1848, he embraced popular sovereignty as an alternative means to achieve his goal, to "take the slavery question out of Congress—where it only kept everybody in an uproar—and banish the accursed problem to the frontier," so that he could concentrate on his important issues—railroad building, a homestead act, and river and harbor improvements.[84] Having adopted the princi- ple, Douglas became a vigorous advocate of popular sovereignty. He argued that the clause in the Constitution giving Congress power over the territories envisioned *territory* as a geographic rather than a political term and held that congressional power over the territories derived only from the section of the Constitution empowering Congress to admit new states. All that Congress could do legally was to organize a territorial government with a view toward ultimate statehood. Popular sovereignty initially was approved as an expedient and was applied in the Compromise of 1850 to the territories of Utah and New Mexico. Douglas played a major role both in introducing the 1850 Compromise bills and in formulating the strategy by which they would be considered separately in order to take advantage of a floating congressional majority.

With the passage of the Compromise measures, Douglas disavowed any further official interest in the slavery question. In December 1850, he told the Senate that he would make no more speeches on the subject. Meanwhile, the Compromise proved to be quite popular across the country, although Fehrenbacher attributes this result to "its general pacificatory effect" rather than to any specific principles.[85] In actual operation, though, things were quite different. Not one of the component parts had the effect that Congress had imagined. But the principle survived, and with it the belief that the Compromise of 1850 was the final, irrevocable settlement of the slavery dispute—a position taken by both parties in their platforms in 1852.

V

American politics underwent great and rapid change during the middle years of the decade, those between the Kansas-Nebraska Act and the *Dred Scott* decision. The immediate cause was the breakup of the Whig party and with it the collapse of the "second party system." Southern Whigs generally supported the Kansas-Nebraska Act, and most of their Northern colleagues opposed it. The Southern Whigs either joined the Democrats, supported one or another new party, or remained in doubt as to their political allegiance. Northern Whigs likewise either remained unattached and uncertain or joined in loose anti-Nebraska coalitions with disaffected Democrats.

For a brief time, however, it seemed as though the new American party, popularly called the Know-Nothings, would emerge as a national force, the beneficiary of turmoil. Between 1853 and 1856, in many parts of the country it was the fastest growing political movement. Its peak came in the 1854 midterm elections, in which antislavery and nativism were strongly linked—so much so that Potter reports, "It was possible to say that the anti-Nebraska men held a majority in the House and also that the Know-Nothings held a majority in the House."[86] Although the Know-Nothings appealed to prejudice against Catholics and immigrants, the party more generally tapped a sense of anxiety and unease that was manifested in a broad distrust of politicians. The Know-Nothing party was antipolitical; its program was to destroy both older parties and to return power to the people. A broadside attack on politicians "provided a persuasive diagnosis of what had gone wrong with local and state government everywhere." Catholics, particularly Catholic immigrants, were visible symbols for resentment, both because they seemed obviously different from older Americans and because they were competitors for jobs and upward social mobility. What they represented "menaced the dearest values of Americans: social order, political democracy, public education, and upward mobility." Moreover, rather than dealing with these threats (and with the immigrants' tendency toward excessive drinking), both established political parties eagerly courted their votes, and the result was an increase in political participation and in bloc voting. Fearful that their own voices would otherwise be lost, many former Whigs turned to the Know-Nothing party as a competing source of organizational and voting strength.[87]

The Know-Nothing movement declined, after 1856, almost as quickly as it had arisen. Antislavery men considered nativism and temperance as distractions from the main issue and found a better vehicle for organizing an antiadministration effort. At the same time, those who wished to escape the rule of established politicians were disillusioned by the ease and speed with which such men as Henry Wilson, Simon Cameron, and Millard Fillmore gained control of the new party.[88] In any case, the nascent Republican party was the beneficiary of this shift in public sentiment against the Know-Nothings. Republicanism was a reformist crusade to restore the principle of majority rule, dethrone Southern dominance of the national government, champion economic growth, and oppose slavery partly on moral grounds but also on the ambiguous argument that the territories should be kept open for free white people.[89] The party's economic principles were appealing to middle-class northerners, and the ambiguity of the party's antislavery doctrine allowed it to appeal "both to those who hated slavery for the black man's sake and to those who hated it because it *brought* black men to the territories."[90] With support from both these groups, the party was able to keep the slavery question in the foreground as a means of uniting its disparate supporters. By 1856, it had begun to unify the various anti-Nebraska factions, and it became a haven for ex-Whigs, who outnumbered former Democrats in the new party by a ratio of about four to one.[91] The new party was also ambivalent on nativist issues, hoping to attract both the support of former Know-Nothings and the vote of German immigrants, who might be wooed as a bloc to counter the Irish.

The formation of the Illinois Republican party mirrored the national trend. At the beginning of 1856, political factions included Nebraska Democrats, anti-Nebraska Democrats (Douglas fit into this category), Americans, Republicans, anti-Nebraska Whigs (Lincoln was closest to this view), Whigs who became Democrats, and conservative Old Line Whigs who revered Henry Clay but were unsure of their current political allegiances. As anti-Nebraska sentiment grew, men realized that its power was dissipated if it were fragmented. So, as George F. Brown wrote to Trumbull, "I continue to hear the most encouraging accounts, and now we want organization." In response to this concern, the free-soil organizers of the Republican party called for a state convention. They hoped to recruit Lincoln to their ranks and placed his name on the list of their state central committee, though without his approval.[92] Among those attracted were Lyman Trumbull, an anti-Nebraska Democrat who had been elected to the Senate in 1854; William H. Bissell, a congressman; Ozias M. Hatch, a former Know-Nothing whom the Republicans slated for secretary of state; Lincoln's law partner, William H. Herndon; and, finally, Lincoln himself, who identified with the new party after its founding convention in Bloomington. In the fall of 1855, Douglas could pronounce the fusion effort "dead *dead*," but, by the summer of 1856, Trumbull was more sanguine about the Republicans' presidential prospects, although he acknowledged that "it is in the Southern counties that we in Ills. will have most trouble, & perhaps there may be some difficulty in reconciling the Whigs through the center."[93] Those would still be the areas of Republican vulnerability in 1858.

The sense of political flux was captured in the 1856 election campaign. The Democrats deposed Franklin Pierce, the only president ever denied renomination by his own party, because of Northern convictions that he had made a deal with the Southern extremists. There was a solid base of support for Douglas, but he withdrew his name in the interest of party unity. Avoiding a choice between Douglas and Pierce, the Democrats nominated James Buchanan, who was uncontroversial because he had been out of the country during the most intense slavery agitation. Douglas assured Buchanan that the nominee would carry Illinois "with entire certainty. I have no doubt but that we shall give you a handsome and decided majority."[94] But Douglas was being challenged in his own state. His candidates, Shields and Richardson, had lost their races for senator and governor, and it seemed as though Douglas himself might be losing his hold on popular opinion. As Lincoln would say of him in June 1857, Douglas had seen his associates, "politically speaking, successively tried, convicted, and executed, for an offense not their own, but his. And now he sees his own case, standing next on the docket for trial."[95] In short, Douglas would need to mend his fences at home at the same time that he sought to retain his national prominence in the Senate and a leadership role within the party.

The Democratic platform was ambiguous, and this ambiguity was essential to its success. It endorsed popular sovereignty, which appeared to be a victory for Douglas. But it permitted an interpretation of that phrase consistent with the Southern view—that local self-government with respect to slavery was not operative until a territory petitioned for admission as a state. Needing both Northern and Southern votes to win, Buchanan hedged on the question of timing, insisting all the while that the matter would soon be settled by the Supreme Court. Northern Democrats, meanwhile, convinced themselves that Buchanan would assure free play in Kansas and that the result would be a free state; throughout the North, banners proclaimed "Buchanan, Breckinridge, and Free Kansas." Buchanan agreed that a referendum undoubtedly would produce a free Kansas, yet, invoking the Democrats' sacred term *nonintervention*, he questioned his authority to force fairness on a duly constituted body.[96]

Despite an ambiguous platform and an innocuous candidate, the Democrats were given a tough race. The new Republican party nominated the popular John C. Fremont, and the Know-Nothings selected former president Millard Fillmore. Democrats stigmatized their Republican opponents as dangerous revolutionaries, and, foreshadowing 1860, some threatened disunion if Fremont were elected. Ultimately, however, Fremont and Fillmore were competing for the same votes. In crucial Northern states, the third-party candidate polled enough votes to deny Fremont a majority, and the electoral votes of these states were decisive in the choice of Buchanan. The Democrats won, appealing to traditional values, but what the election "meant" or its implications for the slavery question were very much in doubt. Buchanan would soon find himself the prisoner of events.

VI

Throughout the early nineteenth century, the political culture of Illinois was a microcosm of the nation. The fastest growing state during the 1850s, it contained a south, a north, and a border region similar to those of the country as a whole. Originally, the state had been settled from south to north. The extreme southern region, known as "Egypt," was strongly Democratic and most sympathetic to slavery.[97] The northern region, site of the latest settlement boom and the most recent immigration, was antislavery, heavily Republican, reform minded, and even tending toward abolitionism. The central region, the swing vote in the 1858 election, was heavily populated by Old Line Whigs who were unsure of their current affiliation. This region would be cultivated assiduously by both Douglas and Lincoln.

Illinois also resembled the nation in the tendency to personalize political questions and in the high degree of popular interest in politics. Beginning in the 1830s, a tradition of stump campaigning developed in which discourse consisted largely of personal arraignments against the opponent. Davidson and Stuve report that the system sacrificed "all principles of honor and sincerity," replacing them with "mutual deceptions of every grade and character, from which the most adroit intriguer emerged with the greatest success."[98] Votes were given not on principle, or as a manifestation of policy preferences, but as a matter of personal reward or favor. But attention was paid to political contests; they were the stuff of public entertainment and instruction. Fehrenbacher comments, "Political discussion filled the newspapers, extended from pulpit to saloon, and fell like monsoon rains from the lips of countless stump orators."[99]

Speeches and debates were particularly popular and had become a recognized part of the Illinois political scene by the 1830s. These were social events as well as opportunities for political persuasion. Audiences were attentive; they "expected plenty of jokes, partisan insults, and extravagant accusations, but they also listened attentively to fine-spun technical arguments and lengthy rehashes of past utterances and events."[100] Public speaking ability was a prerequisite for holding office. The speeches and debates were reported in newspapers that, like those elsewhere, were highly partisan. The leading Democratic papers were the (Springfield) *Illinois State Register*, edited by Charles H. Lanphier, and the *Chicago Times*, edited by James Sheahan. For the Republicans, the best papers were Joseph Medill's *Chicago Press and Tribune* and the (Springfield) *Illinois State Journal*. Newspaper editors played significant roles as advisers to the candidates.

Like the rest of the country, Illinois was marked by ambivalence between nativism and appeals for the immigrant vote. Heckman estimates that in 1858 there were approximately thirty thousand Know-Nothings in the state; in a close election, they could provide the critical margin. But there also were large numbers of Irish and German immigrants, particularly in the north. Both immigrant groups had been sources of Democratic votes, and the Irish still were, but the Germans had been antagonized by extreme states' rights and proslavery views and had begun supporting Republicans.[101] As a result, Republican candidates would need to walk a particularly fine line in order not to antagonize either nativists or immigrants while appealing for votes from both.

Most of all, however, Illinois resembled the rest of the nation in the evolution of the slavery question. In the 1830s, most people preferred to leave the whole subject alone as a way to avoid rancor. In contrast, by the 1850s, slavery was the dominant question in state politics. "Candidates for such offices as mayor, sheriff, constable, and even membership on school boards," Heckman reports, "devoted much of their campaign time to a rehash of what should be done in Kansas rather than to statements on how they intended to run their offices if elected."[102]

Illinois lay within the boundaries of the Northwest Territory, from which slavery had been prohibited by the Ordinance of 1787. But the Northwest Ordinance was also ambiguous, and throughout most of the territorial period it was interpreted as outlawing the introduction of new slaves into the region, without affecting the status of slaves already there or that of their descendants. Accordingly, slavery continued in Illinois until statehood was achieved in 1818. Then the first state constitution outlawed both slavery and long-term indentures, but it did not interfere with existing slaves or indentured servants. Even this action was taken not because of the Northwest Ordinance—which many in Illinois believed not to be binding—but because of the fear that Congress simply would not accept a constitution permitting slavery. Even so, the 1818 constitution was similar to that of Tennessee and more sympathetic to slavery than that of either Indiana or Ohio. The first session of the General Assembly, in 1819, proceeded to pass harsh "black laws" that incorporated many of the provisions of the territorial code that virtually gave a free hand over slaves or servants to the owner or master.[103]

In the mid-1820s, in fact, there was talk of a convention to rewrite the state constitution in order to adopt slavery. This effort reflected the belief that the Northwest Ordinance was binding only during the territorial period and that the state had the right to decide whether it would be slave or free. The call for a convention was defeated, and that disposed of all consideration of becoming a slave state. Afterward, however, there was no strong antislavery movement; the issue just died down. Meanwhile, the legislature left intact the "black laws" of 1819, and, in the 1825 case of *Cornelius v. Cohen*, the state supreme court upheld masters in their right to hold slaves who had arrived in Illinois prior to statehood.[104] Descendants of the original slaves remained slaves, with the result that the 1820 census showed 917 slaves in Illinois (probably including indentured servants) and the 1830 census showed 746. As late as 1845, there were still slaves in Illinois; not until that year did the state supreme court reverse its earlier rulings exempting descendants of the original French slaves from the provisions of the Northwest Ordinance.[105] Even in 1854, an appeal was made on economic grounds for the introduction of slavery as an antidote to panics and depressions.[106]

One searches in vain for evidence that many Illinoisans considered slavery to be a matter of morality or principle. Douglas was closer to the mark when he frequently asserted that Illinois had tried slavery, found that it was not economical, and abandoned it for that reason. Southern Illinois retained a strong proslavery bias, and racial discrimination was widespread throughout the state. In the early 1840s, free blacks "were not allowed to vote, to sue for their liberty in the courts, to serve as witnesses, to hold property, to serve in the State militia, or reside in the State without showing a certificate of freedom at some County Commissioner's Court and giving a thousand dollars bond that they would never become a county charge."[107] Little had changed by the 1850s. The new constitution, adopted in 1847 and ratified by a large majority, forbade free blacks not already in Illinois from entering the state. The legislature moved in 1853 to enforce this clause through fines for entering and compulsory labor if the fines were not paid.[108] Although there were questions about the constitutionality of the exclusion clause, it remained on the books until 1865. A new state constitution in 1862 contained an exclusion clause, and it was adopted by a popular majority of more than 100,000 votes, better than two to one. As late as September 1864, an indictment was brought against a man who allegedly brought a slave into Illinois for the purpose of setting her free.[109] As for free blacks already in the state, they could remain, so long as they were law abiding, but they still could not become citizens, possess property, attend public schools, or hold office.[110]

The fact that Illinois traditionally had been hospitable to slavery was a powerful constraint on speakers discussing the institution during the 1850s, but that was not the full story. An antislavery movement, albeit small and ineffectual, could be traced back to the 1830s. Elijah Lovejoy's *Alton Observer* is credited with helping create the first "general antislavery sentiment" during 1836–37. The Illinois Antislavery Society was organized in October 1837, but the movement did not assume major proportions until some time after Lovejoy's death. A small group of lawyers, among them Lyman Trumbull, brought cases to court challenging the indenture system. In 1849, Illinois, like many other Northern states, instructed its senators and representatives to vote for the Wilmot Proviso (instructions that were repealed in 1851).[111]

During the 1850s, antislavery causes gained much greater adherence, especially in northern Illinois. This was an important shift in public opinion, to which political leaders had to be sensitive. The state's population quadrupled, and many of the new settlers came from the East and from abroad. They lacked the sympathy for slavery that was found among the older generation, who had settled the state from the south. Illinois presented the political candidate with a clear case of public opinion in flux. Candidates who wished to be elected, and not merely to speak to their principles, had to devise a position that somehow could appeal to the growing antislavery sentiment of northern Illinois, to the central tier of counties where the Old Line Whigs were mildly antislavery but strongly antiabolition, and to the voters of Egypt, who were basically sympathetic toward the institution and hostile to any type of government interference. Creating a viable coalition would require attention to nuances and subtle shades of meaning, and there were limits to what any candidate could say.

VII

Lincoln and Douglas were no strangers to Illinois politics, or to each other, when they met in debate in 1858. Douglas was by far the better known, and his record was a string of political successes going almost all the way back to his arrival in Illinois in 1833 at the age of twenty. He taught school, obtained a law license, and spoke for the Democrats at political rallies. He developed an avid interest in politics. Beginning in the mid-1830s, he served as state's attorney, a member of the Illinois legislature, register of the land office at Springfield, secretary of state for Illinois, and a judge of the Illinois Supreme Court. In 1842, he was elected to the U.S. House of Representatives, where, as an ardent advocate of expansion, he was named to chair the Committee on Territories. He assumed the same position in the Senate, to which he had been elected in 1846 and reelected in 1852. In each of the past two presidential elections, he had been considered as a possible candidate. He had experienced only two major defeats: in 1838, when he lost his first race for Congress to Lincoln's law partner, John T. Stuart, and in 1842, before he was even of age to be a senator, when he lost a legislative election for that position by five votes.

Douglas was a man of action, not a philosopher. He sometimes seemed to be an opportunist, defending himself with whatever argument was handy at the moment, without thinking through the implications to which his position might lead. But his actions consistently reflected a set of basic beliefs, including faith that America had a unique destiny to fulfill, complete trust in the popular will, and commitment to national growth and expansion. His fundamental unit of analysis was the community since he believed that rights, privileges, and immunities did not inhere in man but derived from the community in which he had his civic existence.[112] Beyond the community, he had a feel for the nation as a whole, which his biographer ascribed to his combining a New England heritage, maturity in the individualistic West, and marriage into the tradition of Southern aristocracy. "His interests were national," Johannsen concludes, "and this fact shaped everything he said and did."[113]

Douglas's early political campaigns were of the rough-and-tumble variety. In a debate with Stuart in 1838, he "used such offensive language that Stuart picked him up, tucked his head under his arm, and dragged him around the Springfield square; Douglas meanwhile biting Stuart's thumb almost in two." In the 1840 campaign, Lincoln wrote Stuart describing an episode in which Douglas sought to avenge an insult in the newspaper by caning the editor in the street. The editor "caught him by the hair and jammed him back against a market-cart." The whole affair, Lincoln reported, was "so ludicrous" that all but Douglas had been laughing about it since.[114] These same campaigns, however, also revealed Douglas's "power to speak to the people in their own language, his use of frontier metaphors, and his determination to stand by his own convictions." These characteristics made him an effective stump speaker and earned for him the sobriquet of the Little Giant.[115]

In the Senate, Douglas tried to deemphasize the slavery question, confident that it was clearly subordinate to the foremost tasks of filling and building up the expanding country and pursuing a vigorous foreign policy. He refused to own slaves himself, disclaiming title to some his wife inherited, but he consistently opposed abolition or free-soil efforts and said nothing publicly to indicate that he regarded the institution as an evil.

Douglas was an effective speaker. Milton reports that his voice especially attracted fascination: "His tones were marked with a deep, vibrant energy and were effective not only in the legislative hall but also in the open air. . . . Round, deep, and sonorous, his words reached his remotest hearer."[116] His physical delivery, including wild gesticulation and frenzied appearance, was relatively typical of stump speaking on the frontier. His argumentation has been criticized as sophistic, even by sympathetic biographers such as Capers, who wrote that Douglas excelled at the device "of misrepresenting the opposition and of twisting logic which, however obvious to the present-day reader of his speeches, seems usually to have convinced his audiences." Capers adds, however, that these techniques were regarded as perfectly appropriate in the context of the time: "As in physical contests in frontier areas there were simply no rules of fair play; one caught one's opponent as one could and took all the advantages offered, though when the bout was over the loser was expected to accept the outcome with good grace."[117] He was skilled at evading the burden of proof. An early incident in which Douglas had misspelled the name of a county, only to discover that so too had the statute that created the county, convinced him to follow the rule, "Admit nothing, and require my adversary to prove everything material to the success of his cause."[118] He sometimes employed diversionary arguments, and he could be accused of inconsistency. Yet his oratorical prowess was probably his most outstanding attribute. Capers offers the judgment, "From his schooldays until the presidential campaign of 1860, a year before his death, the Little Giant influenced his fellow men chiefly through the spoken word."[119]

Lincoln compared himself unfavorably to Douglas. Reflecting on their acquaintance over twenty years, he wrote, "With *me,* the race of ambition has been a failure—a flat failure, with *him* it has been one of splendid success. His name fills the nation; and is not unknown, even, in foreign lands."[120] So great is the Lincoln legend that it is difficult to remember that for most of his career he was eclipsed by Douglas.

After Lincoln's death, correspondents wrote to Herndon that Lincoln had been a Jackson Democrat when he left Indiana for Illinois and that he converted to the Whig cause shortly thereafter.[121] He remained a Whig for the duration of the party's life, and, since Illinois was a heavily Democratic state, this allegiance limited his prospects for political advancement. He was elected to the state legislature in 1834 and served for four terms, distinguishing himself by his support for internal improvements and for moving the state capital from Vandalia to Springfield. His political philosophy was articulated in an 1838 address to the Young Men's Lyceum of Springfield. His major theme was that the personal heroism of the Revolutionary generation was no longer an adequate source of moral guidance since Americans no longer had personal knowledge of the founders. Instead it must be replaced with fidelity to laws, and respect for law as a civil religion, so that the legacy of the Founders might be extended.[122]

Lincoln's own political participation included working in law partner John T. Stuart's successful campaign against Douglas for Congress. He married in 1842, and his wife, the former Mary Todd, encouraged his political activities and strengthened his ties to the Whig party. In 1844, he agreed with Henry Clay's opposition to the annexation of Texas, but the following year—after Clay had been defeated by third-party defections that allowed James K. Polk to carry New York State—he made light of the issue, finding that not much good would come from annexation but neither would it augment the evil of slavery since slaves taken to Texas would reduce the numbers elsewhere.[123] This was a very different position from the one that he would espouse a decade later in the Kansas conflict.

In 1846, Lincoln was elected as the state's sole Whig congressman. In Washington, he opposed the Mexican War and the slave trade in the

District of Columbia. He supported Zachary Taylor over Clay for the 1848 presidential nomination on the grounds that Taylor was more electable. Each of these was an unpopular position at the time. Lincoln was not returned to Congress, though not because of his record. He had a prior understanding with Whig leaders that he would vacate the post after one term so that it might be passed around among other deserving aspirants.[124]

As a congressman, Lincoln did not become much involved in the slavery controversy, although he generally voted in favor of prohibiting slavery in the territories. He was far better known for his "spot" resolutions, introduced in December 1847 and calling on President Polk to identify the spot where American blood had been shed on American soil—the rationale that Polk had used to justify war with Mexico. These resolutions were disliked by his constituents at home. As Angle explains, "They had gone into the war with enthusiasm, they were proud of the record of their soldiers, and they wanted no one to tell them that they had been in the wrong."[125] A decade later, the Democratic press was still invoking the "spot" resolutions to question Lincoln's judgment.

Out of office, the former congressman returned to private law practice in Springfield. He enjoyed modest success but developed a reputation for his understanding of legal principles, the simplicity of his explanations, and his ability to woo judge and jury alike. When he accepted a case, he worked tirelessly for his client, whether the principles at issue were noble or base. He thought so naturally in legal categories and language that he sometimes expressed himself that way even in political speeches. Like Douglas, he tried whenever possible to shift the burden of proof to the opponent, but, particularly in speaking to juries, he stressed simplicity of presentation. One of his most characteristic traits, Randall writes, was "his knack of taking a complicated subject, going to the core of it, and coming through with a lucid statement of essentials."[126] While practicing law, Lincoln supported the cause of Hungarian freedom by espousing the right to revolution, delivered eulogies for both Zachary Taylor and Henry Clay, and embarked on a program of study to master the first six books of Euclid.[127]

The Kansas-Nebraska Act brought Lincoln back into politics, and he soon became a leader of the anti-Nebraska forces. His first denunciation of the act came in a speech delivered on August 26, 1854 in Winchester, where Lincoln was campaigning for the reelection of Richard Yates to Congress. He followed with speeches at Carrollton and Jacksonville and early in September debated the question with John Calhoun at Springfield. In early October, he spoke at Springfield and Peoria, arguing that Douglas's popular sovereignty actually encouraged the spread of slavery.

At the state fair in Springfield, he and Douglas appeared successively on the same platform, and both previewed the issues that would be developed more fully in the debates four years later. [128]

Lincoln's prominence in the anti-Nebraska cause led to his being considered a candidate for the Senate in 1854, contesting the seat of Democrat James Shields, who was up for reelection. Douglas was confident that Shields could be sustained and urged his friends to portray the Whig opposition as prejudiced: "Throw the responsibility on the Whigs of beating him *because he was born in Ireland.*"[129] But when the legislative elections were completed—Lincoln, incidentally, was among those elected—it became apparent that the Whigs, together with the abolitionists and anti-Nebraska Democrats, held a majority and could elect the senator if they were united. Lincoln agreed to become their candidate. Five anti-Nebraska Democrats, though, could not bring themselves to support an ex-Whig and held out for Lyman Trumbull. Fearing that Shields would withdraw in favor of a more popular Democrat, Lincoln took his name out first and urged his followers to vote for Trumbull, to assure the election of an anti-Nebraska senator and to rebuke Douglas. This episode would be cited by Douglas four years later to support his claim that Lincoln and Trumbull were plotting against Douglas so that Lincoln might have the Little Giant's seat to avenge his own loss in 1854.

Lincoln remained a Whig even as the party disintegrated after 1854. He showed no sign of support for the Know-Nothings, and, although his name was sometimes placed on Republican documents without his knowledge, he did not join the new party until the Bloomington convention of 1856. There he delivered what has become known as his "lost speech," said to be so powerful and eloquent that reporters put down their pens and forgot to take notes. The crowd asked him to speak, expecting to be amused. Instead, he delivered a rousing speech, according to reports, that sought to quiet the extremists and hold the allegiance of the Old Whigs while also proclaiming slavery to be morally wrong, opposing any extension of the institution, and insisting that Kansas must join the Union as a free state. [130] During the 1856 campaign, Lincoln was considered as a prospect for the Republican vice presidential nomination, and he spoke frequently against permitting any extension of slavery.

Lincoln has been aptly described as "a political leader rather than an intellectual," and his thinking about slavery was constrained by the details of the situation. These included devotion to the Constitution, which sanctioned slavery; recognition of property interests in the slave; belief in the rights of local democracies; and understanding the complexity of the matter. [131] He denied adherence to any ideology or doctrine, though he did believe that man had a higher nature and should seek to approximate the divine law for the government of men. Believing that few things were wholly good or wholly evil, he usually took positions based on practical considerations and not on principle alone. He was a conservative who somewhat distrusted the clarion call for reform. As a general principle, he thought it better to preserve the work of the past, at least until men could be found whose understanding was superior to that of the Founding Fathers. He trusted in the ability of people to govern themselves, even as he believed that the affairs of men were generally predetermined and that he was responding to events over which he had no control. Like Douglas, Lincoln regarded economics as important to his political thought, but he concentrated more on individuals' social mobility than on overall economic growth. And, like Douglas, he was committed to the idea of the American Union as unique, endowed by God with the mission to demonstrate that democracy could work, and as an organic whole that could not be separated. [132]

If Douglas's views about slavery remained fairly constant, Lincoln's clearly evolved. Simon's biography of Lincoln's early career traces antislavery convictions to his early childhood, and John Hanks told Herndon in 1865 that Lincoln's opinions on slavery were formed during a trip to New Orleans, when he saw a mulatto being sold at auction and vowed that, given the chance, he would hit slavery hard. But Hanks was not present in New Orleans, and there is no reliable evidence that the incident, part of the Lincoln legend, ever occurred. [133] His first public comment was in 1837 in the Illinois legislature, when he decried slavery as an evil but went on to argue that abolition made matters worse. With few exceptions, he said nothing else about slavery publicly for over a decade. Twice as a lawyer he was involved in claims to slaves. In 1841, he won the case of a black girl who, though residing in free Illinois, was sold. In 1847, he lost the case representing a master seeking to reclaim a fugitive. [134]

Only after 1854 did Lincoln's views on slavery become relatively fixed. He opposed slavery as an evil in itself and as a denial of the right to rise. When southerners compared the condition of the slave favorably to that of the free black laborer in the North, Lincoln insisted that they missed the point. There was no such thing as a fixed laboring class in the North. As he said in Kalamazoo in 1856, "The man who labored for another last year, this year labors for himself, and next year he will hire others to labor for him."[135] In denying this fundamental right to rise, slavery denied the very humanity of the slave. Moreover, to keep one group from exercising its rights would create a precedent for excluding others. Slavery also depressed the wages of white workers, contradicted the ideals of the Declaration of Independence, and violated the law of God.[136]

By the standards of his day, Lincoln's racial thinking was enlightened, although it is easy for a twentieth-century reader of his speeches to find evidence of racism. Fehrenbacher attributes the fact to expediency rather than principle but notes that Lincoln "did plainly endorse the existing system of white supremacy, except for slavery."[137] He continued to define the problem as a matter only of slavery extension, not abolition. He continued to support the colonization movement because of his conviction that the races could not coexist peacefully in America. He was solicitous of the South and held the entire country, not just the one region, responsible for slavery. In his 1854 Peoria speech, he remarked, "I think I have no prejudice against the Southern people. They are just what we would be in their situation. If slavery did not now exist among them, they would not introduce it. If it did now exist among us, we should not instantly give it up."[138] These signs indicated that, even in the 1850s, Lincoln was a moderate on the slavery question. And only a moderate would have a chance of building a winning coalition.

The earliest evidence that Lincoln presented of his rhetorical prowess was as a storyteller in his youth. He would deliver orations from the tree stump, much to the consternation of his father, who begrudged the time lost from work. After Lincoln's death, Nat Grigsby recalled that as a boy he "was figurative in his speeches—talks and conversations. He argued much from analogy and explained things hard for us to understand by stories—maxims—tales and figures."[139] His earliest study of language came during the 1830s when he participated in the New Salem Debating Society and read through Kirkham's *Grammar*.[140] He cultivated a combative style of argument, including mimicry and satire, but in his later years he fused metaphor and analogy with logic, and he became more precise and eloquent.

Lincoln often spoke extemporaneously, sometimes keeping notes afterward so that he could remember a significant statement that he had developed orally. Many of his most-remembered phrases, however, were carefully worked out in advance and then perhaps inserted into an extemporaneous speech. Lincoln used *Lessons in Elocution* by William Scott of Edinburgh as a guide to preparation; Handlin and Handlin contend that the book "reinforced his inclination to figurative modes of speech, peppered with familiar stories, fold characters, and tales of common experience." As for oratorical models, Herndon maintains that Lincoln regarded Daniel Webster's second reply to Hayne as the outstanding example.[141] He continued to use anecdotes and stories—

Herndon wrote that he "saw a philosophy in a story, & a school master in a joke"—but less so in formal speeches and debates.[142] He also made less use of direct quotation than was common among speakers of his time. He had a thorough knowledge of the Bible and made many allusions to Scripture, but he tended to weave them together with his own ideas.[143]

Among the rhetorical figures, Lincoln made extensive use of metaphors and similes, drawn principally from common things and experiences in order to make his arguments clearer and more vivid. "Bears, dogs, other animals, and bees and birds often came to his mind as he sought telling comparisons," Blegen notes. "Douglas was, of course, the victim of his sharpest gibes." In addition, Lincoln characteristically employed repetition of sounds, words, and grammatical structures; alliteration and assonance are frequently to be found in his speeches.[144] When he spoke extemporaneously, his physical response was often vigorous, but his facial and bodily expressions were less intense on occasions calling for formal speeches. Lincoln suffered from stage fright and seemed wooden and afraid for the first few moments of a speech. Once the stage fright wore off, however, he became considerably more animated.[145] The same pattern would be repeated during his debates with Douglas.

VIII

When Lincoln and Douglas met at Bement to arrange their joint canvasses, they had already been engaged in political debate for nearly twenty years. During the 1836–37 session of the state legislature, they took opposite sides on a resolution supporting slavery in the slave states as a "sacred" right and upholding slavery in the District of Columbia. The resolution passed by a vote of seventy to six; Douglas was in the majority, and Lincoln was opposed. Then, during the 1838 congressional contest, Lincoln reportedly substituted for Stuart when the candidate became ill in Bloomington.[146]

The first scheduled debates between Lincoln and Douglas occurred during the winter of 1839–40, at the beginning of the presidential campaign between Martin Van Buren and William Henry Harrison. Each of the Illinoisans spoke as a surrogate for his candidate. A heated political discussion in the back of Joshua Speed's store in Springfield was continued as a public debate. Additional speakers were enlisted and three days reserved for the exchange. Douglas sought to defend Van Buren's subtreasury plan, but Lincoln, quoting statistics from government documents, found factual errors throughout the Little Giant's presentation.

No records were kept. The *Sangamo Journal* contained a report favorable to Lincoln, but Joseph Gillespie wrote Herndon after Lincoln's death that the Whig "did not come up to the requirements of the occasion. He was conscious of his failure and I never saw any man so much distressed. He begged to be permitted to try it again, and was reluctantly indulged, and in the next effort he transcended our highest expectations."[147] There were, indeed, a series of joint debates, focusing especially on the subtreasury plan, and Lincoln sharpened his argument as they proceeded.

One episode from the 1839–40 debates is particularly interesting and ironic. Each man had accused the other's candidate of harboring abolitionist sentiments. Douglas was thought to be involved in the composition of an editorial in the *State Register,* which read, "Whenever an abolitionist is found, he is loud and warm in the support of Harrison."[148] For his part, Lincoln asserted, in a debate on April 30, 1840, that Van Buren supported Negro suffrage under certain conditions. Douglas denied it. Lincoln then read from Van Buren's campaign biography to substantiate his charge; Douglas dismissed the book as a forgery. Not to be outdone, Lincoln produced a letter that a prominent Illinois Whig had obtained from Van Buren and that Lincoln carried in his pocket until the time was right. The letter certified that the account in the campaign biography was accurate. As King relates what happened next, "Nothing daunted, Douglas stepped to the barrel that served as a rostrum, grabbed the book and flung it far into the crowd. 'Any man who would write such a book,' he shouted, 'and send it out to the great West, expecting that it would advance Van Buren's interest was a d——d fool.' "[149] This episode not only revealed the depth of antiabolitionist sentiment and the delicacy with which the issue had to be approached but also pointed up the boisterous nature of the campaigning during the 1830s and the liberty that both men took with the evidence. Considerable maturation took place in later debates.

During the 1840s, the two future candidates, both lawyers, met from time to time on opposing sides of a case. Their most famous confrontation was in the Truett-Early murder case of 1841. Truett had accosted Early in a Springfield hotel, displayed a pistol, and demanded to know if Early had written resolutions attacking Truett's father-in-law. Without answering, Early tried to protect himself with a chair. Truett fired, and Early fell; he died three days later. Seemingly, Douglas, as head of the prosecuting team, had an airtight case, but Lincoln won the case for the defense. He raised reasonable doubt about Truett's guilt by establishing that Early's chair was a deadly weapon and that Truett had shot in self-defense![150] In addition to the Truett-Early case, Lincoln appeared at least once before the Illinois Supreme Court while Douglas was one of the justices.[151]

Lincoln and Douglas did not encounter each other again until 1854, and then it was not directly in debate. Both then and the next year, Douglas declined to debate either Lincoln or Trumbull and suspected them of trying to take advantage of his own crowds. But the two men made speeches at the state fair in Springfield that, taken together, have the characteristics of a debate. Lincoln opposed the Kansas-Nebraska Act and called for restoration of the Missouri Compromise. He denied that popular sovereignty was equivalent to self-government since it denied that right to blacks. Moreover, he did not believe that such a momentous national issue as the future of slavery in the territories should be regarded as a trivial, local question and removed from the halls of Congress. Douglas had spoken the day before and followed Lincoln with another speech, in both of which he set out and sought to defend the theory of popular sovereignty. These speeches contained in embryonic form the arguments that both candidates would hurl at each other in 1858.

Lincoln's speech was virtually repeated two weeks later at Peoria, and it has become known to history as the "Peoria speech." It was notable for its careful staking out of a position. Lincoln did not recite the cruelties of slavery but stuck to the legal aspects of the question. He did not call for abolition, but he was equally uncompromising in his opposition to the Nebraska bill. Moral indignation against that measure was combined with appeals to the Founding Fathers. "The result," Neely writes, "was to legitimize the antislavery movement as conservative and thoroughly American."[152] Lincoln was beginning to demonstrate his ability to find an acceptable position that recognized that many voters were both antislavery and antiabolition.

The final encounter preceding the debates took place in June 1857 in Springfield. On June 12, Douglas spoke on "Kansas, Utah, and the *Dred Scott* Decision"; it was his first public statement about the decision, which had been rendered three months earlier. There was no formal debate; in fact, Lincoln did not reply until two weeks after Douglas had spoken. But the two speeches could be viewed in retrospect as rehearsals for the debates. They contained virtually all the arguments that the candidates would employ in debate the following fall.

It was in his Springfield speech that Douglas initiated the argument that *Dred Scott* established only an abstract right and that friendly local legislation was necessary to make that right effective. Hence, notwithstanding the *Dred Scott* case, a territory could maintain popular sovereignty by withholding friendly legislation. He also vigorously argued for the inferiority of the Negro and portrayed equality and racial amalgamation as the consequences of Republican policy. In 1858, the Buchanan administration's newspaper, the *Washington Union*, would pillory Douglas for his "friendly legislation" escape clause, but in 1857 it printed Douglas's speech in full and said that it deserved "unqualified commendation." To the degree that the *Union* was a reliable guide to Southern sentiment, this endorsement suggested that the "friendly legislation" thesis was not by itself sufficient to antagonize the South.[153]

For his part, Lincoln did not dispute the "friendly local legislation" argument, nor did he yet attribute the *Dred Scott* decision to the work of the "slave power" conspiracy. He also saw no ultimate solution to the slavery problem other than colonization. But he did allege that popular sovereignty was "a mere deceitful pretense for the benefit of slavery." He used his speech to narrow the scope of the *Dred Scott* ruling, contending that only the denial of Negro citizenship was authoritative. He distinguished between undermining the decision and working to reverse it; he eschewed the former and promised the latter. And he resisted Douglas's attempt to portray the Republicans as favoring racial amalgamation, protesting "against that counterfeit logic which concludes that, because I do not want a black woman for a *slave* I must necessarily want her for a *wife*."[154] Finally, he traced his belief in each man's right to control his own labor to the statement in the Declaration of Independence that all men are created equal, and he ridiculed Douglas's contention that the Declaration was meant to assert only that Englishmen who settled in the American colonies had the same political rights as those who remained in England.

The issues were present; ambiguities could not be sustained or challenges avoided indefinitely. The question of slavery would soon be addressed, against the backdrop of mid-nineteenth-century political culture and in the crucible of public debate.

2

The Senatorial Campaign

As the election year 1858 began, Illinois political allegiances were in a state of flux. Douglas, having broken with Buchanan over Lecompton, was persona non grata with the national Democratic administration, and a concerted effort was underway to thwart his bid for reelection. His political base in Illinois had already been threatened by the elections of Lyman Trumbull to the Senate in 1855 and Richard Bissell to the governorship in 1856, both men defeating candidates he had supported. Now he also faced the prospect of a purge by his own party.

I

Administration supporters, sometimes known as Buchaneers after the president, were denigrated by Douglas as Danites, evoking the image of a secret band of Mormons pledging unswerving support for their prophet, Joseph Smith, notwithstanding law or morality.[1] Throughout the year they would excoriate Douglas, calling on him either to declare his support for the administration or else to resign.[2] Failing to defeat him at the state Democratic convention, they held a separate convention in June. They were unable at that time to agree on an alternative candidate but later settled on Sidney Breese, a former senator and now a justice on the state supreme court. Breese held out until late in the campaign but finally agreed to run.[3] He disliked Douglas for both principled and personal reasons, going back to Douglas's support for James Shields against him when he ran for reelection to the Senate. If, as seemed likely, the state legislature were to have an anti-Douglas majority, then Breese could play the same role that Trumbull had played in 1855: another

Democratic candidate, to free Douglas's foes from the need to vote for Lincoln.

Throughout the campaign, both the Republicans and the Danites themselves exaggerated the significance of the Buchanan forces. In April, *Chicago Press and Tribune* editor Joseph Medill predicted that the Buchanan ticket would receive as many votes as Douglas in the election, and Republican papers throughout the fall made what Fehrenbacher judges "fantastic" estimates of the strength of the Buchanan forces. The *Chicago Press and Tribune*, for example, proclaimed in October that Buchaneers were organizing all over the state and faced "flattering prospects of success" in "many of the Democratic strongholds."[4] Obviously, it was in the Republicans' self-interest to portray Douglas as vulnerable within his own party, and for this purpose there were various levels of collusion between the otherwise incompatible Republicans and administration men—strange bedfellows indeed.

Never, however, did the Danites have substantial strength. In July, the pro-Douglas *Illinois State Register* referred to the revolt against Douglas as "an abortion," and, in October, editor Charles H. Lanphier was advised that they would carry few votes even in their stronghold of southern Illinois. Also in October, Vice President John C. Breckinridge broke with Buchanan and endorsed Douglas, a crushing blow to the Danites. In the end, they showed strength in only two counties and polled barely five thousand votes statewide.[5]

The Danites made noise, and probably encouraged the Republicans, but they posed little threat to Douglas, who was more in tune with the mood of Illinois Democrats. After the Trumbull and Bissell embarrassments, he had to be, if he were to have any chance at higher office. At the state Democratic convention, all but one of the ninety-eight counties were represented by anti-Lecompton delegates, a unanimity that was largely a matter of support for Douglas but also a reaction to the vituperative Republican press. The violence of the Republican attacks was a good thing, wrote Democratic congressman Thomas L. Harris; "*It has kept our party together.*"[6]

Douglas, an outcast in the eyes of the Buchanan administration, was the champion of his party at home. Not only that, but his opposition to Lecompton made him attractive to many Republicans—more outside Illinois than in—who saw him as a possible antiadministration "fusion" candidate. Horace Greeley of the *New York Tribune* had urged Illinois Republicans not to oppose him, believing him to be the fittest object for achieving the Republicans' purposes. Some in Illinois took the same line. One wrote to party leader Ozias M. Hatch that Douglas deserved support because of his prominence, his power over public opinion, his opposition to Lecompton, and state pride, concluding that, despite his "temporary mischief," he had "done more to confirm, deepen & justify Free Soil principles than any & all other men." Another wrote to Douglas that he, like "a very considerable number of Republicans," would "do all I can for your re-election." Lincoln later recognized that these defections were "one of the chances I have to run."[7] Other former Whig associates of Lincoln, repelled by what they took to be the abolitionism of the Republican party, saw Douglas as a viable alternative; this group prominently included Usher F. Linder and Judge T. Lyle Dickey.

For the most part, though, Illinois Republicans remained hostile to Douglas. They resented the "outside interference" of the East. Trumbull had written Lincoln in January that "the laudation of Douglas by Republicans" would be short lived, but others were not so sure. The *Chicago Democrat* (a Republican paper) proclaimed that there was "no conflict into which the Republicans of this State have entered so heartily, so thoroughly, so unitedly, as the present." As for "sentimental philosophers and enthusiasts" outside the state, they were asked "to let us alone in this fight." Judd wrote Trumbull that the East would be responsible if Lincoln were to lose the election.[8]

The state Republican leadership was not attracted by Douglas's siren song. At best, they saw him as a recent convert to the cause of freedom who had yet to establish his bona fides. For Trumbull, the litmus test was Douglas's continued endorsement of the *Dred Scott* decision; no one who did that deserved Republican support. "A penitent prostitute may be received into the church," another Republican said, "but she should not lead the choir." The danger was that Douglas, if a Republican, might take over his new party and that the Illinois Republicans would lose their issue. Realizing this possibility, another Republican wrote Trumbull to ask, "*Are our friends crazy* when every thing is so bright in Ill., to have all our hopes and prospects so blasted it is too bad."[9] Some had fancied that Douglas's Lecompton stand was the first move in a sequence by which he would abandon his party and become a Republican; there were even rumors of a bargain between Douglas and Seward that would have brought the Little Giant the 1864 presidential nomination. Few Republicans thought that prospect likely, however, and—especially as long as Douglas endorsed *Dred Scott*—few thought that he would do them great damage.[10]

Besides, Republicans were moving toward consensus on a candidate of their own. Douglas anticipated who it would be, Republican correspondents thought the choice so obvious that no convention was even required, and ninety-five of the county conventions had declared Lincoln to be their choice and sent delegates so instructed to the state convention.[11] There were several reasons for his acceptability. As an ex-Whig, he would balance the ex-Democrat, Trumbull, for whom he had sacrificed the contest four years before. He had done great service for the party, meriting a reward.[12] And it was a strong protest against Greeley and others who were attempting to meddle in the state party's affairs. Lincoln was named by the state convention as the party's "first, last, and only choice," a move that also served to stop a Democratic-inspired interest in John Wentworth of Chicago as an alternative candidate. This nomination—only the second time in American history that a senatorial candidate had been endorsed prior to the election of the state legislature—made the debates possible since it was hard for Douglas to deny a challenge from an officially endorsed opponent.[13]

It *was* confusing. Republicans were uniting with Douglas to defeat the Lecompton constitution, then uniting with the administration to defeat Douglas. The Little Giant, out of favor with Buchanan, attracted some Republican support either on pragmatic grounds or from fear of Republican abolitionism. The urging by some Eastern Republicans for fusion with Douglas backfired, and Illinois Republicans, like their Democratic counterparts, were at odds with influential national leaders within their own party. They coalesced around the candidacy of Abraham Lincoln and officially nominated him at their state convention.

II

Even though there was much prior maneuvering, the opening of the campaign was punctuated by the "House Divided" speech, which Lincoln delivered on June 16, accepting his party's nomination. He espoused the thesis that, in the long run, there was no middle ground between slavery and freedom. The country must become all one thing or all the other, and it was currently tending toward slavery. His motives, most likely, were to drive a clear wedge between Douglas and the Republicans and to minimize the importance of Douglas's opposition to Lecompton. Fehrenbacher's summary explains how each part of the speech contributes to this result: "The concept of 'ultimate extinction' defines Republicanism in terms that exclude Douglas. The conspiracy theory links Douglasism with the onward march of slavery. And the last part of the address demolishes the image of Douglas as an antislavery champion."[14]

Even before the nomination, Lincoln had been invited to speak at the state convention. He had been working on the ideas for some time, but Herndon reports that the speech itself was written between June 5 and June 16. Webster's reply to Hayne served Lincoln as "a kind of model" for the speech, the first occasion when Lincoln wrote an entire speech before its delivery. He spoke, however, without manuscript or notes. When he finished, he took his manuscript to the office of the *Illinois State Journal,* "proofread the galleys, and himself marked the words and phrases to be italicized."[15]

The origin of the key metaphor, the house divided, is biblical. In the New Testament, it appears in Matthew 12:25, Mark 3:25, and Luke 11:17.[16] This speech, however, was not Lincoln's first use of the thought. He had used it in a Whig campaign circular in 1843; he posed the question in an 1855 letter to law professor George Robertson of Transylvania University. He is reported as having used the line in an 1854 conversation with Judge T. Lyle Dickey on the introduction of the Kansas-Nebraska Act.[17] Others, too, had espoused the same idea or even the same phrase. James G. Birney of the Liberty party had written in 1836, "If slavery live at the South, liberty must die at the North. There is no middle ground." Abolitionist Edmund Quincy had used the same biblical quotation in a speech in March 1852. Proslavery literature contained the same theme, beginning with an 1856 editorial by George Fitzhugh that appeared in the *Richmond Enquirer.*[18] The metaphor was not new, but Lincoln put it to new use: not to predict civil war or disunion—possibilities he explicitly denied—but to assert that a united nation would become all one thing or the other and that conspirators were taking it in the direction of slavery.

The speech has three major parts. The short, often-quoted introduction establishes the overall framework for the argument, excluding the middle ground between slavery and freedom. The second, and by far the longest, section of the speech asserted the existence of a conspiracy to make slavery national, by means of a second *Dred Scott* decision that would apply to the states, and identified Douglas among the co-conspirators. This argument was repeated in the opening debate and will be examined in chapters to follow. The final section of the speech discredited Douglas as a champion of the antislavery cause and attempted instead to link the incumbent's position to such odious measures as the reopening of the African slave trade. These three parts are often seen as disjoint, but Fehrenbacher—and, more forcefully, Leff—has argued that they work together to produce a unified whole.[19]

The speech was controversial from the start. Saying that to make the nation all free was the only alternative to making it all slave sounded dangerously close to abolitionism. Lincoln insisted that he was only predicting what would take place. But if he opposed slavery, then his "prediction" seemingly implied a desire for the other alternative. When Lincoln read his draft of the speech, some of his advisers urged against delivering it because it was too radical. Herndon has been represented on both sides of that question, but at least in 1870 his memory was that he had been enthusiastic. Herndon also represents Lincoln as having been doggedly insistent on delivering the speech, on the grounds that the doctrine was true.[20]

The speech and the phrase were widely publicized, both in Illinois and beyond. The Democratic press promptly branded it abolitionism, though cunningly prepared to conceal the full implications of the doctrine.[21] The equation may be unfair since Lincoln was careful not to castigate the South or to propose eliminating slavery where it already existed. Ultimate extinction was to be achieved naturally and gradually, as the eventual outcome of a policy of limiting the institution. Lincoln might well have seen colonization as the means of extinction. At any rate, he wrote Chicago editor John L. Scripps that he was "mortified" that his speech might have been misconstrued, denied the power to interfere with slavery where it already existed, and averred only that keeping slavery out of the territories would have the effect of leading to ultimate extinction.[22]

For a good part of the campaign, Lincoln found himself reexplaining what the "house divided" doctrine really meant. The opposition repeatedly drew the issue back to the doctrine's radical implications, realizing that to do so made Lincoln vulnerable. The *Chicago Times*, for example, described his July 10 speech as "a labored effort to explain away the legitimate construction of his carefully prepared speech to the nominating convention" but concluded that the effect was "to confirm his hearers in their first impression of his abolition tendencies." The *Illinois State Register* articulated a similar view, trying also to see a rift between Lincoln and the abolitionists: "Mr. Lincoln's subsequent explanations of his convention speech are not taken as orthodox by his associate advocates of Negro equality, who are not willing to recognize his quibble making a distinction between his 'wishes' and his 'expectations.'" The paper then explained that Frederick Douglass was giving Lincoln's speech a radical construction, "and the only true one."[23] Such reactions served multiple purposes. They defined Lincoln as an abolitionist and assumed that men such as Frederick Douglass were his close associates. They presumed a correct interpretation of the speech and discounted other interpretations as guile and deceit. They also kept Lincoln on the defensive.

The danger of being perceived as a radical was especially serious in the crucial battleground of the campaign, the central counties running roughly in a band across the state, from Ottawa in the north to Springfield in the south.[24] Both candidates concentrated their attention on this region. Lincoln spoke "at only four places north of Galesburg and at only three south of Alton," and Douglas left the central counties on an extended basis only twice, for the debates at Freeport and Jonesboro.[25] Lincoln's and Douglas's supporters in this area had relatively similar views, mildly free soil but largely determined, as Wells explained, "by a deep-seated suspicion of radicalism of any description."[26] The central counties were heavily populated by former Whigs who were unsure as to their new political affiliation and by the foreign born, whose votes might be solicited en bloc.

In the central counties, Lincoln often eschewed the label *Republican*, instead organizing meetings of "all opposed to Democracy." The Douglas papers made an issue of Lincoln's disavowal of his own party label, but a Pekin Republican was quite frank in writing Lincoln, "You are stronger here than Republicanism and in all of our meetings instead of heading them 'Republican' I shall say 'meeting of the friends of Lincoln.'" In this way, the writer believed, "we can gain something from the old Whigs, who may be wavering, and soften down the prejudice of others."[27] Every vote might matter in this crucial region, and no possible strategic advantage should be foregone.

III

The opening weeks of the campaign saw Lincoln on the defensive. Not only was he under fire for the implications of the "house divided" speech, but he had to respond to accusations that, as a congressman ten years before, he had been unpatriotic in his votes against the Mexican War. Controversial at the time, the war was seen in hindsight as a noble cause, and Lincoln's "spot" resolutions—calling on President Polk to identify the spot where American blood supposedly had been shed on American soil—became objects of ridicule. The *Chicago Times* launched the attack almost immediately on Lincoln's nomination; the *Illinois State Register* took it up a few weeks later. Picking up on the "living dog" reference in the "house divided" speech, the *Times* proposed that Lincoln should be known as "Spot." The *Register* brandished charges of disloyalty on its pages through much of July. Lincoln wrote to Joseph Medill of the *Chicago Press and Tribune* denying the charges but made no public comment for some time. Concerned that Lincoln might not be taking the matter seriously enough, Henry C. Whitney wrote that the attack "is far more dangerous than many persons might suppose" and that the imputation of disloyalty was "the most potent and dangerous weapon that can be used against you in the rural districts."[28]

Nor was that all. Douglas began his campaign in early July, as soon as the Senate adjourned, and was determined to make Lincoln rather than his own record the issue. He followed the advice of Congressman Thomas L. Harris, who wrote him that the Republicans erred "in putting

Lincoln against the field—instead of allowing you to stand against the field." Harris urged that this situation be exploited: "A *severe* canvass against Lincoln is the policy." Republican strategists had anticipated what Douglas might do; they knew, as one wrote, that, if Douglas could focus the issue on Lincoln, then "he will in this way keep public attention away from his past *conduct* & fix it upon his assaults & your defense." Republicans also guessed correctly, as Trumbull said, that Douglas "will seek to create a sympathy among our friends by charging that he is being persecuted by the Lecomptonites."[29]

Douglas delivered his opening campaign speech from the balcony of the Tremont House in Chicago on July 9. Lincoln was present since he was in Chicago for the opening session of the U.S. District Court. Douglas defended his role in the Lecompton imbroglio, explained the *Dred Scott* decision, and expounded popular sovereignty as sacred principle. He attacked the Danites for attempting an unholy alliance with the Republicans, but his strongest fire was saved for connecting Lincoln's "House Divided" speech with radical abolitionism. A Republican might write that Douglas's speech was "just a piece of pettifogging as we might expect from him," but the speech was generally well received.[30] At its conclusion, Lincoln rose to say that he would return to speak the following night. His speech, though forthright, was defensive. He denied any Republican alliance with the Buchaneers, denied that Republicans opposed popular sovereignty as properly understood, and explained his view in the "House Divided" speech. He then forecast several arguments that he would use later, in the debates—the allegation that slavery did not seem to Douglas to be a moral issue, the observation that Douglas was inconsistent with respect to the finality of Supreme Court decisions since he had supported Andrew Jackson's actions during the Bank War, the denial that he favored racial equality, and the proclamation that Douglas's views were akin to the divine right of kings.[31]

The following week Douglas spoke in Springfield. There he cavalierly dismissed the charge that he was part of a conspiracy to obtain a second *Dred Scott* decision. Lincoln was not present at the time but spoke in Springfield the next day. He issued another disclaimer that the "House Divided" doctrine represented his wish; it was only an expectation. He argued at some length that Douglas's support for popular sovereignty was inconsistent with his endorsement of *Dred Scott*. He repeated the conspiracy charge, maintaining that Douglas had not yet answered it. He also repeated his statement that Douglas had not been consistent with respect to the finality of Supreme Court decisions. Again, the speech is largely a forecast of arguments that Lincoln would develop in the debates.[32]

The Republican *Illinois State Journal* praised Lincoln's speech, finding it "a complete and most masterly answer to all the quirks, squabbles, sophistries, misrepresentations and falsehoods of Mr. Douglas." In contrast, the paper declared, Douglas "stoops to low, mean, trickery and resorts to all manner of unfairness in debate, to accomplish his ends but he has not the honesty to meet an opponent squarely in the discussion of great principles."[33] Others, however, were less sanguine. Lincoln's speeches had been defensive and self-justificatory; he had not been able to focus the discussion on the incumbent's record. Leading Republicans, but not Lincoln himself, appealed for help from the other senator, Lyman Trumbull. Trumbull was better known than Lincoln and had a reputation of taking the offensive; his presence would be a real boost to the campaign. Trumbull's agreement to come home to campaign for Lincoln has been described as reluctant, but he wrote Palmer that he felt that his coming was "a duty, & shall take a pleasure in standing by him to the utmost of my ability in the coming contest." He delivered a rousing speech in early August, in which he charged that Douglas had conspired to word the Kansas-Nebraska Act so as to deprive Kansas of a referendum between slavery and freedom. This was the same argument that Lincoln would develop during the Charleston debate.[34]

Throughout this period, however, the momentum of the campaign lay with Douglas. He was gaining endorsements from Old Line Whigs and also from former Know-Nothings. His party was well financed and devoted great energy to impressing voters with pageantry. A correspondent from northern Illinois wrote Douglas, "Mr. Lincoln is not liked here even by the most ultra Blacks. . . . the skies are very bright and we are gaining very fast every day." Lincoln made light of Douglas's claims to momentum; he wrote Gustave Koerner, "It is all as bombastic and hollow as Napoleon's bulletins sent back from his campaign in Russia."[35] But he was trailing. He began following Douglas across the state, taking advantage of the Little Giant's crowds in order to present a rebuttal. David Davis had advised this course, and the candidate himself wrote that "speaking at the same place the next day after D. is the very thing—it is, in fact, a concluding speech on him." But the tactic exposed Lincoln to ridicule. The *Chicago Times*, alleging that Lincoln followed Douglas only because he could not attract crowds on his own, suggested that he join one of the "two very good circuses and menageries traveling through the State; these exhibitions always draw good crowds at country towns."[36] Meanwhile, the *Illinois State Register* launched a new attack on Lincoln, indicting him for saying different things in different parts of the state. This accusation said in effect that Lincoln had no consistent principles but trimmed his sails in order to cater to the prejudices of the audience. This charge, too, would hound Lincoln throughout the campaign.

Republican advisers began counseling the candidate, urging that he must find a way to take the offensive. Norman B. Judd confided in Trumbull his fear that Lincoln "will allow Douglass to put him on the defensive." John Mathers, a prominent citizen of Jacksonville, wrote Lincoln to suggest that he take the role of assailant, "and *keep* this *position* until the close of the fight, & not let Dug, by any *stratagem* drive you from it." (Lincoln found Mathers's suggestion to be "certainly correct. That is a point which I shall not disregard.") J. H. Jordan wrote Lincoln from Ohio, "You are *too easy* on the scamp! You should, you *must* be *severer* on him . . . when you are fairly *driven* to it by his continued rascally perversions and misrepresentations."[37] To regain momentum, Lincoln had to do something dramatic. In this context, he challenged Douglas to debate.

The idea for the challenge sprang from several sources: from Horace Greeley's *New York Tribune;* from Jesse Fell, secretary of the Republican State Central Committee; from the *Chicago Press and Tribune;* and from Lincoln's correspondents.[38] Two motives were reflected in the challenge. First, Lincoln could take advantage of Douglas's prominence and ability to attract crowds. By appearing on the same platform, he could overcome his underdog position. This consideration was particularly important in the light of his difficulty in attracting his own audiences. Second, Douglas's greater prestige and popularity might otherwise enable him to avoid Lincoln's attacks altogether while conducting a unity campaign and weaning away Republican votes. In fact, Douglas was largely ignoring Lincoln, saving his verbal fire for Lyman Trumbull. The challenge to debate would assure that Lincoln was not ignored and that Douglas would be unable to define the terms of the campaign.[39] The proposal sent to Douglas would have involved fifty debates—the *Illinois State Journal* had called for one hundred—and would have virtually preempted the incumbent's calendar for the remainder of the campaign. Conveniently, Lincoln did not issue his challenge until Douglas had just published his schedule of speaking engagements for the balance of the campaign.

The challenge put Douglas in a dilemma. As the better-known candidate, he had nothing to gain by debating, and he risked disappointing supporters whose invitations for him to speak would be preempted by the debates. On the other hand, the frontier West had long employed stump speaking and debates, and Douglas risked serious loss of face if he declined a challenge. "By the middle of the nineteenth century," Heckman writes, "political speeches and debates had become an integral part of the Illinois scene." Debates enlarged the audience, promoted genuine clash of arguments, and saved the voters' time. Applying pressure to Douglas to accept the challenge, the *Chicago Press and Tribune* editorialized that joint canvass was "the usual, almost universal western style of conducting a political campaign, and it has been justly held that the candidate who refused to speak in that way had no better reason than cowardice for declining the challenge."[40]

Douglas replied to Lincoln's challenge on July 24, the same date he received it. His letter referred to "difficulties in the way of such an arrangement" that "recent events have interposed." He noted that he had just released a full campaign schedule and that the arrangements for Democratic meetings "will occupy the whole time of the day and evening and leave no opportunity for other speeches." He expressed surprise that Lincoln had waited until his schedule was released to come forward with the challenge. Besides, he noted, there might be a third candidate—presumably Breese—who would demand the right to debate as well, "and claim the right to speak from the same stand; so that he and you in concert might be able to take the opening and closing speech in every case." These considerations explained why Douglas could not accept the challenge as presented. But neither could he refuse to debate altogether. For this reason, he agreed, "in order to accommodate you as far as it is in my power to do so, [to] take the responsibility of making an arrangement with you for a discussion between us at one prominent point in each Congressional district in the state," except for the Chicago and Springfield districts, where both had recently spoken "and in each of which cases you had the concluding speech." He then proposed a town in each of the seven remaining congressional districts.[41]

There followed a brief "debate about the debates." Republican papers regarded Douglas's letter as an evasion, not an acceptance, of Lincoln's challenge to debate. The Democratic press, meanwhile, asserted that Lincoln's original challenge had been insincere and made only for the purpose of embarrassing Douglas; the speculation, therefore, was that Lincoln would reject the Little Giant's sincere and forthcoming response.[42] Norman B. Judd, who had delivered Lincoln's challenge, sent him Douglas's reply with a cover note stating, "It is a clear dodge, but he has made the best case he could," and passing along Orville Browning's recommendation that he accept the proposed terms.[43]

Lincoln did so, but only after a July 29 letter in which he took issue with the "insinuations of attempted unfairness on my part" in Douglas's letter to him. Indeed, most of Lincoln's letter is a response to Douglas's accusations. He denied knowledge of any move to bring a third candidate into the race. As to why he had not issued the debate challenge earlier, Lincoln said only, "I made it as soon as I resolved to make it," and somewhat disingenuously suggested that he had been waiting to see if Douglas might challenge *him*. As for the charge that Lincoln had already had the closing position in the Chicago and Springfield speeches, that "is hardly a fair statement. . . . in the matter of time for preparations, the advantage has all been on your side; and that none of the external circumstances have stood to my advantage." Nevertheless, Lincoln accepted the offer to speak at Douglas's choice of places and times, "provided you name the times at once." Lincoln's only stipulation was for "perfect reciprocity, and no more. I wish as much time as you, and that conclusions shall alternate."[44] On July 30, Douglas proposed the towns, the dates, and the three-hour format with the candidates alternating the opening and closing speeches. Lincoln accepted these terms the next day, noting, however, "You take *four* openings and closes to my *three*."[45] On July 31, the arrangements were sealed.

In the light of history, the debates would dominate the senatorial campaign, but they were a small part of the campaign as the candidates viewed it. As Mayer summarizes the campaign statistics, "Lincoln covered 4300 miles by train, carriage, and riverboat, and made 63 major speeches and many minor ones. Douglas, crisscrossing the state, piled up 900 more miles than Lincoln and delivered 59 set speeches of two to three hours, 17 shorter speeches, and 37 responses to addresses of welcome."[46] Other politicians both inside and outside Illinois also played significant roles in the speaking of the campaign.[47] Since similar themes and arguments were developed throughout the campaign, it may be appropriate to regard the months from August through November as one continuing debate, of which the seven formal debates were but the most conspicuous part.

IV

The debates were both a serious discussion of the issues and a form of communal entertainment. People arrived early, held picnics and parades, and greeted the arrival of their candidate with frenzied enthusiasm. The debates themselves were carefully managed, however. Timekeepers were strict, and audience demonstrations of anger or applause were discouraged lest they consume time allocated to either candidate. The audiences, in general, did remain attentive for three hours of political debate.

Among the many potential issues of interest to Illinois voters in 1858, only one very narrow question was discussed in the debates. As Wells has observed, neither candidate discussed such important matters as money, banking, securities reform, trade, tariffs, foreign policy, homestead lands, immigration, or the Pacific railroad.[48] The discussion was confined to slavery—and, even there, to a small portion of the issue. There was no challenge to the institution where it already existed, surrounded as it was by legal and constitutional protections. Instead, the debates focused on the territories, where slavery did not yet exist but might someday go. Several factors help explain this narrowing of focus. The candidates were not far apart on several of the economic issues; slavery had been probably the single most prominent issue at least since Douglas had introduced the Kansas-Nebraska Act; both men believed that slavery in the South was constitutionally protected; because of Douglas's chairmanship of the Senate Committee on Territories, he was quite prominently identified with the territorial issue; and the focus on slavery enabled both candidates to assemble coalitions that might have come apart had more immediate interests been at issue.

Even on this narrowly drawn issue, the debates offered little that was new. Each man's basic position had been articulated in speeches throughout the previous year. Moreover, the practical differences between their proposals were small. Whoever triumphed, it was unlikely that any of the existing territories would become slave states—Kansas, where the chances seemed greatest, had finally rejected the Lecompton constitution by a margin of ten to one. But the difference between the abstract principles defended by the two candidates was vast. For Lincoln, the central issue was the extension of slavery per se, whereas for Douglas it was a contest between concepts of popular and congressional sovereignty, the question ultimately being who had the right to decide with regard to slavery in the territories. Moreover, both candidates were competing for essentially the same voters: moderate antislavery Democrats and unaffiliated former Whigs. The conservative cast of both groups dictated each candidate's basic strategy: to portray himself as the man of reason, moderation, and good judgment and to place his opponent in the extreme region of the political spectrum, the province of the fanatic. Capers compares the candidates to "two cautious wrestlers grappling for an opening," both of whom "generally took the defensive in hopes that the other would commit a fatal error. While they spent much of their time defending positions previously taken and reiterating rebuttals, each was seeking to convict the other of inconsistency."[49] The immediate effect was to exaggerate each other's positions and, perhaps, to make the possibilities for compromise seem dimmer. But the greater effect was that the debates made plain the difference between two sharply competing notions of where the nation was heading and how it might get there.

Lincoln had to convince his listeners that there was a basic difference between Douglas and himself; he had to prove that the Republican party was not superfluous in the wake of the Lecompton rejection. To do that, he needed to tarnish Douglas's image as a statesman who could appeal to audiences across party and geographic lines. He wanted to portray Douglas as actually favoring the spread of slavery and to place on Douglas the responsibility for denying the charge. If he could succeed, he would implant the idea that the Little Giant was a radical rather than a conservative, and he would shift the burden of proof to his opponent. This strategy reflected the advice that Lincoln received from his aides and correspondents, one of whom wrote that the strategy must be to "*arraign* him; bring your charges against him, and thus *force* him to *defend* himself—if he can!"[50]

Douglas's basic strategy was similar. He wished to focus attention away from his own Senate record, which he would have to defend, and to concentrate instead on Lincoln, so that he might attack and shift to his challenger the burden of proof. The goal was to engender a perception of Lincoln not as a moderate Republican but as a true ally of the radical abolitionists and therefore dangerous. Douglas frequently charged his adversary with sacrificing American institutions and even the integrity of the Union for the sake of personal ambition. Angle has summarized Douglas's overall strategy, writing that the Little Giant would "stand on popular sovereignty as a basic American principle, harmonize it with the *Dred Scott* decision through his doctrine of unfriendly local legislation, charge Lincoln with advocating sectional conflict, and press the contention that the Negro was an inferior being who was not entitled to the social and political equality which, he alleged, Lincoln sought to bring about."[51]

Both men spoke extemporaneously and somewhat informally. Lincoln refreshed his memory by consulting a book of clippings that included Douglas speeches, quotations from the Framers, and newspaper editorials.[52] He was precise in his word choice and was versatile enough to range "from wit to sarcasm, from homely analogy to solemn eloquence."[53] He made relatively little use of anecdotes or stories, however, and typically avoided any elaborate summary or peroration, choosing instead simply to stop when his time had expired. His voice was described as high pitched and shrill, yet capable of reaching to the edges of the crowd.

Douglas likewise trusted to the inspiration of the moment. He was a master at refutation, particularly employing dilemmas and *reductio ad absurdum*, yet he also sought support by appealing to the audience's sense of fair play. His evidence was drawn either from documentary texts or from the audience's common knowledge of the political events of the day. He spoke in a powerful low bass voice, projecting each word from the chest. The dual nature of his appeal is summed up by Harris's statement that the Little Giant "was ready in repartee, witty, and aggressive, but in criticism he was severe and patronizing by turns."[54]

Far more than most Senate races, the Lincoln-Douglas contest attracted national attention. The primary reason was Douglas's political situation. The nation's two most prominent Democrats, Douglas and Buchanan, had broken with each other over the Lecompton constitution. In publicly challenging the president, the senator hoped to avoid the fate of Democrats who opposed Andrew Jackson only to witness their own political demise. The Illinois race would test both the men and their ideas. Interest was heightened further when it became apparent that Lincoln, not well known outside the state, was an able and adroit campaigner who was a match for Douglas.

The debates received extensive press coverage; in fact, they probably represented the first time that campaign speeches had been reported verbatim. Correspondents from both Illinois and out-of-state newspapers accompanied the candidates, and each also employed stenographers to provide accurate transcripts. The press was highly partisan, so accounts of the debate differed widely from one paper to the next. The major Lincoln papers were the *Illinois State Journal* and the *Chicago Press and Tribune*; for Douglas, the key papers were the *Illinois State Register* and the *Chicago Times*. Southern Illinois was served by the *St. Louis Democrat*, a Republican paper, and the *St. Louis Republican*, a Democratic paper! Horace White and Robert R. Hitt, reporter and stenographer at the *Chicago Press and Tribune*, covered the 1858 debates, as did Henry Binmore and James B. Sheridan, writing for the pro-Douglas *Chicago Times*.[55] Published transcripts varied widely, though, as a paper tended to publish its candidate's remarks in full and then gloss over those of the opponent. Complaints of distortion were widespread; just as commonly, they were deflected. The *Chicago Times*, for instance, contained the assertion that the *Press and Tribune* had accused it of mutilating Lincoln's speeches because "they were ashamed of his poor abilities and wanted to divert public attention from them, under the cry of mutilation and fraud."[56]

Originally, the debates were reported only in the Illinois papers, but they sparked nationwide interest, and soon the speeches were telegraphed and reprinted in the major national organs from coast to coast. Although some editors ignored the debates altogether, Fehrenbacher concludes that even the fragmentary national coverage "greatly exceeded that given most state elections."[57]

V

The first debate was on August 21, at Ottawa. The town was solidly Republican; its congressman was Owen Lovejoy, an abolitionist seeking reelection, and Douglas's biographer has estimated that Republicans made up two-thirds of the audience.[58] Addressing a hostile audience, Douglas sought common ground, and he did so by isolating Lincoln from the political mainstream. He sought to implicate his challenger in the development of an extremist document alleged to be the state Republican platform of 1854. The week before the debate, Douglas had written his friend Charles H. Lanphier to secure information about this platform, and he introduced the matter early in his opening speech, charging Lincoln with conspiracy.[59] Lincoln's strategy for the debate was not so well formed, and to some extent he appeared to be unduly nervous or defensive. He even concluded his speech with fifteen minutes' time remaining.

The debates began with momentum favoring Douglas. Democratic papers seized on this situation and exaggerated Lincoln's discomfort. The *Illinois State Register* cast Lincoln as having "stumbled, floundered, and, instead of the speech that he had prepared to make, bored his audience by using up a large portion of his time reading from a speech of 1854, of his own. He did not 'face the music' upon the points made by Douglas." The *Chicago Times* was even more graphic. Under such headlines as "Lincoln's Heart Fails Him! Lincoln's Legs Fail Him! Lincoln's Tongue Fails Him!" the paper declared:

The exhibition of weakness by Lincoln was humiliating in the extreme: He writhed and twisted, but he could not keep up under the infliction, and at last, long before the expiration of his time, be broke down, and declared—"I have nothing more to say." His friends were deeply mortified at his failure.[60]

The *Chicago Press and Tribune*, by contrast, headlined its story, "Twelve Thousand Persons Present. The *Dred Scott* Champion Pulverized." But, noting that the Republican papers had far more favorable accounts of Lincoln's performance, the *Chicago Times* retorted that their texts had been doctored, probably because "the Republicans have a candidate for the Senate of whose bad rhetoric and horrible jargon they are ashamed, upon which, before they would publish it, they called a council of 'literary' men, to discuss, re-construct, and re-write."[61]

Postmortem judgments of the Ottawa debate were not unlike the "debates about debates" during the 1980s, when rival campaign staffs try to influence public perceptions of an ambiguous event. Richard Yates wrote Lincoln, "We are *well satisfied* with you at Ottawa. Doug evidently felt bad." Judge David Davis likewise regarded the outcome as very positive for Lincoln. A correspondent for the *New York Evening Post* was "convinced that [Lincoln] had no superior as a stump speaker. . . . He is, altogether a more fluent speaker than Douglas, and in all the arts of debate fully his equal." Over thirty years later, stenographer Hitt reminisced that an Ohio politician had judged Lincoln to have "completely worsted the little giant. You have a David greater than the Democratic Goliath." Lincoln himself was more modest, writing the editor of the *Urbana Union* the next day, "Douglas and I, for the first time this canvass, crossed swords here yesterday; the fire flew some, and I am glad to know I am yet alive."[62]

Others, however, were concerned that Lincoln had been overly defensive. A Cincinnati correspondent remonstrated that he was "*too mild*, I fear, on the fellow. You should be more *severe*. . . . Why *dont* you come down on him in a style that he deserves!" Henry Clay Whitney, citing an unnamed source, averred, "You could have vanquished 'Doug' by dissenting from and disapproving of all of that platform that D. read and taking bold ground against its propositions." Another correspondent, anticipating later judgments that Lincoln's Ottawa rebuttal came up short, said, "Until you shall explicitly answer his questions . . . he will from that source derive considerable advantage."[63] Certainly, the Douglas papers claimed for their hero the advantage in the debate. The *Chicago Times*, noting Lincoln's admission that he knew little of dialectic, proclaimed that "his acquaintance with dialectics is quite equal to his knowledge of logic. And his rhetoric is worse than either." The *Illinois State Register*, surveying the aftermath of the Ottawa debate, concluded that Lincoln "will be forced to stand square up to his abolition platform or back clear down. At Ottawa he beat an inglorious retreat, and shirked the issue at the first joust in the lists of his own suggestion."[64]

Six days after Ottawa, both candidates spoke at Freeport, a Republican stronghold in the northwest corner of the state. Lincoln benefited from strategic thinking about how to approach the second debate. He had asked Ebenezer Peck and Norman Judd to brief him about how to handle Douglas's interrogatories from Ottawa. The Republican strategists met in Chicago, and their advice was delivered in a letter handwritten by Joseph Medill, probably written on August 26. It urged Lincoln, "Don't act on the *defensive* at all. . . . hold Doug up as a traitor and conspirator, a proslavery, bamboozling demagogue." It noted that Lincoln would have a friendly crowd and pleaded with him, "For once leave modesty aside." It proposed a rough division of Lincoln's time, indicated that he must reply to Douglas's interrogatories, and then suggested some that might be put to the Little Giant in return.[65] There is a close resemblance between the questions suggested by Medill and those that Lincoln asked at Freeport.

The Freeport debate is remembered most for Lincoln's interrogatories, especially the second question: whether the people of a territory might legally prohibit slavery. Folklore has it that this question placed Douglas in a cruel dilemma: he must lose either his Southern or his Northern support. He might win the Senate seat, but the dilemma would thwart his presidential aspirations. "I am after bigger game," Lincoln is widely thought to have said of his maneuver. But virtually every step in the story is false. Lincoln knew how Douglas would respond since the Little Giant had answered substantially the same question for more than one year. In fact, Lincoln had written in July that Douglas "cares nothing for the South—he knows he is already dead there. He only leans Southward now to keep the Buchanan party from growing in Illinois."[66] Widening the breach between Douglas and the Danites was the probable purpose of the maneuver, which David Potter has described as "one of the great moments of American history."[67]

Strangely, once Douglas had answered the interrogatories, Lincoln did not pursue these themes. He devoted his rebuttal period to further discussion of his own record and to his conspiracy charge against Douglas. The effect was to lose momentum, to convey the attitude that, once Douglas had answered the simple questions, there was little left for Lincoln to argue. The Douglas papers proclaimed their hero's victory with headlines such as "The 'Lion' Frightens the 'Dog!'" (a reference to the "House Divided" speech) and "Lincoln Again Routed! He can't Find the Spot!" (a reference to Lincoln's advocacy of "spot" resolutions during the Mexican War). It was also noted that the Republican *Illinois State Journal* had so far refused to print the complete text of either debate, with the editors themselves "giving their lying versions of the contest."[68] The implication, of course, was that the Republicans had something to hide.

Pro-Lincoln papers took a different view of the debate. Their headlines proclaimed, "Great Caving-In on the Ottawa Forgery," and, borrowing Douglas's own words, explained how the "Dred Scott champion" had been "trotted out" and "brought to his milk."[69] The emphasis of these reports was that Douglas had retreated from his earlier claim to have a genuine 1854 state Republican platform. But his judgment was unduly optimistic. A reading of the transcript of Lincoln's rejoinder suggests that he was not altogether sure what to say in response to Douglas. Willis scored Lincoln's "acceptance of the hair-splitting, logic-chopping methods of his opponent, in which the latter was far his superior," and expressed dismay that the challenger had abandoned "his own natural weapon—the simple and forceful enunciation of broad principles." The same judgment was made by those who were there. Elihu Washburne judiciously stated that "neither party was fully satisfied with the speeches, and the meeting broke up without any display of enthusiasm." Medill was more candid. In a confidential letter written the day after the debate, he admitted that Lincoln was not Douglas's equal on the stump. He then actually predicted Douglas's victory: "I *fear* he will beat us in the *dozen counties* which decide the result. We are doing all we can, but the *ground swell* seems to be with him. The popular sympathy is more on his side than Lincolns." Medill hastened to add, "These are my *private impressions*."[70]

The third debate was held in Jonesboro, in the southern tip of the state, the region known as "Egypt." It was Democratic country but also the area of Buchanan's greatest strength. This region had the most homogeneous population, and the greatest aversion to Negroes, of the state. There were few Republican votes to be had; Fremont had received but 3.8 percent of the county's total vote in 1856.[71] The debate had the smallest audience of the series, and the preparations were the crudest. Heckman reports,

The citizenry did not decorate the town, since there was no community fund from which to secure the money. The platform for the speakers consisted of rough sawed planks from a nearby lumber mill. There were no seats for the audience and very few for the officials on the stand.[72]

Although Lincoln had little to gain from the local townspeople, the Jonesboro debate was important for the larger audience now following the series. Douglas had charged that Lincoln trimmed his views to fit his audience; he had pledged to "trot him down to Egypt" to see if he would disavow the strong antislavery sentiments expressed in northern Illinois. Not only did Lincoln not do that, but he began to reclaim momentum. He analyzed Douglas's responses to the four Freeport interrogatories, focusing especially on the doctrine of "friendly local legislation," the means by which the Little Giant thought territories could exclude slavery despite *Dred Scott*. Lincoln subjected this theory to historical analysis, concluding that it was belied by the facts in the *Dred Scott* case itself. He then added a fifth interrogatory. Douglas believed that protective legislation for slavery was necessary for its spread; Lincoln asked whether he would support such legislation if the slaveholders requested it. Douglas answered in the negative, an answer that, as Heckman points out, offended the South *more* than the original Freeport interrogatory.[73] That one, after all, was ambiguous, but now Douglas's position seemed plain: he would support popular sovereignty only insofar as it tended toward freedom.

Lincoln also sought to subject Douglas to closer scrutiny. The incumbent had stigmatized his challenger by identifying Lincoln with radical Republicans, a valuable form of "negative campaigning" especially in the crucial counties. Now Douglas received a dose of his own medicine. The *Chicago Press and Tribune* had related the cases of two radicals: Thompson Campbell, an antislavery Democrat from Galena, who had been elected to Congress in 1850 with Douglas's support, and Richard S. Molony, supported by Douglas, who campaigned for Congress.[74] Lincoln used this device, most likely, not to tie Douglas to the radicals so much as to deny by example the bond that had been alleged concerning himself.

Shortly before the debate, Douglas had enlisted the aid of Usher F. Linder, an attorney in Charleston and a former supporter of Lincoln. Linder had offered to share the stump with Douglas in order to respond to attacks from both ends of the spectrum, Republicans and Danites. Douglas accepted his offer with a telegram, supposedly saying, "For God's sake Linder, come up into the Northern part of the State and help me. Every *dog* in the State is let loose after me—from the bull-dog Trumbull to the smallest canine quadruped that has a kennel in Illinois." On September 7, a correspondent wrote Lincoln that Linder was planning to come and intimated "that he will be hansomly remunerated or paid for his Services."[75] Republicans got wind of the impending visit and ridiculed the speaker as "God's Sake Linder."

Once again, who "won" the debate depended entirely on which papers one read. The *Chicago Press and Tribune* noted that Lincoln was not "brought to his milk" as Douglas had boasted but said instead "that Doug is 'played out;' that he was completely whipped in the debate." The *Illinois State Journal* thought that "Mr. Douglas rehearsed his stereotyped harangue already delivered whenever he has made a political speech; while Mr. Lincoln came forward with a number of new points, which Mr. Douglas could not and did not meet." On the other hand, the *Chicago Times* reported, "Poor Lincoln was greatly embarrassed," and the *Illinois State Register* thought that the debate resulted in Douglas's complete overthrow of his opponents.[76]

Though few votes were changed in Jonesboro, both candidates gained from the debate: Lincoln demonstrated his underlying consistency and probed the logic of popular sovereignty; Douglas was able to compete successfully with Buchanan for the allegiance of the Negrophobes of southern Illinois.[77] Moreover, the debates began to move past repetition of the same arguments and toward more thorough probing of their foundations.

Three days after Jonesboro, the candidates were in Charleston, a town in east central Illinois that lay squarely within the old Whig region. Republicans had at best a slight advantage over the Whigs, so an appeal to broaden their base of support was critical. An audience of twelve thousand, divided about equally between the two candidates, watched this debate.

By this time Douglas was feeling the pinch of the combined Republican and Danite attack. His Freeport speech was being used by Republicans to convince Buchanan loyalists and southerners that he was not a true Democrat. Lincoln tried to take advantage of his opponent's vulnerability. He followed Judd's advice that "you make your entire opening a Series of Charges against Douglass leaving all Statement of your own views for your reply."[78]

The Charleston debate is interesting because its subject matter is unique. After a few minutes in which he reassured his audience that he did not favor racial equality and that he believed in white supremacy, Lincoln devoted the remainder of his opening speech to developing the charge that Douglas was part of a conspiracy to deprive Kansas of the opportunity to vote on whether the territory would be slave or free. Douglas's part of the plot was the insertion into the Toombs Bill, in 1856, of specific language excluding a referendum—although that language was later removed. This charge was not new; it had originally been made on the Senate floor by Bigler and Trumbull and had been refuted. But Trumbull reintroduced it on August 7 when he returned to Illinois to campaign for Lincoln, and it clearly angered Douglas. At one point, the senator had said that he would hold Lincoln responsible for Trumbull's accusations, and that statement gave Lincoln license to introduce the charge as his own. It also enabled him both to identify with the better-known Trumbull and, by taking over the same charge, to prevent Douglas from ignoring him while campaigning only against Trumbull. In any event, after thorough discussion at Charleston, the argument received hardly any notice thereafter. Only once did either candidate refer to it again, when Lincoln told the Quincy audience that Douglas had been unable to prove his allegation that Trumbull had forged his charges.

The apparent racism in Lincoln's Charleston speech also seems anomalous to today's reader, but it had a simple political explanation. Republicans were being stigmatized by the accusation that they favored Negro equality, a particularly unpopular position in the crucial counties of central Illinois. Their wisest strategy was to distinguish their position from that of the radicals, and that goal could best be achieved, consistently with Lincoln's other beliefs, through denial of a commitment to equality. Even his introduction of the issue—"while I was at the hotel to-day an elderly gentleman called upon me to know whether I was really in favor of producing a perfect equality between the Negroes and white people"—seems contrived, designed more for reasons of campaign politics than for the substantive refinement of the debate issues.[79] Potter describes Lincoln's course as "a minimum antislavery position— one which would make him preferable to Douglas in the eyes of all antislavery men, but which would antagonize as few as possible of those who cared little about slavery." In this way, Lincoln could take the sails out of Douglas's campaign against Negro equality, which the *Illinois State Journal* called "the only thing he harps on, when he knows there is not a Republican in the State that advocates any such odious doctrine."[80]

The danger, however, was that this appeal might backfire, repelling Lincoln supporters in northern Illinois who thought that the candidate's position *did* tend toward racial equality and who favored it for just that reason. Rietveld, for example, has argued that the same ministers who were bothered by Douglas's attacks on the clergy felt that Lincoln's speech had abandoned the moral basis of policy.[81] Lincoln's Charleston remarks were also argued to be inconsistent with his earlier statements. The *Chicago Times*, for example, found the Charleston statement "a most absurd one" in light of the fact that "he had but just asseverated in other towns, his conviction that Negroes and white men are equals." Moreover, this record of inconsistency and vacillation, noted the *Illinois State Register*, should make clear to the people "what little reliance there is to be placed in the modified platforms of black republicanism. Where it is certain of success it clings openly to ultra abolitionism— elsewhere it panders to a conservative sentiment, only to defraud conservative men of their votes."[82]

Lincoln denied that there was any inconstancy in his statements, and to prove it he reconciled his current remarks with what he had said at Ottawa, in the first debate. That only proved, Democrats replied, that *both* the Ottawa and Charleston speeches were incompatible with his Chicago statement very early in the campaign: "I leave you, hoping that the lamp of liberty will burn in your bosoms until there shall no longer be a doubt that all men are created free and equal."[83] These difficulties may help explain why Lincoln did not repeat the racial remarks after the Charleston debate but instead moved to other ground.

One other aspect of the Charleston debate warrants mention. As in the past, Douglas accused Lincoln of having aided the enemy during the Mexican War by refusing to vote for supplies for the troops. Tired of simply denying the charge, Lincoln pulled Orlando B. Ficklin, a prominent Charleston attorney and former Whig, to the stand to respond to the charges. Ficklin, proclaiming friendship for both Lincoln and Douglas, did not respond directly to the question about troop supplies but instead pointed out that Lincoln had voted for Ashmun's resolution declaring that the war had begun illegally.[84] Lincoln took that comment as enough to sustain and vindicate his own patriotism.

Again, the newspaper accounts were sharply divergent. The *Chicago Times* reported that people in the Charleston audience were so satisfied with Douglas's remarks that they left immediately thereafter, "and before Lincoln was half through with his rejoinder not a quarter of the crowd remained to hear him." Among the paper's headlines were "Lincoln Retreats from Egypt," "Trumbull's Slander Refuted! Lincoln's Weakness Exposed!" On the other hand, the *Chicago Press and Tribune* titled its story "Lincoln Tomahawks His Opponent with the Toombs Bill" and "Great Rout of the Douglasites in the Seventh District." The *Illinois State Journal* judged that Lincoln "fairly drove his competitor to the wall" and announced the date and place for the next debate, "if Senator Douglas does not before that time abandon the canvass."[85]

The fifth debate took place in Galesburg, three weeks after the Charleston meeting. In the mid-1850s, Galesburg was a central hub of Illinois abolitionism. Settled by immigrants between 1840 and the early 1850s, it was a solid bastion of Republicanism. It also produced the highest attendance, between fifteen and twenty thousand. Douglas opened the debate, and, although he brought up Lincoln's Charleston proclamations against racial equality as a way to embarrass his challenger, he and Lincoln both addressed issues of principle rather than personality. Perhaps they thought that the voters of Knox County expected an intelligent discussion; perhaps they thought that their earlier positions were now vulnerable; perhaps the first four debates had exhausted the foreplay. In any case, beginning in Galesburg, the debates took on a new tone, with candidates addressing matters of principle. It was in this debate that Lincoln syllogistically "deduced" a second *Dred Scott* decision and foreshadowed his moral argument against slavery. For his part, Douglas strongly articulated the principle of local community self-determination and crystallized his view of Lecompton, the English bill, and the relationship between Buchanan and the Republicans. The last item received special attention, perhaps because the local postmaster had been ousted in a patronage feud.[86]

As before, newspaper accounts of this debate varied immensely. The *Chicago Times* reported that Lincoln's "language is inelegant, his sentences distorted, and his whole phraseology so mixed up that it is tenfold more difficult to render what he says in intelligible English than it would be to report what any other speaker would say." Lincoln was described as "nervous and trembling; . . . he was the most abject picture of wretchedness we have ever witnessed." Lincoln, the paper concluded, "experienced one of the most complete defeats which he has met during the campaign." Headlining its story "Lincoln Again Riddled! His Two Faces Exhibited!" the *Illinois State Register* reported that, on the debate's conclusion, Douglas "was surrounded by an immense mass of people who accompanied him to his hotel, which during the whole evening, was thronged with people going and coming to congratulate him upon his great success; whilst Lincoln, entirely forgotten, was taken care of by a few friends, who wrapped him in flannels and tried to restore the circulation of blood in his almost inanimate body." Both the *Times* and the *Register* claimed that Democrats at the debate outnumbered Republicans two to one.[87]

The Republican *Chicago Press and Tribune* regarded this negative portrayal of Lincoln as the result of misquotation of his speeches. Whereas Douglas himself had admitted that he was being quoted accurately in the Republican organs, he had hired "two phonographic puffers imported from abroad. He instructs them what to say and how to distort and pervert what his antagonist may say, and he pays them for these dishonorable services." As for Douglas's debate performance, to the *Press and Tribune* he "displayed more than his usual effrontery and impertinent pretension." The Republican papers headlined their account, "New and Powerful Argument by Mr. Lincoln. Douglas Tells the Same Old Story" and "The Little Giant Again Badly Worsted in the Encounter."[88]

Six days after Galesburg, the candidates met again at Quincy, a town in west-central Illinois that at one time had been Douglas's home district. Adams County was regarded as "Democratic, though not overwhelmingly so."[89] Located in the disputed central Illinois area, it was a crucial battleground for both sides, and both saw reasonable prospects of victory. There was not much evolution of arguments between Galesburg and Quincy, although Lincoln was more explicit in his delineation of the moral issue. The campaign was taking a physical toll on Douglas, and the Republican papers gloated over his fatigue. To the *Chicago Press and Tribune*, "Douglas grows fainter and weaker. The well directed and firmly planted blows of Lincoln begin to tell, and the Senator is evidently sick." To the *Illinois State Journal*, "All is stale, flat, second handed, and weak. His dodges and quibblings are less adroit than usual. He does not even falsify with his ordinary boldness and ingenuity."[90] By contrast, Lincoln was described as being as fresh as ever, just now hitting his stride. The challenger was again advised not to let Douglas put him on the defensive. James W. Gaines, with whom Lincoln stayed before the debate, remembered years later that he had advised him "that he should assume the aggressive and attack his adversary in turn; that it was useless to defend himself against Mr. Douglas' charge, for as one would be refuted another would be trumped up."[91]

In his account of the Quincy debate, Neely calls attention to two almost tangential features, one that markedly altered the argument and another that might have done so. Douglas, attempting to equate his policy with that of the Founding Fathers, loosely stated at one point that the nation could endure forever divided into free and slave states. Lincoln seized on this remark as a confession that Douglas saw no end to the peculiar institution. Placing the incumbent in that position enabled Lincoln to rally to his cause anyone who believed slavery an evil that ought to end at some time, even if that time be in the far distant future. It was this contrast between himself and Douglas that framed the moral argument that Lincoln developed at Alton.[92]

Douglas did not make as much of his opportunity. He introduced the claim that Lincoln's plan to confine slavery to its current limits would lead to extinction by starvation of the slaves. This contention represented a potentially strong challenge to Lincoln's moral argument, for it suggested that the Republican's means of accomplishing his goal were inhumane, no matter how exemplary the goal. Here was a great opportunity to embarrass the Republicans, especially since, in Neely's phrase, they "always left to the imagination the exact way their platform would end slavery."[93] Douglas briefly repeated this assertion at Alton, but it was never developed into a serious moral alternative to Lincoln's stance.

Again, the newspapers carried quite different accounts of the debate. The pro-Lincoln *Illinois State Journal* reported that Douglas was wearing out, but "Old Abe is as fresh, vigorous and elastic as when the contest began," and the "closing remarks of Mr. Lincoln were perfectly scorching. Douglas was literally flayed alive!" The headline in the *Chicago Press and Tribune* included the judgment, "Lincoln 'Concludes' on the Artful Dodger with a Vengeance." By contrast, the pro-Douglas *Illinois State Register* reported, "Taken together, the arguments of Judge Douglas were of so overwhelmning [*sic*] a character, as to carry conviction to the heart of many a man that day. He spoke with more than usual eloquence and force, and dealt with great power upon the dangerous tendency of sectional doctrines—that could not even be proclaimed by Mr. Lincoln in the land of his fathers."[94]

Only three days later, the candidates traveled together downriver to Alton, in Madison County, twenty-five miles north of St. Louis, for the final debate on October 15. Madison County had a checkered political past. It had voted both Whig and Democratic, and in the 1856 presidential election it had been captured by Millard Fillmore and the American party. It included a vocal Danite faction, one of whose members interrupted Douglas with an embarrassing question as the senator was preparing to speak. There was a large German vote. And there were a significant number of Old Line Whigs, a fact that made the county one of the hotly contested regions for both candidates. Two Republican leaders, Lyman Trumbull and Governor Richard Bissell, both came from the area.

Despite the significance of the region, attendance at the debate was small—approximately five to six thousand, the smallest crowd except for Jonesboro. Perhaps it was the cool fall weather, perhaps the fact that people had become familiar with the arguments and were now eager to cast their ballots. Although Mrs. Douglas traveled by train to hear the debate, the senator was fatigued. His voice was raspy and painful to hear. Lincoln was still in good physical shape and, as Heckman said, even "seemed to gain strength as the campaign progressed."[95]

Douglas had spoken carelessly at Quincy when he implied that slavery could go on forever. At Alton he tried to describe popular sovereignty with an eye to the north, as a device that would result in freedom. Indeed, Neely concludes that "Douglas gave popular sovereignty a more Northern flavor than in any previous debate."[96] His major goals were to capture Whig votes and destroy the effectiveness of Lincoln's moral appeal.[97] He repeated his charge that Lincoln would favor starvation as the way to confine slavery to its current limits, thereby trying to blunt Lincoln's moral claim. He concentrated on three arguments that would place his opponent on the defensive: Lincoln's "House Divided" speech, his attack on the Supreme Court, and his belief that Negroes were included within the ambit of the Declaration of Independence.[98] Douglas also emphasized his differences with Buchanan.

Lincoln's speech at Alton combined the culmination of earlier arguments with the most fully developed articulation of his moral position. He finally took note of Douglas's erroneous statement that the reason Lincoln opposed the *Dred Scott* decision was that it denied Negro citizenship. This was an appeal to the old Whigs to establish that Lincoln was not the radical he had been represented to be; for good measure Lincoln accused Douglas of deliberately misrepresenting him and thereby added a question of character. He followed with another argument well suited to his audience, the claim that he and not Douglas was the legitimate heir of Henry Clay. These contentions he reconciled with his belief that the Negro was encompassed by the Declaration of Independence; he attributed this conviction to Clay as well. He again defended the "house divided" doctrine and attacked that of the Kansas-Nebraska Act. He supported the general principle of local self-government but denied that it applied to the issue at hand, and he also denied that the current turmoil was merely the work of ambitious politicians who had whipped up the people over a false issue. At this point, Lincoln elaborated his sense of the moral issue, "the real issue . . . that will continue in this country when these poor tongues of Judge Douglas and myself shall be silent."[99] He wove together his view of the morality of slavery and his ascription of the same view to the Founding Fathers.

Lincoln may have intended the treatment of the moral issue as his peroration, but he discovered that he had ten minutes remaining. He used it to attack the logic and consistency of Douglas's scheme of "friendly local legislation" as a way to preserve popular sovereignty despite the *Dred Scott* decision. He argued that the distinction was specious if the right to property in slaves is recognized in the Constitution. He then pointed out that Douglas's theory would equally justify Northern states in nullifying the fugitive slave law. With more than a touch of sarcasm, he concluded the debate by saying, "Why there is not such an Abolitionist in the nation as Douglas, after all."[100]

Newspaper accounts were by now quite predictable. The *Chicago Times*, defending Douglas, exclaimed that "this last effort of Mr. Lincoln's is the lamest and most impotent attempt he has yet made to bolster up the false position he took at the outset of the fight." The paper even complained that Lincoln's facial movements during Douglas's closing statement were discourteous and distracting. Its headlines included a reference to Lincoln as the "Artful Dodger" and said that he "Tries to Palm Himself Off to the Whigs of Madison County as a Friend of Henry Clay and No Abolitionist, and is Exposed!" Meanwhile the Republican *Illinois State Journal*, commenting on the same debate, reported, "All accounts agree that Mr. Douglas was badly whipped out. He lost his temper and descended to personalities totally devoid of argument. Lincoln's sledgehammer arguments have been entirely too much for him, and Douglas is glad enough that he is through with the last of the discussions." The *Chicago Press and Tribune*, with less flourish than earlier, included in its headline, "Douglas' Seventh Rehearsal of 'That Speech.' Admirable Summing-Up of the Issues of the Campaign by Mr. Lincoln."[101]

VI

Although there are nuances here and there, Douglas's argument and evidence change little over the course of the debates. His attacks and constructive positions were about the same in Alton as in Ottawa. With Lincoln there is more of an evolution in argument, beginning with the charge that Douglas was conspiring to produce a second *Dred Scott* decision, running through the defensive explanation of his own past record and the seemingly irrelevant Toombs Bill conspiracy charge, and then finally weaving together history and morality in an argument that distinguished between the two men and projected the implications of their positions both backward and forward in time.

Still, a chronological study of the debates will impress on the reader how much is repeated, how little changes. The encounters were largely repetitive, as each candidate tried to make the same basic appeal for different audiences. The arguments were all there at the outset; in fact, they were present in the speeches that each delivered in Springfield in June 1857. But beneath the surface there is a rich interplay of rhetorical forces. If one takes the seven texts as a unit rather than as discrete events, one can discover patterns of argument that build on one another and that evolve and transform over the course of the debates. Capturing the underlying rhetorical action in the text requires that one traverse across the whole field of the debates and that one be alert not just to what is said explicitly but especially to the underlying argument forms and the functions they serve.

3

The Conspiracy Argument

Exposure of alleged conspiracies is a staple of American politics. From colonial times to the present, advocates have accused their opponents of participating in a group secretly plotting to deceive the people in order to bring about a loathsome result.[1] Sometimes the charge may imply only the existence of an ulterior motive, without the further assumption of deviousness. Often, however, it covers activity that is not only concerted but clandestine. Usually the argument is advanced by radicals or fanatics but is not taken seriously by a larger audience. The general public regards the alleged plot as a fantasy in the minds of deluded advocates.[2]

Occasionally, though, conspiracy arguments will become credible to the political mainstream, being advanced by moderates as well as extremists and commanding widespread adherence. For example, the argument that President John F. Kennedy's assassination was the work of a conspiracy has passed beyond the bounds of fantasy and almost become the conventional wisdom. The same pattern of "mainstreaming" the conspiracy argument was evident in the late 1850s. Northern and Southern radicals had introduced the allegations, but Lincoln and Douglas helped make them plausible. They did so by tying together several themes in the political culture of the 1850s: widespread distrust of politicians, who were viewed as scheming and "designing" men; suspicion of extremists, who threatened established mores that linked the current generation with its predecessors; and apprehension about the "slave power," a perceived conspiracy to remake all national politics in the service of the peculiar institution. These arguments were all "in the wind." But Lincoln and Douglas gave them credence by making them the centerpiece of coherent narratives that formed the premises of powerful arguments.

Four substantial conspiracy arguments recur throughout the debates. Each candidate made one major charge—for Douglas, the accusation that Lincoln was plotting to abolitionize the major political parties and thereby the country; for Lincoln, the allegation that Douglas was conspiring to spread slavery all across the land. Each also developed an argument that received less attention. Douglas charged that Republicans were conspiring with the Buchanan administration to exploit federal patronage in order to defeat him. Lincoln insisted that Douglas was secretly working to deny Kansas a referendum on its proposed state constitution, even while publicly proclaiming the opposite.

I

In the opening speech of the first debate, Douglas charged that Lincoln, along with Senator Lyman Trumbull, had plotted in 1854 to convert the two major Illinois parties to abolitionism. Trumbull would rally his fellow antislavery Democrats, and Lincoln would enlist the antislavery Whigs. Having weakened both established parties, Lincoln and Trumbull would unite their forces under the banner of the new Republican party. The terms of the bargain, as Douglas explained it, were "that Lincoln should have Shields' place in the U.S. Senate, which was then about to become vacant, and that Trumbull should have my seat when my term expired." In this way, both Senate seats would be held by abolitionists.

But, as Douglas continued the tale, Trumbull welshed on this bargain. When the state legislature met to elect a senator for the term beginning in 1855, "Trumbull cheated Lincoln, having control of four or five abolitionist Democrats who were holding over in the Senate; he would not let them vote for Lincoln." The only way to elect an abolition senator, then, and prevent the reelection of Shields was for Lincoln to instruct his own supporters to abandon him and vote for Trumbull instead. In this fashion, Trumbull won the Senate seat intended for Lincoln. Now, to hold the new abolitionist coalition together, Trumbull must support Lincoln: "Mr. Lincoln demands that he shall have the place intended for Trumbull, as Trumbull cheated him and got his, and Trumbull is stumping the state traducing me for the purpose of securing that position for Lincoln, in order to quiet him." To obtain Lincoln's assurance that he would not be cheated again, the Republican convention took the unusual step of declaring in advance that Lincoln was "their first, their last, and their only choice" rather than again leaving the election to the wisdom of the state legislature.[3]

This argument served several purposes in addition to its obvious function of stigmatizing Lincoln as an abolitionist. At the outset of the campaign, Trumbull was better known than Lincoln. If the Democrats could explain his support for Lincoln as recompense for his earlier chicanery, they would weaken the credibility of his endorsement of Lincoln and trivialize its significance. Better yet, they might lead Lincoln to distrust Trumbull and thus drive a wedge between the two Republican allies.[4]

Like most conspiracy arguments, this charge was grounded in a factual situation. In 1854, concerned that the Whigs and abolitionists would divide the Democratic party and elect a Whig senator, Douglas advised his friend Charles H. Lanphier, editor of the *Illinois State Register*, that Democrats should unite behind Shields and allege that Whigs refused to support him only because he was born in Ireland. Douglas thought, however, that the Whigs would stick with Lincoln until the last, even if the result was that the legislature was unable to elect anyone.[5] As Douglas predicted, a small group of anti-Nebraska senators refused to support either Shields or Lincoln. Anticipating a deadlock, another pro-Douglas editor, James W. Sheahan, offered to ask Shields to step down, and Shields predicted to Lanphier that the opposition was "holding back to bring out a new man." Shields nevertheless insisted, "I am sanguine and more than that, I tell you my election is certain if well and wisely managed. . . . The opposition is beat."[6] Rather than accept a deadlock, Lincoln instructed his supporters to vote for Trumbull, to assure that an anti-Nebraska senator would be chosen.

There is no evidence that Lincoln harbored resentment against Trumbull, and Trumbull's biographer finds none that he orchestrated his own election.[7] Douglas's accusation to the contrary was based on the statement of James H. Matheny, a former Whig who, Douglas said, was "Mr. Lincoln's special friend." Matheny had been best man at Lincoln's wedding and was a longtime political associate. He had supported Fillmore in 1856, not yet having become a Republican, and Lincoln opposed his nomination for Congress that year. Whatever bitterness had been between them, however, was past history by 1858, and Lincoln supported Matheny for Congress from the Springfield district.[8]

Lincoln responded to this conspiracy charge by denying it, arguing that it could not be proved, and then placing the burden of proof on Douglas. In his reply at Ottawa, he stated, "I have the means of *knowing* about that; Judge Douglas cannot have; and I know there is no substance to it whatever." He ridiculed the charge by pointing out that Owen Lovejoy complained that he was *retaining* the old Whigs and preventing their defection to the Republican party. Yet he added, "Now I have no means of totally disproving such charges as this. . . . A man cannot prove a negative, but he has a right to claim that when a man makes an affirmative charge, he must offer some proof to show the truth of what he says."[9] Presumably in response to this demand for proof, Douglas in the Jonesboro debate quoted Matheny directly. But Lincoln merely enveloped Matheny's statement with his same basic response: just as Douglas had no proof for the claim, Matheny had no proof either. "My own opinion," Lincoln said, "is that Matheny did do some such immoral thing as to tell a story that he knew nothing about." He was exasperated that Douglas would continue to tell the tale despite his repeated denials, noting that "it used to be a fashion amongst men that when a charge was made some sort of proof was brought forward to establish it, and if no proof was found to exist, the charge was dropped. I don't know how to meet this kind of an argument."[10] Lincoln's response was self-sealing: the conspiracy could be proved only by testimony, yet Lincoln could impeach any testimony by claiming that the witness had no direct evidence or did not know what he was talking about.

Although Lincoln tried to impeach Matheny's credentials on the alleged bargain, he did not dispute Douglas's references to Matheny as "Mr. Lincoln's especial confidential friend for the last twenty years."[11] Nor did the allegation of Trumbull's deceit provoke any rift between him and Lincoln. If anything, it increased Republican pressure on Trumbull to campaign for Lincoln, although, as Krug notes, party leaders were even more interested in "Trumbull's experience in debating with Douglas in the Senate, his talents as a speaker, his appeal to the voters in southern Illinois, especially in St. Clair and Madison counties, and his acknowledged organizing abilities."[12]

II

The presumed bargain with Trumbull, however, was not the only basis on which Douglas charged his challenger with being a conspiring abolitionist. He also quoted, in the Ottawa debate, from what he claimed was the 1854 Republican platform adopted in Springfield with Lincoln's name affixed. This platform, which seemed to support abolitionism, was the foundation for Douglas's interrogatories: "My object in reading these resolutions, was to put the question to Abraham Lincoln this day, whether he now stands and will stand by each article in that creed and carry it out." What made the interrogatories necessary, though, was that Lincoln would not "come out and say that he is now in favor of each one of them."[13] Lincoln's unwillingness to acknowledge his own role could be taken as a sign that the plot to convert the parties to abolitionism was secret.

The substance of the interrogatories will be dealt with elsewhere, but the 1854 platform itself became the subject of argument. For Lincoln to be associated with this platform would be embarrassing since it was a far more radical statement than would be palatable, especially to the swing voters of 1858. He first denied that he had anything to do with the Springfield convention, maintaining that he was in court in Tazewell County at the time that it met. Although his name was on the document, he insisted that it had been put there without his knowledge. He did not deny, however, that the statement represented the platform of the Republican party, nor did he indicate whether he agreed with it. The disagreement seemed to center only on the question of whether Lincoln was present. In his Ottawa rejoinder, the Little Giant established that Lincoln had spoken in Springfield on the very day that the platform had been adopted and also pointed out that the Springfield papers at the time reported Lincoln as being in agreement with the platform—a report that Lincoln had never denied. Finally, Douglas told the audience that the question of whether Lincoln had participated on the committee that drafted the platform was "a miserable quibble to avoid the main issue" of whether he endorsed it.[14]

By the Freeport debate, however, Lincoln was ready with a stronger argument. He said that the resolutions "were never passed in any convention held in Springfield. It turns out that they were never passed at any convention or any public meeting that I had any part in." Not only that, but "there was not, in the fall of 1854, any convention holding a session in Springfield, calling itself a Republican State Convention." Where then had the resolutions come from? "Now it turns out that he had got hold of some resolutions passed at some convention or public meeting in Kane County." Lest the discussion focus only on the place of origin, Lincoln hastened to add that he was "just as much responsible for the resolutions at Kane County as those at Springfield, the amount of the responsibility being exactly nothing in either case; no more than there would be in regard to a set of resolutions passed in the moon."[15]

Nevertheless, Douglas replied by confining the issue to the place where the convention met. He caricatured Lincoln as having objected to the resolutions on the basis that the platform was "not adopted on the right 'spot'"—thereby triggering memories of Lincoln's unpopular "spot" resolutions when he was a member of Congress during the Mexican War. Moreover, Douglas assured his listeners, he was not in error in alleging that the platform was adopted in Springfield. His evidence was an undisputed assertion to that effect by Thomas L. Harris in an 1856 congressional debate and by the research of editor Lanphier. There still might be a possibility that he was in error, Douglas volunteered, so he promised to investigate the matter when he next reached Springfield. But it was all really of no consequence since substantially similar platforms had been adopted by Republican conventions across the state—as Douglas proved by reading a platform adopted in Rockford. Finally, the incumbent summed up his argument with a dilemma: either Lincoln is truly committed to these platforms, or the Republicans have compromised their principles by nominating him. [16]

In his rejoinder, Lincoln ignored many of Douglas's specific accusations but introduced a crucial distinction. The incumbent, he said, was reading from various local platforms that bound only their signatories since in 1854 the anti-Nebraska forces had differed on many individual issues. There was no statewide Republican party or platform until 1856, and it was on *that* document that Lincoln based his campaign. [17] With those comments, the discussion of this issue petered out. It had been a dominant focus at Ottawa and Freeport, yet it received no attention at Jonesboro or Charleston.

This bickering over the 1854 platform certainly seemed inconclusive but introduced a number of major concerns: whether Lincoln could be categorized successfully with the abolitionists; the extent to which a written document such as a platform can bind a candidate; and the veracity, thoroughness, and fairness of both Lincoln and Douglas.

Although conspiracy charges were generally in the air during the late 1850s, one of Douglas's biographers has surmised that the Little Giant was prompted to make this particular charge in order to blunt the force of conspiracy allegations that had been made against him. Trumbull, in particular, had charged in 1856 that Douglas had plotted to remove the referendum provisions from the Toombs Bill, and Lincoln had charged in the "House Divided" speech that he was a conspirator to nationalize slavery. [18] If Douglas's moves were intended to deflect attacks, his action illustrates the principle that, since a conspiracy charge is virtually impossible to refute, the most effective response may be to counter with a charge of one's own.

Douglas took the 1854 platform from a congressional speech delivered in 1856 by Thomas L. Harris. Before introducing the matter in the debates, the Little Giant wrote Lanphier and asked that the editor check his files. In a letter dated August 15, Douglas specifically asked "whether Lincoln was present and made a speech and such other facts concerning the matter as you may be able to give." He added, "This information is very important and I want it immediately."[19] Lanphier, in response, thoroughly checked his files, printed the resolutions, attributed them to a Springfield convention, and noted that Lincoln's name was listed among the drafting committee—apparently unaware that Lincoln had disavowed any role.

Although the *Register* was in fact merely reprinting an earlier error, the rival *Illinois State Journal* had not originally challenged the authenticity of the report.[20] It was not until later in August that a correspondent, Charles L. Wilson, alerted Lincoln to the fact that the resolutions that Douglas quoted at Ottawa "were adopted at Aurora by what was then called a Peoples Convention"—although they were similar to resolutions adopted by local Republican groups throughout northern Illinois.[21]

The similarity among local platforms—despite Lincoln's denial that he was bound by any of them—gave credence to the Democrats' allegation that to focus on where a platform was adopted was to evade the central question of whether Lincoln was committed to it. Lanphier, for example, thoroughly unrepentant for any embarrassment he might have caused his patron, wrote Douglas, "I see that your quotation from our old file has made an uproar. *I yet believe the resolutions there given* to be the genuine ones. Whether so or not, the point you made is not affected by their denial of the 'spot.'"[22] Douglas never admitted that the 1854 platforms he quoted might not represent the Republican party in 1858. This refusal, Whan has theorized, was strategically useful. It "cost Lincoln much time and trouble in repeating the charge of 'fraud,' and it allowed Douglas to draw into every discussion a reference to Lincoln's earlier and unfortunate war record. It also allowed Douglas to take a strong offensive on the matter of Lincoln's Abolition tendencies."[23] In short, while neither substantively profound nor conclusive, it was an argument of great strategic value.

III

Lincoln was not finished with the matter of the 1854 platform. Correspondents had advised him to seize on Douglas's error. David Davis, for example, wrote, "I think Douglas in palming off the Aurora resolution is a D___ D___. Pour hot shot into Douglas all the time." Medill had suggested that Lincoln, in the Freeport debate, "give Doug a run on his forging a State platform on you." Republican papers picked up the same theme. Reporting on the Freeport debate, the *Illinois State Journal* asserted that Douglas "*knew* when he read the fictitious resolutions, that they were a forgery. He once tried to quote the same batch of resolutions in the U.S. Senate, on Senator Trumbull, and they were promptly and authoritatively contradicted." The *Chicago Press and Tribune*, which had researched the resolutions and discovered the error, thundered that Douglas's "Ottawa harangue" had become "limp and feeble" once "the lie which was its backbone and muscle is taken out." Even more indignantly, it added, "And this lie—this forgery—the act of a Senator of the United States!"[24]

This was stronger medicine than Lincoln was prepared to administer at Freeport, and neither candidate discussed the 1854 resolutions at Jonesboro or Charleston. But in the Galesburg debate Lincoln re-opened the discussion. Responding to Douglas's charge that he was secretly an abolitionist, the challenger put forward a conspiracy claim of his own. He reminded his listeners that a month had passed since Douglas had promised to investigate the matter and that Douglas had been in Springfield during that time, but, "so far as I know, he has made no report of the result of his investigation." Douglas's silence might itself be taken as an admission on his part that he had misrepresented the platform. Then Lincoln made an even stronger charge. Not only was the 1854 platform fraudulent, but Douglas knew it to be so and was involved in a plot to besmirch the character and reputation of Lincoln and other Republicans by associating them with a fabricated document. "A fraud—an absolute forgery was committed," Lincoln charged, "and the perpetration of it was traced to the three—Lanphier, Harris, and Douglas."

Lincoln agreed that the resolutions in question had indeed been printed in the *Illinois State Register*—the source from which Douglas read them—in the fall of 1854, but he insisted that they were known to be bogus even then. Their insertion was fraud, and not an honest mistake, because Lanphier's paper contained a *portion* of the real proceedings of the 1854 Springfield convention. So the writer of the article must have had access to the true records, but he "purposely threw out the genuine resolutions passed by the convention, and fraudulently substituted the others." The motive behind this act was to defeat the old Whig candidate for Congress, Richard Yates, by making him appear to be supporting an extremist platform and to elect the Democrat, Thomas L. Harris, in his place—an object of great importance to both Douglas and Lanphier.

Having succeeded in their original goal, the three made repeated use of the same fraudulent document. Lincoln related that Douglas had used it against Trumbull in the Senate, Harris had used it in the House of Representatives, and all three had employed it against Lincoln in the Ottawa debate. He concluded, "It has been clung to and played out again and again as an exceedingly high trump by this blessed trio."

Lincoln employed sign reasoning to implicate Douglas in this plot. This form of reasoning infers the existence of what cannot be proved directly—in this case, Douglas's participation in the plot—from some external manifestation that is taken to be a sign of it. Since the incumbent would stand to gain by clearing himself, his silence after promising to investigate the matter is a sign that he was a co-conspirator. Moreover, if Douglas were innocent, he should be angry at Lanphier for embarrassing him by sending him a fake platform and leading him to think it genuine. But, far from being angry, Douglas "manifests no surprise" and "makes no complaint of Lanphier." The three are "just as cozy" now as before; they all find each of the others to be "a most honorable man," and they all continue to repeat the false story. "Now all this is very natural," Lincoln noted, "if they are all alike guilty in that fraud, and it is very unnatural if any one of them is innocent."[25]

Heckman concluded that Lincoln's allegation of forgery lacked substance because Douglas's August letter to Lanphier clearly indicated that the Little Giant was seeking accurate information.[26] Of course, one who believed Lincoln's charge would interpret Douglas's letter as an attempt to give himself the ruse of "deniability"—just what one would expect of a true conspirator. Moreover, Lincoln's argument reached back, beyond 1858, to the original insertion of the wrong resolutions in the *Register*. Though he lacked direct evidence, the effect of his sign argument was to suggest that Douglas was involved in that decision. In the Galesburg debate, he tried to extract an admission from Douglas and also to drive a wedge between the incumbent and Lanphier: "Can Judge Douglas be induced to tell how it originally was concocted? It may be true that Lanphier insists that the two men for whose benefit it was originally devised [Harris and Douglas], shall at least bear their share of it!" Probably not expecting an answer, Lincoln must have hoped that even his innuendo would be sufficient to tarnish Douglas's credibility. He said that "while it remains unexplained I hope to be pardoned if I insist that the mere fact of Judge Douglas making charges against Trumbull and myself is not quite sufficient evidence to establish them!"[27]

Douglas's reply to this accusation, divided between his Galesburg rejoinder and his speech at Quincy, had two essential parts. First, he insisted that he had made an honest error, having been misled by hearing Harris and reading Lanphier's report. Indeed, as soon as he discovered his mistake, not even waiting for Lincoln to call it to his attention, he "frankly explained it at once as an honest man would." Douglas was appalled that this explanation did not satisfy Lincoln since "I did not think there was an honest man in the state of Illinois who doubted that I had been led into the error, if it was such, innocently." Having apologized for his mistake, Douglas sought to compare his conduct with

Lincoln's. At Quincy he said, "I corrected it myself, as a gentleman, and an honest man, and as I always feel proud to do when I have made a mistake. I wish Mr. Lincoln could show that he has acted with equal fairness, and truthfulness, when I have convinced him that he has been mistaken." Here Douglas was trying to turn a potential embarrassment to his advantage by diverting the issue from the truth or falsity of the resolutions to the behavior of each candidate when confronted with error. He likewise tried to turn the issue to his advantage at Galesburg when, after explaining himself, he said, "I do not now believe that there is an honest man on the face of the globe who will not regard with abhorrence and disgust Mr. Lincoln's insinuations of my complicity in that forgery, if it was forgery." The incumbent reminded his listeners that he had treated his opponent "courteously and kindly; I always spoke of him in words of respect, and in return he has sought, and is now seeking, to divert public attention from the enormity of his revolutionary principles by impeaching men's sincerity and integrity, and inviting personal quarrels."

This last comment suggests Douglas's second response to the charge— to minimize it as a diversion from the central issues. He urged the Galesburg audience to "bear in mind that he does not deny that these resolutions were adopted in a majority of all the republican counties of this state in that year . . . and that they thus became the platform of his party in a majority of the counties upon which he now relies for support; he does not deny the truthfulness of the resolutions." Lincoln's only objection, Douglas insisted, was that the resolutions read in the Ottawa debate "were not adopted on the right spot." This rejoinder, of course, enabled him not only to ridicule Lincoln's argument but also to reintroduce his challenger's unpopular "spot" resolutions during the Mexican War. [28]

When Lincoln was accused of conspiracy, he denied the charge and insisted that Douglas prove it. With respect to the countercharge, Douglas newspapers took a similar approach. The *Register*, for example, challenged the rival *Illinois State Journal* to prove from its own files that the 1854 resolutions were not as Douglas had claimed. Otherwise, Lanphier's paper insisted, the "forgery" charge will be regarded as "the noisy fustian of shallow-pated trickstery, caught in a close place, attempting, by bald lying, to shirk a political issue." Two days later, the *Register* crowed that the *Journal* had been unable to answer the challenge: "It blathers in immense capitals about 'forgery' by us, but keeps hidden from view its own version and its comment upon the action of that convention."[29] Douglas himself, however, did not try to renounce the burden of proof. Rather, he sought to turn explanation to his advantage by demonstrating his own standards of gentlemanly conduct, minimizing the issue, ridiculing Lincoln, and attacking his integrity as well.

Lincoln, of course, contested these replies in his Quincy rejoinder. First, he again repeated that Douglas had made no report of his promised investigation. Douglas must have thought that acknowledging his error was enough, but Lincoln was pressing for evidence as to which one or more of Lanphier, Harris, and Douglas was responsible for the original insertion of the fake resolutions into the *Register*. He continued to find the incumbent's silence telling: "I demand of him to tell why he did not investigate it, if he did not; and if he did, *why he won't tell the result*." Then he dismissed Douglas's claims to magnanimity and gentlemanly conduct for freely admitting an error. "I will tell you how he became so magnanimous," Lincoln said at Quincy. "When the newspapers of our side had discovered and published it, and put it beyond his power to deny it, then he came forward and made a virtue of necessity by acknowledging it." Finally, he denied that the only difference between him and Douglas was the spot where the resolutions had been adopted. Instead, it was the difference between "holding a man responsible for an act which he *has not* done, and holding him responsible for an act that he *has* done."[30] There the matter rested. The plot to abolitionize the parties was not discussed at Alton. At other times in the debates, though, Lincoln did use the example of the bogus 1854 resolutions in order to cast doubt on the accuracy of other documents from which Douglas read.

IV

The point of this first conspiracy charge, of course, was to brand Lincoln as an abolitionist. The equation of Republicans with abolitionists was a standard item in Democratic rhetoric. It had been featured that spring in the congressional debates over the Lecompton constitution when Southern Democrats argued that Republicans stood inflexibly against the admission of any more slave states and that this implacable opposition was the first step toward the goal of abolition.[31] It was used against Lincoln throughout the 1858 campaign, including an unsigned pamphlet, *Lincoln and His Doctrines*, that was circulated "to show the full scope of Lincoln's belief in Negro equality and abolitionism." Typically, any expression of opposition to slavery was viewed as support not only for abolitionism but also for racial equality. The party, as Stampp indicates, was often branded as the "Black Republican party," the "nigger party," or the "amalgamation party," and abolitionists were seen as subverting national unity.[32]

Like most similar allegations, these—though tenuous—were not completely without foundation. Republicans in 1856 had not been able to divest themselves of the abolitionist stigma in the central counties, where conservative Whigs went for Buchanan or Fillmore rather than Fremont. In 1858, Republican speakers virtually embraced abolitionism when they were in heavily abolitionist districts, giving Douglas and the Democrats some reason to suspect that they really were abolitionists at heart. In the long run, moreover, confining slavery to its current boundaries might well have made it unprofitable, and if that were not enough the federal government could restrict the interstate slave trade under the broad interpretation of the commerce power that Republicans inherited from the Whigs.[33]

Certainly, it was in Douglas's interest to so stigmatize Lincoln. "To be an abolitionist in antebellum days," Randall has written, "was to be without political influence and to be widely despised in the North"; his analogy was to the power of "communism" as an expression of hatred during the late 1940s and early 1950s.[34] The stigma was particularly strong in the central Illinois counties among former Whigs whose new political allegiance had not yet solidified. Moreover, to the degree that Douglas could focus attention on Lincoln's racial views, he would divert it from detailed inspection of his own record in the Senate.

Lincoln anticipated that Douglas would try to equate antislavery, abolition, and racial equality. Noting in his June 1857 Springfield speech that there was "a natural disgust in the minds of nearly all white people" to the idea of racial amalgamation, he predicted that Douglas's chief strategy would be to exploit this sentiment: "If he can, by much drumming and repeating, fasten the odium of that idea upon his adversaries, he thinks he can struggle through the storm."[35] Like most Republicans, Lincoln recognized that his political survival depended on avoiding the abolitionist label. As a result, he made strong statements—which his supporters today find embarrassing—disclaiming any support for Negro equality.

In 1857, Lincoln had registered his protest "against that counterfeit logic which concludes that, because I do not want a woman for a *slave*, I must necessarily want her for a *wife*." In the Ottawa debate, he proclaimed that "anything that argues me into [Douglas's] idea of perfect social and political equality with the negro, is but a specious and fantastic arrangement of words, by which a man can prove a horse chestnut to be a chestnut horse." Most explicitly, at Charleston, he declared, "I am not, nor ever have been in favor of bringing about in any way the social and political equality of the white and black races." He went on to add that, since coexistence on terms of equality was not possible, "I as

much as any other man am in favor of having the superior position assigned to the white race."[36] In fact, Lincoln tried to turn the tables by
contending that slavery itself was the greatest cause of race mixing, and
Republican papers defended their party's program as "the white man's
platform" since it preserved the territories for settlement by white
people.[37]

The abolitionist stigma recurred in a variety of argument forms and
would cause difficulties for Lincoln throughout the debates. With respect to the conspiracy charge, however, his best strategy was to counter
it with other conspiracy allegations of his own.

V

The second major conspiracy argument was in some respects the reverse
of the first. If Douglas believed that Lincoln was a secret abolitionist, the
challenger accused the incumbent of being a co-conspirator in a plot to
make slavery legal everywhere—states as well as territories, North as
well as South.

Alleging the existence of a "slave power" conspiracy was not a new
idea in 1858. The argument had been advanced by the early abolitionists, had passed into the political mainstream during the debates over
the Wilmot Proviso, and was rendered credible by the events of the
1850s, particularly by the *Dred Scott* decision. By the late 1850s, as Eric
Foner has noted, it had become a standard Republican rhetorical stance
"to accuse the slave power of a long series of transgressions against
northern rights" and to predict that, unless halted, the slave power
would result in "the complete subordination of the national government
to slavery and the suppression of northern liberties."[38]

Historians have tended to give little weight to the argument since no
evidence of overt conspiracy was subsequently discovered. But that is to
miss the point. The idea of a conspiracy was real and meaningful to antebellum advocates, moderate as well as extreme. Rawley lists Henry
Wilson, Horace Greeley, Joshua Giddings, Thomas Hart Benton,
William Lloyd Garrison, William Henry Seward, and Lincoln as be-
lievers in the existence of the conspiracy. The argument was articulated
by the Liberty party in 1839 and 1842, expressed in an 1846 pamphlet by
John Gorham Palfrey, a Unitarian minister running for Congress, and
promoted in the 1854 *Appeal of the Independent Democrats*. Zachariah
Chandler of Michigan developed the idea in his maiden Senate speech.
Several references to it were made during the congressional debates
over Lecompton in early 1858. Finkelman correctly concludes that,
since "a winning presidential candidate and hundreds of other successful politicians and editors" took the idea seriously, it should not be

dismissed "as political rhetoric, as an 'absurd bogey' designed to arouse northerners and gain votes."[39]

The power of the theory, like that of any conspiracy argument, lay in its power retrospectively to explain confusing or troublesome events. Looking backward from the perspective of 1858, Ohio senator Benjamin F. Wade explained the Texas annexation controversy by accusing the slave power of "seizing upon Texas, and bringing her into this Union for no other purpose than to uphold, strengthen, and render predominant in this Government the institution of slavery, and that in derogation of the political rights of the North." Elihu Washburne, speaking in the House, saw the work of the "slave power" conspiracy in the election of Franklin Pierce. Senator William Pitt Fessenden reminded his colleagues that in 1854 he had regarded popular sovereignty as a mere pretext for repeal of the Missouri Compromise in order to promote the spread of slavery; Lincoln alluded to the same general theme in his Peoria speech of October 1854 when he said that the future use of the popular sovereignty principle would be "the planting of slavery wherever in the wide world, local and unorganized opposition cannot prevent it." Both Seward and Lovejoy, convinced that there had been collusion between Buchanan and Chief Justice Taney in formulating the *Dred Scott* decision, saw this decision as the work of the slave power.[40] With each new event that the theory helped explain, its plausibility grew.

Slavery had a double meaning in the antebellum political culture. To be sure, it referred to the institution of chattel slavery. But it also had an older, eighteenth-century meaning: subjection to tyranny or, in Bailyn's phrase, "the inability to maintain one's just property in material things and abstract rights."[41] It connoted loss of one's ability to control one's own choices. Consequently, Gienapp notes, "slavery symbolized the antithesis of republicanism, and thus when Republicans denounced slavery, they often meant the threatened loss of *white men's* liberties."[42] In this latter sense, slavery was the penalty for insufficient vigilance, the price paid by people who fail to notice danger signals and to heed alarms. Advocates of the "slave power" conspiracy thesis appealed to both meanings. Chattel slavery was the common self-interest of the conspirators, and their ultimate aim was the destruction of Northern political rights.

The prevalence of this argument in Northern political culture can be explained by the variety of functions it performed. First, it rendered the issue of slavery both more immediate and more graphic for the North. The dramatic structure of conspiracy, climaxing in the exposure of a secret plot, captures and holds attention more effectively than does an impersonal, expository argument.[43]

Second, the argument helped exclude a middle ground and thereby radicalize Northern moderates on the slavery issue. As Nye described it, the conspiratorial cast identified the slaveholder "with a conspiracy of infinitely dangerous designs" and thereby "robbed the pro-slavery position of any possible appeal to the immigrant, the workman, and the lower middle class in the North."[44]

Third, the slave power conspiracy argument enabled northerners to oppose slavery without needing to abandon their own race prejudice. Neely points out, for example, that 70 percent of Illinois voters had voted to exclude Negroes from the state under the 1848 constitution. In such a climate, one could not expect appeals grounded in humanitarian sympathy for the Negro as a person to be persuasive. The slave power argument enabled advocates to ground their concern not in a moral obligation to the Negro but in a threat by the Southern political system to their own self-interest. Seward, for example, was able to proclaim to an Iowa audience that the Negro had less to do with the whole controversy "than anybody in the world." Lincoln was able even to turn the tables, citing fear of racial amalgamation as *support* for his position. Had Douglas not opened the way for slavery in Kansas, he asked in a speech early in the campaign, "could there have been any amalgamation there?"[45] The conspiracy argument widened the ground between freedom and equality, so that it was possible to attack slaveowners without embracing abolitionism.

Fourth, the attack on the slave power conspiracy could easily be extended to an argument against wealth. By expansive definition, the slave power consisted not only of slaveholders but also of the commercial and manufacturing interests, in the North as well as the South, that benefited from the products of the slave system. This broadening of the issue made the conspiracy thesis persuasive to immigrants, farmers, lower-class workingmen, and mechanics, all of whom were already disposed "to doubt the motives of the rich and powerful." In this respect, as Foner has explained, the slave power became the successor to the money power of the Jacksonian period as the symbol for the fears and resentments of the poor against the rich. In turn, it enabled Republicans such as Seward "to tap the egalitarian outlook which lay at the heart of northern society," presenting their own position as essentially conservative since it aimed to protect Northern free labor and democratic values. Some Republicans even believed, erroneously as it turned out, that the antiaristocratic thrust of the argument would attract support from slaveless Southern yeomen.[46]

Finally, the conspiracy argument was capable of creative embellishment. Since it emphasized the threat to the self-interest of Northern whites rather than to the slaves, the threat could be rendered more urgent and the need for action more immediate. If Northern rights were threatened, it would be much harder for a northerner to claim that the conspiracy was not his affair. As another example, the slave power could be seen as leading to *white* slavery; by means such as the Nebraska bill's denial of citizenship to aliens for five years, involuntary servitude might be made a prerequisite for citizenship. Beyond that, as Nye pointed out, the slave power would "make the free white man a virtual slave to a privileged aristocracy of Southern slaveholder and Northern capitalist"—an appeal that again relies on the dual meaning of the word *slave*.[47] Yet another example was the suggestion that the slave power, having overwhelmed Northern free society, would next move to reopen the African slave trade, on the basis that there was no moral distinction between buying a slave in Virginia and buying one in Africa. Similarly, the slave power could be cited as the cause of foreign-policy embarrassments, as when Lincoln maintained in his 1854 Peoria speech that "covert *real* zeal for the spread of slavery . . . deprives our republican example of its just influence in the world—enables the enemies of free institutions, with plausibility, to taunt us as hypocrites."[48]

The allegation of a slave power conspiracy had a long history by 1858. It was a versatile and flexible argument that contributed powerfully to the Northern antislavery arsenal.

VI

Lincoln made two major contributions to the conspiracy argument. He presented elaborate explanations of the legal means by which the conspiracy could work its will, and he linked Douglas to the plot.

Lincoln's first specific formulation of the charge came in the "House Divided" speech, although it appeared in fragmentary form in a draft he wrote probably in December 1857 or January 1858. Fehrenbacher theorizes that several specific events in early 1858 led Lincoln to sharpen the charge: editorials in the *Mattoon National Gazette* urging that Illinois legalize slavery, a California Supreme Court decision holding that a slave remained the property of his master even though the master was a virtually permanent resident of that free state, a February Senate speech by Fessenden elaborating the conspiracy theory, and a March speech in which Douglas himself developed the charge against the *Washington Union* and by implication against the Buchanan administration.[49]

In the "House Divided" speech, Lincoln hedged his charge through indirection. He told a story of four men–conveniently named Stephen, Roger, Franklin, and James—who were building a frame house. If all the pieces fit together, with a single piece missing and the frame exactly fit-ted to bring that piece in, then "we find it impossible to not believe that Stephen and Franklin, and Roger and James, all understood one another from the beginning, and all worked upon a common plan or draft drawn before the first lick was struck." The frame house, of course, represented national slavery; the "common plan or draft" was the conspiracy to produce this result; and the missing piece was the means by which it would be achieved—a future Supreme Court decision that would extend the principle of *Dred Scott* to the states as well as the territories. Lincoln repeated this statement, almost word for word, in the Ottawa debate, thereby entering the conspiracy argument into the debates.[50]

The "news" in Lincoln's use of the argument was his assertion that Douglas was in on the plot. This was part of a general strategy described by Holt of making Northern Democrats "surrogates for the Slave Power." Since Republicans campaigned only in the North, their opponents were other northerners rather than southerners. This fact made it necessary for them to establish "that Republicans alone, and not simply any Northern politicians, were needed to resist and overthrow the slavocracy."[51] Portraying their opponents as co-conspirators would certainly achieve that end.

Lincoln had received specific advice early in the campaign to stress this theme. For example, William C. Phillips of Carlinville wrote him in July that many old Whigs were leaning toward Douglas and advised, "Our tactics must be changed or the day is lost. . . . We must directly charge and keep charging Douglas with a conspiracy in favor of Slavery extension."[52] The *Chicago Press and Tribune* expressed delight when Lincoln made the charge in a July speech in Clinton, telling its readers that "Catiline, the world-renowned conspirator, never writhed more under the majestic eloquence of Cicero, than does Douglas under this charge of conspirator."[53] Lincoln repeated the charge in an August 12 speech at Beardstown and then introduced it into the Ottawa debate.

But by what means could Douglas be linked to the conspiracy? Surely not by his own testimony or his overt acts, but by either of two approaches that Lincoln developed. One portrayed the Little Giant as the perhaps unwitting tool of the slave power, the other as its active agent.

The first approach depended on the premise that public opinion was essential to the execution of Supreme Court decisions. "In this and like communities," Lincoln said at Ottawa, "public sentiment is everything. With public sentiment, nothing can fail; without it nothing can succeed." Therefore, it was the molder of public opinion who made it possible or impossible for statutes and decisions to be executed. Douglas, as "a man of vast influence," had a great role in shaping public sentiment; indeed, "it is enough for many men to profess to believe anything, when they once find out that Judge Douglas professes to believe it." And Douglas had maintained that the *Dred Scott* decision should be respected, not because of its merits, but simply because it had been propounded by the Court. If the people generally accepted this reasoning, they would be uncritical of Supreme Court decisions and thus quiescent. Into the breach caused by public indifference the Supreme Court would step at a propitious time with "*Dred Scott* II," a decision holding that the Constitution denies *states* the right to outlaw slavery. And Douglas would be powerless to oppose that decision, for the very reason he listed for supporting the original *Dred Scott* decision. "Committing himself unreservedly to this decision," Lincoln told the Ottawa audience, "*commits him to the next one* just as firmly as to this. . . . The next decision, as much as this, will be a *thus saith the Lord.*"[54]

But Lincoln went further. He professed to find, in Douglas's role in developing the Kansas-Nebraska Act, evidence of Douglas's active role as a ringleader of the conspiracy. The Little Giant, he contended, had deliberately created niches to accommodate both the *Dred Scott* decision and a future "*Dred Scott* II." First, during the Senate debate in 1854, Chase of Ohio had proposed an amendment that would permit the people of a territory to exclude slavery if they wished. Douglas, as chairman of the Senate Committee on Territories, had voted the amendment down and caused it to be defeated. Since the Chase amendment only made explicit a feature of Douglas's popular sovereignty, what possibly could have been the Little Giant's motive for objecting—if not to create an opening for the first *Dred Scott* decision? There was a second niche as well. The Kansas-Nebraska Act contained a clause disavowing the intent "to legislate slavery into any territory or state" or to exclude it therefrom, subject only to the dictates of the Constitution. Why the reference to *states* in an act dealing with territorial organization? As Forgie has pointed out, legally the reference to states was superfluous language.[55] It must have been put there, Lincoln surmised, to invite a second *Dred Scott* decision that would parallel the first. Just as the 1857 decision held that the Constitution prevented the territories from outlawing slavery, the imagined future decision would apply the same constraint to the states. Douglas must have been preparing for just this result; otherwise, why would he have introduced the superfluous language?

The possibility of a second *Dred Scott* decision was not as farfetched as one might suppose. To be sure, the Southern political program did not include slavery for the free states. Still, the idea of a "*Dred Scott* II" was in the air. An editorial in the *Washington Union*, the administration organ, had advocated such a course in November 1857. Titled "Slavery Must Go North," the editorial laid out the logic of a second decision under the "privileges and immunities" clause of the Constitution.[56] The possibility of such a move had been suggested in the *Bloomington Pantagraph* as early as March 10, 1857, four days after the original *Dred Scott* decision. Harlan of Iowa, Fessenden of Maine, and Chandler of Michigan all spoke in the Senate of the possibility of a second decision.[57] Douglas himself had charged the editors of the *Union* with conspiring to produce the result. Lincoln had been convinced for some time that the 1857 *Dred Scott* decision itself contained all the premises needed for a second decision. All that was needed were a motive and an appropriate case.

The motive was easy to find. A generation of "slave-state presidents or their northern 'doughface' allies," as Finkelman describes them, had appointed lower court judges who sympathized with the South on the slavery question. "By the 1850's," he concludes, "there was reason to believe that the federal courts were intent on protecting slavery, even in the free states." Southerners would not be likely to invoke states' rights to thwart a federal move in their own interest; as Jaffa notes, they sounded the states' rights theme only in order to protect slavery and were quite willing to condone even positive federal action to accomplish the same end. So the clamor for states' rights came instead from northerners who wanted to free any slave brought into their state.[58]

The "appropriate case" was also working its way through the courts. *Lemmon v. the People* involved eight slaves brought from Virginia to New York for shipment to Texas. They sued for their freedom, citing the state's personal liberty laws, and the state supreme court eventually affirmed "that on being brought to free soil a slave automatically becomes free." Republicans worried, though, that the Supreme Court under Taney would overturn the New York decision and establish "the right of transit of slaves through the free states."[59] It is not hard to imagine that the same reasoning used in the *Dred Scott* case would have led to a decision for the plaintiff. In fact, Fehrenbacher judges it "very likely" that a majority of the Taney Court would have issued a proslavery decision had the case reached them before it was rendered moot by the secession crisis.[60] If the right to travel with one's slaves through the free states were established, the distinctions among the concepts of transient, visitor, sojourner, and resident would be fuzzy indeed. *Lemmon* might well be the opening wedge by which the principles of *Dred Scott* would be applied to the states. The *Lemmon* case was nationally famous, and it is quite possible that Lincoln knew of it at the time of the debates.

Lincoln's difficulty was less in imagining the case than in linking Douglas to the plot. The niches the challengers claimed to find in the Kansas-Nebraska Act could be interpreted in other ways consistent with

Douglas's commitment to popular sovereignty—as the Little Giant proceeded to argue. But Lincoln used a Douglas inconsistency against him. Angered by the practice of polygamy in Utah, Douglas had proposed that the federal government intervene and revoke the territorial charter. His willingness to intervene in Utah, while denying the federal government's authority to do so in Kansas, proved to Lincoln that popular sovereignty was not truly a neutral principle but "a mere deceitful pretence for the benefit of slavery."[61] Several correspondents had even advised Lincoln to portray Douglas, just like the minions of the slave power, as really an *enemy* of popular sovereignty by virtue of his support for the *Dred Scott* decision and his covert interest in extending slavery nationwide.[62] Lincoln did not follow this advice, but its object would have been not only to expose Douglas as a hypocrite but to turn the appeal of his popular sovereignty principle against him.

Although one of Douglas's biographers found it unlikely that Lincoln himself believed the conspiracy charge, the preponderance of evidence indicates that he sincerely did. Lincoln cited the fear of the slave power conspiracy, not the desire for personal preferment, as his reason for undertaking the Senate campaign. He acknowledged that his evidence was all circumstantial but asserted that "nevertheless it seemed inconsistent with every hypothesis, save that of the existence of such conspiracy. I believe the facts can be explained to-day on no other hypothesis. . . . From warp to woof his handiwork is everywhere woven in."[63] Although convinced of his argument, he hedged his claim. He was careful to state that he did not know the charge to be true but that he believed it to be. And he tried to shift the burden of proof. When Douglas accused him of conspiring to abolitionize the parties, Lincoln insisted that the burden of proof was on the affirmative claim. When the charge was his own, he took a different tack; he stated his beliefs and then challenged Douglas to disprove them. Appearing magnanimous, he stated at Ottawa, "If, in arraying that evidence, I had stated anything which was false or erroneous, it needed but that Judge Douglas should point it out, and I would have taken it back with all the kindness in the world. . . . If I have reasoned to a false conclusion, it is the vocation of an able debater to show by argument that I have wandered to an erroneous conclusion."[64] If he could prevail in this stratagem, the virtual impossibility of disproving the conspiracy argument would work powerfully in his favor.

VII

At first, Douglas did not take this accusation seriously. Although he devoted much of his Chicago speech opening the campaign to the radical implications of the "House Divided" speech, indicating that he was familiar with Lincoln's remarks, he took no notice of Lincoln's arraigning him as a conspirator to spread slavery across the land. At Springfield a week later, he dismissed the charge, saying, "I have no comment to make on that part of Mr. Lincoln's speech," but indicating that he did not think so badly of the other named principals "as to believe that they were capable in their action and decision of entering into political intrigues for partisan purposes." Not satisfied with this reply, Lincoln repeated the charge in the conclusion of his own Springfield speech the same day. He noted that Douglas "has not, so far as I know, contradicted those charges" and therefore declared, "On his own tacit admission I renew that charge. I charge him with having been a party to that conspiracy and to that deception for the sole purpose of nationalizing slavery."[65]

Meanwhile, the pro-Douglas *Chicago Times* admonished readers that the charge rested on flimsy evidence indeed. The argument was said to have been "fabricated by unscrupulous men for use in this State," but there was nothing to sustain it. "How can Mr. Lincoln justify himself in pronouncing it?" the paper asked. "He does not attempt to sustain or justify the base assertion; on the contrary, he proclaims it on his own individual account, and thus takes to himself all the odium of a foul and unexcusable libel." Douglas himself, speaking at Clinton, branded the charge "unfounded and untrue from the beginning to the end of it."[66] Nevertheless, Lincoln repeated the accusation in the Ottawa debate, and Douglas now found it necessary to reply more specifically.

This time, Douglas tried to throw the burden of proof back to Lincoln. As he put it, "I am not green enough to let him make a charge which he acknowledges he does not know to be true, and then take up my time in answering it, when I know it to be false and nobody else knows it to be true." Instead of disproving Lincoln's claim, he would "say that it is a lie, and let him prove it if he can."[67] He went on, however, to offer alternate explanations for the historical circumstances that Lincoln had cited.

His vote against the Chase amendment, for example, was a matter of simple fairness. Chase had refused a request by Lewis Cass to modify his amendment so that it would allow the territories to permit as well as to exclude slavery. That being the case, the Chase amendment was one sided, and no senator whose career was based on the premise that the people had the absolute right to decide could endorse that amendment. Besides, the Chase amendment was superfluous since the original bill "already conferred all the power which Congress had, by giving the people the whole power over the subject."[68]

Lincoln was not satisfied by this answer. In his opening speech at Freeport, he regarded it as only a pretext. "They very well knew that

Chase would do no such thing" as modify his amendment because Chase insisted that freedom "was *better* than slavery." The Democrats "very well knew they insisted on that which he would not for a moment think of doing, and that they were only bluffing him." The motive must have been to have a pretext for rejecting the Chase amendment and thereby leaving in the Kansas-Nebraska Act the niche to be filled by the *Dred Scott* decision. The challenger was confident that his view of the matter was better than the incumbent's because he recognized that Chase's inflexibility did not prevent Douglas from having the amendment adopted through other means, had he really wanted it. For example, Lincoln wanted to know "*if they wanted Chase's amendment fixed over, why somebody else could not have offered to do it?*" Or why not pass the Chase amendment and then add *another* amendment to the modified bill so that the final result would be what Douglas wanted. But the Democrats chose instead "to quibble with Chase to get him to add what they knew he would not add, and because he would not, they stand upon that flimsy pretext for voting down what they argued was the meaning and intent of their own bill. They left room thereby for this Dred Scott decision."[69]

Douglas rebutted these accusations with a similar argument of his own. Though Lincoln's attack was an inference drawn from the Democrats' failure to choose what to him were reasonable alternatives, Douglas's was based on assertions. The Chase amendment was not genuine: "He offered it for the purpose of having it rejected." Chase's motive, as Douglas put it, was,

as he has himself avowed over and over again, simply to make capital out of it for the stump. He expected that it would be capital for small politicians in the country, and that they would make an effort to deceive the people with it, and he was not mistaken, for Lincoln is carrying out the plan admirably.[70]

There the matter rested, with charge and countercharge. Nothing more was said about the Chase amendment.

In addition to the Chase amendment, Lincoln had also cited the anomalous presence of the words *or state* in the Kansas-Nebraska Act, a measure adopted to regulate territories. Far from anticipating a second *Dred Scott* decision, this language was inserted to defeat the abolitionist proposal that there be no more new slave states even if the people want them. This proposal was not an idle threat since the whole basis of the Missouri controversy of 1819–21 was Northern objection to a slave-state constitution even though that was the will of the people. To avert any replay of this crisis, the Kansas-Nebraska Act stipulated, "not only [that] the people of the territories should do as they pleased, but that when they come to be admitted as states, they should come into the union with or without slavery, as the people determined."[71] Lincoln either was satisfied with this answer or forgot about it since no more was said in the debates about this particular link alleged between Douglas and the slave power.

Although he had no more time at Ottawa, Douglas commented on two other aspects of the charge at Freeport. Earlier, Lincoln had complained that Douglas had no right to belittle or ignore *his* conspiracy charge when, after all, the Little Giant had just recently made a similar complaint against the editor of the *Washington Union* in a Senate speech on March 22. The incumbent's reply was simple and direct: just because he had made a true charge against the *Washington Union*, that did not justify Lincoln in making a false charge against him. Moreover, Douglas's complaint was confined to the editor of the *Union;* that was a far different matter from alleging the existence of a conspiracy including Douglas, Taney, Pierce, and Buchanan. Seizing on the word *authoritative* in Douglas's March 22 speech, Lincoln protested that the *Union* could not have acted alone but must have published its advocacy of national slavery under someone's authority. That meant, Lincoln said, that there were other conspirators in the plot. Since it was well known that the *Union* was the administration paper, it was not necessary to specify who the co-conspirators were. An argument that rested so heavily on the ambiguity of the word *authoritative* was a tenuous argument; Lincoln's protest was neither answered nor repeated.

Finally, at Freeport Douglas turned directly to the figurative accusation that he, Pierce, Buchanan, and Taney were all involved in a plot. Lincoln must have meant that the conspirators were active at the time of the Kansas-Nebraska Act. But that charge was clearly false. Buchanan was not even in the country; he was representing America at the Court of St. James. Indeed, it was his very lack of involvement in the vexed slavery question that recommended him as the Democratic presidential candidate in 1856. The *Dred Scott* case—the supposed object of the conspirators—was not even before the Supreme Court at the time of the Kansas-Nebraska Act, so Taney presumably could not have been involved. "As to President Pierce," Douglas went on, "His honor as a man of integrity and honor is enough to vindicate him from such a charge, and as to myself, I pronounce the charge an infamous lie."[72] That was the end of that particular charge.

One common answer to the slave power charge, however, was not available to Douglas. It is always hard to defeat a conspiracy claim by denying the alleged motives because the advocate of the claim usually can reinterpret adverse evidence as supporting evidence. A firmer objection might be to argue that, whatever the motives, there was no means by which the conspirators could succeed. Applied to the slave power charge, the response would be not that no one wanted national slavery but instead that there was no way to bring it about. It was alleged to be physically impossible to introduce slavery in much of the North and West because of the conditions of soil and climate. If that were so, it was pointless to oppose "popular sovereignty" since it could produce no more than symbolic gains for the South anyway. An "isothermal line" would protect the territories from slavery.

This theory of "natural limits" to slavery was advanced most prominently by the revisionist historian Charles W. Ramsdell, but it was a popular argument at the time.[73] Douglas probably believed in the theory. In 1854, he had written the editor of the *Concord, N.H., State Capitol Reporter*, "All candid men who understand the subject admit that the laws of climate, and production, and of physical geography, . . . have excluded slavery" from Kansas and Nebraska. The specter of an extension of slavery "has been raised for mere party purposes by the abolition confederates and disappointed office-seekers." His biographer George Fort Milton attributes to Douglas the belief that the Kansas-Nebraska Act, far from extending slavery, would have weakened Southern opposition to the formation of new free territories. The new territories would undercut the cost of slave labor, and slavery would die a natural death. "But during the process," Milton explained, "the South would have no *legitimate complaint*, for the honor would have been carefully respected, its constitutional rights scrupulously observed and maintained."[74]

The "isothermal theory" was controversial. Few Republicans believed it; Lincoln specifically denied it. The Northwest Territory would have adopted slavery if not prevented by law; moreover, free and slave states lay at similar latitudes. Accordingly, he deemed the theory "a *palliation—a lullaby*." Besides, the experience of the nineteenth century was the repeated transcending of "natural limits." In particular, industrial growth would open up new opportunities for the peculiar institution.[75]

Nevertheless, the isothermal theory had considerable appeal since it seemed to offer the way out of an irreconcilable conflict. But it was not available to Douglas since it would undermine his contention that popular sovereignty was a purely neutral principle under which the cause of slavery had as good a chance as the cause of freedom. He could not contend, therefore, that national slavery was out of the question, even though he found the idea preposterous. Instead, he had to argue that people who wanted to keep slavery out could *choose* to do so, notwithstanding the *Dred Scott* decision or the work of any conspiracy, by refusing to pass "friendly local legislation." This line of argument would create its own difficulties.

Douglas was on strong ground in denying the links that his challenger had hypothesized between the incumbent and a conspiracy; few of them were even repeated by Lincoln. But Douglas could not deny the possibility of national slavery, nor could he indicate whether he would favor or oppose such a result. Republican papers noticed this omission. Late in the campaign, the *Chicago Press and Tribune* pointed out that, "though entreatied times without number to say which side of these questions he would take, his only answer has been a sneer."[76] This constraint became his undoing.

Lincoln changed his tactics. He virtually abandoned the slave power conspiracy charge after Freeport, returning instead to the milder claim that Douglas was the unwilling ally of the slave power by preparing public opinion to accept that slavery was a matter of moral indifference. He asked in one of the Freeport interrogatories whether Douglas would support a *"Dred Scott* II" in deference to the authority of the Supreme Court, as he had supported the actual 1857 decision. When Douglas avoided the question but insisted instead that such a decision would be preposterous, Lincoln demonstrated at Galesburg that it was not at all preposterous—that it followed with the deductive force of a syllogism from the logic of the *Dred Scott* case itself. Douglas then said that the Taney Court had explicitly disavowed any *"Dred Scott* II" and said as much in the *Dred Scott* decision itself, but he could not document this assertion when Lincoln handed him a copy of the decision and asked him to find the pertinent passage. If there was an ultimate victor on the possibility of a second *Dred Scott* decision, it was Lincoln rather than Douglas.

The charge that Douglas was part of a slave power conspiracy, then, was valuable less for what it established directly than for its contribution to a rhetorical trajectory. The concept of "rhetorical trajectory" acknowledges that arguments and persuasive appeals have their own "natural" curve of development. For example, the arguments used in the 1850s to oppose slavery would later lend themselves to use in attacking other forms of racism. In the case at hand, a preposterous charge may not be accepted, but even to consider it as a possibility is to increase the weight given to other, less serious charges. It might not have been credible to view *"Dred Scott* II" as Douglas's conspiratorial aim. But even discussing the question in that context may have made it more credible for listeners to imagine *"Dred Scott* II" coming about in less sinister ways that were the natural outgrowth of Douglas's position. Following the Little Giant's program might lead to national slavery, in effect if not by design. And that was all that Lincoln needed to prove.

VIII

The two primary conspiracy arguments, then, were Douglas's contention that Lincoln was part of a plot to abolitionize the parties and Lincoln's insistence that Douglas was plotting to spread slavery across the land. Each candidate also developed a second conspiracy charge that received less attention. For Douglas, it was the allegation that Lincoln and the Republicans were in unholy alliance with Buchanan Democrats to exploit the federal patronage in order to defeat him.

Although Douglas openly broke with Buchanan over the Lecompton constitution, relations between the two had never been cordial. Douglas withdrew as a presidential candidate in 1856, enabling Buchanan to capture the nomination, but received no political reward for doing so. The president ignored Douglas's advice on national appointments and may have deliberately antagonized the senator in making lesser appointments.[77] The vendetta intensified in early 1858, when the president, aided by Frances J. Grund, began to remove Douglas supporters from federal office and to mobilize the state's postmasters against the Little Giant. Other Buchanan loyalists included "Ike" Cook, who was named postmaster of Chicago, and Dr. Charles Leib. Special efforts were directed at newspaper editors. Heckman reports that the Peoria *Union* opposed the Lecompton constitution but reversed its position after being offered a federal printing contract. Other Douglas papers, such as the *Chicago Times* and the *Illinois State Register*, were hurt by the withdrawal of official advertising and post office printing. When Douglas editors could not be converted, rival papers were started; in July 1858, David Davis wrote that the Buchanan forces had launched six new newspapers in the preceding two weeks alone. "Buchaneers" even tried to wrest control of the 1858 state Democratic convention.[78]

Perhaps because Douglas had clearly demonstrated his strength at the state convention, talk of reconciliation was in the air. Congressman Thomas Harris reported to Lanphier in early May, "It is understood that the administration will make no more removals—will order their tools in Illinois to obedience—& support of the state ticket—will restore even those removed, if necessary to power." Republicans had a similar sense of the situation, for Trumbull wrote John M. Palmer in May that "there seems to be a sort of a truce between the President & Douglas just now. No removals are being made in our state of late." Douglas's own correspondents wrote that "the administration have determined to touch no more of your friends in Illinois" and that "*all* are now anxious to bring about a reconciliation, in Illinois, of the Democracy. . . . By a little management you can control the affairs of your state, *by your former enemies coming to the rescue.*"[79]

Douglas, however, dissolved any hope for reconciliation. On his return to Chicago, he discovered that Buchanan was widely disliked in Illinois and, therefore, that his hatred "was too valuable to lose and any concessions would gain him more enemies than friends."[80] Rather than extend the olive branch, Douglas threw down the gauntlet in his July 9 Chicago speech, proclaiming victory over the administration's effort "to force a constitution upon the people of Kansas against their will."[81] With this declaration, the rift was permanent, and there were new threats of reprisal by the administration against Douglas supporters. Daniel McCook, for example, wrote Harris that Buchanan had reportedly ordered "that immediately after the Election Every Post Master in the State who Sympathizes with Douglas are to be removed."[82]

The implication of the conspiracy charge was that the administration was secretly acting in concert with the Republicans to embarrass Douglas. Trumbull warned in June that Douglas would try "to create the impression that there is an alliance between a few Lecompton office holders & the leading Republicans to defeat him," and Sheahan's *Chicago Times* made the allegation repeatedly during August. On August 26th, for example, the paper reported that Danite federal officeholders were explicitly declaring in favor of Lincoln, and on August 29 the *Times* alleged that money was exchanged between Republican leaders and Leib. In a Senate speech, Douglas had specifically named Leib as a conspirator.[83]

The contribution that the debates made to this argument was to connect the Lincoln campaign to the conspiracy. Douglas indirectly suggested a link in the course of his Freeport response to the slave power charge. When Lincoln cited the *Washington Union* against him, Douglas asked why his challenger should be defending Buchanan. "Is he so interested in the federal administration," he asked, "that he must jump to the rescue and defend it from every attack that I may make against it?" It was all very clear, Douglas said. The *Union* had endorsed Lincoln, so he felt compelled to defend it. "This only proves what I have charged," Douglas surmised, "that there is an alliance between Lincoln and his supporters and the federal office-holders of this state, and presidential aspirants out of it, to break me down at home."[84] Lincoln's only reply was to deny that he was defending Buchanan particularly.

In the Galesburg debate, Douglas was more explicit. Although Lincoln's position on Lecompton was the same as his own, Douglas charged that Republicans and Buchaneers had submerged their differences and that Lincoln was receiving aid from officeholders "who are using their influence and the patronage of the government against me in revenge for my having defeated the Lecompton constitution." Douglas's imagery was vivid: "You know that the axe of decapitation is suspended over every man in office in Illinois, and the terror of proscription is threatened every Democrat by the present administration unless he supports the Republican ticket in preference to my Democratic associates and myself." As an example, he cited the postmaster of Galesburg and "every other postmaster in this vicinity, all of whom have been stricken down simply because they discharged the duties of their offices honestly, and supported the regular Democratic ticket in this state in the right." He alleged that Republicans were stooping to such treachery because they know "that if they let this chance slip they will never have another." Without this aid from administration hacks, Douglas averred, Lincoln "has no hope on earth, and has never dreamed that he had a chance of success." Douglas asked the Republicans present what they thought "of a political organization that will try to make an unholy and unnatural combination with its professed foes to beat a man merely because he has done right."[85]

This conspiracy charge was not without foundation. It is clear in retrospect that there was indeed close coordination between the Buchanan administration and the Lincoln campaign. Leib kept close relationships with Republican strategists, and Republican funds helped launch new anti-Douglas newspapers. Attorney General Jeremiah Black declared his preference for Lincoln. A correspondent wrote Lincoln, "The Buchanan folks will give you a cordial welcome, on the score of undying hostility to Douglas." Ozias M. Hatch, Illinois secretary of state and a Republican leader, was informed that Republicans were submitting editorials to the *Springfield State Democrat*, a Buchanan paper, and that a $500 contribution was expected from Lincoln himself. John Wentworth, a leading Chicago Republican, offered advice to the Buchaneers in the pages of his newspaper, and in Springfield the father and brother of Lincoln's law partner, William H. Herndon, were prominent Buchaneers. Republicans boosted the attendance at Buchanan meetings. Their own newspapers publicized Danite events, as Wentworth explained, in order to satisfy potential bolters from Douglas "that the Buchanan men are in earnest." Trumbull was told throughout the spring that Buchanan was gaining daily at Douglas's expense; the senior senator himself assured Buchanan's emissary, John Slidell, that he would vote for anybody the president appointed "to replace anywhere one of Douglas' supporters."[86]

In the idiom of the 1980s, Lincoln was able to maintain "deniability" about his role. At Galesburg, he found it hard to conceal his amusement. He admitted, "I have no objection to the division in the Judge's party," but added, "He got it up himself." The popular sovereignty doctrine and the Lecompton constitution had produced the split, not anything that Lincoln had said or done. He put the burden of proof on Douglas to produce evidence "that I have in any way promoted that division." He then reminded listeners that in 1856 Democrats had been delighted to see the Republicans divided between Fremont and Fillmore. What the Democrats felt then, the Republicans feel now, but "that is all there is of it."[87] This stance was consistent with Lincoln's private letters, in which he told correspondents that he was pleased by the division in the Democratic ranks but was unaware of any collusion to bring it about and that there was no alliance "by which there is to be any concession of principle on either side."[88]

Others likewise denied the existence of a conspiracy—including, however, the most likely conspirators. The *Illinois State Journal* proclaimed in June that the Buchanan forces "are no allies of ours. We spit upon and execrate their doctrines." Herndon wrote Trumbull, "We have no understanding with either faction of the so-called Democracy as to what shall be done or what shall be left undone, either directly or indirectly, and upon this you may depend." In a document whose very existence almost denies what its content asserts, Leib wrote Trumbull, "When Douglas in the Senate Charged an alliance between your friends and mine he charged what he well knew was a *lie.*"[89]

Even these denials, however, tend to overstate the case. On July 8 Lincoln did meet with John Daugherty, the Buchanan candidate for state treasurer. It can be inferred from Angle's report that Daugherty announced plans to run Buchanan candidates in every county and election. Lincoln seemed quite pleased and thought that the action would give him the election.[90] On the whole, though, Lincoln did manage to stay aloof from any collusion and yet obtain the benefits of a divided opposition.

Those benefits, however, were less than they appeared to be. Lincoln's two conspiracy arguments were on a collision course. The more he emphasized the break between Douglas and Buchanan, the harder it would be for Lincoln to depict Douglas as the captive of the slave power. Moreover, in the end the Buchanan forces received only a few thousand votes.[91]

Perhaps as a diversion from this conspiracy argument, some of the Danites insisted that Douglas was in a conspiracy with the Republicans against *them.* This charge too had some foundation. During the Lecompton struggle, Douglas claimed to be fighting the Republicans' fight, pleaded for Republican cooperation, and pleaded with the *Chicago*

Press and Tribune to desist from attacking him during the Lecompton fight. Iowa senator George W. Jones and other administration supporters spread the rumor of a secret deal whereby Republicans would support Douglas for the Senate with the understanding that he would then shift allegiances and run for president as a Republican.[92] This rumor appeared to lack foundation, and Douglas denied it categorically.

IX

Lincoln's subsidiary charge was more complex; it occupied virtually the entire Charleston debate, but it appears only there. He elaborated on an allegation made earlier in the Senate by Trumbull that Douglas had been party to a plot to prevent the Kansas constitution from being submitted for a vote by the people, thereby denying his cherished principle of popular sovereignty. The original bill for territorial organization provided that the constitution be approved by popular vote, but Douglas and other senators removed this provision and inserted instead a clause preventing a referendum. To be sure, this new clause was subsequently stricken, but still Douglas had inserted it. Unless his object was to deprive the people of Kansas of a fair election, why did he put it in?

This argument was not new. Senator William Bigler of Pennsylvania had advanced it on the Senate floor in December 1857, although Bigler's reference to Douglas was oblique. Referring to the Illinoisian, he said, "I cannot be persuaded that the Senator intended to secure to the people the right to vote on the constitution, by striking from the bill the words making that policy necessary." Senator Hale of New Hampshire took up the theme in January 1858, indicating that the deletion from the Toombs Bill "was not accidental," and in March Bigler alluded vaguely to his earlier allegations. The charge was made most specifically by Trumbull on his return to Illinois. In a speech on August 7, he pointedly named Douglas as a co-conspirator. At that time, Lincoln had said that he knew nothing of the matter but would vouch for Trumbull's integrity. That being the case, Douglas said, he would not waste his time answering Trumbull but would hold Lincoln responsible for whatever his compatriot said. That was the reason that Lincoln used to justify his bringing the matter into the Charleston debate. There it occupied the full time of his opening speech, save the first few minutes, in which he disavowed racial equality.[93]

The facts in the Toombs Bill dispute can be grasped easily. The Kansas-Nebraska Act specified no procedure by which the territories would become states. Senator Robert Toombs in Georgia proposed in 1856 to remedy this defect, and thereby defuse the Kansas question, by proposing a bill stipulating procedures for a constitutional convention and a vote on slavery. Rawley has described this bill as "the highest act of states-manship on Bleeding Kansas that the times produced" since it provided federal supervision of the process and sought to determine the will of the people fairly. When Douglas's Committee on Territories reviewed the bill, it deleted a clause that would have required submission to a referendum. Douglas had argued that the clause was unnecessary; everybody knew that there would be a referendum. His biographer, Robert Johannsen, has pointed out that Douglas's opposition noticed but did not object to this omission at the time and states that all assumed Douglas's position on this matter to be correct. On July 2, 1856, the Senate passed the Toombs Bill thirty-three to twelve. The very next day, the House, controlled by an anti-Nebraska coalition, not only refused to pass the bill but instead voted ninety-nine to ninety-seven to admit Kansas as a state under the rival Topeka constitution, which outlawed slavery. The Senate, of course, would not accept the Topeka document as legitimate, and a stand-off resulted.[94]

What is less clear is why this impasse resulted. Some suggested that Republicans could not bear to have the question settled; as Crissey put it, "'Bleeding Kansas' was their best issue. They intended to keep it."[95] The same reason was given for Republican opposition to the Lecompton constitution itself by Buchanan in his February 1858 message and by Democrats on the floor of the Senate.[96] On the other hand, Republicans alleged that the Toombs Bill as it emerged from the Senate was a fraud, an attempt to force slavery on the people of Kansas by denying them the opportunity to vote it out. They could not possibly support such a deceitful move.

The controversy over the submission clause may seem arcane, but its implications were crucial. By 1857, when the Kansas territorial legislature was elected, it was abundantly clear that any referendum would produce a decisive defeat for the proslavery forces. The Lecompton convention was composed as it was only because free-state supporters had boycotted the election for delegates—and they may well have done so on the expectation, encouraged by Territorial Governor Walker, that they would have an opportunity to vote down the final document itself. Whether Kansas went slave or free thus turned on the question of whether a referendum was required. Whether other states had been admitted without referendum was ultimately beside the point, as Congressman John Hickman exclaimed: "Kansas is a case standing by itself; it has no parallels; it is not to be illustrated by precedent."[97] The issue was important for another reason. Douglas opposed the Lecompton constitution, and by his opposition he threatened to take votes from the Republicans. If it could be shown that he conspired to prevent a referendum in the first place, then his opposition to Lecompton would be exposed as being expedient rather than principled and hence as no guide to his future conduct. He would be exposed as hypocritical and opportunistic, and his doctrine of popular sovereignty would be exposed as deceitful. Much was at stake.

Partly for this reason, Trumbull's charge received wide attention. Whan reports that most Illinois newspapers gave more space to it than to any of Lincoln's other arguments—perhaps suggesting why Lincoln devoted the Charleston debate to this charge.[98] Correspondents urged Lincoln to make the argument. M. W. Delahay wrote that, although the accusation "seems to be somewhat new to many," still Douglas would have to defend the alterations in the Toombs Bill, "and whenever he does you have got the *Word on him.*" Ozias Hatch wrote that, after Trumbull's August speech, the Democrats *"are all mad."* J. H. Jordan of Cincinnati crisply advised Lincoln, "Don't forget that charge of *altering Toombs' Bill*—taking out the 'Popular Sovereignty'—It is *true*—therefore *make him eat it!*"[99]

Lincoln's Charleston speech is a masterful exercise of refutation. He never advanced the conspiracy charge himself; he stated only that Trumbull had done so and that he would vouch for Trumbull's integrity. Instead, he sought to cast doubt on Douglas's reply to Trumbull and by residues to reinstate the charge. If all attempts to refute a claim fail and are themselves refuted, then the original claim remains—not because it has been actively resubstantiated but as the residue of the attempts to overthrow it. Seven specific refutations make up Lincoln's speech. First, Douglas had said that the Kansas bill was similar to other acts for the admission of new states. Not so, replied Lincoln: other acts had been silent on the matter of a referendum, but there was no other case in which such a clause had been first inserted and then removed. Moreover, it was a curious coincidence that the clause was stricken "almost simultaneously with the time that Bigler says there was a conference among certain Senators, and in which it was agreed that a bill should be passed leaving that out." Douglas has ignored Bigler's testimony, but his simultaneous action "will make a pretty fair show of proof" that he truly was in the plot.[100]

Second, Douglas had said that the Toombs Bill never did contain a clause requiring submission. But he did not deny that the words had been stricken—and, in case he did, Lincoln produced "what I suppose to be a genuine copy of the Toombs bill, in which it can be shown that the words Trumbull says were in it, were, in fact, originally there." The only question was whether the stricken words actually would have required a referendum on the constitution. Here Lincoln quoted Trumbull's argument. True, the reference was indirect, but the implication was clear. The bill provided for voting on various land provisions "at the election for the adoption of the constitution," and how could that be done if no such election were held?[101] The meaning and intent were clear.

Third, Douglas had tried to impugn Trumbull's credibility. In post-conference floor debate, Trumbull had said that he supposed that the constitution would have to be submitted to the people. Why does he think differently now? To this question Lincoln replied simply that Trumbull, in haste, may have missed the alteration and that whether he saw it or not does not change the fact that the bill was altered.

Fourth, Douglas had asked why Trumbull did not seek to amend the bill if he had found it flawed. To do so would have been pointless, Lincoln answered: "Why, I believe that everything Judge Trumbull had proposed, particularly in connection with this question of Kansas and Nebraska, since he had been on the floor of the Senate, had been promptly voted down by Judge Douglas and his friends. He had no promise that an amendment offered by him to anything on this subject would receive the slightest consideration." Moreover, Lincoln repeated that the issue of Trumbull's motives "does not reach the question of fact *as to what Judge Douglas was doing.*" Even if Trumbull himself had been part of the plot, "it would not at all relieve the others who were in it from blame." Drawing the analogy to a murder trial, Lincoln noted that he could not establish his own innocence by proving that others were guilty too.[102]

Fifth, Douglas had accused Trumbull of shifting ground in his charges, once saying that Douglas had deleted the clause and once that it was deleted in committee. This was not a shift at all, Lincoln said, but the amassing of new evidence consistent with what had been proved initially.

Sixth, Douglas had maintained that he himself had moved to strike from the bill those provisions that prevented an election "and that on his motion it was stricken out and a substitute inserted." Lincoln granted that fact; so indeed had Trumbull. But this statement was in no way inconsistent with Trumbull's charges. As Lincoln put it, "I presume the truth is that Douglas put it in and afterwards took it out." But whether Douglas later removed the offending language is really beside the point: "The question is, what did he put it in for?"[103]

Finally, Douglas had said that Trumbull "forges his evidence from beginning to end, and by falsifying the record he endeavors to bolster up his false charge." But the hard evidence denies the allegation. Lincoln referred to copies of the bill before and after it was considered by Douglas's committee and to statements by Bigler and by Douglas himself that had been printed in the *Congressional Globe*. After offering a definition of forgery, he challenged Douglas to explain, "How do you make this a forgery when every piece of evidence is genuine?"[104] With but three minutes left, he then returned to the central question. Why did he take out the clause requiring an election, and why did he substitute a new one preventing it?

Douglas's reply was selective and lacking in depth, and many of his defenses had already been anticipated and preempted by Lincoln. The incumbent began by accusing Lincoln of trivializing the debate through introducing a matter unrelated to current public policy and two years old at that. Lincoln was bringing it up now, when Trumbull did not do so earlier, because Trumbull was also part of the plot, but if that is so then Trumbull should not be believed now "when he turns state's evidence and avows his own infamy in order to implicate me."[105] Yet Lincoln had no independent basis for alleging the conspiracy; his proof depended entirely on Trumbull.

Douglas proceeded to lash at Trumbull, accusing his colleague of knowing that Bigler's charge was a lie but repeating it nonetheless. "He waited until I became engaged in this canvass," the Little Giant said, "and finding that I was showing up Lincoln's Abolitionism and negro equality doctrines, that I was driving Lincoln to the wall, and white men would not support his rank Abolitionism, he came back from the East and trumped up a system of charges against me, hoping that I would be compelled to occupy my entire time in defending myself, so that I would not be able to show up the enormity of the principles of the Abolitionists."[106] Distraction from the issues was the only motive for Lincoln's raising the charges, Douglas insisted, but his vitriolic references to Trumbull risked his being caught in just that trap, battling against Trumbull rather than Lincoln.

When he got to the substance of the conspiracy charge, Douglas had less to say. He explained to the audience that territorial bills usually do not specify that there will be a referendum, so the original clause in the bill was superfluous and its removal innocuous. In committee, it had been commonly assumed that of course there would be a referendum. If there was a conspiracy in this case, then every previous president who had supported a bill for territorial organization was likewise implicated. The original bill had required a referendum only on a land grant, not on the entire constitution. Trumbull knew the clause was missing at the time the bill was passed. He had indeed shifted his charges against Douglas after the *Chicago Times* had exposed the original charge as faulty. Douglas was the one who finally struck out the clause preventing elections and substituted an amendment permitting them. Douglas ignored Lincoln's argument about the futility of a Trumbull amendment, and he ignored Lincoln's refutation of the claim that the Toombs Bill was a complete forgery.

Lincoln responded to Douglas's opening remarks. Far from his having raised a diversionary issue, it was *Douglas* who had started the matter by holding Lincoln responsible for Trumbull's statements. As for Douglas's assertion that the Toombs Bill was a dead issue, Lincoln found it odd that the incumbent, if he were so concerned, would continue to raise the *ten-year-old* issue of Lincoln's Mexican War record. "Isn't he a pretty man," Lincoln asked, "to be whining about people making charges against him only *two* years old."[107] With respect to Douglas's attacks on Trumbull's character, Lincoln noted that nothing in his charge depended on Trumbull's veracity; the evidence was independent.

For the most part, Douglas's substantive arguments were easily dealt with. His remarks about the unusual nature of submission clauses did not deny that one had been there and that the incumbent senator had taken it out. The issue over the land grant was, as he had said earlier, a quibble over the meaning of words; since the land grant was to be voted on at the election for the adoption of the constitution, such an election must be held, or the provision would be meaningless. The fact that Douglas struck out the offending clause did not deny that he originally had put it in. Finally, Lincoln repeated his answers to Douglas's claim that Trumbull's charges were forged. Referring to the individual pieces of testimony, Lincoln noted, "*Not one of them has he shown to be a forgery,*" and then asked, "if each of the pieces of testimony is true, *how is it that the whole is a falsehood?*"[108]

Prominent though this argument was at Charleston, it received virtually no attention thereafter. At Quincy, Lincoln noted that the incumbent had been unable to substantiate the charge of forgery, and, at Alton, Douglas repeated his harangue about Lincoln's voting record during the Mexican War. Otherwise, the issue disappeared seemingly as fast as it had developed. Lincoln had used the argument in place of the "frame house" conspiracy claim. Soon he would abandon the conspiracy argument altogether.

Most readers of the Charleston debate have concluded that the conspiracy charge against Douglas was without foundation. That view was taken at the time by the Democratic press. The *Illinois State Register*, for example, interpreted the debate to mean "that Lincoln has become satisfied that he cannot cope with Douglas" because "Lincoln had nothing to say for himself . . . but he repeated the charge made by Trumbull and reproduced the falsehoods of that renegade from democracy." Even Douglas's early and sympathetic biographer Allen Johnson recognized, however, that the incumbent had hurt himself by the nature of his defense. The vindictiveness and venom of his responses backfired, in Johnson's opinion, and "his words did not carry conviction to the minds of his hearers. . . . Democrats seemed ill at ease after the debate."[109] It is worth noting that, of all the central Illinois area, only in the eastern region, around Charleston, did Lincoln score well on election day. Surely, Douglas's principles were called into question. He now demanded a referendum for Kansas after having rejected the need for it in the Toombs Bill. Even as he insisted on a referendum in Kansas, he denied the need for one in Minnesota. Surely, Republicans could feel confident that they had knocked Douglas off balance.

The Charleston debate was dominated by the conspiracy argument, but the form largely disappeared from the remaining three debates. Except for brief references back to positions developed earlier, little more is said about the designs of scheming men. Why this is so will be the subject for speculation later. It is noteworthy, though, that the three final debates are characterized more by legal, historical, and moral arguments, and it is in these exchanges that the clash between Lincoln and Douglas reaches its climax.

X

Taken together, these four conspiracy claims illustrate the dynamics of the argument form. They tell a story that is vivid and plausible. Even though there are lacunae in the supporting acts and documents, these are woven together in a believable narrative. Conspiracy arguments depend on the inventional genius of the arguer in perceiving patterns of experience. They illustrate strategic considerations in the placement of presumption and burden of proof. And they reveal that a countercharge is frequently the most effective refutation because explicit denials only show the cunning of the conspirators and hence can be reinterpreted as support for the charge.

Most of the conspiracy arguments in the Lincoln-Douglas debates would be dismissed as absurd by most historians because there is little if any objective evidence to support them. But that is the easy out. The greater challenge is to explain why, in the light of their limited support, they were taken seriously by intelligent advocates and audiences at the time. Several answers suggest themselves.

First, conspiracy arguments become widely accepted when they explain an otherwise ambiguous evil. In the most thorough rhetorical study on the genre of conspiracy arguments, Creps contends that they resolve the paradox of evil in a presumably good society. By locating the cause of evil in a plot, the argument removes the guilt from the community at large.[110] When there is a simpler explanation for evil, conspiracy claims will not get a widespread hearing. But sometimes the evil is not clear cut. It may have persisted for generations, or it may have been so sudden and instantaneous that it escaped accurate reporting, or the whole society may be implicated in it, or it may be intangible. Both the sudden renewal of slavery agitation in the mid-1850s and the persistence of slavery in a nation dedicated to freedom fit several of these conditions. In circumstances such as these, a society's tolerance for ambiguity weakens. The conspiracy claim provides a convenient alternative to living with uncertainty. It identifies agents (usually outsiders) who have a clear motive to afflict society, and it sets out the means by which they do so. The argument thereby provides clear targets for resentment, reproach, or punitive action, and society, by thwarting the plot, can arrest the evil.

Second, conspiracy arguments become widely accepted when they explain a pattern of anomalies. Perfect order and logic never reign in any society; there are always some discordant notes. Normally, these difficult-to-explain events are simply accepted as "noise" in the system. But when a large number of such events occur and the anomalies seem to have a pattern, the search for an explanation intensifies. The conspiracy argument is able to explain paradox and incongruity. Given surface plausibility, the argument's "theory" of events is almost self-sealing.

By the late 1850s, events did seem to fit a pattern. New York congressman Clark B. Cochrane, for example, exclaimed on the House floor, "This Lecompton conspiracy is not an isolated wrong. . . . It is but the culmination of a *system* of atrocities."[111] Southerners likewise saw a pattern of systematic insult to honor and prestige as well as to the status of the peculiar institution itself. Finding in conspiracy the explanation for an anomalous pattern was commonplace by the time of the Lincoln-Douglas debates.

In the debates, the conspiracy argument does make sense out of an otherwise confusing array of circumstances. It shows Democrats why Republicans would depart from custom and proclaim Lincoln their "first, last, and only choice" rather than leaving the selection to the legislature. It explains why Lincoln would deny his role in the 1854 Republican platform when the "facts" seemed to show otherwise. It explains why Lincoln took a hard-line abolitionist stance in northern Illinois but softened his position as he went south. On the other side, the conspiracy charge explains for Republicans why Douglas would not report the results of his "investigation" in Springfield even when he could clear his name by doing so. It explains why Douglas would object to the explicit acknowledgment of the power to exclude slavery, which he conceded to be implicit. It explains why Douglas would insert a clause preventing a referendum into the bill for the admission of Kansas and then remove the clause again.

Third, conspiracy arguments are plausible when they provide a plausible narrative. Indeed, the narrative form is precisely the pattern that the argument bestows on events, giving them a plot, heroes and villains, and movement through past, present, and future. The value of the narrative, as White explains it, grows "out of a desire to have real events display the coherence, integrity, fullness, and closure of an image of life that is and can only be imaginary."[112] The narrative structure of the slavery conspiracies was not unlike the popular melodrama of the early nineteenth century.[113] Besides, the conspiracy narrative made it possible to set individual events in a broader context, to see them as first steps toward some larger end.

Fourth, conspiracy arguments become generally accepted when polarizing positions helps resolve ambiguity. A situation that requires choice, yet in which the alternatives are not very different, produces uncertainty and confusion. Merelman has written that American politicians often have relatively narrow bases of disagreement. "For this reason," he concludes, "unmasking often involves attempts by both sides to magnify their differences. A favorite unmasking tactic . . . is to label each other as 'really' more 'extremist' than their present identities may appear to make them." During the 1850s, the sense of polarization was heightened, as Davis explains, "by contrasting one's own unconditional loyalty to the nation with the essentially subversive character of some reference group."[114] The conspiracy argument goes beyond more general forms of challenging an opponent's character because of its focus on what is *secret* as a basis for inducing polarization.

The polarizing function of the conspiracy argument can be seen clearly in the case of the Lincoln-Douglas debates. The practical effects of the two candidates' positions were similar. Even if Lincoln had triumphed, slavery would not have been abolished anywhere it then existed. Even if Douglas won, popular sovereignty was not likely to result in any new slave territories—Kansas, where the prospects seemed greatest, had just rejected the Lecompton constitution by a margin of eight to one. And both candidates subscribed to the popular sovereignty principle as it applied to new states. But neither candidate could take comfort in the similarity of positions because it offered voters no clear basis for choosing one over the other. The conspiracy argument creates fundamental differences by suggesting that the apparent similarity of views is only the tip of the iceberg. A wedge is forced between apparently similar positions, and the people are required to make a real choice.

Fifth, conspiracy arguments are more generally accepted when they furnish the basis for appeals to loyalty or unity. In the manner of the scapegoat, the alleged conspirator becomes the object of the people's fears and apprehensions and provides the threat in whose face people stand as one. Portraying one's own motives as open and sincere, in contrast to the guile and deceit of an adversary, was a way to reaffirm basic democratic values. By exposing subversion, David Brion Davis has written, the individual could not only clarify national values but also attribute to oneself "a sense of high moral sanction and imputed righteousness." Moreover, in depicting a challenge to any institution as a challenge to such fundamental verities as law and justice, one strengthens adherence to those basic values.[115] In the confused political culture of the 1850s, conspiracy arguments led separate factions to see their interests as identical to the interests of the whole as a result of portraying their opponents as threats to the whole.

Sixth, conspiracy arguments become generally accepted in times of social stress and strain. These are times when it is hard to get a clear picture of the world. Previously shared norms are questioned, life is difficult, and the signs are not clear. The conspiracy argument offers a measure of reassurance. It is alarming to think that a secret cabal is afoot, but some stability is provided by the belief that one knows what is going on, can make sense of difficult and complex phenomena, and hence can be on one's guard. We know that the 1850s were a time of great uncertainty and stress, and this pressure was reflected in the debates. Strozier dismisses Lincoln's conspiracy arguments as paranoid but suggests that perhaps "he was simply seizing the public's mood and giving it voice." A more charitable reading is offered by Baker, who concludes that the failure of the "second party system" was a stressful situation that could not be explained save by reference to a conspiratorial plot.[116]

These considerations suggest that external conditions have much to do with whether conspiracy arguments are credible and enter the mainstream of American political discourse. So they do, but their influence is not total. Events furnish arguers with a context, possible premises, and "the facts," but then arguers make choices about how to use those materials in constructing arguments. The Lincoln-Douglas debates also reveal the internal dynamics of successful conspiracy arguments.

To begin with, successful arguments shift the burden of proof to one's opponent while minimizing one's own burdens. By conventional standards of proof, a conspiracy charge is virtually impossible to prove. It deals with acts committed in secret to achieve a purpose usually known only through inference. But the charge is also virtually impossible to disprove. One cannot prove a negative; moreover, acts or events that seem to challenge the existence of the conspiracy can be reinterpreted as the work of clever conspirators to conceal their true intentions. Since the argument can be neither proved nor disproved, who "wins" will likely depend on who shoulders the burden of proof. Consequently, much of the argumentation is the attempt by both parties to claim presumption and to force the burden of proof onto the antagonist.

The Lincoln-Douglas debates illustrate this jockeying for presumption. When attacking a conspiracy claim, either man was likely to insist that "he who asserts must prove." But when offering a claim, either man would present his evidence and reasoning and then defy the opponent to disprove the claim. Which advocate succeeds will depend both on what arguments are marshaled to support his claim to presumption and on how sensitive his opponent is to the importance of the claim.

Conspiracy arguments are often about motives; the argument will not be persuasive unless the alleged conspirator is shown to have had a motive for participating in the plot. Whan has suggested that the Lincoln-Douglas debates were not finally about slavery in the territories but instead about the motives of the candidates. Each sought to build his own prestige and call the other's consistency and honesty into question.[117] The debates reflect a contrast between two quite different ways to establish motive.

Douglas explicitly identified Lincoln's motive as selfish desire for office. That impulse, the incumbent alleged, led his challenger both to ally himself with federal officeholders and to conspire to convert the Whigs to abolitionism. By contrast, Lincoln usually argued motives by residues. For example, he asked what motive Douglas would have had for defeating the Chase amendment other than his participation in a conspiracy or why he wrote the Kansas-Nebraska Act as he did other than because he anticipated a future *Dred Scott* decision. Inability to offer alternatives would prove the existence of the alleged motive.

Strategic considerations suggest the superiority of arguing motive by residues. First, the audience has participated in considering and rejecting other plausible accounts of motive. Listeners should be more inclined to accept the proffered motive since they, together with the speaker, have ruled out all other possibilities. Second, this form of argument saddles the opponent with the need to find some new, unthought-of alternative explanation and render it persuasive. Of course, the person arguing from residues must be able to defeat any and all other interpretations, but the self-sealing nature of the conspiracy argument means that alternative theories usually can be reinterpreted to fit within the framework of conspirational design. Third, the initial advocate may be able to "poison the wells" by preemptively discrediting other likely explanations of motive, thereby increasing the odds that the motive argued by residues will emerge persuasive.

Another consideration affecting the dynamics of the conspiracy argument is the nature of proof offered. In general, inferences are a more persuasive form of evidence than documents. This statement may seem counterintuitive; documenting texts, as primary source materials, are often thought the most incontrovertible form of evidence. Sometimes they are, particularly when the issue turns on their existence rather than their meaning. For example, when Douglas asserted that the Toombs Bill never contained a clause preventing a referendum and Lincoln produced an authentic copy indicating that it had, that ended the argument about whether the words existed.

But most disputes involving documents turn on their meaning, and, as Clark has observed, texts "do not speak; they must be spoken for."[118] In other words, the power of a document depends on the context in which it is placed. To some degree, contexts can be chosen by the arguers themselves, and one debater can effectively dismiss a document by redefining its context. On the other hand, the debate itself furnishes the context for inferences validated by the audience; one cannot object to the context without impugning their reasoning and judgment.

Although both men used various types of evidence, Douglas tended more to produce documents, and Lincoln—aside from reading his own previous speeches—resorted more to inferences. Douglas quoted from Matheny's speech, from the *Illinois State Register*, from the *Washington Union*, and from the Toombs Bill. Lincoln, drawing his inferences from Douglas's actions or inactions, reinterpreted ambiguous or even seemingly trivial events to make them fit into a larger pattern. Interestingly, neither man really came to grips with the other's pattern of support. Lincoln dismissed Douglas's documents by contending that the writers were not qualified to speak or that they themselves had no evidence. Douglas dismissed Lincoln's inferences as speculation and conjecture unsupported by any evidence. He denounced the charges as lies and waited for Lincoln to prove them.

But Douglas faced an additional problem. As with any enthymeme— an argument whose premises are drawn from the beliefs of the audience—listeners participated along with Lincoln in reasoning through his inferences. Not only was active participation likely to incline the audience toward Lincoln's conclusions, but, when Douglas derided Lincoln's reasoning as preposterous, he was implicitly criticizing the audience as well. His own documents, meanwhile, were more passive forms of evidence. As listeners reasoned through with Lincoln to his conclusions, they were developing the materials with which to discredit or dismiss the incumbent's documentary evidence.

A final aspect of the conspiracy argument bears mention. Countercharges are the most effective responses to a conspiracy claim. When a speaker alleges the existence of a conspiracy, there seem to be three basic ways that an opponent may respond: deny it outright, offer an alternative account of the events that allegedly prove the existence of the plot, or make a countercharge that one's opponent is really the true conspirator. The first of these approaches is effective only if coupled with successful shifting of the burden of proof onto one's adversary. Otherwise, it is merely an attempt to balance one's word against the array of evidence, and one hardly would be a competent witness in support of one's own case. The second approach, offering an alternative explanation, is effective to some degree, particularly in response to tenuous inferences. It is harder to sustain in reply to documentary evidence, for the predictable result is that the authenticity of the documents rather than their interpretation becomes the central point at issue. But more effective than either of these approaches is the counterclaim, the *tu quoque*. Since the accused conspirator cannot absolutely disprove the existence of a plot, what better response than to make the same charge against one's accuser, saddling him with the same difficulties? If both charges appear reasonable, one can at least hope for a wash, and one charge sometimes may be used effectively to deny the other. Douglas alluded to several conspiracies in the course of his response to Lincoln, but for the most part these counterclaims were not developed thoroughly. Lincoln's most obvious use of this tactic was to allege a conspiracy to forge the supposed 1854 Republican platform in reply to Douglas's charge that this platform was the work of a conspiracy to abolitionize the Whigs.

Notwithstanding all that has been said, one might question whether either candidate really took the conspiracy argument all that seriously. Two years before the debates, Lincoln had expressed doubts about the utility of the form. "True, each party charges upon the other, *designs* much beyond what is involved in the issue," he had written, and then concluded, "but as these charges can not be fully proved either way, it is probably better to reject them on both sides, and stick to the naked issue, as it is clearly made up on the record."[119] As the debates progressed, he gave less attention to deliberate plots and focused instead on the natural tendency, unless arrested, toward national slavery. This charge may have reflected his assessment that his charges were not persuasive to his audiences and that they were outweighed by Douglas's efforts to paint him as an abolitionist. That charge was nothing but trouble. He could not win the old Whig vote if it stuck, and he might not hold on to his Northern support if he disavowed it too energetically. To overcome this dilemma he must find a new way to distinguish himself from Douglas, one that would be more effective than the somewhat tenuous, and tedious, conspiracy charge.

For Douglas's part, the *Chicago Times* judged the conspiracy charge to be "the whole stock in trade of the arrant adventurer. He seeks notoriety and position, and to hide his own former ignominious career behind the portentous cloud of some mysterious conspiracy." Republicans, the paper alleged, "who mistake notoriety for honor," were all over the state "belching forth their accusations of conspiracy."[120]

Still, the argument was effective. It had been used in a context in which charges and recriminations had become a staple of political discourse. As Rawley summarizes the political culture,

Douglas and the South had violated the sacred Missouri compact, New England had leagued with abolitionist emigrants, the South had leagued with Border Ruffians, Presidents had been putty in the hands of a southern Directory, Black Republicans supported Osawatomie Brown, fanatical Puritan abolitionists were inciting a race war, northerners obstructed the Fugitive Slave Law with their personal liberty laws and Underground Railroad, southerners were bent on spreading slavery through all the territories and into Central America and Cuba, and on reviving the infamous African slave trade.[121]

In such an atmosphere, the conspiracy argument was at home. And it worked. A correspondent wrote Lincoln after the Ottawa debate that the Douglas men so far had been "staggered" by three things, all of them conspiracy arguments: the plot to nationalize slavery ("keep it going for it is true as God's own word"), Trumbull's charge that Douglas conspired against popular sovereignty in amending the Toombs Bill, "and now the fact, (if true,) that he has passed a forgery upon the Ottawa meeting in regard to the Springfield convention of 1854."[122] As for Douglas, his charge that Lincoln was part of an abolitionist plot, coupled with the historical argument that he would develop later, was his strongest and most successful appeal in the campaign.

4

The Legal Argument

If the conspiracy argument seems unusually graphic, the arguments about law and the Constitution will strike the modern reader as arcane. But in the mid-1850s they were unsettled and important issues. Legal arguments came easily to two such experienced lawyers as Lincoln and Douglas, but veneration of the Constitution and the desire to identify current issues with its principles were values widely held among their audiences as well.

The slavery question raised several significant legal issues: whether the commitment to equality in the Declaration of Independence should control interpretation of the Constitution; whether the three-fifths clause in the Constitution represented de facto acceptance of slavery; whether the provisions related to suppression of the slave trade were intended to support or weaken the institution; and whether the fugitive slave clause was concerned only with relations among state executives or whether it, too, lent sanction to slavery.[1] The debates, however, addressed a smaller number of legal questions, beginning with the interpretation of the *Dred Scott* decision but expanding outward to larger questions about the nature of the territories and the reach of the national government within a system of federalism. They also exhibited the use of the interrogatory, which adapted legal cross-examination to the form of public debate.

I

Although questions were raised on occasion during the 1980s, it is now generally held that Supreme Court decisions on constitutional grounds are final, except for the possibility of constitutional amendment. But the principle of finality had not been firmly established in 1858. The *Dred Scott* decision was only the second in which the Court had overturned an act of Congress, *Marbury v. Madison* being the first. Whether the earlier case authoritatively established judicial supremacy is unclear. As Jaffa has noted, it had concerned the extent of the Court's own powers, whereas *Dred Scott* was the first to address the powers of another branch of the government and to have significant consequences for policy.[2] Was the Supreme Court to be only one voice in a discordant political chorus, or was it to be the decisive voice?

On the face of it, the decision favored the Southern slaveholding interests, so it is not surprising that Southern voices were raised insisting on the finality of the decision. Douglas also argued that it was final partly because, as a national politician with presidential aspirations, he could not afford to alienate the South; partly, no doubt, because he was constrained by agreement at the time of the Kansas-Nebraska Act to submit to the courts the timing of popular sovereignty and then to abide by the decision.[3] But his public rationale for endorsing the decision referred to the integrity of the Court itself. He reflected a traditional belief that legal and political questions were distinct. The only alternative that he saw to acceptance of the decision was anarchy, with Everyman his own judge of the Constitution. Ironically, this was the same theme that Buchanan had struck in his Lecompton message, when he predicted that "a general spirit" against enforcement of the laws would "prove fatal to us as a nation."[4]

According to Carl Sandburg, Douglas developed this line shortly after the decision was announced. He introduced it into the 1858 campaign in a speech at Edwards Grove on July 17, and he related it to Lincoln in the fifth and sixth debates. At Galesburg, he charged his opponent with seeking "to appeal from the Supreme Court of the United States to every town meeting in the hope that he can excite a prejudice against that court." But the result of that action, "destroying public confidence in the court, so that the people will not respect its decisions, but will feel at liberty to disregard them," would be to "have changed the government from one of laws into that of a mob, in which the strong arm of violence will be substituted for the decisions of the courts of justice." At Quincy, Douglas asked rhetorically, "By what tribunal will he reverse [the *Dred Scott* decision]? Will he appeal to a mob? Does he intend to appeal to violence, to lynch law? Will he stir up strife and rebellion in the land and overthrow the court by violence?"[5] Meanwhile, Douglas's supporters went even further. The *Illinois State Register* put forward the thesis, attributed to the Little Giant, "that the attack on the supreme court was an attack on that government the foundations of which our fathers so carefully laid" and that Lincoln's disparagement of *Dred Scott* was part of an abolitionist plot "to keep up the agitation of the slavery question, and unless they could succeed in carrying out their particular measures in favor of the negro, to overturn this government, and nullify the constitution of the country." The best means to this end, the paper asserted, was "to begin by destroying the confidence of the people in the tribunal of last resort on constitutional questions."[6] Questions of legal authority could also be cast in the form of conspiracy arguments.

Douglas's position, however, had not been sustained consistently by the Democratic party or even by the incumbent himself, and Lincoln drew on these discrepancies to refute the theory. He had received advice from correspondents that he cite examples in which Andrew Jackson, Douglas's political hero, did not regard Court decisions as final. Hugh Gordon Seymour suggested that Lincoln mention the expulsion of Indian tribes from the South "in open disregard of the opinion of the Supreme Court of the United States as to their obligation," and Schuyler Colfax quoted Jackson's Bank Veto Message as an example that could be used against Douglas's doctrine of acquiescence.[7] Lincoln himself had pursued the same theme. In his 1857 Springfield speech, he referred to the Court's decision upholding the constitutionality of the Bank of the United States and argued that Douglas's recent denunciation of Republicans on the finality of Court decisions applied to himself as well. "Again and again," Lincoln gloated, "I have heard Judge Douglas denounce that bank decision, and applaud Gen. Jackson for disregarding it. It would be interesting for him to look over his recent speech, and see how exactly his fierce philippics against us for resisting Supreme Court decisions, fall upon his head." He went on to suggest that, if—as Douglas believed—the finality of court decisions was "a distinct and naked issue between the friends and the enemies of the Constitution," then the incumbent had placed *himself* among the document's enemies![8]

Lincoln was on solid ground in developing this *ad hominem* argument that sought to hoist Douglas on his own petard. As Rush Welter has noted, Democrats were frequently disturbed by decisions during the tenure of John Marshall as chief justice and responded by attacking the authority of the Supreme Court.[9] Nevertheless, Lincoln was frustrated at his inability to engage Douglas with this inconsistency. In notes for speeches, Lincoln wrote, probably in August 1858, "I point out to him that Mr. Jefferson and General Jackson were both against him on the binding political authority of Supreme Court decisions. No response. I might as well preach Christianity to a grizzly bear as to preach Jefferson and Jackson to him."[10] He persisted, however, and introduced the counterexamples into the debates.

At Galesburg, for example, Lincoln not only noted that Jackson had disagreed with Douglas's view but quoted Jefferson against the Little Giant as well and cited the Cincinnati platform, which Douglas supported, in its opposition to Jackson on the Bank. Douglas responded only on the example of the Bank. As he noted, the analogy was not perfect because the Bank case involved action that was permitted rather than required, as in the case of the slaveholder's access to the territories.[11] But it was adequate to Lincoln's purpose to show that Supreme Court decisions were not sacrosanct. If he could demystify the Court's authority, he would then be in a better position to attack the *Dred Scott* decision itself.

For purposes of demystifying the Court, Lincoln had an even more graphic example drawn from local politics in Illinois. In 1840, the Democrats had captured the legislature, but the state supreme court remained under Whig control. Mindful of an 1838 decision denying the right of a Democratic governor to remove a Whig secretary of state, and anticipating a decision depriving unnaturalized aliens of the right to vote after six months' residence (a move that would cost the Democrats thousands of votes), the legislature added five new justices, all Democrats, to the four already on the supreme court. Douglas himself, as one of the principal supporters of the measure, became one of the five new justices.[12]

W. S. Frinke of Taylorville, a supporter of Lincoln's, wrote to his candidate to suggest that this particular discrepancy in Douglas's behavior be exploited in the debates. Frinke urged that Douglas be shown up, when "making it almost sacrilege to even call in question the purity and justice" of the Court, by Lincoln's "citing his mind and recollections to events that occurred in this state—but a few years ago—when a Supreme Court was legislated out of existence—a new one legislated into existence—and judge Douglas—one of the members of the new Court."[13] Indeed, Lincoln developed just this theme in almost every debate. At Ottawa, for example, he told the basic tale of how Douglas had become a justice on the Illinois Supreme Court, adding, "It was in this way precisely that he got his title of Judge." Then the challenger added, "When he says a court of this kind will lose the confidence of all men, will be prostituted and disgraced by such a proceeding, I say, 'You know best, Judge; you have been through the mill.'" Likewise, at Galesburg Lincoln reminded the audience, "I have asked his attention to the fact that he himself was one of the most active instruments at one time in breaking down the Supreme Court of the state of Illinois, because it had made a decision distasteful to him—a struggle ending in the remarkable circumstance of his sitting down as one of the new Judges who were to overslaugh that decision—getting his title of Judge in that very way."[14]

For the most part, even this accusation failed to goad Douglas into reply. The Little Giant repeated his statement that Supreme Court decisions should be regarded as final in order to protect the integrity of the Court. To Lincoln, that position was an evasion of the issue, and he had a reply for it too. As he portrayed the situation, Douglas supported *Dred Scott* not on the merits of the case but merely because the decision emanated from the Supreme Court. The decision, Lincoln caricatured, "was for him a 'Thus saith the Lord.'" The difficulty with this position is that it is neverending; the same logic would commit Douglas to support the next decision just as he did this one: "The next decision, as much as this, will be a *thus saith the Lord*. There is nothing that can divert or turn him away from this decision." At Galesburg, Lincoln amplified his prediction: "So he takes the next one without inquiring whether *it* is right or wrong. He teaches men this doctrine, and in so doing prepares the public mind to take the next decision when it comes, without any inquiry.[15] Douglas's unqualified support for any decision, if he were to instill that attitude in others, would create the very state of public indifference that would be likely to prompt "*Dred Scott* II." Even if Douglas disavowed a conspiracy to make slavery national, still his own legal theory would require him to accept such a decision.

On several counts, then, Douglas's position on the finality of court decisions was vulnerable. But so was Lincoln's. The challenger argued that the court, like the executive or legislature, was a political instrument and that each branch of government must determine constitutionality according to its own lights. Therefore, while he accepted the Court's specific judgment that Dred Scott, being a slave, was not a citizen and had no standing to sue, he rejected the broad implications of the decision as a rule of political action. Lincoln had made this distinction clear in his Springfield speech a year before the debates when he said, "We know the court that made it, has often over-ruled its own decision, and we shall do what we can do to have it to over-rule this. We offer no *resistance* to it." As Fehrenbacher explained the distinction, Lincoln accepted judicial review but not judicial supremacy: "He denied that the rationale of such a decision instantaneously and automatically became constitutional law, binding even upon the legislative and executive branches of the federal government."[16]

Certainly, Republicans had every incentive to challenge the *Dred Scott* decision since denial of congressional power over slavery would invalidate the primary plank in their platform. The difficulty was that too intemperate a reaction would leave them undistinguishable from radical abolitionists. If they attacked the Court as an institution, they ran the risk of losing the Old Line Whigs, who were "more sensitive to the constitutional and legal proprieties than to the need for reform," on whose votes their future success depended.[17] (This sensitivity, of course, also made it in Douglas's interest to emphasize acquiescence in Court decisions as a matter of principle.) Moreover, Lincoln had pledged in 1856 to submit to a decision by the Supreme Court;[18] were he to change course now, he might with good reason be accused of hypocrisy.

Like other Republicans, Lincoln seemed in a box. He could not deny the authority of the Supreme Court, but he could not accept it either. Some worked their way out of this dilemma by contending that the Court had exceeded its authority by involving itself in a political question; this involvement forfeited the claim it otherwise could make for support of its decisions.[19] But a more common position was to accept the decision that Dred Scott was not a U.S. citizen and therefore not entitled to sue for his freedom in federal court and then to dismiss the rest of the decision as nonbinding *obiter dictum*. The Supreme Court decides cases on the narrowest possible grounds. If Scott had no standing to sue, then the rest of the decision was moot and served only as an expression of individual opinions by the justices. This distinction was of obvious benefit to the new party. Particularly in the Old Northwest, Republicans' antislavery sentiments had strong racial undertones. They did not want blacks to be U.S. citizens and often did not want blacks in their midst whether free or slave. But surely they could not agree that Congress lacked plenary authority over the territories. The *obiter dictum* argument enabled Republicans to have their cake and eat it too. It had been developed most prominently by Illinois senator Lyman Trumbull, who told his colleagues,

Judge Taney says in so many words that this case is dismissed for want of jurisdiction; and yet, after dismissing the case because the court had no right to pass on it, the majority go on and undertake to express opinions about the slavery question. Their opinions are worth just as much as, and no more than, the opinions of any other gentlemen equally respectable in the country.[20]

To make sure that the constitutional theory espoused in *dicta* did not become final, Lincoln and the Republicans proposed a practical remedy. Election of a Republican president would lead to the appointment of Republican justices who would overturn *Dred Scott*. Lincoln's stance on this question reflected advice he received from J. F. Alexander of Grenoble, who had written, "It might be well to explain how we propose to get the right kind of decisions from the Supreme Court, that is, just as we would if the Supreme Court of our State were in the habit of giving wrong decisions, at the proper time and place, to put better men in their places." The prospect of several impending Court appointments was real since in 1858 seven of the nine justices were in their middle sixties or older.[21]

This distinction between rule and *dicta* was useful in some quarters, but it did not prevent the Republican position from being misconstrued or its authors from being charged with hypocrisy. The real reason the Republicans opposed *Dred Scott*, according to Democratic papers, was that the Court decision denied black citizenship and hence racial equality—goals attributed to their opposition. Republicans proved themselves to be hypocrites because they did not exert themselves to remove similarly "offensive" provisions in state constitutions, which were under their control. Typical of the Democratic press was the *Illinois State Register*, which noted with significance that Republicans "no where make the practical proposition of amending our own state constitution so as to accord with their notions of the decision which they depreciate."[22]

II

Closely related to the finality of the *Dred Scott* decision is the question of what the decision actually established. Here, too, the answers were unclear. To say the least, the decision was complex; there were multiple concurring opinions and several discrete points at issue. Three major elements of the decision can be identified. First, Dred Scott as a Negro was not a citizen and therefore had no standing to sue in federal court. Second, his brief residence in the free state of Illinois did not make him a free man. By the principle of interstate comity, he became subject once again to the laws of Missouri when he returned there. Finally, Dred Scott's residence in the Wisconsin territory (then free by the terms of the Missouri Compromise) did not make him a free man because Congress had no authority to prohibit slavery in the territories; for this reason, the Compromise was unconstitutional.[23] The decision effectively denied blacks the right to sue, denied free states the right to emancipate slaves passing through, and denied Congress the right to outlaw slavery in the territories.

From the time it was issued, the *Dred Scott* decision became the object of vigorous and sharp criticism. Some dismissed it as an abstraction since it outlawed the already-repealed Missouri Compromise yet left intact the Kansas-Nebraska Act, which was then the governing law. It had little effect even on the life of Dred Scott, who was freed in May 1857, less than three months after the trial, and who died on September 17 of the following year.[24] Citing Justice Curtis's dissenting opinion, historians Morison, Commager, and Leuchtenburg find fault with each of the major elements of Taney's decision. Since Negroes were considered citizens in most northern states, they had the right to sue in federal courts. Utilizing the principle of interstate comity, Missouri on seven separate occasions had recognized slaves' claim to freedom on the basis of their residence in free states. And every branch of government, for seventy years or more, had accepted the principle of congressional authority over slavery in the territories.[25]

Lincoln and Douglas differed substantially on the meaning of this decision. As noted above, Lincoln believed that only the first part of the decision was binding. But, if he had regarded the decision as final, he would have had to embrace it all. That was the position in which he wanted to place Douglas—a task seemingly made easy by the incumbent's acknowledgment that he endorsed the decision in all respects. To Lincoln, this endorsement undermined Douglas's cherished principle of popular sovereignty. If Congress could not prohibit slavery, then neither could the territorial legislature, which was after all a creature of Congress. As the challenger frequently gloated, under *Dred Scott* "squatter sovereignty has just squatted out of existence."

Douglas, of course, was hardly ready to accept this declaration of his irrelevance and labored mightily to square the decision with his cherished principle. At the same time he claimed to support the decision, he minimized the scope of its application. Yes, he acknowledged, the decision prevented Congress from outlawing slavery, and it thereby undercut the Republican program. But it did not prevent the territorial legislature from doing so and therefore was consistent with Douglas's own program. Even though the territorial legislature was a creature of Congress, in some respects it possessed powers independent of those granted to it by the national government. The *Illinois State Register* announced that "the supreme court has not yet decided that the people of a territory do not possess the power independent of the action of congress," and one of the Little Giant's biographers concedes "that Douglas made an advocate's case of some cogency and of definite originality. The court had never passed on the question of the exact relation of the national government to the territories, . . . In 1857 the court did not consider the power of territorial legislatures over slavery, nor did it ever pass upon the question."[26]

To Lincoln, this was all hairsplitting. True, *Dred Scott* did not involve the act of a territorial legislature. But the legislature was a creature of the Congress, and the principle articulated in the case was broad enough to cover both. Ironically, Lincoln used the concepts of *dicta* and *rule* to explain his point. The application of *Dred Scott* to the action of a territorial legislature might be *dicta*, but the only thing lacking is another case involving action by a legislature. When that case comes, it is a sure thing that the decision will be extended since the principle of the case already has been asserted to cover the territories.[27] Indeed, attempts were made to bring a test case involving action by the Kansas territorial legislature unfavorable to slavery.

In attempting to square *Dred Scott* with popular sovereignty, Douglas first focused on the distinction between Congress and territorial legislatures. His second effort involved a far broader claim: that the practical application of rights depends on friendly local legislation. He distinguished abstract acknowledgment of rights from positive measures of protection.

III

Although the concept of "friendly local legislation" is associated most prominently with Douglas's response to the Freeport interrogatories, his basic argument recurs throughout the debates and had been articulated since the announcement of the *Dred Scott* decision. Before that, however, he had evaded the question asked by Lyman Trumbull in Senate debate during 1856: whether popular sovereignty empowered a territorial legislature to exclude slavery. Douglas refused to state his own views but replied that it was a judicial question. Fehrenbacher described the Little Giant's reply as acknowledging that his concept of popular sovereignty might be found unconstitutional and agreeing in advance to accept a decision of the Supreme Court.[28]

In the aftermath of the *Dred Scott* decision, however, Douglas needed to recapture the ability to speak to multiple audiences. He could demonstrate loyalty to party by endorsing the *Dred Scott* decision while at the same time upholding his theory of popular sovereignty by interpretive restriction of that decision. To achieve both goals, he advanced the thesis that *Dred Scott* established an abstract legal right that could be rendered meaningful only through the enactment of friendly local legislation. Since the territorial legislature was at liberty to grant or withhold such laws, popular sovereignty remained a viable principle.

This ambiguity had a long history. Under questioning in 1848, Lewis Cass had refused to clarify the Nicholson letter. In the 1856 campaign, Buchanan sometimes spoke as though the territorial legislature could exclude slavery (the Douglas view), and at other times as though that prerogative existed only when the territory sought admission as a state (the Southern position). Douglas himself had first suggested that local police power could be used to regulate slavery in the Eells case of 1843, contending that states could legislate concerning fugitive slaves notwithstanding federal legislation on the same subject. He applied the doctrine to the territories during discussions of the 1850 compromise measures and then revived it in his June 1857 Springfield speech. Anxious to avoid further angering administration spokesmen, Douglas made little use of the argument during the Lecompton debate in the Senate, even though Trumbull again put to him a version of the Freeport question. Not until he returned to Illinois did the incumbent resume arguing the friendly local legislation thesis. In the campaign, it first surfaced in Douglas's July 16 speech at Bloomington, and it figured prominently in the debates. Johannsen reports that the goal of the argument was to appeal to Old Line Whig and German voters.[29]

Douglas drew the analogy to liquor. In the Jonesboro debate and again at Galesburg, he stated that he might have the property right, protected by the Constitution, to take liquor into Kansas but that this right would be of no avail if he discovered that Kansas had a prohibition law once he got there. Likewise, the *Dred Scott* case gave him the right to take slaves into Kansas, but that right too was barren unless positively protected. A territorial legislature hostile to slavery, Douglas predicted at Freeport, "will by unfriendly legislation effectually prevent the introduction of it into their midst." Later, he softened his claim, asserting at Galesburg that even the absence of friendly legislation would block the introduction of slavery: "If the people of a territory want slavery, they make friendly legislation to introduce it, but if they do not want it, they withhold all protection from it and then it cannot exist there."[30]

Douglas's view was widely shared. Russel reports that, during debate over the 1850 Compromise, "Southern congressmen frankly admitted that, no matter what the Supreme Court might say, slavery could not exist in the territories unless sustained by positive law and effective police action." Berwanger maintains that, recognizing the validity of Douglas's claim, few slaveholders would migrate to the new territories in the absence of protective legislation. At various times, other spokesmen—both North and South—advocated the Douglas doctrine. The *Washington Union*, the administration paper that would lead the attack on Douglas during the Senate campaign, printed in full Douglas's June 1857 Springfield speech and said that it deserved "unqualified commendation."[31] In the 1858 campaign, however, the friendly legislation theory proved highly controversial, as Lincoln attacked its thesis, its logic, and its implications.

First, the challenger asserted that the thesis of the argument was empirically false. In August, Schuyler Colfax had written Lincoln, "One point which I find tells in all my speeches is that our whole History proves that Slavery goes wherever it is not prohibited. There were 13 States at the outset; 32 now. *Not one of the whole 19 of new States has come in as a Free State, except where Slavery has been expressly prohibited* by local or territorial laws."[32] Lincoln himself had been thinking along similar lines. In his 1854 Peoria speech, he said, "Wherever slavery is, it has first been introduced without law. The oldest laws we find concerning it, are not laws introducing it; but *regulating* it, as an already existing thing." Fehrenbacher notes that "legislation dating back to 1790 had established the rule that slaveholding could be practiced anywhere in federal territory if it was not positively forbidden by federal law," and empirical evidence indicated that slaveholders went to the territories even in the absence of friendly legislation. Finally, Lincoln pointed out in the Jonesboro debate that the *Dred Scott* case itself illustrated the falsity of Douglas's thesis. The case arose from "a negro being taken and actually held in slavery in Minnesota Territory . . . not only without police regulations, but in the teeth of congressional legislation supposed to be valid at the time."[33]

Second, Lincoln challenged the logic of the friendly legislation thesis, which seemed to him to be a patent contradiction. In notes that he probably prepared before the Jonesboro debate, the Republican wrote that territorial legislatures are sworn to uphold the Constitution. Therefore, he asked, "How dare they legislate unfriendly to a right guaranteed by the Constitution? And if they should how quickly would the courts hold their work to be unconstitutional and void!" The same conditions would hold, he went on, for withholding friendly legislation as for passing unfriendly legislation. Lincoln continued to refine the argument after the debates. It found its most succinct expression during his Ohio speaking tour the following year. At Cincinnati, he dismissed the doctrine by citing "a very well known principle to all lawyers, that what a legislature cannot directly do, it cannot do by indirection. . . and that any attempt to do so would be held by the *Dred Scott* Court unconstitutional." He was even more pithy at Columbus. Referring to the friendly legislation theory, he said, "When all the trash, the words, the collateral matter was cleared away from it, all the chaff was fanned out of it, it was a bare absurdity—*no less than a thing may be lawfully driven away from where it has a lawful right to be.*"[34]

Most significantly, however, Lincoln challenged the implications of the incumbent's theory. In the Jonesboro debate, he argued that anyone supporting the *Dred Scott* decision must also support whatever friendly legislation is deemed necessary to enforce it. With this argument, Lincoln tried to collapse Douglas's distinction between abstract and concrete rights. He developed his claim through rhetorical questions. Suppose, he asked his listeners, "you were elected members of the legislature, what would be the first thing you would have to do before entering upon your duties? *Swear to support the Constitution of the United States.* Suppose you believe, as Judge Douglas does, that the Constitution of the United States guarantees to your neighbor the right to hold slaves in that territory. . . . how can you clear your oaths unless you give him such legislation as is necessary to enable him to enjoy that property?"

The dilemma was even more acute in the case of unfriendly legislation: "How could you, having sworn to support the constitution, and believing it guaranteed the right to hold slaves in the territories, assist in legislation *intended* to defeat that right? That would be violating your own view of the constitution."[35]

The genius of this argument, aside from blurring the distinction between abstract and concrete, is that it enabled imaginative Republicans to conjure up all manner of extreme measures as friendly local legislation that Douglas would presumably be committed by his doctrine to support. For example, the clearest form of friendly legislation would be a federal slave code for the territories, affirmatively acting to protect slaveholders in their property rights. In the Jonesboro debate, Lincoln explicitly asked Douglas whether he would support such a code if requested by the slaveholding citizens of a territory. The incumbent's answer was evasive, referring to the Democrats' Cincinnati platform calling for "non-interference and non-intervention by Congress with slavery in the states or territories." As the *Chicago Press and Tribune* noted, this answer was taken in Illinois as evidence of Douglas's opposition to a federal slave code, while in Virginia it was taken as support for the very same measure. Earlier, the same paper had alleged a slave code to be "a logical sequence of the Calhoun dogmas respecting the federal constitution and of the decision of the Supreme Court in the Dred Scott case, both of which Senator Douglas indorses." The Republican paper predicted that, notwithstanding his current ambiguity, Douglas would support a federal slave code if reelected.[36] Particularly for the central Illinois voters looking for moderation, this line of argument enabled Republicans to portray Douglas as a dangerous extremist.

Another example of offensive friendly legislation was a move to reopen the African slave trade, prohibited since 1808. Lincoln maintained that such a move would be legitimized by Douglas's constitutional theory. In his 1854 Peoria speech, Lincoln had previewed this argument. As he said then, "If it is a sacred right for the people of Nebraska to take and hold slaves there, it is equally their sacred right to buy them where they can buy them cheapest; and that undoubtedly will be on the coast of Africa." In Senate debate in March, Lyman Trumball made a similar argument, contending that to claim that the due-process clause extends slavery into the territories would also require one to claim that the abolition of the slave trade was unconstitutional; otherwise, the Constitution would be in contradiction with itself. Lincoln returned to the same theme in September. "If a Kentuckian may take his slave into a new territory," he said, "any other citizen of the United States may." If he has no slaves, he may buy one for the purpose, and may buy him where he can buy him cheapest."[37]

On other occasions, Lincoln argued that removing the moral condemnation from slavery would remove it also from a reopening of the slave trade, but here he attempted to suggest that the two were entailed by the same legal principle. The fact that Douglas specifically opposed such a measure only went to show that his legal argument was inconsistent and untenable. Lincoln's argument on this score was given added weight by the announcement that Pierre Soule, a Louisiana advocate for the revival of the African slave trade, was supporting Douglas for reelection and by news reports that slave ships were landing Africans in Southern ports notwithstanding the prohibition.

With some reason, then, the *Chicago Press and Tribune* judged that a Douglas reelection could be interpreted as support for reviving the African slave trade. Newspaper editorials immediately before the election gave credence to this fear. Northern papers gleefully reprinted a call by the pro-Douglas *Richmond Enquirer* for repeal of the federal law equating the African slave trade with piracy. The argument from the *Charleston Mercury,* that it was morally the same to buy slaves in Africa as in Virginia, seemed to support Lincoln's contention that popular sovereignty would lead naturally to the reopening of the slave trade.[38]

Both these examples illustrate Lincoln's attempt to portray Douglas as an inevitable advocate of extreme measures on the assumption that the friendly legislation thesis was not viable. Alternatively, however, one might suppose that Douglas *could* establish the validity of his distinction between abstract and concrete rights. That possibility too, Lincoln alleged, would lead the Little Giant to an unfortunate result: the friendly legislation thesis would justify Northern states in acting effectively to nullify the fugitive slave law. Douglas's theory, after all, was based on denial of the power of Congress over local institutions. This same reasoning would justify Northern states in adopting personal liberty laws that made reclaiming escaped slaves impossible within their borders.

Authority for such laws could be found in the 1842 *Prigg v. Pennsylvania* Supreme Court decision, which acknowledged the separation of state and federal functions. As Hamilton explained the verdict, "State officials need not execute a constitutional requirement applying to federal authorities alone."[39] Since the Constitution did not specify that reclaiming fugitive slaves was a state obligation, and since this clause was the only protection afforded the slaveholder against action by the states, Northern states were free to legislate as they wished. They could pass laws freeing all slaves entering the state, notwithstanding the federal property right of the slaveowner protected in the Constitution. When Douglas argued that constitutional rights are abstract and barren unless redeemed by friendly local legislation, he implicitly sanctioned just such an evasion. It was for this reason that Lincoln concluded his speech at Alton—his last in the debate series—with the challenge, "I defy any man to make an argument that will justify unfriendly legislation to deprive a slaveholder of his right to hold his slave in a territory, that will not equally, in all its length, breadth and thickness furnish an argument for nullifying the fugitive slave law." He then added the sarcastic boast, "Why there is not such an Abolitionist in the nation as Douglas, after all."[40]

What might have avoided this result was respect for the principle of comity—"the courtesy or consideration that one jurisdiction gives by enforcing the laws of another, granted out of respect and deference rather than obligation."[41] This long-standing legal practice had been on the wane, however, as fidelity to the proslavery or antislavery argument came to outweigh fidelity to an abstract notion of law. Both Northern and Southern states had become increasingly intransigent with regard to each other's laws, and Douglas's friendly legislation theory seemed to legitimize this intransigence.

This discussion bears out the often-noted observation that the appeal to states' rights was a double-edged sword. "Both sides appealed to the doctrine of state rights and both to national supremacy, depending upon the question," Jaffa has written. He notes that the demand for a federal slave code for the territories "was one that never could have been justified by the strict constructionist thesis."[42] The weakness of Douglas's friendly local legislation theory was that it could not hold either side of this argument. Either it called for positive federal protection, overwhelming the doctrine of self-government, or else it cast too broad a net and justified resistance to the fugitive slave law as well as to the *Dred Scott* decision. Here was the heart of Douglas's dilemma, which ambiguity could conceal only for a time: he could not appeal simultaneously to both a Northern and a Southern audience. The argument that he alone remained a truly national politician was losing its credibility.

IV

Behind the question of whether *Dred Scott* applied to territorial legislation, or whether friendly local legislation was needed, loomed a far more fundamental issue. What was the proper relation between the federal government and the territories? Where did the responsibility for decision lie? Or, to put the matter most bluntly, who "owned" the territories? As Johannsen has noted, these are not simple questions: "The Constitution did not provide easy answers. . . . The one provision that seemed to apply, Article IV, Section 3, was vague and ambiguous."[43]

Both Douglas and Lincoln rejected the extreme Southern view that the territories are the common property of the existing states. By this reading, Congress, as the agent of the states, was obliged to extend to the territories whatever protection of property rights was desired by the states. In Bestor's account, "the slaveholding states, as sovereign, were to make policy not for themselves alone, but for the country as a whole, except within the boundaries of such sovereign states as had chosen to abolish the institution.[44] While rejecting this position, though, the two candidates otherwise had quite different views of the relation between the federal government and the territories.

Following in the tradition of Lewis Cass, Douglas saw the territories as incipient states, waiting only for the attainment of sufficient population. If the territories were basically like states, then they should stand in the same relation to Congress as do the states. Since in 1858 there was no equivalent of the Fourteenth Amendment, a stricture against the federal government did not automatically apply to the states as well. The Constitution protects slavery, yet it does not prevent New York from becoming a free state. In the same manner, Congress might not be able to disallow slavery from Kansas, but the Kansas legislature could do so quite effectively. So long as the Supreme Court did not decide another *Dred Scott* case that came from the act of a territorial legislature, Douglas could retain this distinction.

Douglas grounded Congress's right to govern the territories in the power to admit new states, not from Article IV, Section 3. Since territories were inchoate states, they were entitled to self-determination over matters that were their own business. Slavery clearly belonged in that category. In 1854, he had written to Chicago clergymen: "If a slave should be removed from Kentucky to Nebraska, the effect would be to reduce the number on the east side of the Mississippi to the same extent that it was increased on the west, without enlarging the political power of the master or producing any injurious consequences to the slave. . . . His presence in the new territory could not in any mode or degree affect or injure any human being in any other Territory or State." He himself declined invitations to lecture on slavery because it was one of "the domestic institutions of sister States, with which, under the Constitution and laws of the land, I have no right to interfere, and for the consequences of which I am in no wise responsible."[45] In these and similar statements throughout the period of the debates, Douglas made no distinction between states and territories.

Crucial to his position was the assumption that the word *states* in the Constitution refers to both the later concepts of "states" and "territories," and that the word *territory* in that document refers to geographic, not political, units. This usage may seem tortured, but it had some basis in fact. The temporary Western governments established under the Articles of Confederation were based on such usage, and Douglas reasonably might argue that that was the context known to the drafters of the Constitution.[46] Both Lewis Cass and John A. Quitman had subscribed to this view in earlier years. Its clear implication was that congressional power over the territories was limited to preparing them for admission as states and did not extend to the regulation of their domestic institutions.[47]

From these premises, Douglas derived popular sovereignty not just as an expedient but as a constitutional doctrine. Thus, for example, he could write a newspaper editor in 1854 that the Kansas-Nebraska Act is based on "the great fundamental principle of self-government upon which our republican institutions are predicated."[48] Nevertheless, it was an expedient doctrine, largely because of its ambiguity. As Forgie has noted, while allowing its supporters to assert that they were making a decision based on principle, popular sovereignty "unlike any other plan . . . permitted both extensionists and restrictionists to support it with the hope that it would facilitate their own opposing goals."[49]

The key ambiguity involved what *nonintervention* meant and, accordingly, when the residents of a territory could exercise their right to self-determination. For Douglas, the decision could be made before slaves arrived in the territory in appreciable numbers, but for the southerners not until they were already there. The difference was crucial since, as Lincoln explained in his 1854 Peoria speech, if slavery gets into a territory, as a practical matter it cannot be voted out: "The facts of its presence, and the difficulty of its removal will carry the vote in its favor." On the other hand, Lincoln was convinced, "Keep it out until a vote is taken, and a vote in favor of it, can not be got in any population of forty thousand, on earth, who have been drawn together by the ordinary motives of emigration and settlement."[50]

Despite, or perhaps because of, the importance of the question, Douglas did not resolve it. In the 1848 disputes between Calhoun and Cass, and in discussions of the Compromise of 1850, Democrats had allowed the term *nonintervention* to cover two quite different political doctrines, and Douglas followed in this tradition. For this reason, Southern and Northern Democrats were able to unite behind the Kansas-Nebraska Act. The 1856 Democratic platform, adopted at Cincinnati, was likewise imprecise. And when it appeared to confirm the Southern view of nonintervention, Douglas did not contest the language but continued to argue for the contrary interpretation.[51] Much of Lincoln's debate strategy was to force Douglas to choose between the two views of the matter. That was the apparent purpose behind the question whether

Douglas would support a federal slave code for the territories. From this perspective it is clear that the Little Giant's answer, that he stood on the principle of nonintervention, was evasive.

Usually, Douglas argued in just this fashion that the federal government lacked the power to regulate for or against slavery in the territories. Sometimes, however, his argument was different. Particularly in his earlier years, as in the Wilmot Proviso debates, he had conceded that Congress did have regulatory authority over the territories but had argued, purely on practical grounds, that this power ought not be exercised. At one point during 1857, to the shock of a number of his supporters, Douglas announced "that popular sovereignty was a gift from the federal government to the people of the territories and as such could be revoked by Congress at any time."[52] To say the least, he was not perfectly consistent in applying his principles.

What gave the Little Giant such difficulties was the legalization of polygamy in the Utah Territory. Deeply offended by the immorality of this action, Douglas "proposed that Utah's organic act be repealed and the territorial government blotted out of existence so that the offenders could be apprehended and punished." As Johannsen has noted, these were "strong words for an advocate of non-intervention."[53] The congressional power that Douglas was proposing to use against Utah was a power that his theory of territories as incipient states explicitly denied. Although Lincoln seized on this discrepancy as proof that Douglas's commitment to popular sovereignty was not genuine and that the doctrine was really a pretense for the extension of slavery, it is more likely that it merely illustrated the tension between principle and pragmatism that marked Douglas's entire career.

No ambiguity marked Lincoln's own view of the matter. His answer to the question, who owns the territories? was that they belonged to the federal government, acting in trust for the people. He derived his answer from Article IV, Section 3, of the Constitution, which gave Congress the power "to make all needful rules and regulations respecting the territory or other property belonging to the United States." If territorial governments were the creatures of Congress, then they could not possess powers denied their creator. From this perspective, Douglas's contention that the *Dred Scott* decision did not apply to the territorial legislatures carried no weight.

The whole question of popular sovereignty had no application to the territories anyway. Lincoln often said, as at Bloomington in 1854, that he appreciated the right of self-government as well as anybody but that it had no application to the current controversy, which concerned "whether slavery, a moral, social, and political evil, should or should not exist in territory owned by the Government, over which the Government had control."[54] To say otherwise would be to make an untenable moral and legal distinction. As Lincoln put the challenge to Douglas four years before the debates, "What better moral right have thirty-one citizens of Nebraska to say, that the thirty-second shall not hold slaves, than the people of the thirty-one States have to say that slavery shall not go into the thirty-second State at all?" More pointedly, he wrote in a speech fragment in the spring of 1858, "I do not understand that the privilege one man takes of making a slave of another, or holding him as such, is any part of 'self-government.' To call it so is, to my mind, simply absurd and ridiculous."[55]

Certainly, there were historical precedents for Lincoln's view of the matter. In a Senate speech in March 1858, Lyman Trumbull cited five specific Supreme Court decisions locating sovereignty over territories in the Congress. There were not many cases on record, but all seem to grant plenary authority to Congress. Referring to a statement by Henry Clay, Nevins suggests that "for fifty years every branch of the government, legislative, executive, and judicial, had acted on the postulate that Congress held a broad power over slavery in the common domain."[56]

There was one major difficulty with Lincoln's approach, however. If the territories were the property of the federal government, their status was little different from that of colonies. Extending the analogy, the federal government stood in the same relation to them as Britain had to its American colonies. Anti-British prejudices were strong, particularly in the Northwest, and there was little gain for Lincoln in seeming to replicate the pattern of government that had led to the American Revolution. The danger in this comparison was suggested in 1856 by the *Illinois Sentinel*, a Democratic newspaper in Jacksonville:

We think the assertion made by Mr. Lincoln, that the territories occupy the same relative position to the States as did the Colonies to the mother country, an unfortunate one for himself, his principles and his party. If this parallel be a true one, then do the black republicans seek to enforce the very doctrines which caused the American revolution and a separation from the mother country.[57]

Douglas pressed this embarrassing parallel in his closing speech of the final debate. "Did not these colonies rebel," he asked, "because the British Parliament had no right to pass laws concerning our property and domestic and private institutions without our consent?" He then observed, "Now, Mr. Lincoln proposes to govern the territories without giving the people a representation, and calls on Congress to pass laws controlling their property and domestic concerns without their consent and against their will. Thus, he asserts for his party the identical principle asserted by George III and the Tories of the Revolution."[58] The argument was developed too late to have a major effect in the debates, but it became a centerpiece of Douglas's *Harper's* article and his speeches during 1859 and 1860.

V

Just as the *Dred Scott* decision opened the way to discussion of broader issues about the nature of the territories, so the territorial question led to broader issues of federal-state relations. In the logical tendency of each candidate's position on the territories could be found significant implications for the nature of federalism. Moreover, it was in the candidates' interest to emphasize these implications because they helped each to stigmatize the other's position as extreme.

Douglas found the extensions of Lincoln's position in uniformity among state laws on all subjects, destroying the cherished principle of federalism. In the opening speech of the first debate, the incumbent boldly asserted "that uniformity in the local laws and institutions of the different states is neither possible nor desirable" because "the laws and regulations which would suit the granite hills of New Hampshire would be unsuited to the rice plantations of South Carolina."[59] If territories were basically like states, a central government that denied their authority to regulate their own affairs would do the same to the states as well. There was still widespread suspicion of "consolidated" government, so, if Douglas could persuasively accuse his challenger of leveling distinctions among the states, he would be on solid ground.

In addition, Douglas argued on historical grounds that uniformity among the states was undesirable, and he used an example that might have turned the tables on Lincoln. At Galesburg, he noted that twelve of the thirteen states permitted slavery at the time of the Constitutional Convention. That being so, if the convention labored under the influence of Lincoln's doctrine, "would not the twelve slaveholding states have outvoted the one free state, and under his doctrine have fastened slavery by an irrevocable constitutional provision upon every inch of the American Republic?"[60] Lincoln's doctrine would have led to the very result he most abhorred; therefore, it is an unsound doctrine and should be rejected.

Lincoln delayed his strongest refutation of this argument until the final debate, in which he insisted that Douglas was in error in deriving from his arguments any principle of uniformity. He at once accepted the main premise of his opponent's argument, denied its applicability to the case at hand, and trivialized it through careful choice of examples. He "very readily agree[d]" that "it would be foolish for us to insist upon having a cranberry law here, in Illinois, where we have no cranberries, because they have a cranberry law in Indiana, where they have cranberries," and that "it would be exceedingly wrong in us to deny to Virginia the right to enact oyster laws where they have oysters, because we want no such laws here."[61] But he denied that the analogies were apt. First, territories were different from states. They were the common trust of all people, so all had an interest in their affairs. (Like Douglas, he was reverting to a first principle about the nature of states and territories, not defending that principle.) Second, other subjects had not produced the discord or quarrel accompanying the issue of the extension of slavery; differences on other matters could be tolerated easily.

For his part, Lincoln found the logical extension of Douglas's position in the aforementioned "*Dred Scott* II" decision, which *also* would have imposed uniformity on the states by denying them the ability to exclude slavery. In the earlier debates, his efforts to link Douglas with an active conspiracy to bring about this result were relatively unpersuasive. In the fifth debate, at Galesburg, he shifted his tactics and simply "deduced" a second *Dred Scott* decision from the legal principles embodied in the first. It all proceeded with the elegance of a syllogism:

Nothing in the constitution or laws of any state can destroy a right distinctly and expressly affirmed in the Constitution of the United States.

The right of property in a slave is distinctly and expressly affirmed in the Constitution of the United States.

Therefore, nothing in the Constitution or laws of any state can destroy the right of property in a slave.[62]

Lincoln insisted that there was no flaw in the form of the argument; if there was an error, it lay in the truth of the premises. But Douglas supported the *Dred Scott* decision, which found the right to property in a slave affirmed in the Fifth Amendment's protection against deprivation of property without due process of law. That being so, the conclusion followed automatically. The only missing element was a court case testing the power of a state to outlaw slavery. The pending case of *Lemmon v. Virginia*, involving interstate transit, might have furnished just such a test. More generally, by incorporating the Bill of Rights in the Fourteenth Amendment, twentieth-century Supreme Court decisions have applied many protections in the Bill of Rights against actions by the state governments as well as the federal. Had the Taney Court been so inclined, then reasoning from the *Dred Scott* decision would have led it in exactly the direction that Lincoln surmised.

Douglas, of course, could not accept this syllogism, and it was in response to this presentation that the Little Giant overplayed his hand, contending that the justices of the Supreme Court, in the *Dred Scott* decision itself, had explicitly denied any intention to issue a ruling such as *"Dred Scott* II." When no such disclaimer could be found, Douglas's credibility was hurt, and greater credence was given to Lincoln's legal argument if not to his conspiracy charge.

A second issue involving the states was the question of whether Lincoln would countenance any more slave states in the Union even if the people wanted them. For Douglas there was no issue since the principle of popular sovereignty was absolute, but for his challenger there was considerable tension between opposition to the spread of slavery and acknowledgment of the right to self-determination. Not surprisingly, Lincoln's correspondents urged him to duck this issue. Trumbull, for example, wrote, "In my judgment it will be best to say nothing about the admission or non-admission of any more slave states. It will be time enough to decide that question when it arises, which it never will if Republican principles prevail & slavery is kept out of the territories."[63]

The question arose, however, as one of the seven interrogatories Douglas propounded at Ottawa. In his opening speech, the Little Giant challenged, "I desire him to answer whether he stands pledged to-day, as he did in 1854, against the admission of any more slave states into the Union, even if the people want them."[64] The year 1854, of course, referred to the alleged Republican platform that Douglas cited to prove a conspiracy to abolitionize the nation. Even leaving that aside, however, the question was difficult for Lincoln. He waited until the Freeport debate to respond, and then he answered a slightly different question. First he said, "I state to you very frankly that I would be exceedingly sorry ever to be put in a position of having to pass upon that question." Then he added that, if a territory from which slavery has been excluded during the territorial period proposes a proslavery state constitution, he would have no choice but to support it.[65] Douglas did not regard that as a fair answer and condemned Lincoln for evasiveness, for failing to admit that his true intent was that there be no more slave states. In a later debate, at Quincy, the incumbent alleged directly that the purpose of Lincoln's answer to his query was to mislead the Old Line Whigs into believing that he would stand by the Compromise of 1850 while also convincing the abolitionists that he shared their opposition to any more slave states. Then, at Alton, he made light of Lincoln's answer, saying, "Here, permit me to remark, that I do not think the people will ever force him into a position against his will."[66]

As Douglas pointed out, Lincoln's answer did not apply to any territory then in existence. Why, then, was the issue so important? Why did he treat it so gingerly? The answer is both that this question distinguished the two candidates' positions on the Lecompton constitution and that it symbolized a contest between moderation and radicalism for the allegiance of the Old Line Whigs. Douglas and Lincoln both opposed the Lecompton constitution, but for very different reasons. It was deficient for Lincoln because it extended slavery and for Douglas because it did not truly represent the will of the people. Whereas Lincoln had earlier wanted to heighten the contrast between them in order to stop talk that Douglas might be a viable fusion candidate, now it was the incumbent's turn to suggest that he was far more in keeping with the moderate, compromise-seeking Old Line Whigs. His opponent, notwithstanding his protestations to the contrary, really wanted to freeze the slave states as a first step toward implementation of the "house divided" doctrine.

VI

The dispute over "no more slave states" illustrates the use of the interrogatory, a characteristic form of legal argument that is present throughout the debates. Although there were no formal cross-examination periods, the interrogatories enabled the candidates to transfer to public debate the questioning characteristic of opposing attorneys in the courtroom. Both Lincoln and Douglas believed "that the human mind is best swayed by argument following information gained by question and answer."[67]

Douglas introduced the interrogatories at Ottawa, posing seven questions intended to put Lincoln on record with respect to what the incumbent took to be "the 1854 Republican platform." Douglas asked whether Lincoln favored unconditional repeal of the fugitive slave law, a ban on admitting more slave states, admission of a new state with whatever constitution her people desired, abolition of slavery in the District of Columbia, abolition of the interstate slave trade, prohibition of slavery above and below the Missouri Compromise line, and a ban on acquiring more territory unless slavery were prohibited therein.[68] Lincoln did not answer these questions immediately—according to Herndon, because "he was too sharp and guarded to do so."[69] He pondered the questions during meetings with his advisers in Chicago and then offered responses at the outset of the Freeport debate. There his answers were crisp and precise. So, for example, he denied that he "stood pledged" against admission of more slave states even though that clearly was his wish. Following his answers, Lincoln acknowledged, "I have answered in strict accordance with the interrogatories, and have answered truly that I am not *pledged* at all upon any of the points to which I have answered." The challenger added, "But I am not disposed to hang upon the exact form of his interrogatory," and then proceeded to amplify his own beliefs about the points at issue.[70]

Meanwhile, fearing that their candidate had been too much on the defensive at Ottawa, a group of Republican strategists took advantage of Lincoln's request that they meet in Chicago and provide him ammunition for the second debate. They advised not only that Lincoln answer the incumbent's challenges but that he also put forward some questions of his own. Charles L. Wilson had written Lincoln that he thought the Republican was entitled to an equal number of questions as Douglas. The collective wisdom of the Chicago meeting was contained in a letter from *Tribune* editor Joseph Medill, who suggested questions similar to those Lincoln actually used and urged, "Don't act on the defensive at all," and, "Be saucy with the 'Catiline' & permit no browbeating—in other words give h——l."[71]

Having answered Douglas's questions, Lincoln also believed that he had the right to pose an equal number. At Freeport, he posed the questions, "so far as I have framed them. I will bring forward a new installment when I get them ready." Four questions followed. Would Douglas vote to admit Kansas before it had the required population under the English Bill? Could the people of a territory lawfully exclude slavery in the aftermath of the *Dred Scott* decision? Would the incumbent support an extension of the *Dred Scott* decision to the states? Would Douglas favor acquiring more territory regardless of how doing so would affect the slavery question? At Jonesboro, he added a fifth question. Would Douglas support a federal slave code for the territories?[72]

Douglas complained about these questions. His own had been prompted by the desire to place Lincoln on record with respect to his party's platform, but these questions have "no other foundation for them than his own curiosity." Nevertheless, the Little Giant proceeded to answer each question, and Lincoln had no immediate rejoinder to his opponent's answers. This silence left some supporters convinced that the Republican was still on the defensive; Medill for example, wrote a confidential letter predicting Lincoln's loss of the election.[73]

Considerable folklore has developed around the second Freeport question, in which Lincoln asked, "Can the people of a United States territory, in any lawful way, against the wish of any citizen of the United States, exclude slavery from its limits prior to the formation of a state constitution?" Legend has it that, although advised against asking this question, Lincoln did so anyway, throwing the election by enabling Douglas to escape the dilemma with the friendly legislation thesis but knowing that this thesis would doom him in the South and make him unelectable for president in 1860. "I am after bigger game," Lincoln is reported to have said.[74] This legend is based largely on Medill's 1895 recollection that he had advised Lincoln *against* asking the question—a recollection clearly contradicted by his own 1858 correspondence—and William H. Herndon's 1890 recollection that Lincoln had said, "I am fighting for bigger game."[75] There is little if any contemporary evidence that Lincoln was looking ahead so consciously to 1860. Moreover, Fehrenbacher has demonstrated that the Freeport legend lacks logic. Lincoln's chances in 1860 would have been better served by *defeating* Douglas in 1858; Douglas's position on what came to be known as the "Freeport doctrine" was well known at the time of the debate and had been endorsed by both North and South; and the immediate judgment of contemporaries was that Douglas had answered the question ably, particularly in the light of Lincoln's subsequent silence.[76]

What *can* be said about the famous Freeport question? First, several people had suggested it to Lincoln. Henry Asbury, a Quincy lawyer, suggested that the Republican ask how slavery would be protected once it spread to the territories. Charles Wilson gave Lincoln a clipping from the *Chicago Journal* suggesting the question. A similar version had appeared in the *Bloomington Pantagraph* on June 15. Finally, Medill specifically urged that Lincoln ask, "What becomes of your vaunted popular Sovereignty in Territories since the Dred Scott decision?"[77]

Second, neither the question nor the answer was new. In his Chicago speech at the beginning of the campaign, Lincoln had noted the effect of the *Dred Scott* decision and asked, "When that is so, how much is left of this vast matter of squatter sovereignty I should like to know?" A week later, in Springfield, he touched on the same theme, noting that the *Dred Scott* decision "forbids the people of a territory to exclude slavery. . . . So far as all that ground is concerned, the Judge is not sustaining popular sovereignty, but absolutely opposing it."[78]

Likewise, Douglas's answer was well known. He had provided it in his Bloomington speech of July 16 and in other speeches in Lincoln's hearing. His newspaper, the *Chicago Times*, surprised at the furor over the question, correctly noted that Douglas "did not express himself at Freeport otherwise than he did, fifteen months ago, at Springfield, and as he did in his speech in Chicago, on the evening of the 9th of July last." Douglas himself wrote the following year, "I could fill many columns . . . with extracts of speeches made by me during the discussion of the compromise measures in 1850, and in defense of the principles embodied in those measures in 1851 and 1852, in the discussion of the Kansas-Nebraska Bill in 1854, and of the Kansas difficulties, and the Topeka revolutionary movements in 1856, in all of which I expressed the same opinion and defended the same position which was assumed in the 'Freeport speech.'"[79]

Lincoln had followed the lawyer's rule not to ask a question for which one does not know what the answer will be. But why did he ask the question? Thomas suggests that greater attention would be drawn to Douglas's answer through repetition and that the Freeport answer might widen the breach in Illinois between Douglas and the Buchanan forces, who were trying to defeat him and might even support Lincoln. Frank has indicated that Lincoln might have wanted to escape the stigma of resistance to a Supreme Court decision by pointing out "that Douglas was also following a path of resistance," at least in its logical implications.[80] There is merit to both these speculations. Certainly, it is far more plausible to see the Freeport question against the backdrop of Illinois politics in 1858 than to project forward to the next presidential election.

Third, because the debates attracted national attention, raising the question in that forum dramatized it and give it focus. Nevins believes that for the first time it "arrested the attention of millions"; particularly in the South it attracted notice and subtly began to reshape Douglas's image. Nichols concludes, "He had said it earlier, but never before such a nation-wide audience. Yancey was right; the South could not trust national compromise legislation."[81] In this regard, however, one might wonder whether Freeport was the most appropriate venue for the question. Freeport was in the far northern part of the state, where abolitionism was the strongest. Audiences there might be expected to applaud Douglas's claim that slavery could be excluded by unfriendly legislation and thereby fail to appreciate the dilemma posed by the question with respect to *Dred Scott*. On the other hand, the advantage of Freeport as a site was that Lincoln could try to put Douglas on the defensive before Douglas would have the chance to "trot him down into Egypt," in the Jonesboro debate.[82]

Fourth, although Lincoln asked about the legality of territorial action, Douglas's reply focused on the question of its practicality. In his 1859 Ohio speaking tour, the Republican would note this difference— but not in the debates. In fact, he did not pursue Douglas's answer at all. The Little Giant had replied immediately, not waiting a week to ponder his answers, and Lincoln did not follow up his questions in the next speech. For its part, the Democratic *Illinois State Register* gloated that Lincoln "seems to have learned a 'Yankee trick' . . . of *asking* questions in response to those put to him. In this he was foiled. Douglas promptly replied, while Lincoln again shuffled and quibbled upon the leading points of the black republican creed."[83]

Finally, in the light of these considerations one must question the legend that the Freeport response was fatal to Douglas. It did not doom him in the South, and it did not strengthen the Buchanan forces in Illinois.

Douglas, after all, had espoused a position that several moderate southerners had taken themselves. Jefferson Davis, John C. Breckinridge, Howell Cobb, Robert Toombs, Alexander H. Stephens, and Judah P. Benjamin were among those who had held the same view. Douglas himself, in an 1859 letter, quoted statements from the prominent politicians, mostly southerners, that were essentially similar to the Freeport doctrine.[84] Not surprisingly, then, Douglas's answer was received favorably in some quarters in the South. A Virginia correspondent wrote the senator a week after the Freeport debate, *"Popular sentiment* here & thro-out the South has under gone a great change, amounting to a complete *reaction* in your behalf." And Fehrenbacher cites the *Louisville Democrat, Richmond Enquirer,* and *Augusta Constitutionalist* as examples of southern papers that opposed Douglas on Lecompton but defended his position on the Freeport doctrine. Fehrenbacher also notes, "A surprising number of Southern newspapers . . . took little or no notice of the doctrine in the weeks after its enunciation, and some, like the Memphis *Appeal* and the Montgomery *Confederation,* even became more friendly toward Douglas after the debates began."[85] Southerners who opposed Douglas, by and large, had opposed him since his opposition to Lecompton. For those still giving him the benefit of the doubt, his evasion at Jonesboro about a federal slave code probably did far more damage than did his answer at Freeport.[86]

As for the Danites in Illinois, the Freeport answer hardly enlarged their ranks. Throughout the campaign, Republicans consistently exaggerated the split among Illinois Democrats between Douglas and Buchanan. In the end, the Danite faction produced significant vote totals in only two counties.[87] Even if these votes were attributed entirely to the Freeport doctrine, ignoring all other causes, that is not a very great effect for an answer that became the stuff of legend.

One consequence of historians' fixation on the second Freeport question is that insufficient attention has been paid to Lincoln's third and fifth interrogatories. The third asked about *"Dred Scott* II" and the fifth about a slave code for the territories. Douglas ridiculed one and evaded the other. To the third question at Freeport, he replied, "I am amazed that Lincoln should ask such a question. Yes, a school boy does know better. . . . He might as well ask me, suppose Mr. Lincoln should steal a horse would I sanction it. . . . He casts an imputation upon the Supreme Court of the United States by supposing that they would violate the Constitution of the United States. I tell him that such a thing is not possible."[88] Obviously, if Douglas would discredit even the remote possibility of such a hypothetical decision, he need not answer Lincoln's query about whether he would support it if it came to pass. But the danger of such a response is that, if the opponent can establish even the plausibility of the hypothesized event, the arguer's credibility is undermined seriously. Lincoln achieved this result, first, by "deducing" a second *Dred Scott* decision during the Galesburg debate and, second, by calling Douglas's bluff when the incumbent stated that the Taney Court specifically had disavowed any possibility of "*Dred Scott* II."

The fifth interrogatory was put forward at Jonesboro and might be conceived as the follow-up question to the Freeport doctrine. Douglas had alleged that friendly legislation would be needed to make the *Dred Scott* rights meaningful; would he be willing to support such legislation if it came before the Congress? A negative answer would expose the hypocrisy of his attempted reconciliation of popular sovereignty with *Dred Scott*, but an affirmative reply would lean far more toward the extreme southerners than the central Illinois moderates were prepared to go. Douglas retreated to the ambiguous defense of congressional nonintervention. The best reading one can give to this answer is that Douglas wished to emphasize the inappropriateness of congressional action and that he did not mean to speak to the wisdom of a territorial legislature's adopting a slave code.

Douglas's moves can be explained by reference to the classical concept of *stasis*, referring to the "seat" or "resting place" of the argument, its focal point. In addition to the *stases* of conjecture, definition, and quality, which involved issues of the nature, meaning, and value of the object in dispute, there was a *stasis* in place, raising the issue of whether the dispute was being considered in the proper forum. Raising the procedural *stasis* preempts consideration of the substantive ones since it is idle to consider a matter until it is clear that one is entitled to do so—that one has jurisdiction over the matter. In distinguishing between congressional and territorial action, Douglas wished to redirect the issue to the classical *stasis* in place or procedure rather than focusing on the substance of the issue. But Douglas never drew the procedural *stasis* explicitly, with the result that Lincoln was able to reinterpret Douglas's answer as suggesting the patent absurdity that a thing may be lawfully driven out from where it has a lawful right to be.

Douglas frequently boasted, as he said at Ottawa, "My principles are the same everywhere. I can proclaim them alike in the North, the South, the East, and the West. My principles will apply wherever the Constitution prevails and the American flag waves."[89] Lincoln went a long way toward undercutting Douglas's national appeal by demonstrating that it rested on ambiguous statements that North and South could

interpret in diametrically opposite ways. This line of argument ultimately was far more damaging to Douglas than was the legendary
second interrogatory at Freeport.

VII

The legal arguments developed as a series of concentric circles: from the
specific contents of the *Dred Scott* decision to the finality of judicial interpretation, the ownership of the territories, and the proper relation
between the federal government and the states. The form of the interrogatory sharpened these questions and brought them into focus. In this
way, the Lincoln-Douglas debates were a microcosm of the legal and
constitutional issues facing the nation in the first half of the nineteenth
century.

The prevalence of legal and constitutional argument indicates that
two experienced lawyers were on the stump discussing what were unsettled legal issues. Both men introduced legal concepts and terminology,
almost as if—in Heckman's phrase—"they were trying a case with the
audience as jury." Lincoln regarded slavery as fundamentally a legal
problem. What Frank says of him, though, is also true of Douglas: he
"conceived of the debates as a kind of tussle with another lawyer for the
purpose of persuading a jury of electors." That being so, the debates became "a stupendous kind of ambulatory trial with the two men
interrogating each other as witnesses and with the other evidence coming very largely from public documents."[90] To conduct a trial in the
forum of a public debate requires great skill in translating intricate and
technical legal concepts into a public language so that the audience can
understand and adjudicate the questions. Both men were gifted in this
respect and were able thereby to hold public interest and attention.

But beyond the character of the two debaters, the prevalence of legal
arguments indicates the great reverence for the Constitution characteristic of early American culture. Conceived in controversy and
narrowly obtaining ratification, it quickly became glorified. Rather than
being something fought over, it was fought for. As a consequence, there
was great advantage for any party or advocate who could identify his own
partisan positions with the Constitution and denigrate opponents as tra-
ducers on that sacred document. The Constitution was the dominant
symbol of mid-nineteenth-century politics; in an 1848 speech, for example, Lincoln urged his House colleagues not to tamper with the
Constitution because doing so "may lead to a habit of altering it. Better
rather to habituate ourselves to think of it as unalterable."[91]

The result of venerating the Constitution was that political issues
were converted into constitutional issues. Fehrenbacher attributes this

transformation to the actions of minorities who shifted the terms of public debate lest they face certain defeat on the immediate political issues at stake. He cites the examples of the Jeffersonians in the 1790s and the New England Federalists after 1800.[92] But the effect seems to have been more general. Both the Missouri debate of 1819–21 and the later debate on Arkansas were carried out largely in constitutional terms, as was the dispute over nullification in 1832–33. In his study of the American Whigs, Daniel Walker Howe notes that "political dialogue proceeded by reference to the meaning of the Constitution" and that the sectionally divisive nature of the slavery controversy accentuated the tendency to redefine public issues as constitutional questions.[93]

What made reliance on the Constitution both predictable and troublesome was that the great document was fundamentally ambiguous. Written by one generation for future generations, it was necessarily general in its language so that it might cover unforeseen situations. Embodying ideals and hopes as well as describing a pragmatic structure of government, it contained conflicting values within the same text. Terms such as *sovereignty* and *rights* have well-known connotations but cover a full range of denotations, so that—for example—"'sovereignty' can bestow a majestic tone to a political argument, without implying any precisely definable constitutional theory," as Arthur Bestor explained. The Constitution was equivocal as to the status of blacks and unclear about whether "the people" constituted the nation or whether it was the other way around. Most significantly for the Lincoln-Douglas debates, the constitutional text does not speak clearly to the extent of federal power intended for the territories.[94]

Consequently, the Constitution was always the subject of debate. Writing on the occasion of the constitutional bicentennial, novelist E. L. Doctorow wrote that one cannot engage the text without getting into an argument with it. Surely that was true of the antebellum period. Hyman explained that "to debate made sense because . . . laymen understood that the stakes of power were inseparable from one interpretation or another of the Constitution." Brock, noting that "interpretation all too readily became a substitute for realistic appraisal of social and political issues," added that "in practice these exercises in constitutional logic invariably applied external criteria. The most fervent appeals for adherence to the Constitution meant loyalty to concepts that were not found in the document."[95]

Reliance on legal and constitutional arguments, in turn, changed the nature of the public debate. True, it did tend to domocratize legal concepts and make them accessible to the general public, as was illustrated by the audience of the Lincoln-Douglas debates.[96] But it also overlaid a constitutional dimension on a political dispute. As Arthur Bestor explained, "Questions of policy give place to questions of power; questions of wisdom to questions of legality." The result, however, is to harden positions and make compromise more difficult since any compromise would involve basic principles rather than mere expedients. "If one calls an opponent's proposals unconstitutional," Daniel Walker Howe writes, "it makes them seem more dangerous and illegitimate than if they were simply unwise."[97] The constitutionalization of public discourse is both cause and effect of a raising of the stakes and a growing defensiveness. It was not surprising, therefore, that, as the controversy over slavery grew in intensity, the arguments would be cast increasingly in constitutional terms. The prevalence of the legal argument in the Lincoln-Douglas debates illustrates this development.

5

The Historical Argument

Douglas saw in the "House Divided" speech a great rhetorical opportunity. At best, his challenger had failed to make himself clear and had led audiences to regard his mere prediction about the future course of slavery as a fervent wish. Barely a week after the speech, correspondent John Locke Scripps wrote Lincoln that some Kentucky friends regarded the speech as "an implied pledge on behalf of the Republican party to make war upon the institution in the States where it now exists." The writer continued, "They do not perceive that you refer to a moral tendency but insist that your meaning goes to a political warfare under legal forums against slavery in the States."[1]

In reply, Lincoln, though flattered by Scripps's overall assessment of the speech, was "much mortified that any part of it should be construed so differently from anything intended by me." Although he could not imagine that his reference to slavery's ultimate extinction "asserts, or intimates any power or purpose, to interfere with slavery in the States where it exists," he proceeded—or so he thought—to set the matter to rest with a straightforward statement:

But, to not cavil about language, I declare that wether [sic] the clause used by me, will bear such construction or not, I never so intended it. I have declared a thousand times, and now repeat that, in my opinion, neither the General Government, nor any other power outside of the slave States, can constitutionally or rightfully interfere with Slaves or Slavery where it already exists.[2]

Lincoln might be excused for finding little new or radical in his speech. The biblical quotation was an often-repeated favorite; parts of

141

the introduction and conclusion were paraphrases from Webster; and the claim that the nation could not survive half slave and half free was a staple of debate in the Senate, on the stump, and in the newspapers—he himself had been convinced of the idea by reading editorials in the *Richmond Enquirer*.[3] But Lincoln had strung the thoughts together in a new, simpler, and clearer way. The very reasons that cause modern readers to see the speech as prophetic made it a liability in its own time. The aspirant for the Senate, accused of being a secret radical abolitionist, seemed to have proved the charge in his own words. The charge of radicalism was particularly serious in the central part of the state. So the "House Divided" speech, as Fehrenbacher describes it, "seemed likely to alienate the very votes that Lincoln needed in order to unseat Douglas."[4]

Here, then, was the incumbent's opportunity. He riveted attention on the "House Divided" speech. Except for Lincoln's opening remarks at Charleston, the speech is cited or quoted in every one of the twenty-one debate speeches. It was also a set piece of Douglas's campaign. On the stump, he would read the doctrine "from a little note-book in which he had posted the statement as it had been printed in Lincoln's own organ, the *Illinois Journal*."[5] Meanwhile, Douglas's newspapers made short shrift of Lincoln's distinction between expectation and wish. "We submit," proclaimed the *Illinois State Register*, "that a man who acknowledges an *expectation* that the Union cannot exist with the states part slave and part free," who declares that slavery is the paramount question of the day and proposes to revise decisions of Congress and the courts, "will not be long without the *wish* to see the Union divided unless he can succeed."[6]

The best strategy for Douglas was not only to keep the "House Divided" speech in the minds of his hearers but to emphasize its radical nature. This purpose was served by the historical argument, enabling him to claim that Lincoln was not just an abolitionist but a deviant from the wisdom of the past, that his way was the opposite of that favored by the Founding Fathers. Lincoln would abandon them; Douglas would revere them. Much of the argument, then, centered on the questions of what the Founders thought of the issue in their own time and what they would have done had they been present in 1858.

One might wonder why this question would seem important to the audiences of the debates. The ultimately unknowable views of long-dead ancestors hardly ever control contemporary public debate. But, with the possible exception of the "Young America" movement during the 1840s, the early nineteenth century was an age that venerated the Founders. In part, one could see "idealization of the nation's founders" as "an attempt to establish paternal substitutes." In part, the historical forces embodied in the Founders were still thought to be operative; history was a power "which somehow takes possession of men and works out its intentions through them."[7] On this view, the significance of the founding events of the nation was that they set the normative standards for all future public conduct. Therefore, as Rush Welter explains, "appeals made to the electorate could logically state the issues of any given election as a mere *reprise* of issues already settled at an earlier day. . . . the object of any political campaign was to revive public virtue by invoking the precedent of the founding fathers."[8] The Founders were seen as the source for the triumph of a Union over the diverse interests of colonies and states, "so awesome an accomplishment that succeeding generations ought to pray that eternal vigil before such achievement might cause the elders' wisdom to linger."[9] The values of the achievement and of the Founders were inseparably linked so that to question either would be to reflect impiously on both. The closest modern parallels would be the wave of emotion following the deaths of Franklin Roosevelt and John F. Kennedy, when identifying a proposed policy with the late president served as a compelling argument for the proposal. Douglas's strategy, then, was to draw on the filiopiety of the age in suggesting that the "House Divided" speech put Lincoln at odds with the revered Fathers, further proving that the challenger was a dangerous radical who could not be trusted with a seat in the U.S. Senate.

II

Douglas wasted no time in introducing the argument. In the opening speech of the first debate, he quoted the "House Divided" speech and then attributed to Lincoln the view that "this government cannot endure permanently in the same condition in which it was made by its framers—divided into free and slave states." This rephrasing had Lincoln directly impeaching the Framers. Douglas went on, "Why can it not exist divided into free and slave states? Washington, Jefferson, Franklin, Madison, Hamilton, Jay, and the great men of that day, made this government divided into free states and slave states, and left each state perfectly free to do as it pleased on the subject of slavery. Why can it not exist on the same principles on which our fathers made it?" Later in the speech, he was more emphatic: "Our fathers intended that our institutions should differ. They knew that the North and South having different climates, productions and interests, required different institutions."[10]

How did Douglas claim to know the views of the Fathers? For him it was a simple matter of sign evidence. At the time of the adoption of the

Constitution, twelve of the thirteen states permitted slavery. Had the Founders really believed the "House Divided" doctrine, "the twelve slaveholding states would have overruled the one free state, and slavery would have been fastened by a constitutional provision on every inch of the American Republic, instead of being left as our fathers wisely left it, to each state to decide for itself." This passage was used to suggest that uniformity was the ultimate consequence of Lincoln's legal doctrine. But it also reveals that, for Douglas, the key founding event was the drafting of the Constitution. Although his litany of heroes includes men not present at the Philadelphia convention, he refers to that epochal event as the formation of "the government under which we live" and looked to the deliberations of 1787 to validate his view that the people should be left free to determine their own domestic institutions. In contrast, "this doctrine of Mr. Lincoln's of uniformity among the institutions of the different states is a new doctrine, never dreamed of by Washington, Madison, or the framers of this government."

In the peroration to his Ottawa opening speech, Douglas sharpened the contrast between Lincoln and the Founders. Knowing that his audience would reserve for the Fathers the highest place in the pantheon, he asserted, "Mr. Lincoln and the Republican party set themselves up as wiser than these men who made this government, which has flourished for seventy years under the principle of popular sovereignty, recognizing the right of each state to do as it pleased." Reciting the nation's accomplishments, he assured his listeners that "if we only adhere to that principle, we can go forward increasing in territory, in power, in strength and in glory until the Republic of America shall be the North Star that shall guide the friends of freedom throughout the civilized world."[11] Fidelity to the past, which Lincoln sought to violate, was also the surest guide to the future.

Douglas took this same basic position in most of the debates. At Freeport, he told an unsympathetic audience, "Mr. Lincoln lays does the doctrine that this Union cannot endure divided as our Fathers made it, with free and slave states." That being so, Lincoln would seem obliged to vote against the admission of any more slave states. Yet the challenger would not declare himself distinctly on that question, instead saying only that he would hate to be put to the test. Douglas reassured his listeners, to great laughter, "I do not think he will be put to the test."[12] Since Douglas believed that Congress was bound to admit any state whose government was republican and whose constitution reflected the popular will, he sought to place Lincoln in a dilemma. Either the challenger did not really believe his historical claim, or else the claim was clearly wrong because it would lead to an unconstitutional consequence.

In the Jonesboro debate, Douglas exploited the fact that the "house divided" line was quoted from Scripture and sought to portray Lincoln as suggesting antagonism between the Constitution and the Bible: "Washington and his compeers in the convention that framed the constitution, made this government divided into free and slave states . . . each having sovereign authority over its local and domestic institutions, and all bound together by the federal Constitution. Mr. Lincoln likens that bond of the federal Constitution joining free and slave states together to a house divided against itself, and says that it is contrary to the law of God and cannot stand." He then again recited the litany of national achievements over the past seventy years, all of which took place under a constitution that, according to Lincoln, "is in violation of the law of God." No listener should miss the sarcasm in the statement, "Surely, Mr. Lincoln is a wiser man than those who framed the government."[13]

The Charleston debate was dominated by argument about whether Douglas had conspired to deny Kansas a referendum on the Toombs bill. Nevertheless, even in this debate the Little Giant managed a moment for the historical argument. At the end of his speech he quoted the "house divided" line and then asked, "Why cannot this government endure divided into free and slave states, as our fathers made it? When this government was established by Washington, Jefferson, Madison, Jay, Hamilton, Franklin, and the other sages and patriots of that day, it was composed of free states and slave states, bound together by one common constitution. We have existed and prospered from that day to this thus divided." Douglas asked why such progress could not continue indefinitely, answering, "We can if we will live up to and execute the government upon those principles upon which our fathers established it."[14]

At Galesburg, Douglas was largely occupied in refuting Lincoln's historical argument, and, at Quincy, he offered but a brief restatement of his own position. In the final debate, at Alton, he repeated his analysis of the consequences if the "house divided" doctrine had been persuasive at the constitutional convention, and he proclaimed that it was the principle of state sovereignty that had allowed the North to reach its present position of prominence. He summarized the effectiveness of his own argument throughout the debates: "In regard to [Lincoln's] doctrine that this government was in violation of the law of God which says, that a house divided against itself cannot stand, I repudiated it as a slander upon the immortal framers of our Constitution."[15]

Douglas consistently grounded his position in the fact of regional differences in climate and soil. He insisted that the Founders had recognized these and for this reason had allowed each state to control its own institutions in its own way. This acknowledgment of local sovereignty, in turn, enabled the disparate regions to come together under a common Constitution. The principle of self-government, Douglas often asserted, was the very principle for which the Revolution had been fought; to violate the principle would be to replicate the tyranny of the British.

III

Douglas's introduction of the historical argument was a powerful strategic move. It effectively shifted the burden of proof, focusing attention on the "house divided" doctrine and forcing Lincoln on the defensive, freeing Douglas from the need to stand on his own Senate record. Moreover, by suggesting that sectional warfare was the only alternative to a divided nation, he placed Lincoln in opposition to the symbol of Union that—like the Founders—excited a strong pull on Americans' loyalties during the Middle Period.[16] Lincoln could not ignore the charges or dismiss the Framers; his only recourse was to claim that *his* policy was really consistent with the Founding Fathers. The incumbent had defined the argumentative ground.

Lincoln, however, was not without rhetorical resources. Chief among them was that the Founders' attitudes on the future course of slavery were equivocal. Since the Constitution was silent on the matter, every constitutional argument was—in Bestor's phrase—"a structure of pure inference." Or, as Forgie puts it, the record "is so complex and ambiguous that only someone with the desire to make a political case, combined with a high talent for explaining away the starkest contradictions, could torture the record into a single—let alone coherent—position for or against slavery."[17] Yet so great was the regard for the Founders that one could not allege that they had been mute on the issue. Rather, one must divine their intentions; "one of the standing debates of the ante-bellum generation was whether the Constitution had been meant by them to be a pro- or an antislavery document."[18] Since the record is shrouded in ambiguity, though, there were *topoi* to which each side could appeal.

Lincoln's argument is remarkably similar to that of Salmon P. Chase's 1854 *Appeal of the Independent Democrats*.[19] Like Chase, Lincoln regarded the Founders as profoundly antislavery. He made frequent mention of his views between 1854 and 1860. In his 1854 Peoria speech, for example, he cited Jefferson's role in drafting the Northwest Ordinance, which had preceded the Constitution. He was "the most distinguished politician of our history; a Virginian by birth and continued residence, and withal, a slave-holder" who conceived the idea of prohibition; "with the author of the Declaration of Independence, the policy of prohibiting slavery in new territory originated." Like Douglas,

Lincoln employed sign evidence to establish the wisdom of this policy, noting that no states have surpassed in growth of "population, wealth, the arts and appliances of life" the five states carved out of the Northwest Territory and "deprived of the blessings of 'popular sovereignty,' as contained in the Nebraska bill."[20] Similarly, in his July 1858 Chicago speech, Lincoln pointed to the clause permitting prohibition of the African slave trade in 1808 as "a clear indication that the framers of the Constitution intended and expected the ultimate extinction of that institution."[21] In speeches throughout this period, he grouped Washington, Jefferson, and Madison as early opponents of slavery.[22]

Lincoln saw the American Revolution as a crusade against slavery— not an unusual view since *slavery* was the key devil term of the Revolution. John Hope Franklin has described some colonists' intellectual movement from toleration of slavery to the belief that it was incompatible with the fight against England, and Winthrop D. Jordan has noted the frequency of the colonists' complaint "that ministerial tyranny tended to make 'slaves' of freeborn Englishmen." Bernard Bailyn finds the linkage between the colonists' and the slaves' causes "an identification built into the very language of politics."[23] For his part, Lincoln had noted the connection in an 1855 letter to Judge George Robertson of Lexington, Kentucky: "When we were the political slaves of King George, and wanted to be free, we called the maxim that 'all men are created equal' a self-evident truth; but now when we have grown fat, and have lost all dread of being slaves ourselves, we have become so greedy to be *masters* that we call the same maxim 'a self-evident lie.' "[24] Lincoln, like others, may have equivocated the terms *equality* and *slavery* in order to claim the Declaration of Independence as the key founding document and to use it against Douglas. The Declaration did not discourage the continuation of chattel slavery, but the equivocations permitted Lincoln "to manipulate the history of the Revolution to fit his partisan needs."[25]

In the debates, then, Lincoln flatly denied Douglas's claim that the Fathers *made* the nation half slave and half free. Rather, they *found* it in that condition and, not knowing what else to do, left it that way. He was most succinct in the Quincy debate. The Framers "found the institution of slavery existing here. They did not make it so, but they left it so because they knew of no way to get rid of it at that time. When Judge Douglas undertakes to say that as a matter of choice the fathers of the government made this nation part slave and part free, *he assumes what is historically a falsehood*."[26] By proclaiming Douglas's theory false, Lincoln could claim for himself all the veneration attaching to the Fathers, turning the tables and placing the incumbent on the defensive, possibly even vindicating the "House Divided" speech.

It followed from Lincoln's argument that the vision of the Fathers somehow had been lost and must be regained. This too had been a common theme in Lincoln's rhetoric, reaching back at least as far as the Springfield Lyceum speech of 1838. He applied the argument to the slavery question in the 1854 Peoria speech, in the famous line, "Our republican robe is soiled, and trailed in the dust. Let us repurify it. Let us turn and wash it white, in the spirit, if not the blood, of the Revolution." Likewise, he wrote to Robertson in 1855, "That spirit which desired the peaceful extinction of slavery, has itself become extinct, with the *occasion*, and the *men* of the Revolution."[27] Lincoln saw his mission as the recovery of the Founders' vision. In June 1858, the Republican *Illinois State Journal* had stated the key campaign issue as, "Shall we return to the policy of Washington, Jefferson, Madison, and Jackson?"[28] Not only was this appeal an example of what Wilson has called "a periodic movement . . . to make an 'eternal return' to the original design of the fathers, but it was also wonderfully symmetrical.[29] Douglas had branded Lincoln as the deviant from the vision of the Fathers; now the challenger could make precisely the same charge against the incumbent.

Lincoln also regarded the Constitution as an antislavery document, observing that the word *slavery* was nowhere to be found in it. Distinguishing between constitutional principle and political expediency, he had asserted in 1854, "All legislation that has recognized or tolerated its extension, has been associated with a compensation—a Compromise—showing that it was something that moved forward, not by its own right, but by its own wrong."[30] What sanctioned the subsequent expansion of slavery was not any design of the Founders but the later invention of the cotton gin.[31]

Lincoln's vision of the antislavery nature of the Constitution was open to challenge, however. For example, the contention that the Framers sought to restrict slavery from the territories is overstated. As Allan Nevins has written, "The fathers had not forbidden the expansion of slavery into areas to which it was manifestly suited; the Southwest Territory had been opened to it while the Northwest was closed."[32] Even the Northwest Ordinance did not altogether stop the spread of slavery north of the Ohio. The ordinance "explicitly protected the property of the French inhabitants and other settlers who 'professed themselves citizens of Virginia,'" and in any case slaves were brought into the territory notwithstanding the prohibition. Douglas argued that slavery had been tried in Illinois and was abandoned when it became clearly unprofitable.[33] On this point, the history of the state bears him out. The 1818 state constitution, which Congress accepted, recognized the property rights of slaveowners already in the state. By 1820, the state included over 700 slaves, and, in Harris's judgment, "slavery existed in the territory of Illinois as completely as in any of the Southern States" and was practiced as far north as Sangamon County, then in the early stages of settlement.[34]

On other counts, too, Lincoln's view of the Founders overstated the case. The sage of Monticello who authored the Northwest Ordinance also opposed the Missouri Compromise partly because it restricted the spread of slavery.[35] The Constitution, while omitting the term *slavery*, nonetheless legitimized the institution. The Founders appear to have regarded the slavery question primarily as a matter of expediency rather than principle. In fact, they were hardly confident that the Union itself would last. It was described as an experiment whose future was uncertain; the case for the perpetuity of the Union was not advanced strongly until the nullification crisis of the 1830s.[36]

None of this is to suggest that Lincoln's view of the Framers of the Constitution was untenable. But it did rest on scant evidence—primarily the omission of the term and the contemporaneous passage of the Northwest Ordinance—and it was open to serious challenge. He was on stronger ground with his other historical argument, which was rooted in the Declaration of Independence.

IV

The phrase "all men are created equal" was central to Lincoln's argument, his primary evidence for the antislavery intentions of the Fathers. He regarded the Declaration not just as a historical document but as a living political creed.[37] He explained repeatedly that American history began with the Declaration, not with any earlier event, and not with the Constitution. The Declaration was the apple of gold, the Constitution the picture of silver that frames it.[38] The Declaration had no legal status, though Lincoln sometimes spoke of it as though it did, but it was more fundamental than any law as an expression of American values. It embodied the transcendent vision of the Union that preceded the Constitution and that could not be altogether captured in any written document. In this respect, Lincoln followed other Republicans and free-soil orators who had regarded the nation as the creator of the Constitution rather than the other way around.[39]

Lincoln's regard for the Declaration is most evident in a speech he delivered at Lewistown, Ill., just a few days before the first debate. He went so far as to identify the document with the Genesis doctrine that man is created in the divine image and then closed with the peroration:

Think nothing of me—take no thought for the political fate of any man whomsoever—but come back to the truths that are in the Declaration of Independence. You may do anything with me you choose, if you will but heed these sacred principles. You may not only defeat me for the Senate, but you may take me and put me to death. While pretending no indifference to earthly honors, I *do claim* to be actuated in this contest by something higher than an anxiety for office. I charge you to drop every paltry and insignificant thought for any man's success. It is nothing; I am nothing; Judge Douglas is nothing. *But do not destroy that immortal emblem of Humanity—the Declaration of Independence.*[40]

Having established the cardinal importance of the Declaration, Lincoln contended that blacks were encompassed within the phrase "all men are created equal." In the Galesburg debate, he asserted that prior to 1854 no one had thought otherwise. "I think I may defy Judge Douglas," the challenger boasted, "to show that he ever said so, that Washington ever said so, that any President ever said so, that any member of Congress ever said so, or that any living man upon the whole earth ever said so, until the necessities of the present policy of the Democratic party, in regard to slavery, had to invent that affirmation."[41] From this standpoint, it was easy for the challenger to turn the tables against the incumbent, by contending at Jonesboro that Douglas "has himself been chiefly instrumental in changing the policy of the fathers" by retreating from the ideals embodied in the Declaration.[42] As with his argument about the Constitution, Lincoln here tried to reach beyond the fact that the nation at its origin was part slave and part free and to discuss instead the Founders' intent or motive.

Douglas tried to discredit these claims through argument from sign. Many of the Founders, including Jefferson, were slaveowners and continued to hold slaves after drafting the Declaration. How could they have written the statement "all men are created equal" intending it to apply to blacks and yet continue to hold slaves themselves? Either the Founders stood exposed of the basest hypocrisy—an inconceivable position in an age that venerated them so—or else Lincoln was simply incorrect. At Galesburg, the incumbent was most specific. Noting that all the signers of the Declaration represented slaveholding constituencies, and reminding his audience that "no one of them emancipated his slaves, much less put them on an equality with himself, after he signed the Declaration," the incumbent asked whether "every man who signed the Declaration of Independence declared the negro his equal, and then was hypocrite enough to continue to hold him as a slave, in violation of what he believed to be the divine law?"[43]

Although he did not use it explicitly until the last debate, Douglas had another argument at this point that turned the tables against Lincoln. He had compared Lincoln's belief in federal ownership of the territories with the colonialism of King George III. Now he invoked the same comparison to Britain in order to illustrate the falsity of Lincoln's historical view and the correctness of his own. Referring to popular sovereignty, he had written a group of Chicago clergymen, "It is the principle upon which the thirteen colonies separated from the imperial government. It is the principle in defence of which the battles of the Revolution were fought."[44] On this reading, it was he rather than Lincoln who adhered to the principles of the Declaration.

Still, Douglas faced a problem. He might quibble with Lincoln's interpretation, but there were the plain words "all men are created equal." How was he to account for them? In his view, as he said at Jonesboro, the signers of the document "had no reference to the negro whatever when they declared all men to be created equal. They desired to express by that phrase, white men, men of European birth and European descent, and had no reference either to the negro, the savage Indians, the Fejee, the Malay, or any other inferior and degraded race, when they spoke of the equality of men."[45] The purpose of the phrase, Douglas insisted, was to establish the political equality of men born in America and in Britain. The Declaration, as Lanphier's paper had stated in July, "was a political document, speaking of *political rights*," not an enunciation of moral principle.[46]

Douglas's reading of the "created equal" phrase is open to dispute. Jaffa has described it as self-contradictory to claim as unalienable what were rights only of British subjects: "For a right enjoyed in virtue only of the British constitution may be taken away by that same constitution. And rights which inhere independently of the British constitution are not inherently British, nor may they properly be called such."[47] At the time, the Republican *Illinois State Journal* was more scathing if less thorough in its critique: "The principle stock in trade of Douglas and his satellites consists now-a-days in denunciations of the glorious old Declaration of Independence. . . . their chief card against Mr. Lincoln is that he is a believer in that ancient and venerable instrument."[48] On the other hand, even though colonial dependence on the mother country was described as "slavery," still there is no specific evidence that the Founders passed judgment on this nation's peculiar institution. If not, and if they were not hypocrites, then there must be some other reading of the "created equal" phrase besides Lincoln's. In this respect, Anderson concludes that Douglas "was much more closely in touch with the realities of 1776 than was Lincoln."[49] The challenger, not the incumbent, once again could be placed in the role of deviant from the wisdom of the Fathers and threat to the Union.

To avert such a judgment, Lincoln would need to elaborate and defend his own theory of history. He did so by the device that Perelman and Olbrechts-Tyteca have labeled *dissociation*. A previously unitary concept is broken into parts, one of which is more negatively valued than the other. The opponent's position is then equated with the disfavored term and one's own with the preferred.[50] Lincoln made two strategic dissociations. First, he took the equivocal term *equality* and examined its various aspects. At Ottawa, and again at Quincy, Lincoln explained that his reading of the Declaration of Independence did not entail *social* equality for the negro. Remarking that there was a physical difference between the races and that he agreed with Douglas that his own race should have the superior position, he then added "that notwithstanding all this, there is no reason in the world why the Negro is not entitled to all the natural rights enumerated in the Declaration of Independence, the right to life, liberty and the pursuit of happiness." He then proceeded to make the dissociation explicit: "I agree with Judge Douglas [that the Negro] is not my equal in many respects—certainly not in color, perhaps not in moral or intellectual endowment. But in the right to eat the bread, without leave of anybody else, which his own hand earns, *he is my equal and the equal of Judge Douglas, and the equal of every living man.*"[51] Social equality was one thing, but equality in basic rights was another, and Douglas was chided for failing to see the difference. "Not content with spitting upon the great truths of the Declaration of Independence," thundered the *Illinois State Journal*, Douglas supporters "stoop to the further infamy of assailing all those who do believe in that old instrument and charge them for that reason with being in favor of 'nigger equality.' "[52]

This distinction enabled Lincoln to reduce the apparent radicalism of his position. The equality he defended was, after all, a flimsy reed. He was saying only that the Founders opposed slavery, without implying that either they or he would favor any other change to improve the status of the Negro. Even so, Lincoln was not yet able to answer Douglas's charge that the challenger must be accusing the Founders of hypocrisy since so many of them were slaveowners. For this purpose, Lincoln drew a second distinction, one between empirical description and ideal principle, between the Declaration as fact and as norm.

The material for this second dissociation was contained in Lincoln's year-old Springfield speech of June 26, 1857, but it did not surface in the debates until the last encounter, at Alton, where Lincoln read from his earlier speech. The Founders, he noted, "did not mean to assert the obvious untruth, that all were then actually enjoying that equality, nor yet, that they were about to confer it immediately upon them. . . . They meant simply to declare the *right* so that the *enforcement* of it might follow as fast as circumstances should permit."[53] The phrase was not a description of empirical conditions but a standard to which to aspire—a construction that, as Jaffa notes, was prefigured in the Lyceum speech of 1838.[54] Lincoln reached this conclusion about the proper meaning, he explained in the earlier Springfield speech, by residues. Like any sacred text, the Declaration was taken to be perfect, without superfluous words or phrases. The "created equal" phrase could be "of no practical use in effecting our separation from Great Britain; and it was placed in the Declaration not for that, but for future use."[55]

What Lincoln was suggesting was that the phrase "all men are created equal" was not a fact but a proposition—in precisely the same sense in which he would use that term in the Gettysburg Address. It was a statement to be proved, and the proof would come over time in the life of the country. As Basler explained the idea, "American democracy, as an active, living thing, meant to Lincoln the verification or proving of the proposition to which its very existence was in the beginning dedicated."[56] To prove the proposition, however, history should be a path of steady progression toward the goal; retrogressive moves especially must be avoided. As Lincoln quoted himself at Alton, the signers of the Declaration "meant to set up a standard maxim for free society which should be familiar to all; constantly looked to, constantly labored for, and even though never perfectly attained, constantly approximated and thereby constantly spreading and deepening its influence."[57]

This formulation made it easier for Lincoln to answer Douglas's taunt that the Republicans must be accusing the Founders of hypocrisy. If the Founders had endorsed a tendency rather than an end state, then one could reconcile their belief with their own ownership of slaves. They judged slavery to be an evil that ultimately must end, even though they acknowledged that the world was not yet ready for abolition. So long as people generally believed that slavery someday must and would end, its actual presence in American society was not of central concern to Lincoln. That is what he meant in asserting in at least four of the debates "that the fathers of this government placed that institution where the public mind *did* rest in the belief that it was in the course of ultimate extinction."[58]

Lincoln thereby portrayed Douglas as the transgressor against the Fathers and himself championed a return to the Founders' vision. He made the charge explicit in the Alton debate: "I now say that willingly or unwillingly, purposely or without purpose, Judge Douglas has been the most prominent instrument in changing the position of the institution of slavery which the fathers of the government expected to come to an end ere this."[59] This argumentative stance was consistent with a prominent nineteenth-century theme, that reform was conservative, "an effort to restore an America which had somehow been lost or subverted."[60] In this case, it was clear that the subverter was Douglas himself, first because he needlessly encouraged agitation over the slavery question by introducing the Nebraska Bill, then because he proclaimed that he "don't care" whether slavery was voted up or down. His stance was required by the logic of popular sovereignty but was at odds with the moral judgment that Lincoln attributed to the Fathers. So Douglas was the deviant, and the way to restore the spirit of the old Union was by supporting his Republican challenger.

For all that, however, Lincoln's argument still fundamentally begged the question. It began with an argument from residues: the "created equal" phrase was not put into the Declaration for immediate needs (itself a disputed point); therefore it must have been intended as a maxim for the future. Moreover, this future maxim must have been that the Founders expected the eventual end of slavery, and that assumption then "proved" that Douglas was the apostate. All in all, it was a thin reed on which to build an elaborate historical argument. But Douglas's position likewise depended on inconclusive assumptions: that the Constitution rather than the Declaration was the true origin of American government and that the Framers of the Constitution, in the name of the popular sovereignty principle, deliberately made the new nation part slave and part free.

V

The debates exposed the potency of the historical argument, convincing each candidate "that his position would be unassailable if he could trace it back to the Founding Fathers."[61] But each probably was unsatisfied with the conclusiveness of the claim since each argument rested at key points on assumption or unsupported inference rather than evidence. During 1859, each sought to remedy that defect by studying early American history. Douglas wrote to the historian George Bancroft to request authoritative evidence that the popular sovereignty principle was analogous to the colonial complaint against England, and he borrowed the first six volumes of Bancroft's *History of the United States* as well as *The Federalist* and Elliot's *Debates on the Federal Constitution* from the Library of Congress. The result of his inquiry was an article published in *Harper's* that fall. For his part, Lincoln spent time in the Illinois State Library and read Elliot's *Debates*, a research program whose fruits were evident in February 1860 when he spoke at Cooper Union.[62]

Meanwhile, however, there was a second historical argument in the debates, which not only was important in its own right but also served symbolically to fill some of the gaps in the discussion of the Founding Fathers. Henry Clay, the sage of Ashland, had been in the grave only six years, but already his place in the pantheon of national heroes was secure. The growing national discord over slavery brought his compromising spirit into sharp relief and—as with the Founders—led many to conclude that there had been a deterioration in the political dialogue since the days when Clay walked the halls of the Senate. Clay was a symbolic link to the Founders for the mid-nineteenth-century generation who came to maturity just as the last of them had passed on. If a candidate could demonstrate that his position was in line with Clay's, then by extension it would be viewed as linked with the Fathers as well.

There was another, more practical reason for appealing to the memory of Clay. Central Illinois, the crucial battleground of the election, contained thousands of Old Line Whigs for whom he was the patron saint. Some had joined the new Republican party. Many were attracted briefly to the Know-Nothings, partly because of nativism, but largely because of a Unionist emphasis that avoided the need to choose between North and South. Particularly following the demise of that movement, many of the old Whigs were unaffiliated. The Republican party held some attraction for them since they were long-standing opponents of "locofoco" Democracy, but they were deterred both by the Republicans' simultaneous appeal to immigrant voters and by suspicions that the Republicans really were abolitionists. Like Clay, the Illinois Whigs such as John T. Stuart and Usher F. Linder were mildly antislavery but strongly antiabolition. Republicans therefore emphasized their moderation while Democrats tried to tar their opponents with the abolitionist brush. Sheahan's *Chicago Times* had boasted that "the thousands of old Whigs who, under cover of the 'American' organization, until now have stood out against the seductions of the Republicans, cannot be abolitionized," and one correspondent even suggested that Douglas might draw both the nativist and the immigrant vote.[63]

In 1856, the Whigs had been the swing voters. With some foreboding, Lincoln had written Trumbull, "Nine tenths of the Anti-Nebraska votes have to come from old whigs. . . . So far they have been disregarded," and they split almost evenly between Fremont and Fillmore, with a small number favoring Buchanan.[64] It appeared that they would again be the swing voters in 1858 and that the key question might be whether Republicans could be distinguished from abolitionists. Democratic editors were confident that the link could be sustained, and one

Douglas correspondent can be forgiven for the exaggeration, "All old Whigs are warmly for you, & we will not rest untill we perfect an organization under your leadership."[65] Certainly, a powerful appeal for this crucial audience would be the ability to claim the mantle of Henry Clay. If Lincoln could successfully compare himself to Clay, Whigs would have a hard time portraying him as an abolitionist. Conversely, if Douglas could emerge as the more likely successor to Clay, there would be no dissonance in regarding the Republican challenger as a dangerous rival.

One might think that Lincoln would have had the easier time in this contest. He had been a Whig, indeed became one because of Clay. He served in Congress as a Clay Whig, the only Whig in the Illinois delegation. He supported Clay's position on internal improvements, on the Mexican War, and on colonization. Like Clay, he dismissed the retort that colonization of freed slaves in Africa was impractical. And Lincoln had delivered Clay's eulogy in Springfield in July 1852. Clay, he said then, "never spoke merely to be heard," but "all his efforts were made for practical effect." With respect to slavery, Clay was "cast into life where slavery was already widely spread and deeply seated" and an owner of slaves himself; he "did not perceive, as I think no wise man has perceived, how it could be at *once* eradicated, without producing a greater evil, even to the cause of human liberty itself." Nevertheless, Clay "even was, on principle and in feeling, opposed to slavery," as is evident from the fact that both early and late in life he sought the gradual emancipation of slaves in Kentucky.[66] On all these points, Lincoln claimed to stand where Clay had stood.

Throughout the senatorial campaign, Lincoln stressed his attachment to Clay. The cane he carried reportedly was made from the wood of Clay's house. He began a speech by showing that his and Clay's views on slavery "coincided, exactly." As Fredrickson summarizes, Lincoln "quoted Clay, paraphrased him, and at times virtually plagiarized from him, not merely for the practical political purpose of winning recalcitrant Whigs to the Republican cause but because he indeed thought of himself as taking up where Clay had left off."[67] Republican newspapers represented the party as endorsing "every word which Mr. Clay then uttered" so that "Lincoln and Clay stand upon the Same Platform," while Democratic papers chided Lincoln for trying "to suit himself to the locality and to conceal his Abolition sentiments, whilst pretending to be the friend of Henry Clay."[68]

In the debates, Lincoln made at least forty-one references to Clay and his political philosophy.[69] He emphasized his own Whig heritage and proclaimed Clay his "beau ideal" of a statesman. More to the point, Lincoln insisted that Clay's views on slavery were similar to his own. In his peroration in the Ottawa debate, Lincoln maintained that Clay encompassed blacks within the scope of the Declaration of Independence. Without acknowledging the source, he loosely quoted from Clay's 1827 American Colonization Society address, accusing Douglas of "going back to the era of our Revolution, and to the extent of his ability, muzzling the cannon which thunders its annual joyous return. When he invites any people willing to have slavery, to establish it, he is blowing out the moral lights around us." In the Galesburg debate, Lincoln quoted the same passage and acknowledged the source.[70] Far from being radical, Lincoln implied, his views were only those of the most venerated of the Old Line Whigs.

There was an obvious retort, however. If the Great Compromiser really had shared Lincoln's beliefs, why had he not emancipated his own slaves? Lincoln's rendering of Clay in the Quincy and Alton debates answers that question by distinguishing between tolerating an existing institution as a matter of expediency and extending the institution over virgin territory as a matter of principle. To bolster his statement that Clay saw blacks under the rubric of the Declaration, Lincoln quoted him: "Now as an abstract principle, *there is no doubt of the truth of that declaration*, and it is a principle in the *original construction* of society, and in organized societies, to keep it in view as a great fundamental principle."[71] Lincoln's discussion in Alton was the most complete, perhaps because he acknowledged that "we are surrounded to some extent today, by old friends of Mr. Clay, and they will be glad to hear anything from that authority." He then quoted at length from Clay's remarks on the Declaration, concluding with the words, "If a state of nature existed and we were about to lay the foundations of society, *no man would be more strongly opposed that [sic] I should be, to incorporating the institution of slavery among its elements.*" Since Lincoln regarded the territories as virgin land, his inference was that Clay's 1827 remarks precisely covered the question of expanding slavery in the territories. As he asked rhetorically, "What have I done, that I have not the license of Henry Clay's illustrious example here in doing?"[72]

The pageantry surrounding the debates reinforced the identification of Lincoln with Clay. Banners proclaiming "Westward the Star of Empire winds its way / The girls link-on to Lincoln, as their mothers did to Clay," appeared at the Charleston debate.[73] And Lincoln's other campaign speeches contained the same theme. The *Chicago Press and Tribune* reported on a speech at Tremont, "He then entered into a comparison of the principles of the Whig party as expounded by its great leader, Henry Clay, and those of the Republican party of the present day, showing that there was no difference."[74]

Douglas's rhetorical problem was clear. If Lincoln could identify himself with Clay, and if Clay was regarded as the symbolic link to the Founding Fathers, then Lincoln could establish that his position was the true descendant of Washington, Jefferson, Madison, and the rest and hence that the "House Divided" speech offered no radical doctrine that the Old Line Whigs must fear. The incumbent must break the links in this chain, and to do so required a twofold approach: discredit Lincoln's claim to be Clay's successor, so that ample doubt would be cast on his link back to the Fathers, and then claim that Douglas was really the proper heir of the sage of Ashland.

Democratic newspapers helped in executing the first part of the strategy. The (Jacksonville) *Illinois Sentinel* in 1856 had noted that Lincoln quoted Clay out of context. Clay indeed was opposed to legislating slavery into the Western territories, but he was also opposed to prohibiting its entry there, and he did not regard the Western territories as virgin land.[75] This, of course, was not the same portrayal of Clay's views that Lincoln offered in the Alton debate. The *Chicago Times* went even further, alleging (without evidence) in September 1858 that "Lincoln never was a friend of Clay's. He was one of those men who used to advocate Clay's cause by arguing that he was a first rate abolitionist, and thus during Clay's entire life furnished the Democratic party with the power to defeat him."[76]

There was a specific historical episode that could be used to weaken the Lincoln-Clay bond. After three times supporting the Kentuckian for the presidency, Lincoln had deserted him in 1848, presumably because he had come to the reluctant conclusion that Clay could not be elected. To Douglas papers, though, Lincoln's shift of allegiance was proof of his dishonesty. According to the *Chicago Times*, Lincoln, at a secret meeting in Springfield, "cut the throat of the old Kentuckian, and became the instrument for defeating him the year after at Philadelphia."[77]

But beyond this single note, if Lincoln could be portrayed as a radical abolitionist, his tie to Clay would be broken since the Kentuckian was known for his ability to forge compromises. The *Illinois State Register* reported Clay as having said shortly before his death that he would join the Democrats if the Whigs were abolitionized—a circumstance that the paper alleged to have occurred. Lincoln was not with Clay on the slavery question "but always stood with the class of whigs who looked to 'provisos' and other clap-trap of northern agitators wielded for *party* advantage, as against the peace and best interests of the country." Hence, "the idea of palming Mr. Clay off as being the friend of a sectional abolition party, against his well known sentiments and speeches, is not only amusing but ridiculous."[78] The presumptive link between Whigs and Republicans was countered with the presumptive Whig antipathy to radicalism, and Lincoln was made to appear radical because of the "House Divided" speech.

It was, by contrast, the penchant for compromise that enabled Douglas and his supporters to claim the mantle of Clay. To make the point, Douglas exaggerated Clay's role in framing the Compromise of 1850, minimizing his own considerable contribution to that result. Moreover, the Kansas-Nebraska Act was seen as but an attempt to apply the same principles of the 1850 Compromise.[79] In disrespect to Clay, Lincoln and the Republicans were trampling on those principles.

At Freeport, for instance, Douglas charged, "Lincoln went to work to dissolve the Old Line Whig party. Clay was dead, and although the sod was not yet green on his grave, this man undertook to bring into disrepute those great compromise measures of 1850, with which Clay and Webster were identified." The argument was developed at greater length at Charleston, in the heart of the Whig country, where Douglas accused Lincoln and Lyman Trumbull of leading "the crusade against national principles" in Illinois. The Alton debate saw Douglas succinctly summarize his position, albeit with exaggeration. As Douglas there recalled history, in 1850 "we Democrats, with Cass at our head, welcomed Henry Clay, whom the whole nation regarded as having been preserved by God for the times. He became our leader in that great fight, and we rallied around him the same as the Whigs rallied around Old Hickory in 1832, to put down nullification."[80] Douglas was engaging in hyperbole since the Democrats had rallied around not Clay's version of the compromise measures but his own separation of the omnibus bill and since the Whig party had not even been formed in 1832. But it was an effective appeal to Clay's memory, all the same.

Not surprisingly, Lincoln was upset at Douglas's pretension to Clay's mantle. He did not voice his resentments during the debates but returned frequently to the theme in other speeches of the time. At Lewistown, shortly before the first debate, he found Douglas's view to be so opposite to Clay's "as Beelzebub to an Angel of Light." In Bloomington in September, he spoke of the many contrasts between Douglas and Clay. In a speech at Monmouth shortly before the Charleston debate, he said that, "as to Douglas being of any kin to [Clay], everybody knows they never had a single feeling in unison, and that Douglas was one of his most virulent abusers while living."[81] Republican newspapers took up the theme, contending that Douglas was hypocritical in revering Clay, "a man whom he pursued with wolfish malignity for twenty years," and pointing out that Lincoln had been a lifelong Whig while Douglas had been traveling the state calling Clay "an 'abolitionist,' 'a gambler,' 'a duelist,'" and "'a traitor brought up with British gold.'"[82] While these protests represented genuine resentment, they may also have been indirect evidence of the effectiveness of the Little Giant's argument to the old Whigs.

VI

What *were* Clay's views on the question of slavery in the territories? Appropriately enough, they were ambiguous. One biographer describes his attitude as "a practical acceptance of the institution and a theoretical opposition to it."[83] Lincoln was right in saying that Clay believed slavery to be wrong in principle, that he favored gradual emancipation, and that he would not vote to establish slavery where it did not exist—if he were starting a new governmental structure. He also supported colonization as the necessary accompaniment to gradual emancipation, a position from which he never wavered. On the other hand, by the late 1830s Clay had become a conservative. He saw the preservation of the Union as paramount, and he recognized what Cooper has called a great irony: he "proclaimed slavery essential for American liberty . . . for the South, he believed, would choose slavery over the nation, if forced to make that choice." Most of all, he wanted an end to agitation that might destroy the Union.[84] Moreover, like Douglas, Clay used humor and sarcasm, and he used technical points of law to his own advantage. As was true of the Founding Fathers, Clay's legacy was uncertain, but it furnished materials from which to argue. In the case of the Founders, however, there was no external documentary evidence to confirm or deny their intentions authoritatively. Advocates had to reason from the texts themselves. They employed what Aristotle called "artistic proof," meaning that it came from the artistry of the advocates. But, when it came to Clay's intentions, a powerful inartistic proof was available—a source beyond the texts themselves. If Clay was the symbolic protégé of the Founding Fathers, his own protégés were tangible—and they were prepared to speak out.

Judge T. Lyle Dickey, a Whig ally of Lincoln's, had been distressed in 1856 when his compatriot, in a speech in Bloomington, proclaimed that the government could not last part slave and part free. As he recalled years later, he had remonstrated with Lincoln "that the proposition was not necessarily true—& second if true—no good to the country could come from its promulgation and I thought very much harm might be done by teaching the people that doctrine." Lincoln had then promised Dickey not to utter the same sentiment in that campaign.[85] But two years later, when Lincoln delivered the "House Divided" speech and Dickey lost a battle to deny the Republican nomination for Congress to

Owen Lovejoy, he concluded that the new party had veered too far to-ward abolitionism. Dickey believed that a deal had been made between Lovejoy and Lincoln. He could not reconcile himself to Lovejoy's openly professed abolitionism, and he interpreted the "House Divided" speech as reflecting the same sentiment.[86] On August 2, David Davis warned Lincoln, "I fear that Judge Dickey is for Douglass—through-out," and, indeed, five days later, a letter of endorsement from Dickey was published in the *Chicago Times*.[87]

Reactions to this move were predictable. Democrats gloated, the *Illinois State Register* proclaiming that Dickey, who "has always been an old line Henry Clay Whig," was "well known throughout Illinois as one of the ablest of our lawyers, and one of the most zealous of our politi-cians." His endorsement of Douglas certainly meant something. Republicans, on the other hand, minimized the significance of Dickey's move. The *Illinois State Journal* ridiculed his endorsement letter as "a most incoherent jumble" and imputed to Dickey the motive of office seeking. Davis reassured Lincoln that Dickey's desertion "can't do any harm if the candidates for the Legislature are rightly selected."[88] But Dickey was not the only defecting Whig. James W. Singleton, Henry Clay's personal friend; Cyrus Edwards, previously a Whig candidate for governor and U.S. senator; E. B. Webb, the last Whig candidate for gov-ernor; and John T. Stuart, Lincoln's first law partner and the Whig who had defeated Douglas for Congress in 1838—all rallied behind the Little Giant. Stuart, because of his personal relationship with Lincoln, would not campaign against him but wanted it known that "on the slavery ques-tion he coincides with Mr. Douglas, that he is wholly opposed to the republican party, and to any fusion by Whigs with them."[89]

Not only did Dickey support Douglas, but he obtained for the incum-bent the endorsement of Kentucky senator John J. Crittenden, widely regarded as Clay's political heir and the nation's most influential ex-Whig. This endorsement had been feared since early in the summer. Lyman Trumbull reported a June conversation with Crittenden, who "said that I ought to have no controversy with Douglas, that he was op-posing the administration." In July, Lincoln wrote to the Kentuckian to ask about rumors that he was endorsing Douglas. Crittenden's reply, dated July 29, indicated that Douglas's opposition to Lecompton "was highly gratifying to me. The position taken by him was full of sacrafice [sic] & full of hazard, yet he took it, and he defended it, *like a Man*." Crittenden went on to state that Douglas's reelection was important "as a rebuke to the Administration, and a vindication of the great cause of popular rights & public justice." Though he held these views, the Kentuckian added, he would not be active in the Illinois campaign. "Since the adjournment of Congress," he said, "I have not written a single letter to any person in Illinois."[90]

Meanwhile, Democrats had discussed how to use Crittenden's influence. Early in July, Thomas L. Harris wrote Douglas that Crittenden had said "that he would do any thing we desired—He would write to any body—& give his views and wishes in your favor in any mode in which they would be most effective." Harris went on to state that a Crittenden letter or speech would "control 20,000 American and old Line Whig votes in the center & south." Before anything had been made public, the *Illinois State Register* informed its readers that "Mr. Crittenden has openly expressed his desire for the re-election of Douglas." The paper went on to chide the Republicans for "impudently" using Crittenden's name once "their abolition sectional card proves a failure."[91]

Soon after telling Lincoln that he had written no letters, Crittenden wrote one to Dickey. The judge received the letter in August but delayed publicizing it until mid-October, just after the seventh debate and just two weeks before the election. Speaking at Decatur on October 19, Dickey quoted from Clay's speeches and charged "that Lincoln was just as hostile to Clay's doctrines in 1858 as he was to Clay's person in 1847" and then read Crittenden's letter endorsing Douglas.[92]

Republicans were nonplused by this development. They called the document a forgery because it had been written several months earlier but withheld. Why hold it back if not to make it impossible in such a short time for Crittenden to denounce it as fraud? They also minimized the significance of the letter, contending that its aim was only to praise Douglas's handling of the Lecompton imbroglio, not necessarily to endorse his reelection.[93] The *Illinois State Journal* called the endorsement an "old lie." Crittenden may have supported Douglas before the campaign began, as did several newspapers. With a bit of wishful thinking, the *Journal* proclaimed, "since the canvass has opened, and they have seen Douglas renounce his anti-Lecomptonism and return to the Administration party, they have all denounced him and denounce him now."[94] At least in Crittenden's case, there was no evidence for this alleged reversal.

The Crittenden endorsement hurt Lincoln. With some reason, the *Illinois State Register* admonished that the "incessant cry of 'fraud' and 'forgery,' without the evidence to sustain it, will have no other effect but to show that the republicans are so far driven to the wall that they have become perfectly reckless." The *Register* crowed that this letter "was fast determining hundreds and thousands of old line whigs and Americans, who were before indifferent or undecided as to this election, *to vote for Douglas."* This judgment has been supported by historians; Fehrenbacher, for example, holds that the letter "undoubtedly hurt Lincoln most in the very places where he was beaten—that is, in the old whig strongholds of central Illinois." It is not likely that Crittenden's late October letter to Lincoln, protesting that he had not authorized publication of his letter to Dickey, did much to soothe the situation.[95]

The controversy over the Whig endorsements of Douglas took place outside the debates, but it greatly affected evaluation of the historical argument within the debates. Crittenden, in particular, was close enough to Clay that he was thought able to speak authoritatively about his mentor's intentions. If he and other Whigs were now endorsing Douglas, it was a reasonable inference that Clay would have done so as well. Though Lincoln had been a Whig throughout his adult life, the Crittenden letter seemed to deny him the mantle of Clay. If Clay were the symbolic link to the Founding Fathers, then it was all the more difficult for Lincoln to maintain that he rather than Douglas was their true descendant.

This episode suggests an important limitation on the historical argument. For maximum effectiveness, it must be grounded in a past sufficiently out of reach so that there are no authoritative eyewitnesses. The appeal to the Founding Fathers met this requirement ideally. The positive symbolic value of the Fathers was nearly universal, but the "text" was ambiguous enough to generate an array of rival interpretations whose effectiveness depended on the ability of competing arguers to weave together a plausible narrative. The availability of eyewitness testimony or designated heirs weakens this ambiguity and turns the historical argument from a hermeneutic pursuit into an inartistic proof. When that happens, the historical argument is skewed in the direction of the authoritative source. It is no longer a balanced stance available to both sides of such a basic dispute. The Lincoln-Douglas debates illustrate both the artistic and the inartistic variations of the historical argument, and they also reveal the relative effectiveness of documents and stories as forms of support.

VII

The historical argument was significant not just for strategic reasons and not just because the 1850s were a decade marked by great reverence for the Founding Fathers. It was also a guide to the future. Nineteenth-century Americans saw history as continuous rather than static; it was a set of vectors rather than a set of events. It was a sign of an active public that the country connected itself to its roots and regarded those roots as somehow determinative of future conduct.[96] The past was something to be fought

over, not for antiquarian reasons, but because the successful interpretation of the past would entail a controlling influence on future policy.

Both Lincoln and Douglas believed that the nation stood at a
crossroads since long-recognized historical forces were threatened by
recent developments. For Douglas, the force of local self-determination
over an expanding geographic area was being arrested by Lincoln's attempt to impose uniformity on a territory's domestic institutions. For
Lincoln, the moral condemnation of slavery that he attributed to the Fathers was threatened by the "don't care" attitude of Senator Douglas.
For both men, the stakes were high, and there was no turning back.[97] All
the more important, then, to establish that the forces of history really
were on one's side.

Lincoln and Douglas argued from history in significantly different
ways. Douglas took the past on its own terms, finding in it factual confir-
mation for his claims about the origins of the present condition. For him
history was a source of documentary evidence. Lincoln, in contrast,
viewed history as dynamic and projected forward into the future from
motives uncovered through a reflective reading of the past. In this way,
history has a narrative continuity; it is a source of stories rather than of
documents. The appeal of Lincoln's historical argument is largely in its
story of degeneration from the vision of the Fathers, a calamity for which
Douglas is identified as the chief villain. The moral argument on which
Lincoln ultimately triumphs is both embedded in and bolstered by the
historical narrative, and the narrative form enhances Lincoln's credibility.[98]

Implicit in each man's historical argument was a vision of the future.
Although Douglas was portrayed as approving slavery forever, his real
hope was that national growth, economic development and integration,
and the working out of manifest destiny would dwarf the slavery question into insignificance. Thereby, he would return to the vision of the
Fathers, who were sage enough to compromise on matters that could not
be settled and who wanted wherever possible key political decisions to
be made at the local level by those who would be affected by them.

Lincoln argued that restricting the spread of slavery in the territories
would lead naturally but gradually to the abolition of slavery itself,
thereby returning to the wisdom of the Founding Fathers. His desire to
see slavery end could be reconciled with a pledge not to disturb it where
it already existed. As Fehrenbacher explained Lincoln's thinking on
these two propositions, they "were like lines extending into the future,
seemingly parallel, but capable of being brought together gradually and
gently."[99]

Each man portrayed his vision as the wave of the future and yet portrayed the vision as being in danger of defeat if the threat were not arrested and the country returned to the vision of the Fathers. Both men's historical argument was an appeal for restoration of a lost sense of united purpose. Describing the desire of Americans to escape the complexities and ambiguities of slavery by escaping from time, Wilson has written, "Existing evils, in this view, could best be understood as signs of degeneration, of deviation by the nation through the course of time from its true 'nature.' The chief task of the statesman was thus to absolve the nation from the evil accretions of time by the reaffirmation of its seminal principle."[100] Hence, an appeal to the spirit and vision of the Fathers was both a surrogate for future policy and the means by which one's vision of the future could best be achieved. Following the policy of the Founding Fathers, ironically enough, was the means to achieve fundamental change. In this way, the historical story pointed toward its natural conclusion and gave moral meaning and significance to the events it related.[101]

In recent years, it has become fashionable to decry the historical analysis of policymakers who fail to learn adequately from the mistakes of the past.[102] Analogies often do not fit; principles may be misapplied. On the public platform in the mid-nineteenth century, history was used quite differently. It spoke directly to the present, it exerted force and influence, it made judgments, and it ultimately grounded one's vision of morality in public affairs.

6

The Moral Argument

A contemporary reader, recognizing that slavery was ultimately a moral issue and expecting to find the moral question thoroughly discussed in the Lincoln-Douglas debates, would be both disappointed and puzzled. There are few points at which the two candidates discussed the moral question, and even on those occasions their underlying notions of morality were not so much competing as incommensurable. The puzzle is greater because it was quite common during the pre–Civil War period for issues of public policy to be cast in moral terms. The Jacksonian crusade against the Bank of the United States and the expansionism of the 1840s were presented as moral struggles. And it was the moral issue that made the extension of slavery to new territories so controversial since one cannot oppose the spread of an evil without acknowledging it to be an evil.[1] Surveying these and other examples, Wright has concluded that the "special and peculiar quality" of American politics has been "a tendency to state questions and issues in terms of right and wrong—to endow them with a moral quality."[2] This tendency has the effect of setting issues in a broader context and increasing their significance. It raises the stakes of victory or defeat and helps rally the faithful.

Why, then, did Lincoln and Douglas not approach the moral issue head-on? Such a course might have left little room for the development of argument beyond asserting the rightness of one's own position and the error of the opponent's. More important, there was not a single moral argument, and the texture of the discussion was richer and deeper than one might at first suppose. Lincoln and Douglas had different moral hierarchies, and the debates were a search for grounds for choice between them.

I

For Douglas, morality lay in neither slavery nor abolition but in the procedure of local self-government—what he meant by popular sovereignty. This does not mean that he was an apologist for slavery. In a private conversation he had called it a "curse beyond computation"—though, in fairness, less because of its inherent evil than because of its disruptive effect on national politics.[3] He declined the opportunity to inherit slaves from his father-in-law, causing the inheritance to be passed solely through his wife. But he did not regard slavery as a public moral issue, and he did not believe that policy decisions should be based on whether slavery was right or wrong.

As his biographer has expressed it, slavery as a moral question "had no practical value within the framework of American politics; indeed, it was a question fraught with danger to the very existence of the Union."[4] Both parts of the statement are important. Douglas approached the slavery issue in a pragmatic, almost opportunistic way. If slavery produced material well-being, it was satisfactory; if it drained the economy, he was opposed. When Lincoln cited the Northwest Ordinance as evidence of moral sanction against slavery, Douglas responded that the institution was introduced to Illinois anyway. As he said in the Alton debate, "We in Illinois . . . tried slavery, kept it up for 12 years, and finding that it was not profitable we abolished it for that reason, and became a free state."[5] When Lincoln cited prohibition of the African slave trade as evidence of moral condemnation, Douglas answered that this prohibition had been merely a pragmatic compromise by the Constitutional Convention to hold the Union together, not an expression of moral principle.[6]

The incumbent consistently underestimated the moral significance of the issue, whether in failing to appreciate the extent of Northern opposition to the Kansas-Nebraska Act or in failing to recognize the growing sense of outrage on the part of the Northern moderates. His fundamental error, Wells has theorized, "lay not so much in appearing indifferent toward the future course of slavery, but in failing to realize how his country would react once its conscience was aroused."[7]

But, if Douglas neglected the moral dimension of slavery, it was because he fixed his gaze on his own key moral principle: popular self-government. This was not just a procedural matter but the prerequisite for preserving and expanding the Union, more important to Douglas than slavery or any other domestic issue. Rebuking Chicago clergymen who in 1854 had opposed the Kansas-Nebraska Act, he had written, "The sovereign right of the people to manage their own affairs in conformity with the Constitution of their own making, recedes and disappears, when placed in subordination to the authority of a body of men, claiming, by virtue of their offices as ministers, to be a divinely-appointed institution for the declaration and enforcement of God's will on earth."[8] Of course, if men of God had no special insight into morality that might supersede the will of the people, so much less would the statesman, politician, or reformer. Douglas opposed all "who on their assumption of superior moral rectitude and judgment were bent on removing motes from the eyes of their brothers."[9] Against all such intolerance, Douglas championed the right of a community to regulate its own affairs. This principle was an outgrowth of commitments to democratic decision making and particularly to states' rights; as Jaffa explained, by "seizing upon the old and deep connection of the idea of morality with the idea of local self-government," Douglas might be able "to neutralize, if not to defeat, the moral fervor of the anti-slavery crusade."[10] Douglas found the moral authority for his principle in the second chapter of Genesis, where God set good and evil before man "and empowered him and his descendants in all time to choose their own form of government, and to bear the evils and enjoy the blessings of their own deeds."[11]

Like any procedural issue, Douglas's was preemptive; it subsumed the moral aspect of slavery by focusing on who had the right to determine whether it was moral. To Douglas, that right lay with the inhabitants of a state or territory, who, after all, would have to live with the results of their decision. As Jaffa characterizes this position, "The political judgment of popular majorities need not be controlled by any moral law 'higher' than the procedural basis of majority rules as embodied in such a document as the Constitution." Douglas himself had written to the Chicago clergymen that the principle of popular sovereignty was unaffected by the fact "that human slavery is, in your opinion, a great moral wrong." He explained that states and territories were called on to decide other issues of moral wrong for themselves, and he assumed that this case was no different.[12] The most grievous moral transgression was to enforce uniformity on the states and territories. Doing that was wrong, both because it trampled on the principle of local self-determination and because it kept the slavery issue at the forefront of controversy rather than banishing it from the federal government's purview. Jaffa aptly characterizes Douglas's view:

In short, the movements against slavery, against expansion, against foreigners were all movements for British interests and for those Americans who conceived their own interests in kinship to England's. The high moral tone which permeated all three was nothing but snobbishness. The crocodile tears that were shed for the Negro were only pretexts for destroying the constitutional equality of the states, that equality which alone guaranteed that a large republic could remain a free republic; and which, hence, alone permitted the extension of our boundaries as far as the fulfillment of our republican mission to the world might require.[13]

If local self-government meant anything, it meant that those not affected directly by a decision had no business expressing themselves or trying to influence that decision. When Douglas said that he "don't care" about slavery, he meant not that he was personally indifferent but that federal policy should be officially indifferent since the federal government had no proper jurisdiction over the matter. Even a person opposed to slavery might accept Douglas's procedural morality since it rested on the commonly understood theory of dual citizenship. One was a citizen both of a state and of the United States, but neither automatically entailed the other. Therefore, as Brock explains, "As citizens of the United States they could discuss and ask for decisions on all questions that came under the authority of Congress, but as citizens of a state they had no right to discuss the domestic affairs of a sister state. Even if it were right to discuss the morality of slavery as an abstract proposition, it would be wrong to condemn others for thinking differently."[14] Douglas's moral position, then, was a rule for assigning jurisdiction over the issue.

This orientation shaped Douglas's moral argument in the debates. At Ottawa, he explained the need for diversity among the states and the dangers of uniformity with the previously cited contrast between "the granite hills of New Hampshire" and "the rice plantations of South Carolina." This statement not only proved the wisdom of the Founders but asserted a great principle: the public forum should be neutral. Douglas's statements mixed the prevalent anti-Negro sentiment of the time with concern for the well-being of the slave. In the Ottawa debate, he proclaimed, "I am opposed to negro citizenship in any and every form. I believe this government was made on the white basis. I believe it was made by white men, for the benefit of white men and their posterity for ever." But, immediately after this acknowledgement of the inherent inferiority of the Negro—a view widely shared by his listeners—he added, "I do not hold that because the negro is our inferior that therefore he ought to be a slave. . . . On the contrary, I hold that humanity and Christianity both require that the negro shall have and enjoy every right, every privilege, and every immunity consistent with the safety of the society in which he lives."[15] The juxtaposition of these two statements made clear that Douglas's concern was not with slavery per se; he neither endorsed nor denounced the peculiar institution. His interest was jurisdictional or procedural. The key question was what rights, privileges, and immunities were compatible with the public good, and that question could best be answered by the inhabitants of each territory or state. Some might make the Negro a slave; some might make him a citizen; and some, like the state of Illinois, might follow a middle course. Immorality consisted in imposing uniformity among the states and territories, denying each the right to decide its domestic institutions according to its own lights.

In the Jonesboro debate, Douglas took up the same theme, allying his own view with that which he attributed to George Washington. The first president

did not believe, nor did his compatriots, that the local laws and domestic institutions that were well adapted to the green mountains of Vermont were suited to the rice plantations of South Carolina; they did not believe at that day that in a republic so broad and expanded as this, containing such a variety of climate, soil and interest, that uniformity in the local laws and domestic institutions were either desirable or possible. They believed then as our experience has proved to us now, that each locality, having different interests, a different climate and different surroundings, required different local laws.[16]

The difficulty with his opponent's position, as has been noted, was that it tended toward such enforced uniformity, which was a moral as well as a legal error.

Finally, in the Alton debate, the incumbent drew together his position into a succinct statement: "If the people of any other territory desire slavery let them have it. If they do not want it let them prohibit it. It is their business not mine." In his closing speech, Douglas made his hierarchy of values even clearer:

I look forward to a time when each state shall be allowed to do as it pleases. If it chooses to keep slavery forever, it is not my business, but its own; if it chooses to abolish slavery, it is its own business—not mine. I care more for the great principle of self-government, the right of the people to rule, than I do for all the negros in Christendom.

Lest anyone miss the point, Douglas repeated himself: "I would not endanger the perpetuity of this Union. I would not blot out the great inalienable rights of the white men for all the negroes that ever existed."[17]

Douglas's emphasis on procedural rather than substantive morality reflected, no doubt, his own sincere conviction. But it was also a strategically useful rhetorical stance. Douglas was convinced that moral questions could not be settled within the realm of practical politics because their injection raised the argument to such a level of abstraction that competing beliefs became intractable and compromise impossible. Such a chain of events would threaten the destruction of the Union, the preservation of which was his highest political objective. In his view, preserving the Union required preserving the Democratic party, which by the late 1850s was the single remaining national political institution. That, in turn, required the continued allegiance of the South, and Douglas was convinced, reasonably so, that the slaveholding states "would not countenance any step of national policy premised on the sinfulness of slavery."[18] For the South, the struggle was less over the desire actually to take slaves to Kansas than over the need to avoid the stigma and public humiliation implied by a national judgment of the immorality of their domestic institutions. If anything in the Compromise of 1850 particularly satisfied the proslavery forces, it was the fact that there was no express or implied denunciation of slavery.[19]

Consequently, Douglas must have reasoned, if he could keep the moral issue off the agenda, the bond between Southern and Northern Democrats would not be shattered. The Democratic party would be held together as a national political instrument, and that would assure the preservation of the Union. Douglas's best hope for keeping the morality of slavery off the agenda was to do precisely what he did— proclaim that he "don't care" about the substantive outcome so long as the right procedure was used. By transforming this defensive stance into an argument for diversity and not uniformity, Douglas took a far more constructive and appealing position, challenging the use of one set of moral categories by drawing on another of a very different kind.

II

Douglas's position has not fared well at the bar of history. Yet, as Jaffa points out, there is an unfairness to some of the criticism. To denounce the Little Giant's view of morality, he has written, one must show, "first that it was wrong to subordinate the slavery issue, upon which North and South could not agree, to an aim and purpose upon which they could agree; and, second, that the aim upon which sectional agreement and subordination of slavery was pitched was itself immoral."[20] Douglas's goals were objectives for which most Americans strove, and his line of reasoning was not implausible, provided that one believes that in 1858 it was still possible to subordinate slavery to any other issue.

Certainly, the Republicans did not observe Jaffa's strictures. From their vantage point, the critique of Douglas began with the premise that slavery was morally wrong and the conviction that the essence of the incumbent's system was an attempt to legitimize a moral wrong. On the Senate floor, James Harlan of Iowa proclaimed, "No vote, either by large or small communities, can make slavery right or wrong. If slavery is in itself wrong . . . no number of votes can ever make it good, because its rightfulness or wrongfulness depends on an original principle. . . If slavery is right, no people have a right to annihilate it by a vote; if it is wrong, it cannot be made right by a vote."[21] Anderson recently has contended that the right to do wrong is exactly what the Constitution guaranteed "by defining liberty only as the absence of restraint, and by introducing no test of right and wrong other than a consensual one: right and wrong would be measured by the political strength of contending forces."[22] But common sense would regard "the right to do wrong" as paradoxical if not absurd, and Republicans in 1858 appealed to this level of public understanding. The only way to resolve the paradox was to conclude that Douglas did not think slavery morally wrong. And if he did not think it wrong, then he must find it right. Identifying the Little Giant with this cluster of values would enable Republicans to blunt the incumbent's attempt to rank procedural above substantive morality.

The linchpin of the Republican attack was Douglas's statement that he "don't care" whether slavery was voted down or up. The line came from Douglas's Senate speech of December 8, 1857, in which he announced his opposition to the Lecompton constitution. "If Kansas wants a slave-State constitution she has a right to it, if she wants a free-state constitution she has a right to it," the Illinois Senator had declared. "It is none of my business which way the slavery clause is decided. I don't care whether it is voted down or voted up."[23] As Fehrenbacher has noted, Republicans lifted the "don't care" phrase out of context. Douglas was referring specifically to the slavery clause in the Lecompton constitution and explaining that his opposition to the document was not confined to that one clause. He opposed Lecompton because it did not fairly represent the will of the people, and that would be true whether the slavery clause were voted down or up. "Nevertheless," Fehrenbacher surmises, "Lincoln believed that the phrase was an accurate summary of popular sovereignty."[24] It certainly allowed Republicans to excoriate their opponent for his moral indifference.

Lincoln denied that slavery was a trivial issue. Shortly before the debates, Lovejoy had written him, "I think you said the whole in a word when you said that the mistake of Judge D. was that he made slavery a *little* thing when it was a great thing."[25] In the debates, the challenger hammered at the similarity that Douglas assumed between slavery and other domestic institutions. If slavery were like any other economic interest, why would it alone produce such an uproar? In his Chicago speech on July 10, 1858, Lincoln answered that question by reference to the power of public opinion. Vast numbers of people, he said, do not see slavery as being "only equal to the question of the cranberry laws of Indiana," devoid of moral significance.[26] That being the case, he ridiculed Douglas's attempt to thwart public discussion of the moral issue by making "the ignoring of principled differences itself a principle," in Jaffa's phrase. In the Alton debate, he taunted him for "false statesmanship that undertakes to build up a system of policy upon the basis of caring nothing about *the very thing that every body does care the most about.*"[27] Douglas's refusal to engage the moral argument would itself be an argument against him; he was not only wrong on principle but personally at fault.

Referring to Douglas's "don't care" position, Lincoln suggested that it was not truly neutral. He observed, "Any man can say that who does not see anything wrong in slavery, but no man can logically say it who does see a wrong in it; because no man can logically say he don't care whether a wrong is voted up or voted down. He may say he don't care whether an indifferent thing is voted up or down, but he must logically have a choice between a right thing and a wrong thing."[28] The last sentence is crucial. Douglas's posture was one of indifference to the morality of slavery, but Lincoln was arguing that on matters of right and wrong there is no middle ground. Not to condemn slavery as wrong necessarily meant that it was condoned as right. If one regarded it as right, then there was no reason to suppose it might not go on indefinitely. Lincoln tried to push Douglas to that position, knowing that the Old Line Whigs, however much they might hate abolition, started with the fundamental premise that slavery was wrong and would disappear in God's good time.

Not only would Douglas's moral indifference permit slavery to continue; it would enable it to spread. For if there is no evil in slavery, then why not allow the slaveowner to take and hold his property in whatever territory *or state* he chose? How could the Northern states justify outlawing slavery if there were no compelling moral interest to offset the right to property enumerated in the federal Constitution. Lincoln's principal charge, in Richard Weaver's view, was "that his opponents, by straddling issues and through deviousness, were breaking down the essential definition of man." In a speech shortly after the debates, Lincoln developed a sequence of events to explain that the natural consequence of Douglas's moral neutrality was the nationalization of slavery.[29]

Lincoln was quite specific about the causal chain. Douglas's proclamation that public policy should be indifferent to the morality of slavery would lead individuals to conclude that they had no basis to oppose slavery as a matter of personal moral judgment. By narcotizing public opinion, Douglas was effectively removing the only obstacle to the spread of slavery across the land. In a speech in Chicago in 1856, Lincoln had previewed this line of argument:

Our government rests in public opinion. Whoever can change public opinion can change the government, practically just so much. Public opinion, or [on?] any subject, always has a "*central idea*," from which all its minor thoughts radiate. That "central idea" in our political public opinion, at the beginning was, and until recently has continued to be, "the equality of men."[30]

It was Douglas who was crucial to the erosion of that "central idea" by denying the primarily moral aspect of the slavery question. That denial would create the moral climate in which a future Supreme Court might entertain such a travesty as a second *Dred Scott* decision denying a state the power to outlaw slavery. In the Galesburg debate, Lincoln specifically charged that his opponent "is also preparing (whether purposely or not), the way for making the institution of slavery national!" He went on to explain, "for I wish no misunderstanding, that I do not charge that he means it so; but I call upon your minds to inquire, if you were going to get the best instrument you could, and then set it to work in the most ingenious way, to prepare the public mind for this movement, operating in the free states, where there is now an abhorrence of the institution of slavery, could you find an instrument so capable of doing it as Judge Douglas? or one employed in so apt a way to do it?"[31]

In the debates, Lincoln left this argument with a rhetorical question; the next year, he proceeded to answer it. In notes for speeches on his Ohio tour, he wrote that Douglas's chief effect had been to change the prevailing moral tone since those who accept his position are also influenced by his reasoning and sentiments: "The reasoning and sentiments advanced by Douglas in support of his policy as to slavery all spring from the view that slavery is not *wrong*." He concluded that, if the free-state people were to adopt those sentiments, they then would see no reason to prohibit slavery in their own states.[32] This line of reasoning enabled Lincoln, far more persuasively, to round out the argument that began with the "frame house" analogy, suggesting that Douglas, Pierce, Taney, and Buchanan had conspired to bring about a second *Dred Scott* decision.

In attacking Douglas for moral indifference, Lincoln and the Republicans had hit a sensitive nerve. They had presented a value that arguably transcended the Little Giant's concern for procedure. As Johannsen has explained, by opposing consideration of the moral dimension Douglas "sowed the seeds of his own political repudiation, for he satisfied neither those who regarded slavery as immoral and desired its restriction nor those who looked on slavery as a good and sought to guarantee its expansion."[33] Certainly a lasting influence of the debates was to make clear that, while both men sought strenuously to preserve the Union, their fundamental disagreement was over the morality of slavery and their divergent policy recommendations followed from that difference. For his part, Lincoln continued to stress this difference, writing in notes for his 1859 Ohio speeches that Douglas's concealed basic assumption was "that slavery is a little, harmless, indifferent thing, having no wrong in it, and no power for mischief about it." He added that Douglas's policy might be appropriate if all viewed slavery in this light, but reassured himself that "neither all, nor half the world, so look upon it."[34]

III

Just as Douglas had an interest in preventing discussion of the morality of slavery, Lincoln had an interest in promoting it—so long as he was careful not to present himself to the voters of central Illinois as a radical abolitionist.

Lincoln's was a morality of natural rights that overpowered questions of procedure. His sense of human rights was not fully developed in his speeches and is sometimes ambiguous, but there is little doubt that he regarded the moral dimension of slavery as the most fundamental. In his 1854 Peoria speech, he grounded his opposition to the Kansas-Nebraska Act in the fact that "it assumes that there CAN be MORAL RIGHT in the enslaving of one man by another . . . —a sad evidence that, feeling prosperity we forget right—that liberty, as a principle, we have ceased to revere." Midway through the 1858 debates, he spoke at Edwardsville and prefigured his peroration at Alton by stating that the leading difference between the parties was in whether they considered slavery wrong and that "the action of each, as respects the growth of the country and the expansion of our population, is squared to meet these views."[35]

Natural rights, by this view, were the cornerstone of the political system. Hence, Lincoln, while generally supporting the same principle of local self-government that Douglas championed, made an exception in the case of slavery. Foner explains that, "because of its essential immorality, it tainted the entire nation," and therefore its treatment was properly a matter for national and not merely local concern.[36] Lincoln himself had written his friend Joshua Speed in 1855 that it was untrue "that I have no interest in a thing which has, and continually exercises, the power of making me miserable." If northerners refrained from giving voice to their moral concerns, that was because they "do crucify their feelings, in order to maintain their loyalty to the constitution and the Union."[37] Like Douglas, Lincoln thought in terms of biblical analogies. Jaffa explains that men under free government lived like man in the Garden of Eden; freedom was contingent on denying oneself the forbidden fruit. This awareness of human limits, of what man is commanded not to do, was what made democracy work toward justice.[38] To condone slavery was to taste the forbidden fruit of despotism and to blind man to his own limits.

Lincoln denied that slaves were property in order to deny that the constitutional protections of property rights were dispositive of the moral question. In his 1854 Springfield and Peoria speeches, he alleged that not even in the South were slaves treated like hogs or horses, citing as evidence Southern support for making the African slave trade a capital crime, Southern shirking from the presence of the slave dealer, and the very existence of free blacks. Moreover, Fehrenbacher has noted, criminal law held the slave fully responsible for his own actions, and, for that matter, "the principal moral justification for slavery—that it lifted savages up toward civilization and heathens up to Christianity—certainly contemplated slaves as men."[39]

If slaves are human, then, whatever other rights they may have, they share at some fundamental level in whatever it is that makes men human, and that is the level that enables one to say that "all men are created equal." Sometimes Lincoln articulated what this view implied as a political principle, as when he stated at Peoria in 1854 that the essence of self-government was "that no man is good enough to govern another man, *without that other's consent.*" Sometimes he developed the less radical economic implication "that whatever any one man earns with his hands and by the sweat of his brow, he shall enjoy in peace."[40] There is considerable difference between these two statements; one seems to imply political equality and the other nothing beyond the end of slavery. This difference illustrates the difficulty of fully comprehending Lincoln's views of human rights. But there is a basic similarity between them. Whether in a political or an economic sense, both hold that there is a natural right to improve one's own condition. In nineteenth-century parlance, this was referred to as "the right to rise," and the immorality of slavery lay in the fact that it denied that right.

In a speech in Kalamazoo, Michigan, in 1856, Lincoln celebrated America as "the wonder and admiration of the whole world" and inquired "what it is that has given us so much prosperity, and we shall understand that to give up that one thing, would be to give up all future prosperity. This cause," he concluded, "is that every man can make himself." Morality and economics were fused; the Jeffersonian ideal of equality became equality of opportunity to get ahead in life.[41] But slavery violated this right by permanently consigning the slave to a dependent status. When southerners argued that the slave was better cared for than was the hired laborer in the North, Lincoln pointed to the fallacy in the argument: it assumed that the laborer would always remain a hired laborer, whereas in fact, "the general rule is otherwise. . . . the poor, honest, industrious, and resolute man raises himself, that he may work on his own account, and hire somebody else." That progress, Lincoln went on, "is that improvement in condition that is intended to be secured by those institutions under which we live, is the great principle for which this government was really formed."[42] Moreover, denial of this right to blacks would effectively jeopardize it for whites as well, as Lincoln eloquently argued. Speaking at Edwardsville in September 1858, he warned, "Destroy this spirit [the love of liberty], and you have planted the seeds of despotism around your own doors. Familiarize yourself with the chains of bondage, and you are preparing your own limbs to wear them. Accustomed to trample on the rights of those around you, you have lost the genius of your own independence, and become the fit subjects of the first cunning tyrant who rises." The next year, he wrote Henry L. Pierce and others, "This is a world of compensations; and he who would *be* no slave, must consent to *have* no slave. Those who deny freedom to others, deserve it not for themselves."[43]

The only protection of fundamental liberties for whites, then, lay in recognizing that these liberties derived from their status as human beings and hence were shared by all other people, including blacks. But slavery denied the rights of man and, in this very fundamental sense, threatened the entire edifice of natural rights. Perhaps because of the fundamental nature of the threat, Lincoln, like other Republicans, sometimes took on a prophetic tone and suggested that slavery violated the will of God. When quarreling with proslavery theologians, he was more restrained, indicating, for example, in notes made after the Charleston debate, "Certainly there is no contending against the Will of God; but still there is some difficulty in ascertaining, and applying it, to particular cases." He further mused that "slavery is strikingly peculiar in this, that it is the only good thing which no man ever seeks the good of, *for himself*." But he was far more forthright in his Chicago speech in July. He quoted the biblical maxim, "As your Father in Heaven is perfect, be ye also perfect," and added that Jesus had set the admonition up as a standard to be "as nearly reached as we can." At least one correspondent applauded Lincoln's high moral tone, noting, "As I view the contest (tho we say it is between Douglas & Lincoln) it is no less than a contest for the advancement of the kingdom of Heaven or the kingdom of Satan."[44]

Lincoln's position on the morality of slavery developed in the years after 1854. Though always convinced that slavery was an evil, he felt no compulsion to act against the institution until after the passage of the Kansas-Nebraska Act. The Springfield and Peoria speeches of 1854 are the first in which he criticized slavery on moral grounds. The 1858 debates reveal a curious pattern. Although he had referred to the issue in speeches in Chicago in July, Lewistown in August, and Edwardsville in September, he made almost no mention of it in any of the first four debates. The only exception was in his conclusion in the Ottawa debate, where he referred to Henry Clay's address to the American Colonization Society, suggesting that one who would repress all tendencies toward ultimate emancipation "must blow out the moral lights around us."[45] Although this passage prefigures Lincoln's later moral argument, in its context it aims as much to put Douglas at odds with Clay, Lincoln's "beau ideal of a statesman," as it does to develop the argument in its own right.

Fuller development of Lincoln's view awaited the fifth debate, at Galesburg. At Charleston, he had publicly proclaimed his belief in Negro inferiority and his opposition to Negro citizenship. Those sentiments may have helped counter a perception among old Whigs that he was really an abolitionist, but they dismayed more antislavery Republicans in places such as Knox County, where the fifth debate was held. There Lincoln was able, in Rietveld's phrase, "to appeal to the 'Christian consciences' of Whig-Americans, as well as Republicans and Democrats."[46]

After protesting that he, just like Douglas, opposed making "odious distinctions" between free and slave states, Lincoln went on to identify the true difference between Douglas and the Republicans:

The Judge is not in favor of making any difference between slavery and liberty . . . and consequently every sentiment he utters discards the idea that there is any wrong in slavery. Everything that emanates from him or his coadjutors in their course of policy, carefully excludes the thought that there is anything wrong in slavery. All their arguments, if you will consider them, will be seen to exclude the thought that there is anything whatever wrong in slavery.

At this point the argument is incomplete. It does not lay out a Republican position on the moral issue but merely notes the omission of the moral consideration from Douglas's argument. Lincoln then advances the view that the "don't care" position of the incumbent depends on the assumption that there is nothing wrong in slavery, for, as Lincoln put it, Douglas "cannot logically say that anybody has a right to do wrong." Only if slavery is not wrong can slaves be viewed as equal to "horses and every other sort of property."[47]

Douglas passed over this line of reasoning in his Galesburg rejoinder, so Lincoln returned to the same theme in his opening speech at Quincy. Acknowledging Douglas as "the leading man" of the Democratic party, Lincoln credited him with "the high distinction, so far as I know, of never having said slavery is either right or wrong." He described the Democratic policy as "a careful, studied exclusion of the idea that there is any-thing wrong in slavery."[48] Perhaps angered by the accusation of moral callousness, Douglas returned to the defense of the Founding Fathers, declaring that "this republic can exist forever divided into free and slave states, as our fathers made it and the people of each state have decided." That gave Lincoln the opening to advance the argument in his rejoinder, when he gave to the incumbent "my profound thanks for his public an-nunciation here to-day, to be put on record, that his system of policy in regard to the institution of slavery *contemplates that it shall last forever.* " Even the conservative old Whigs generally shared Clay's belief that slavery must someday end, and that conviction resulted from a least a general feeling that there was something wrong in slavery. But Douglas's prediction that slavery could last forever made sense only if one assumed that there was no wrong in it. With good reason, Lincoln could gloat, "We are getting a little nearer the true issue of this controversy, and I am profoundly grateful for this one sentence."[49]

The argument was then fully developed at Alton, but only in Lin-coln's reply. After insisting that Douglas's charges that his challenger favored racial equality or wished to make war on the slave states were false issues, he stated directly;

The real issue in this controversy—the one pressing upon every mind—is the sentiment on the part of one class that looks upon the institution of slavery *as a wrong*, and of another class that *does not* look upon it as a wrong. The sentiment that contemplates the institution of slavery in this country as a wrong is the senti-ment of the Republican party.

Recognizing all the difficulties posed by the actual existence of slavery and its protection in the Constitution, still the Republicans proposed to treat the issue on the basis that it *was* a wrong by containing it and there-by convincing the public that it eventually must end. On the other hand, the Democrats did not propose to treat slavery as a wrong—either be-cause they believed it to be right or because, like Douglas, they were indifferent to whether it was right or wrong. Lincoln repeated his claim that "the Democratic policy in regard to that institution will not tolerate the merest breath, the slightest hint, of the least degree of wrong about it" and again went through his analysis of how the "don't care" position required excluding the belief that slavery was wrong since, "if it is wrong, he cannot say people have a right to do wrong."[50]

Then Lincoln came to his climax, to the passage that—though atypical of the debates as a whole—is often quoted as evidence of their eloquence:

That is the real issue. That is the issue that will continue in this country when these poor tongues of Judge Douglas and myself shall be silent. It is the eternal struggle between these two principles—right and wrong—throughout the world. They are the two principles that have stood face to face from the beginning of time, and will ever continue to struggle. The one is the common right of humanity and the other the divine right of kings.

As he had done at Quincy, Lincoln thanked his opponent for acknowledging *"that he looks to no end of the institution of slavery. That will help the people to see where the struggle really is. It will hereafter place with us all men who really do wish the wrong may have an end."*[51]

Interestingly, in the "these poor tongues" passage Lincoln redefined the alternatives to exclude the very position that Douglas defended. Lincoln alleged that the contest was between those who think slavery right and those who think it wrong. But Douglas's position, as Lincoln had just acknowledged, was that he was indifferent to whether it was right or wrong. Indifference had been assimilated to a positive defense of slavery so that Douglas could be portrayed as akin to Southern defenders of the institution and Lincoln could bid for the support of all who harbored the belief that there was any evil in the peculiar institution.

IV

Like Douglas, Lincoln sincerely believed in the moral position he espoused; like him as well, there was strategic gain in introducing the morality of slavery into the discussion. It served to distinguish between two candidates whose views otherwise were quite similar. As Thomas summarizes the likenesses, "Neither man favored Negro equality, though Lincoln was more liberal, as well as more uncertain, than Douglas on this point. Both deplored sectionalism. Both wanted to quiet the slavery agitation. Neither wished to see slavery extended. Both desired fervently to preserve the Union of the states."[52] But, if the two were basically alike, why should a voter prefer the relatively untried and inexperienced Lincoln over the powerful incumbent, chairman of the Senate Committee on Territories and leading aspirant for the 1860 Democratic presidential nomination?

This was a crucial problem for Illinois Republicans. Since Douglas had broken with the Buchanan administration over the Lecompton constitution, he had become attractive to antislavery elements who believed that, whatever the senator might say publicly, the practical effect of popular sovereignty would be to make all new territories free. Indeed, some prominent Eastern Republicans, such as Horace Greeley, were encouraging *their* party to nominate the Little Giant as a fusion candidate. Fehrenbacher describes the possibility that all or part of the

Republican party "might become a tail fastened to the Douglas kite" as "a real and imminent danger" in 1858 because the Lecompton dispute had softened the hostility of many antislavery leaders to popular sovereignty in principle.[53]

Lincoln thought such a course disastrous for his party, his personal fortunes, and the antislavery cause. His objective, therefore, must be to drive a wedge between the Republicans and Douglas, preventing rapprochement. Yet he could not do so by supporting radical abolition doctrine, so he must try to push Douglas to the other extreme and portray him as an apologist for the spread of slavery. He could not distinguish himself from the Little Giant on the territorial question alone, for—in the aftermath of Lecompton—the differences between the two on that matter were slight. In Fehrenbacher's analysis, as the debates proceeded, Lincoln recognized that "a much sharper distinction could be drawn if the discussions were shifted to the more expansive domain of moral principles."[54] Even though both candidates were men of the center and favored policy positions that were essentially similar, at the level of moral principle the difference between them was vast.

Although there was benefit to Lincoln in raising the moral issue, there were risks as well, which required that he be exceedingly careful in how the argument was drawn. Chief among these constraints were the racial attitudes of Illinoisans, which by late-twentieth-century standards must be deemed racist. There were pockets of abolitionist support, and mild sympathy for the Negro, in some of the northern counties, but hostility in the south. As Mayer explains, the crucial middle counties "had drawn numerous settlers from Kentucky and Tennessee, who, like most Southern whites, took the inferiority of blacks for granted and enthusiastically supported the policy of excluding the Negro from Illinois," whether free or slave.[55] Lincoln himself had acknowledged, in his 1854 Peoria speech, that the reason that slavery in the territories was a national issue and not just the concern of settlers who go there was that the territories were wanted "for the homes of free white people. This they cannot be, to any considerable extent, if slavery shall be planted within them."[56] The possibility that free *blacks* might move to the territories appears not to have been considered. In particular, the Old Line Whigs resented the moralizing of the abolitionists. Recognizing this vulnerability, and seeking as well to exploit the reaction to the "House Divided" speech, the Democratic press spread the message that—whatever Lincoln's own protestations might be—his election would symbolize to the nation a declaration that Illinois favored political equality between the races. In July, the *Illinois State Register* accused him of playing "'fast and loose'" and admonished, "It will not do to lay down texts for abolition support, and then attempt to evade the force of his premises by vague conclusions, to be adapted to different localities." By October, the *Chicago Times* was more trenchant: "In case Lincoln was elected Senator, Illinois would at once, and by irresistible unanimity, become known, all the world over, as a State in favor of placing Negroes upon an equality with her white people."[57] The "House Divided" speech already had given cause for concern; surely Lincoln must do nothing more to abet the perception of himself as an abolitionist. His stance on the morality of slavery, therefore, must clearly avoid supporting abolition.

Another constraint on Lincoln's moral advocacy was his own view of compromise. He believed moderation to be a virtue in itself and shied away from confrontation. Randall has characterized Lincoln as a liberal because of his regard for the established order and his commitment to gradualism, and commitment that he could sustain because he "believed in and expected human betterment. . . . he had confidence that reasonable change would come."[58] There were many precedents in his earlier life for his commitment to compromise as a principle in its own right. His 1837 protest in the Illinois legislature against an antiabolition petition has been described by Strozier as "gentle": it was "clear, even courageous, in statement of essential moral purpose but moderate in dealing with political realities." Jaffa has extensively analyzed Lincoln's 1842 temperance speech, which reflects his conviction that political moderation is itself a virtue. During his time in the House of Representatives, Lincoln spoke on internal improvements, saying, "There are few things *wholly* evil or *wholly* good. Almost every thing, especially of government policy, is an inseparable compound of the two."[59]

Undoubtedly, then, Lincoln and his supporters resented Douglas's efforts to label him an abolitionist. In July, the *Illinois State Journal* lectured its readers, "There is a vast an[d] illimitable difference between Abolitionism and Republicanism," but noted that "misapplication of the word 'abolitionist' has lost its power and sting. The people know better, and despise the meanness which uses it."[60] This last statement may have reflected wishful thinking.

Both because of the racial attitudes of the state and because of his own instinct for moderation, Lincoln had to be cautious in defining a moral stance. His supporters urged him explicitly to disavow Negro equality. For example, his friend David Davis wrote on August 3, "All the orators should distinctly & emphatically disavow *negro suffrage*, negro holding office, serving on juries, & the like." He added, "For God's sake don't let Lovejoy go into Tazewell"—although Lovejoy wrote Lincoln the next day, "I believe that the bugaboo of Negro Equality has pretty much lost its power." Another correspondent urged that more use be made of the

Declaration of Independence but took pains to note that commitment to the Declaration did not imply negro equality.[61]

Lincoln accepted this advice. He disavowed racial equality and even opposed citizenship for the Negro, even though most of his arguments for emancipation served equally as arguments for citizenship. He managed, however, to distinguish between the rights of a man and those of a citizen. In speeches at Augusta, Macomb, and Greenville during August and September, he denied that he favored abolition or amalgamation. Much to the embarrassment of his twentieth-century admirers, Lincoln's statements on this point were put most starkly during the Charleston debate. Using as his pretext a question asked at his hotel by an elderly gentleman, he said:

I will say then that I am not, nor ever have been in favor of bringing about in any way the social and political equality of the white and black races,—that I am not nor ever have been in favor of making voters or jurors of negroes, nor of qualifying them to hold office, nor to intermarry with white people; and I will say in addition to this that there is a physical difference between the white and black races which I believe will for ever forbid the two races living together on terms of social and political equality. And inasmuch as they cannot so live, while they do remain together there must be the position of superior and inferior, and I as much as any other man am in favor of having the superior position assigned to the white race.[62]

He went on to say that just because he did not want a woman for a slave did not mean he must take her for a wife; he could just leave her alone. Leaving the blacks alone was what Lincoln's position amounted to; he was prepared to extend blacks no civil or political rights beyond freedom itself.

This was the smallest possible departure from a position condoning slavery. It stopped short of any practical program—whether compensated emancipation, colonization, or whatever—that might hasten the demise of slavery. As Wells characterizes it, Lincoln "expressed and focused the latent discontent of thoughtful, reasonable men, without ever explicitly prescribing a radical cure for the ills of conscience."[63] This reticence reflected both the political situation and the likelihood that the Republicans genuinely did not know what to do about the larger issue of race adjustment. A year after the debates, Lincoln's law partner, William H. Herndon, wrote that "my *Colored brethren* are asking 'What are you going—you white folks to do with the darky?'; and . . . I must confess that I can't answer the poor Sambo's simple question."[64]

Lincoln limited himself not only in the ends he pursued but also in the geographic scope of their application. He did not attack slavery where it existed but developed his moral position only to combat its possible extension. He also occasionally argued, as in the 1854 Peoria speech cited above, that slaves should be kept out of the territories so that white people could go there since exercising the right to rise requires room, but he did not feature this argument as prominently as did other Republicans who wanted to divert attention from the moral issue. Only once during the debates, at Alton, did he argue that blacks should be kept out of the territories for reasons of political economy.[65]

A final constraint on Lincoln was the obvious fact that the moral aspect of slavery was not the only value in his hierarchy. He gave special weight to the sanctity of the Constitution and the preservation of the Union. As he saw it, the actual presence of slavery in the land limited the reformer's options. When, at Galesburg, he previewed the moral argument, he was careful to note his "due regard for its actual existence amongst us and the difficulties of getting rid of it in any satisfactory way, and to all the constitutional obligations which have been thrown about it." At Alton, he drew the analogy between the Union afflicted with slavery and a person suffering from cancer: "You may have a wen or a cancer upon your person and not be able to cut it out lest you bleed to death; but surely it is no way to cure it, to engraft it and spread it over your whole body."[66]

These constraints on Lincoln's advocacy created a paradox of rhetorical strategy. Lincoln's moral beliefs, derived from a theory of natural rights, seemed to be absolute, but the actions he supported were limited and gradual. His arguments seemed to call for abolition if not social and political equality, yet the measure he defended was more limited: containment of slavery where it already existed, opposing its extension to the territories. How could he justify his condemnation of the institution without joining in the call for its immediate repeal?

Lincoln answered this question by reference to a theory of the public and public opinion that evolved during the debates. In Ottawa, though speaking about Douglas, he made a statement that applied to himself as well: "In this and like communities, public sentiment is everything. With public sentiment, nothing can fail; without it nothing can succeed. Consequently, he who moulds public sentiment, goes deeper than he who enacts statutes or pronounces decisions."[67] From this standpoint, the necessary and sufficient condition for Lincoln's program was public confidence that slavery, however gradually, would disappear—or, as he carefully phrased it, slavery must be placed "where the public mind shall rest in the belief that it is in course of ultimate extinction."[68] Yet how could the public conclude that slavery was on the way out? The answer, for Lincoln, lay in the public condemnation of the institution on moral grounds, precisely because one did not have a right to do wrong. Remove that condemnation, and there was no reason why slavery could not be expected to last forever, just as Douglas had said. Or, as Jaffa put it, "Without a moral decision against slavery, no guarantee for the future was possible," presumably because one could not be sure of the direction of the public mind.[69]

In this way, morality and practical action were connected. Slavery is immoral; therefore, it should not be extended. Refusal to extend it will symbolize that the country intends it to end, and the force of that intention will hasten the day of voluntary emancipation where slavery now exists. Since the Constitution prohibited direct interference with slavery in the states where it exists, this chain of events was not only consistent with morality but the best result for which one could hope. The construct of the public mind created the conceptual space between acquiescence and abolition. Conveniently, too, in Smith's phrase, "With magnificent eloquence Lincoln had expressed the highest moral ideals in language which required no sacrifice from anyone."[70] In fact, since the Republican party was the embodiment of antislavery sentiment, identification with the new party and commitment to its program was sufficient to satisfy the moral demands of the issue.

If one way in which Lincoln adapted to the constraints he faced was to rely on the middle ground of "public mind" and "course of ultimate extinction," a second was to focus not on the moral evil of the slaveowner but instead on his opponent, Douglas. The slaveowner was, if anything, an innocent victim of history. The villains in Lincoln's moral drama were the politicians who kept the slavery issue unsettled by trying to rid it of its fundamental moral dimension. For those concerned that an antislavery platform would invite unrest and agitation, he turned the tables. Social unrest resulted not from putting slavery on the road to extinction but from upsetting the traditional stance of moral condemnation.

As evidence, Lincoln cited the calm resulting from the Compromise of 1850, which left the Missouri Compromise intact, comparing that calm with the agitation stirred up by the Kansas-Nebraska Act, which repealed the Compromise. Referring to the Missouri Compromise, Lincoln plaintively asked in the Jonesboro debate "why he could not have left that Compromise alone."[71] Moreover, by treating the issue so purely as one of procedure and by arguing that laws regulating slavery were essentially no different from those regulating liquor and cranberries, Douglas really did offer no reason to believe that slavery could not go on indefinitely.

Focusing on Douglas in this manner had two benefits for Lincoln. First, it enabled him to redefine the moral issue in order to occupy the higher ground. It is not that he is at one extreme of the political spectrum favoring abolition; rather, Douglas is at the *other* extreme, opposing any end to slavery, ever. Portraying one's opponent as a dangerous radical would make one appear moderate by comparison. Lincoln neatly reversed the position of the two candidates at the outset of the debates. He could make a claim for the support of all who view slavery as an evil, even if it is a necessary evil. He was willing to see it end a hundred years or more in the future, but unlike Douglas he favored a course of action that began with the commitment that it ought to end.

Lincoln was frank in acknowledging that his purpose in putting the issue in this fashion was to realign the audience by winning over to his own side some who now supported Douglas. As he explained in the Alton debate, each man currently numbered among his supporters some who thought slavery to be at its root an evil. But, "whenever we can get rid of the fog which obscures the real question," this element can be brought to the Republican side.[72] That shift in allegiance, Lincoln thought, would be sufficient to set slavery on the course of ultimate extinction, and to do so peaceably, too.

The other benefit to Lincoln from focusing his moral argument on Douglas rather than on slavery was that it made his earlier conspiracy arguments, which had dominated the first four debates, seem more credible. Although Lincoln could ask leading questions and draw inferences from circumstantial evidence, the assertion that Douglas was an active participant in a proslavery cabal seemed preposterous. But far more effective was Lincoln's later argument that Douglas was the unwitting dupe—the "instrument"—of this conspiratorial design who was nevertheless behaving just as effectively as if he were in on the plot. Douglas's specific role was to anesthetize the public mind as to the moral significance of the issue. Jaffa, for example, believes that public opinion would not have stood for the *Dred Scott* decision had it been issued in 1854. The way had to be prepared, by the Kansas-Nebraska Act and the 1856 election campaign. Only then, "when the old idea of the moral objectionableness of slavery . . . had been replaced by the idea of the moral indifference of slavery could the Court have attempted what it did attempt," Jaffa concludes.[73]

Now history was repeating itself. By insisting that, as a matter of public policy, he "don't care" whether the territories were slave or free, Douglas would induce his listeners not to care, as a matter of individual moral judgment. Since "public sentiment is everything," the dulling of the public conscience was a vital prerequisite to the subsequent extension of slavery. Then, and only then, could a future Supreme Court consider such a travesty as the hypothetical "*Dred Scott* II," which would hold that no state had the power to outlaw slavery.

Besides focusing on the "public mind" and on Douglas, Lincoln had a third adaptation to the constraints of his situation in the timing of his discussion of the moral issue. Except for the brief reference at Ottawa to Henry Clay and "blowing out the moral lights," he did not introduce the issue until Galesburg, the fifth debate. The timing is all the more curious since Lincoln had not just stumbled on the moral issue; he had been arguing it since 1854. In his Peoria speech decrying the Kansas-Nebraska Act, he said, "This *declared* indifference, but as I must think, covert *real* zeal for the spread of slavery, I can not but hate. I hate it because of the monstrous injustice of slavery itself." Moreover, Lincoln had included the moral argument in the "House Divided" speech. He invoked it in his Chicago speech of July, when he concluded, "I leave you, hoping that the lamp of liberty will burn in your bosoms until there shall no longer be a doubt that all men are created free and equal." Even during the fall campaign, in less public settings than the debates, Lincoln returned to this theme, arguing, for instance, at Edwardsville, between the Freeport and the Jonesboro debates, that the precise difference between the two parties was to be found in their view of the morality of slavery.[74] Why, then, did he wait so long to bring the issue into the debates?

Lincoln knew his audience. However much Illinoisians might disagree about slavery, they still disdained the Negro. A large part of the population was Southern in origin and in settling the prairie state brought with them a Southern outlook and Southern values. Moreover, many whites opposed slavery because they opposed the Negro and wanted him kept out of Illinois, whether free or slave.[75] Consequently, it would be difficult for Lincoln to summon up moral outrage over the slavery issue; a careful and gradual progression of the argument would be needed. Although he was speaking of Douglas when he said that "public opinion is everything," Lincoln realized that he was bound by these strictures, too. Even as he sought to influence public opinion, he was molded and constrained by it and thus careful not to advance too far beyond it. In his 1854 Peoria speech, he had said that "a universal feeling, whether well or ill-founded, can not be safely disregarded." Fredrickson has traced to Lincoln's early career "the conservative principle that firmly established public opinion on any question must be respected because it was providential and would therefore change only in God's good time," and one of Lincoln's friends reminisced to Herndon after the president's death that Lincoln "had great faith in the strong sense of country people. . . . If he found an idea prevailing generally amongst them, he believed there was something in it."[76] Lincoln was constrained by public opinion even when it led to such paradoxes as men exercising their right to self-government by denying that all men are created equal.

For these reasons, Lincoln had to prepare public opinion for what was to come later. That task was accomplished by placing Douglas on the side of slavery—via the conspiracy charges—and then by insisting that there was a middle ground between slavery and the opposite extreme, Negro equality. After denying that he favored political and social equality for the Negro, Lincoln added, as at Charleston, "I do not understand that because I do not want a Negro woman for a slave I must necessarily want her for a wife."[77] It was this middle position, once established, for which Lincoln far more easily could stake out a moral claim. Ironically, while seeking a middle ground as to policy, Lincoln denied that there was any middle ground with respect to the basic moral judgment.

V

Douglas had virtually no answer to Lincoln's arguments based on the immorality of slavery. Indeed, his silence was required by the logic of his own position, which emphasized the inappropriateness of collective moral judgments in public affairs. There are only two occasions, at Quincy and at Alton, when the Little Giant grappled directly with his opponent's claims. First, he tried to make a virtue of his silence by insisting that the whole topic is outside the purview of any action that might be taken by a U.S. senator. As the incumbent put it,

He tells you that I will not argue the question whether slavery is right or wrong. I tell you why I will not do it. I hold that under the Constitution of the United States, each state of this Union has a right to do as it pleases on the subject of slavery. . . . Hence I do not choose to occupy the time allotted to me in discussing a question that we have no right to act upon. I thought that you desired to hear us upon those questions coming within our constitutional power of action. Lincoln will not discuss these. What one question has he discussed that comes within the power or calls for the action or interference of an United States Senator? He is going to discuss the rightfulness of slavery when Congress cannot act upon it either way.[78]

Douglas was here attempting to reestablish the primacy of the procedural question by contending that Lincoln was deliberately evading the issue, focusing on matters not pertinent to the office that both men sought. In the same way, he sought to dismiss his challenger's critique of the *Dred Scott* decision by noting that it was a Supreme Court decision and hence that there was no higher tribunal to which to appeal—unless, of course, Lincoln wished to proceed from a decision by the Supreme

Court to the action of the mob. The difficulty with this line of argument was that it was easily refuted. Lincoln explained precisely how he sought to revise the *Dred Scott* decision as a political rule. And if Douglas could rebuke him for ignoring the issues that a senator can affect, Lincoln was able to ridicule the incumbent for the far more serious error, as noted above, of "false statesmanship that undertakes to build up a system of policy upon the basis of caring nothing about *the very thing that every body does care the most about.*"

Douglas's other response is more intriguing. It is his one effort to grapple with the substance of Lincoln's position, by examining what the "course of ultimate extinction" means and how it would be achieved. He previewed it at Quincy and then repeated it in his rejoinder at Alton—the last speech of the last debate. Douglas asked and answered, "How he is going to put slavery in the course of ultimate extinction everywhere, if he does not intend to interfere with it in the states where it exists." The answer follows: "His idea is that he will prohibit slavery in all the territories, and thus force them all to become free states, surrounding the slave states with a cordon of free states, and hemming them in, keeping the slaves confined to their present limits whilst they go on multiplying until the soil on which they live will no longer feed them, and he will thus be able to put slavery in a course of ultimate extinction by starvation." The Little Giant drew analogies: "He will extinguish slavery in the Southern states as the French general exterminated the Algerines when he smoked them out. He is going to extinguish slavery by surrounding the slave states, hemming in the slaves, and starving them out of existence as you smoke a fox out of his hole." Then the coup de grace: "And he intends to do that in the name of humanity and Christianity, in order that we may get rid of the terrible crime and sin entailed upon our fathers of holding slaves."[79]

This is a potentially powerful argument. It is what Henry Johnstone has labeled an argument *ad hominem* and described as the only valid way to refute a philosophical argument, by showing that it leads to conclusions that its maker would not accept.[80] Lincoln was defending on moral grounds a course of action that would lead to results that he surely would not regard as moral. What this response enabled Douglas to do was to refute Lincoln's moral position without yielding to the temptation that the challenger had placed before him—that is, without entering Lincoln's assumptive framework and defending slavery as morally right. Douglas could remain "above the battle" while insisting that Lincoln's moral position is wrong because it self-destructs.

Had this argument been developed earlier and pursued vigorously, it would have invited searching examination of the assumptions underlying Lincoln's claim that slavery would be put in the course of ultimate extinction. Fredrickson attributes to Lincoln the belief that containing slavery would promote colonization: it "had the long-range benefit of denying slaveholders a chance to sell their surplus bondsmen at high prices in new slave territories, thus encouraging them to begin the process of gradual emancipation by sending the excess to Liberia."[81] Neither colonization nor, for that matter, "ultimate extinction" was taken seriously as a Republican political program, however. True, Republicans wished to contain slavery, but not as a step toward extinction. Benson has written that "antebellum economic realities made the 'containment = ultimate extinction' equation nonsensical, or, at most, so distant a prospect (1900? 2000?) that it cannot be taken seriously" as evidence of an idealistically inspired political program.[82]

If colonization was not a viable option, yet Lincoln was committed to the containment of slavery, one might quite legitimately ask the consequences of implementing his moral position. The "starvation" attack does not appear to have been taken seriously by the Republicans since there is no evidence that they ever answered it directly. Perhaps that neglect was wise; after all, anyone who cared could recognize that starvation was not the inevitable outcome of their moral position. But Douglas's attempt to inquire after the consequences, though not fully exploited, was a valuable strategic maneuver, offering at least the possibility of turning Republican moralism against itself.

While not directly challenging Lincoln's argument about the morality of slavery, Douglas introduced a quite different sort of moral claim, grounded in the morality of individuals rather than systems. Specifically, he charged his opponent, Lincoln, with inconsistency, pandering to his audiences by saying different things from one part of the state to another. The clear implication was not only that Lincoln was not to be trusted but that he was morally at fault for deceiving his listeners and concealing his true beliefs.

Douglas developed this accusation early in the campaign. In the Ottawa debate, he boasted, "My principles are the same everywhere. I can proclaim them alike in the North, the South, the East, and the West. My principles will apply wherever the Constitution prevails and the American flag waves." He then put to Lincoln his original interrogatories in order to get his opponent on the record so that the incumbent could embarrass Lincoln later with his own words. Believing that the Ottawa audience had cheered abolitionist sentiments that he had attributed to the Republican party, Douglas warned, "Your affirmative cheers in favor of this abolition program is not satisfactory. I ask Abraham Lincoln to answer these questions, in order that when I trot him down to lower

Egypt I may put the same questions to him. . . . I desire to know whether Mr. Lincoln's principles will bear transplanting from Ottawa to Jonesboro?" Again and again the incumbent repeated the charge that his opponent could not sustain a consistent moral vision. At Jonesboro, he proclaimed that "I would disdain to hold any political principles that I could not avow in the same terms in Kentucky that I declared in Illinois, in Charleston as well as in Chicago, in New Orleans as well as in New York."[83]

Now Lincoln answered the charge, although in an indirect way. He treated the argument as if it referred to differences among Republicans rather than to inconsistencies in his own statements. This decision allowed him to respond, reasonably enough, that he should not be held accountable for all actions by all supporters. To add emphasis to the point, he claimed that not all of Douglas's supporters were in agreement either. He referred to Thompson Campbell and R. S. Molony, Democratic candidates for Congress whose views on slavery were the opposite of Douglas's. He cited the resolutions passed by a Democratic district convention at Naperville, similar resolutions by a Vermont convention, and the case of Judge Mays, a candidate for the legislature. All three said that they were Democrats, yet all held views of slavery that were quite at odds with Douglas's.[84] The clear implication is that, since neither man can control his followers, neither should be responsible for everything the advisers say.

Douglas was not taken in by this twist in the argument. He disavowed Molony and Campbell, calling the former a renegade and noting that the latter published his offensive remarks only after he was safely elected. But he trained his fire on Lincoln, pointing out that the Republican party currently was advocating different programs in the different parts of the state, supporting abolition in the north while denouncing it in the south. All this proved was that the Republican party was a "house divided against itself" and hence unfit to govern.[85]

The same charges were repeated, and even sharpened, at Charleston, where Douglas noted that Republicans went by various names in different parts of the state. "What object have these Black Republicans," he asked, "in changing their name in every country? . . . I would like to know why it is that this great free soil abolition party is not willing to avow the same name in all parts of the state?" Developing this theme, he said of the Republicans, "Their principles in the north are jet black, in the centre they are in color a decent mulatto, and in lower Egypt they are almost white. Why, I admired many of the white sentiments contained in Lincoln's speech at Jonesboro, and could not help but contrast them with the speeches of the same distinguished orator made in the northern part of the state." Lincoln, replying, this time confined the charge to himself and simply denied that there was any inconsistency in his speeches: "I will not charge upon Judge Douglas that he wilfully misrepresents me, but I call upon every fair-minded man to take these speeches and read them, *and I dare him to point out any difference between my printed speeches north and south.*"[86] This was a dangerous invitation since in Chicago Lincoln had proclaimed that all men are created free and equal whereas in Charleston he had proclaimed the superiority of the white race. But, of course, following up on Lincoln's challenge depended on just what was meant by a "difference" between the speeches.

The argument reached its climax at Galesburg. Douglas took up Lincoln's challenge and cited the difference between the Charleston and Chicago speeches while also repeating the allegations that the Republicans were not a national but a sectional party and that they did not even use the same name in all parts of the state. Lincoln gave the charge of inconsistency the care of a detailed response and in so doing put some parts of this argument on the course of ultimate extinction. For instance, he charged that the Democrats had used different names in different parts of the state, too: "I have the honor to inform Judge Douglas that he spoke in that very county of Tazewell last Saturday, . . . and when he spoke there he spoke under a call not venturing to use the word 'Democrat.'" Lincoln then scored on the incumbent by drawing attention to his break with Buchanan and relating it to the changing of names: "In the contest of 1856 his party delighted to call themselves together as the 'National Democracy,' but now, if there should be a notice put up anywhere for a meeting of the 'National Democracy,' Judge Douglas and his friends would not come."[87] Lincoln did not complete his argument, but the likely inference is that shifts of name in either party were, not signs of inconsistent principles, but rather testimony to the general political flux of the 1850s. It was also a period marked by widespread distrust of politicians as a class, one in which widespread variations in names may have helped mask ambiguity about one's principles. Lincoln is suggesting that it is not only his supporters who practice this deception, if that indeed is what it is, but that it is part of the common political culture of the time.

Likewise, Lincoln's answer to the charge that the Republicans were wrong because they were a sectional party put that issue to rest. Part of the answer was farfetched. In order to show that no political position had universal appeal, the Republican surmised "that Judge Douglas could not go into Russia and announce the doctrine of our national democracy; he could not denounce the doctrine of kings, and emperors, and monarchies, in Russia," just as in some parts of the United States the Republican doctrine could not get a fair hearing. Douglas bluntly denied the analogy, saying, "I would remind him that Russia is not under the American Constitution," and then asserting, "If Russia was a part of the American republic, under our federal Constitution, and I was sworn to support that Constitution, I would maintain the same doctrine in Russia that I do in Illinois."

Lincoln dropped the analogy, but Douglas had no response to the more substantial part of his argument. Lincoln posed the matter as a question: "Is it the true test of the soundness of a doctrine, that in some places people won't let you proclaim it? Is that the way to test the truth of any doctrine?" Rather, he suggested, the fact that southerners (and Douglas) would not grapple with Republican principles must mean that there is nothing wrong with them—if the principles were in error, surely an opponent would draw attention to that fact. But, he said, referring to Douglas, "The only evidence he has of their being wrong is in the fact that there are people who won't allow us to preach them." Finally, Lincoln noted, if the test of a position was its universal appeal, Douglas would fail the test, too. Not only was it true that "at one time the people of Chicago would not let Judge Douglas preach a certain favorite doctrine of his," but Douglas's shifting national political position was also worthy of note: "I ask his attention to the fact that his speeches would not go as current now south of the Ohio River as they have formerly gone there. . . . I see the day rapidly approaching when his pill of sectionalism, which he has been thrusting down the throats of Republicans for years past, will be crowded down his own throat."[88] No more was said by the Little Giant about this allegation.

With these two parts of the argument discussed in the Galesburg debate, the sole remaining contention was that Lincoln had made inconsistent statements in different parts of the state. Lincoln denied it, pointed out that he obviously knew that his speeches would be printed and circulated throughout the state, and asserted that a careful reading of all his speeches would show that there was no contradiction. He did not refer directly to either the Chicago or the Charleston speech, but he did emphasize the fundamental distinction that he thought Douglas overlooked, the middle ground between slavery and racial equality. It was this middle ground that enabled him to say (as at Charleston) that blacks and whites were not socially or politically equal and also to say (as at Chicago) that all men were created equal and therefore entitled to the rights enumerated in the Declaration of Independence. Douglas missed the distinction and concluded that the only way that the Chicago and Charleston speeches could both be right is, "not because he is consistent, but because he can trim his principles any way in any section, so as to secure votes."[89]

The Quincy debate saw only a shadow of this argument. Lincoln read short passages from his speeches to show that they were consistent and asserted that the Charleston speech—which Douglas thought was intended only for Egypt—was repeated in the northern abolition districts, indeed within Douglas's hearing, at Ottawa. Douglas's only answer was that Lincoln made no reference to the Chicago speech, thereby proving that he "has twice, instead of once, held one creed in one part of the state and a different creed in another part." Lincoln repeated that he had met the incumbent's charge by quoting the same speech in different parts of the state, and there the matter ended.[90]

This part of the dispute helps illumine Douglas's perspective on morality in public argument. Morality was not a function of institutions such as slavery; indeed, on that score the Little Giant held doggedly to the belief that the public forum must be neutral. Rather, it was a feature of individuals, and its tests were a consistent set of principles that could be proclaimed anywhere. Lincoln never denied the appropriateness of this standard of morality; he argued instead that he met the tests as well as did Douglas.

Although Lincoln, strictly speaking, was not inconsistent, his discussions revealed marked differences in emphasis. As Johnson explained years ago, "In Chicago he said nothing about the physical inferiority of the negro; he said nothing about the equality of the races in the Declaration of Independence, when he spoke at Charleston. Among men of anti-slavery leanings, he had much to say about the moral wrong of slavery; in the doubtful counties, Lincoln was solicitous that he should not be understood as favoring social and political equality."[91] But Douglas was unable to sustain the momentum of this argument—first, because he allowed important parts of the argument to drop after Lincoln's responses at Galesburg; second, because he never came to grips with Lincoln's explanation that the "middle ground" between slavery and equality made his Charleston and Chicago speeches consistent; and, most important, because Douglas failed even to articulate how individual consistency really was a moral principle to be weighed in the scales against the Republican claim that slavery was wrong. Calling the opposing party a "house divided against itself" was an adroit tactical move, but it failed to establish the ultimate moral significance of Lincoln's alleged impropriety.

VI

Douglas and Lincoln clearly had different approaches to the moral argument. For the incumbent, morality was a procedural matter, embodied in the principle of local self-government and the consistency of principles championed by advocates in public discussion. For Lincoln, morality was a substantive matter, and it was expressed in the containment of slavery, a "message" symbolizing that the institution was wrong and that it must someday end. Although there are occasional efforts by each man to grapple with the other's view, for the most part each of these competing notions of morality escaped direct challenge. Quite likely, the two debaters did not fully realize that they were not arguing on the same plane.

Nevertheless, it was the introduction of the moral issue that made the dispute between Lincoln and Douglas ultimately incapable of compromise. Not only is it difficult at any time to compromise moral right and wrong at the expense of personal integrity, but as Smith points out, early nineteenth-century Americans were an especially moralistic people, "thoroughly steeped in the tradition of religious salvation through righteousness and eternal damnation through wickedness."[92] If one's own position is seen as divinely inspired and the opponent's as threatening the integrity of a Union seen in familial terms, the rigidity of discussion is even greater. Furthermore, when the positions are not just different but incommensurable, compromise is even more difficult because it would require adapting an alien set of categories and language. Each participant in a dispute would need to see the world in terms and categories that that participant's own beliefs deny. The impossibility of genuinely imagining the other's beliefs and values, even "for the sake of the argument," helps explain why arguments sometimes find each advocate frozen in a position that seems to be expressed as the repetition of stale slogans. The contemporary abortion controversy illustrates the problem. The "pro-life" claim that life is sacred and begins at conception and the "pro-choice" claim for self-determination and the woman's right to control her own body simply do not meet; they are on different planes altogether. Neither participant can imagine the other's categories as relevant to the matter ultimately at hand. So the dispute cannot proceed, much less find resolution. As Pearce and his colleagues observe about such a moral dispute of the 1980s, "Neither side is willing to lose gracefully because it must avoid the very way of thinking and talking adopted by the other."[93]

Most twentieth-century readers of the debates will see the moral issue as dispositive and Lincoln as the decisive victor on that issue. In part, this judgment reflects his great ability to simplify and clarify the issue. As Sigelschiffer writes, Lincoln "reduced the moral aspect of slavery to the prime requisite of unqualified acceptance of the Negro as a human being who was entitled to his liberty, without complicating the issue by questions of political and social status."[94] In part, a judgment for

Lincoln reflects the obvious fact that his view of morality has received the sanction of time and is now held by almost all Americans, as, if not a description of their society, at least a goal for which to strive.

In part, too, a claim for Lincoln as the victor reflects his skill in the ability to work from an absolute value position yet avoid the need to take an absolutist stance in public debate. Absolute values make compelling claims on a listener's attention and belief, but to be taken seriously they should be linked to a program of action that is *not* absolute. Otherwise, as the abolitionists and other radicals before and since have discovered, the effort may be stigmatized as extreme. Yet the link between absolute value and limited action must seem natural and appropriate, or it will undermine the credibility of both. In this light, the genius of Lincoln's position emerges. By paying homage to the value of public sentiment (which Douglas the majoritarian could hardly oppose), Lincoln was able to suggest that a public judgment that slavery was on the way out would have the same ultimate effect as would its immediate abolition. He was thus permitted the luxury of defending an absolute value position to be achieved in the world of prudential conduct by no absolute means.

Still, these judgments for Lincoln must be tempered by reference to context. Few audiences ever enjoy being called to account for their moral lapses. The moral argument was especially uncomfortable if Rawley is right in saying that "historical evidence is lacking to prove that the moral division ran deep" and that it is doubtful that northerners "were moved to adopt nonextension of slavery in the territories or popular sovereignty because they believed slavery immoral."[95]

A contemporary analogue may be useful. During the 1970s and 1980s, one of the most troublesome moral issues involved the question of abortion. Aside from such issues as the definition of life and the balancing of rights, one of the stickiest disputes has involved the appropriateness of using public policy as a means of expressing individual moral judgments about an issue in dispute. Prominent politicians such as Governor Mario Cuomo of New York have proclaimed their own strong moral opposition to abortion yet also have insisted that they would oppose legislation or constitutional amendment to restrict abortions on the grounds that it is not appropriate to enshrine in law what is essentially one side of a dispute over moral or religious values.[96] This distinction, which many sectors of mainstream public opinion find perfectly appropriate, is in many ways not unlike the position espoused by Douglas in the debates. Yet few of the "pro-choice" advocates in this controversy would probably find themselves comfortable as allies of Douglas. Abortion, of course, is only one example, but—whatever the issue—those who are more willing to pass judgment on slavery than to confront the moral dilemmas of our own time should remember that there were equally strong pressures for the public forum to avoid the great unsettled question of 1858.

All this is to suggest the need to appreciate that many were undoubtedly influenced by the appeal that Douglas made most clearly in the Quincy debate. Attempting to justify his effort to put the moral issue beyond the pale of public discussion, he told his listeners, "I do not discuss the morals of the people of Missouri. . . . I hold that the people of the slaveholding states are civilized men as well as ourselves, that they bear consciences as well as we. . . . It is for them to decide therefore the moral and religious right of the slavery question for themselves within their own limits." Moral judgment of the slaveowners, then, was a matter not for public political debate but for their consciences and their God.[97]

7

The Aftermath of the Debates

The debates concluded on October 15, but the campaign had nearly three weeks to run. In the closing days, both candidates spoke frequently, repeating what had become well-worn arguments but still attracting crowds and attention. Last-minute innuendo and warnings of impending vote fraud also marked the campaign's denouement. It ended on November 2 with an election whose ambiguous results fueled new controversy about the importance and influence of the debates.

I

After the Alton debate, Lincoln spoke ten times, mostly in small towns but concluding on October 30 in his home town, Springfield. His final rally was publicized in the *Illinois State Journal,* which appealed to old Whigs to attend and give Lincoln a hearing. Sensitive to Whig fears that Lincoln was too radical, the paper intoned, "Hear him, and you will be satisfied that the charge of NIGGER EQUALITY is as false against Lincoln, as the charge of *Toryism* and *Abolitionism* was against Clay."[1] This appeal was directed to the group whose votes Lincoln needed most and was intended to portray his position as conservative. In the speech, only a fragment of which remains, the challenger once again reassured listeners that he recognized the constitutional protections thrown up around slavery and that he had no desire to disturb the institution where it already existed. He then took up Douglas's repeated statement that base motives of office holding lay behind the current crisis. "Ambition has been ascribed to me," Lincoln admitted. He acknowledged that he was sensitive to political honors, but, "could the Missouri restriction be restored" and should unyielding hostility to the further spread of slavery become the norm, then "I would, in consideration, gladly agree, that Judge Douglas should never be *out,* and I never *in* an office, so long as we both or either, live."[2]

Republicans concentrated fire on Douglas during these closing weeks. Just as he had lambasted Lincoln for taking different views on slavery in the north and the south, they leveled the same charge at him. The *Illinois State Journal,* referring to an article in *De Bow's Review,* a Southern journal, noted that Douglas "says that slavery already exists in the Territories" and predicted that he would "doubtless aid in introducing it into the Western States, under the plea that the interests of Democracy require it"—all this despite the expectation of moderate Northern Democrats that popular sovereignty was really the means to encourage *freedom* in the new territories.[3] Another Republican paper, the *Chicago Press and Tribune,* cited the fact that Douglas originally championed the Missouri Compromise and then proposed its repeal as evidence that one had "no certainty that Mr. Douglas' present professions are fair expositions of his political creed, or an index to his future political action."[4] The power of this argument lay not just in the fact that Douglas could be shown to be as changeable as Lincoln. It also mocked the Little Giant's proclamation that his political principles were the same everywhere and suggested instead that Douglas was an opportunist and a hypocrite.

Adding to the attacks on Douglas were the disaffected Buchaneers. George W. Jones, an administration Democrat in Dubuque, wrote to Danite candidate Sidney Breese that "Douglas is playing the last game in the rubber—has become desperate and of course has resorted to all kinds of corruption and collusion." Jones asserted that Douglas had entered into a pact with the Republicans whereby they would bail out his faltering reelection prospects and he in turn would endorse Seward for president in 1860 and expect to follow him in 1864. Jones had already written Breese that Douglas had secretly quit the Democratic party, though he dared not admit it to his supporters in Illinois.[5]

But the Danites' most powerful assault on Douglas was far more public. Around the time of the Jonesboro debate, Buchanan operative John Slidell appeared in southern Illinois with rumors of mistreatment of slaves on a Mississippi plantation owned by Douglas's late wife and bequeathed to his sons. Their ownership of a cotton plantation containing over one hundred slaves was well known but not widely publicized. In July, for example, a correspondent wrote the senator, "There is a few Republicans who claim that you hold slaves in the state of Mississippi now I wish to know whether you do or not."[6] In mid-October, the *Illinois State Journal* tweaked Douglas with respect to his campaign statements expressing fears of racial amalgamation and castigating Lincoln as an advocate of racial equality. What Douglas was doing, the paper declared, was to "foully and villainously slander the men and women of Illinois . . . who have in no respect the opportunities much less the desires for any such schemes as he has, with his Southern plantation of negroes and mulattoes." The threat of amalgamation, the *Journal* seemed to suggest, came not from banning slavery from the territories but from having blacks and whites living in close proximity, as they did "at his own door and at the door of that Southern Democracy with whom he is in close communion."[7] It was an elegant attempt to turn the racist argument against itself.

The matter of Douglas's plantation took a particularly ugly turn the weekend before election day, when the *Chicago Press and Tribune* gave wide publicity to Slidell's charges that the slaves were mistreated. The paper reported Slidell's declaration "that the condition of these slaves was a disgrace to their owner; *that they were badly fed, badly clothed, and excessively overworked!*" This fact helped explain, the paper said, Douglas's "sneers at the Declaration of Independence, at the idea of Universal Human Liberty, at the efforts of Humanity in behalf of both the oppressed and the oppressor." After all, Douglas had "a large and immediate personal interest in the perpetuation and extension of the bondage which the Declaration and the common sentiment of the world so pointedly condemn." The *Press and Tribune* even proposed that the money saved by the neglect of these plantation slaves was the source of Douglas's campaign funds.[8] The power of this story, of course, lay largely in the fact that it was published right before the election, when it would be fresh in voters' minds and when time would not permit publication of a rebuttal.

What were the facts of the matter? Douglas's first wife had been the daughter of a Southern planter. Her father desired to bequeath his plantation and slaves but, noting in his will that Douglas did not wish to own property in slaves, left them in his daughter's name alone. When she died, the property passed to Douglas's sons and was held in trust for them until they reached legal age. There was absolutely no substance to Slidell's rumor that the slaves had been mistreated, as was made clear immediately after the election. The very fact that the plantation was in the family might have proved eventually to be a more serious embarrassment, but it is unlikely that the whole matter of the treatment of the slaves swayed many votes in 1858. The charge did, however, add an element of last-minute drama to the campaign.

In trying to rally supporters, Republicans often stressed the symbolic significance of the Illinois race. All eyes were said to be on the prairie state; as the *Chicago Press and Tribune* editorialized, "Illinois may be regarded as the centre battle ground, or turning point, between the hosts of Freedom and the powers of Slavery."[9] The election was nothing less than a contest between good and evil. This same sharp division was also employed by the Democrats, for whom the struggle was not between freedom and slavery but between principle, which Douglas defended, and the raw political power of the Buchanan administration, which was invoked to benefit the Republicans. As early as mid-September, for example, a correspondent had written Springfield congressman Thomas L. Harris, Douglas's close political ally, "All eyes are turned toward the canvas [sic] in Illinois, all other elections and results are nowhere compaired [sic] with the bold defiant movement of Douglas and his friend in Illinois."[10] Although they defined the central issue differently, both sides saw the contest as crucial on the larger national scene.

For their part, the Democrats sensed victory in the air. Their candidate, too, gave ten speeches after the Alton debate, culminating with an election eve speech on November 1 in Chicago. The campaign had taken a physical toll; Douglas was fatigued, and his voice cracked so that it was difficult for audiences to hear or understand him, but he kept up the pace and audiences continued to turn out. He had recently remarried, and his wife, the former Adele Cutts, joined him in Alton and appeared with him in several towns during the campaign's final days—a novelty in the political climate of the time. After they appeared in Bloomington, C. R. Parke wrote, "Douglas is Sure to be elected. . . . He spoke here on last friday to a large concourse of people about 8,000— Mrs. D— was here, She is beautifull."[11] Rallying Democratic support, the pro-Douglas *Chicago Times* identified the issues as "whether the free people of Illinois will permit the federal government to strike down a representative who, in the hour of peril, stood manfully in defence of the rights of the people, and resisted successfully a wanton outrage." When the paper asked, "Will the people of Illinois permit the independence of the representative to be sacrificed?" it stated the issue in a way that would best mobilize support for the incumbent.[12] Of course, Democrats repeated the charge that Lincoln favored racial amalgamation. On election day, the *Chicago Times* printed a warning, all in capital letters, "A VOTE FOR THE REPUBLICAN CANDIDATES IS A VOTE TO CROWD WHITE LABORERS OUT OF, AND TO BRING NEGROES INTO THE CITY."[13]

The Democrats, too, had a last-minute surprise. Early in the campaign, they had secured an endorsement for Douglas from Kentucky senator John J. Crittenden, the political heir of Henry Clay. Although Crittenden had written his endorsement in a private letter, it was published in the Democratic press in the closing weeks of the campaign. It was harmful to Lincoln not only because of Crittenden's own prestige but also because it cast doubt on Lincoln's claim that he rather than Douglas was following in the tradition of Clay. Republicans alleged that the endorsement, printed so late in the campaign, must be a forgery, or they suggested wishfully that the endorsement was taken out of context—it was a statement of general support for Douglas, not a preference for him over Lincoln in the current contest. These were weak retorts, though; the endorsement was genuine, even if possibly hasty. It was damaging to Lincoln in the central Illinois counties. Crittenden could reply to Lincoln, as noted, only that he had not authorized the letter's publication.

Both parties courted the immigrant vote, but that was a tricky matter. Democrats wooed the Irish, who had already established a record of party loyalty. Republicans had few supporters among the Irish, and Democrats fanned that antagonism. Throughout the campaign, the Republicans were accused of prejudice against the Irish. In early September, the *Illinois State Register* reported a remark attributed to Lincoln's law partner, William H. Herndon: "God damn the Irish, I want it distinctly understood that *we* are willing to have war with them."[14]

Republican antipathy toward the Irish stemmed in large part from the conviction that Irishmen were being used by the Democrats to perpetrate vote fraud. Many owners of railroads favored Douglas, the argument ran, so they offered the Irish free rides from the Republican cities, where their votes would do no good, to the central Illinois counties where their votes would be most useful. Republicans were warning against this impending fraud throughout the month of October; they believed that things were going well for Lincoln and that vote fraud would be the Democrats' desperate means to snatch victory from the jaws of defeat. One of the Republican field operatives wrote to John C. Bagby in mid-October that the principals of the railroad were "flooding the road with the Irish in every County in this district that a road passes through. We must watch this it will play the devil with us." Referring to Carthage, he added, "Douglas made a complete failure here there is nothing against us in this county unless it is the Irish importation look Sharp to this." Bagby asked another local worker to check on suspicious Irish immigration. Back came the reply: "I inquired . . . about those Mc-Murphys—O'Flanagans and other McDouglas. . . . I am inclined to think that you are mistaken—however we will not forget to keep a look out for this new feature of 'Squatter Sovereignty.' "[15]

The *Chicago Press and Tribune* asserted on October 12 that "hordes of wandering Irishmen" were already "seeking, under the guidance of their leaders, the places where their ballots may do most service in the cause of the Pope, Slavery, and Douglas." Ten days later, the paper reported that more than one hundred Irishmen had left safely Republican Ottawa "for a destination in some of the closely contested counties in the State, not yet ascertained."[16] Lincoln was particularly concerned about this danger. He heard a rumor in mid-October that four hundred Irishmen were being brought into Schuyler County to work on a new railroad, and of course to vote Democratic. He gave a speech in which he referred to his fear of "imported Irishmen," and he wrote to Norman B. Judd on October 20 about his fear of illegal voting by Irishmen who falsely swear residence in the district in which they seek to vote. Lincoln was especially concerned because it would be hard to challenge these new voters since perjury in such a matter would be extremely difficult to prove.[17]

These charges were not taken seriously in the Democratic press. Making light of the accusations, the *Chicago Times* in early October maintained that there was but one wandering Irishman traveling about the state, "and he is a Republican." Later in the month, the same paper intoned that the Republican charges of fraud were but a diversion from Lincoln's imminent defeat at the polls. The charge was common "on the eve of an important election which they know will result disastrously to them"; it was a device "to let the duped adherents of Lincoln down as early as possible."[18]

Another response to the Republican warnings was more serious. The *Jacksonville Sentinel*, a Douglas paper, reported on Lincoln's October speech voicing the fear of fraud. The paper cast Lincoln's remarks as an attack on the Irish and tried to portray him as a Know-Nothing.[19] This was a serious charge because it might disrupt the Republican strategy of appealing especially for the German vote while also attracting those Whigs who had supported Fillmore in 1856. Achieving that goal was a difficult balancing act in any case, but all the more so if Douglas supporters were able to cast Lincoln as being in one camp or the other. Correspondents had written Douglas earlier in the summer that he might get some German votes but that the Know-Nothings would be arrayed against him. That being the case, there was political gain in spreading the rumor that Lincoln was a Know-Nothing. It would be hard for him to deny the accusation vigorously and yet also appeal for Know-Nothing votes.[20] In the end, however, Republicans received much of the German vote, probably—as Whan theorizes—because of the antislavery convictions of those immigrants "who had fled their native lands to escape oppression."[21]

Not to be outdone, Democrats also charged that the Republicans were the ones perpetrating vote fraud. Their charges, however, were far more general and usually left the agency for this misdeed unspecified. Beginning in late September, columns in the *Illinois State Register* asserted that Republican allegations that Democrats were "colonizing" the Irish were "only thrown out to cover precisely such rascality now being contemplated by the republican leaders." In October, the *Register* warned, "Beware of these republican gentlemen, we are satisfied that they are maturing a plan to commit the most monstrous frauds on the purity of the ballot-box." It was all a diversionary tactic, concluded the *Chicago Times:* if Republicans "can once set the eyes of the honest public to watching the Democracy, then their own frauds and rascalities will be concealed and consequently successful." These reports reflected word received by editor Lanphier from his correspondents, one of whom, for example, wrote that "it will be the most glorious political victory ever achieved on the continent" if Douglas won the election but cautioned that "every possible scheme is resorted to to cheat us out of a representative or two."[22]

The level of discourse in the campaign's final weeks was not equal to that of the debates themselves. Familiar patterns of partisan accusation and invective developed, without the constraints of cross-questioning and the physical presence of the opponent on the platform. The stories of Douglas's alleged mistreatment of his family's slaves and of Crittenden's endorsement, which seemingly established that Lincoln was a dangerous radical, weighed with special force as voters waited to cast ballots on November 2.

II

Lincoln won a plurality of the popular vote. The Republican received 125,430 votes, compared to 121,609 for Douglas and 5,071 for the Buchanan Democrats represented by Sidney Breese. But Douglas carried more legislative districts—fifty-four to forty-six—and so, in the era before the Seventeenth Amendment, won reelection to a third Senate term.

What role the debates played in this result it is difficult to say. Voter turnout was higher than in 1856, in part probably because of the drama of the debates, but there is little reason to believe that the debates changed many votes. Then as now, they were more likely to attract attentive voters already committed to a candidate, whereas the election would be decided by the votes of the relatively indifferent and uninvolved. The debates, as Rothschild correctly notes, were only one ingredient in the campaign, and it is not possible precisely to measure the influence of each ingredient on the final result. For that matter, what the final result itself meant was not so clear. The election did not settle what Randall called the "vexed question" of slavery in the Territories. As a practical matter, barring further expansion to the south, that question had been answered by the decisive rejection of the Lecompton constitution two weeks before the debates began. Other factors also muted the mandate of the election; Johannsen lists "the divisions and defections, the blurring of party lines, the outside interference and clandestine management."[23]

All this is to suggest that the election results, like the outcome of each debate, were ambiguous. Who really won or lost depended on the subsequent struggle for interpretation of the results, and this struggle favored Douglas. Democratic papers were jubilant in reporting the election results; Republican papers buried the announcement in brief editorial comment or obscured its significance.

Two factors particularly influenced a pro-Douglas interpretation. First, the senator had prevailed in his challenge to the president of his own party. A year earlier, Buchanan had admonished him that no Democrat had broken with an administration "of his own choosing" and survived. Now the Little Giant had not only survived but triumphed, and his victory over Buchanan seemed at least as important as his defeat of Lincoln. The victory was all the sweeter because Douglas won in the face of Republican gains elsewhere in the North. It all seemed to suggest that popular sovereignty *was* the great unifying principle and the foundation for further Democratic victories.[24]

Second, Republicans lost the crucial counties of central Illinois. Except in the east central part of the state, Democrats rather than Republicans picked up most of the old Whig vote. Republican legislative candidates were defeated in the five counties closest to Springfield and strongly identified with Lincoln: Sangamon, Morgan, Madison, Logan, and Mason. Douglas also carried his legislative candidate in formerly Whig Tazewell County. These were all narrow votes; had five of the six counties gone the other way, Lincoln would have won.[25] The *Chicago Times* credited editor Charles H. Lanphier of the *Illinois State Register* with swaying opinion in Douglas's favor in the central counties. Certainly he was active, but the debates may also have had an influence there. Whan, for example, notes that, relative to the 1854 vote, Democrats improved their performance over Republicans in all counties where both Lincoln and Douglas spoke.[26] It is a reasonable inference that conservative Whigs were swayed by Douglas's repeated assertion that the "house divided" doctrine was a cloak for abolitionism. The endorsement that Douglas received from Clay's political heir, Kentucky senator John J. Crittenden, undoubtedly helped as well.

Republican leaders were openly angry about the loss of the central counties. After acknowledging, "We are beat, and I am one of the Sickest men you ever Saw," G. W. Rives asked Ozias M. Hatch, "What in the D—l was the matter in Sangamon, Madison and Morgan—! Was there any foul play—." An answer was provided by John Tillson, who wrote Hatch two weeks after the election that, as Lincoln attracted support from Buchanan Democrats who wished to punish Douglas, he risked the loss of support from the old Whigs and that this risk had been demonstrated most graphically in central Illinois. With an eye to the future, the correspondent admonished Hatch that unless the Republican party could "secure that conservative part of the old Whig party which the Democrats have been fishing after for the last three years we may as well 'hang up de fiddle and de bow.'" Writing with less tact, Judge David Davis exclaimed to Lincoln, "The Pharisaical old Whigs in the Central Counties, who are so much more righteous than other people, I can't talk about with any patience."[27]

Republican despondency was general. Davis, who had written Lincoln the previous summer that, if Lincoln were defeated for the Senate, "the bottom will fall out of the thing," was clearly surprised by the results; he wrote Lincoln that the outcome "has both astonished and mortified me beyond measure."[28] The resentment felt by the leaders is evident in the dispatch from G. W. Rives to Hatch. Rives reflected that Lincoln "is too good a man to be thus treated by these D— Sons bitches, he has done is [sic] duty nobly—! Is he not like Clay too good and Great to advance." As if to answer his own question, Rives proposed to avenge Lincoln's defeat by making him the party's candidate for president in 1860.[29] But there was work to be done first. The Republicans ended the campaign $3,000 in debt; "what is to be done," Norman B. Judd asked Hatch. Judd even raised the possibility of assessing Lincoln personally for his campaign debts, although he dismissed this option "except as a last resort." Meanwhile, the party must figure out how to modify its appeal. William H. Herndon wrote Trumbull that Lincoln's fate would await *him* two years hence as well unless he could determine how to "wring victory out of the fates." Herndon explained that Lincoln lost because of the old Whigs and admonished Trumbull, "this class of timid, but good, men beat Lincoln, and you must reach them."[30]

In seeking to explain their defeat, Republicans cited several possible causes. Vote fraud was one. The morning after the election, L. H. Waters wrote Hatch, "Our Republican Precincts all did better than we anticipated but by illegal voting they have beaten us. We have some now under arrest for Perjury and shall run them through to the bitter end." Davis, in a letter to his son, cited the influence of the "Irish Colonization," along with the Catholic church and the slave-state influence on the central counties.[31]

Illinois Republicans also found fault with easterners in their own party, particularly with Horace Greeley, whose New York editorials had urged the reelection of Douglas as a fusion candidate. Greeley and William H. Seward, then the Republican front-runner, were political allies, so Illinois Republicans engaged in a kind of guilt by association. If Greeley were responsible for Lincoln's defeat, they would avenge the loss by punishing Seward. At the same state convention that had nominated Lincoln for senator, Republicans by straw vote overwhelmingly favored Seward for president in 1860, but in the aftermath of Lincoln's defeat their support for the New Yorker waned appreciably. Letters to Hatch, the secretary of state, reveal the measure of the Republicans' determination. John Tillson wrote, "I could name a Score of men here as ardent Republicans as ever breathed who swear they never will vote for Wm. H. Seward or any other man that the New York Tribune favors for the Presidency." To Grimshaw, "Seward and Greeley Republicans who voted for Douglas" were worse even than the Know-Nothings or the imported Irish." Rives likewise wrote, "I say D—m Greeley & Co.—they have done more harm to us in Illinois than all others besides, not excepting the D—m Irish." Ben L. Wiley joined his frustrations against both Greeley and Crittenden. "I feel very much like d—g" them both, he wrote; "had they have kept their hands in their breeches it would have all gone OK and we would have sent Stephen into retirement."[32]

In addition to vote fraud and Greeley's influence, another explanation of Lincoln's defeat was that the Republican party had gone too far in trying to appeal to extremists. Tillson wrote that "we have deferred too much to the Democratic element and the Ultra Anti Slavery elements of our party." This course would lead to repeated disasters since, he reminded Hatch, "*you* know as well as I do that the back bone of the Republican Party is the Whig portion of it."[33]

Even the weather was blamed for Lincoln's defeat. It was cold and rainy across much of the state on election day, and Cole contends that the inclement weather cost Republicans at least ten thousand votes. This possibility occasioned some frustration at the time. Thomas C. Sharpe, for example, wrote, "Our Republicans are too many of them of the dry weather sort. I don't often swear but I say Damn a man that will talk big before election and then excuse his supineness on the day, because of the weather."[34]

One often-cited explanation for Lincoln's defeat, especially in the light of his plurality in the popular vote, is that the legislature was malapportioned. It was, but a properly apportioned legislature would not likely have elected Lincoln either. The legislature had been redistricted in 1852 on the basis of the most recent federal census, but the apportionment did not reflect the rapid growth in northern Illinois during the decade, and a Republican redistricting bill based on an 1855 state census had been defeated. Nevertheless, the distribution of legislative seats in 1858 closely mirrored the distribution of the popular vote—if one excludes the thirteen state senators who were "holding over," not up for reelection. Eighty-seven legislators were chosen that fall, forty-six Democrats and forty-one Republicans. The Republican share was but a few percentage points lower than their popular vote share. What made the difference were the holdover senators, eight of whom were Democrats. Even if the eighty-seven contested seats had been distributed exactly according to the popular vote, the holdovers would have provided enough votes to elect Douglas by a two-vote margin.[35]

For his part, Lincoln was calm and reassuring to his supporters. His early fall, he assured them, was nothing if the cause they represented would triumph eventually. Of that he had little doubt. He admonished Charles H. Roy, "I believe, according to a letter of yours to Hatch, you are 'feeling like h—ll yet.' Quit that. You will soon feel better. Another 'blow-up' is coming; and we shall have fun again." His confidence derived from his assessment of Douglas's peculiar stance. The Little Giant was able, his challenger thought, "to be supported both as the best instrument to *put down* and to *uphold* the slave power; but no ingenuity can long keep these antagonisms in harmony."[36] To Anson Henry, Lincoln wrote, "I am glad I made the late race" because it had given him a hearing on the great issue of the time and had afforded him the opportunity to make a difference. To Judd he wrote that he "is convalescent," admonished, "Let the past as nothing be," and urged work on Trumbull's behalf so that he might be able to withstand the assault two years hence. To Alexander Sympson, a month after the election, he wrote, "I have an abiding faith that we shall beat them in the long run," and added, "I write merely to let you know that I am neither dead nor dying."[37]

The Senate election had to be concluded, and that required an official vote by the newly elected legislature. Both Lincoln and Douglas backers spread the story that administration Democrats were trying to woo legislators committed to Douglas to prevent the Little Giant from receiving a majority. Trumbull wished the Buchaneers well, "but have not faith in all they say."[38] In the end, these schemes came to naught. On January 6, 1859, Douglas was duly reelected by a vote of fifty-four to forty-six. Lanphier immediately telegraphed the good news: "Glory to God and the Sucker Democracy." Back from Baltimore, where he was staying at the time, came the senator's reply: "Let the voice of the people rule."

III

In some respects, neither candidate "lost" the debates. Both benefited from the public attention directed to Illinois, the drama of the contest, and the closeness of the vote. Douglas benefited as the only major Northern Democrat to score well in 1858; his version of popular sovereignty rather than Buchanan's platform seemed to be the wave of the future. Already twice having been considered a presidential possibility, he quickly emerged the front-runner for 1860. He made a Southern tour after the 1858 election, most likely to mend his fences.[39] Then—to reassure Northern supporters that he had not abandoned them—he released the famous "Dorr letter" in 1859. This document acknowledged his interest in the presidency—but only if the convention reaffirmed its popular sovereignty platform of 1856 and did not propose reopening the slave trade or drafting a slave code for the territories.[40]

Douglas was in some difficulty, though. Even after the 1858 elections, Buchanan had many loyal supporters, and those who had been defeated usually had lost by very close votes. Rather than congratulate Douglas for his victory over Lincoln, administration supporters blamed him for the divisiveness that meant losses elsewhere. Even before he returned to Washington from his reelection victory, Buchanan loyalists united to strip him of his chairmanship of the Senate Committee on Territories.[41] Moreover, his standing in the South was eroding to precisely the degree that southerners saw popular sovereignty as a one-sided bar to the expansion of slavery. Testing him on the issue, they narrowed the range of ambiguity that he might be permitted. Eventually, the Kansas issue led to what one biographer has called "a break as bitter as that with northern politicos after the Nebraska Act."[42] It was increasingly necessary for Douglas to reconcile popular sovereignty with positive protection of slavery, in order to appeal to Southern audiences, yet also to reduce the sense of moral callousness that popular sovereignty conveyed to northerners. That combination of results required ambivalence that was difficult for Douglas or anyone to sustain.

But it was not the debates themselves that eroded Douglas's position. Many southerners regarded the dispute between Douglas and Buchanan as a personal feud rather than a question of principle, and they admired the scrappy nature of Douglas's attacks on Lincoln. In the opinion of one of his biographers, even in 1859–60 Douglas offered more to the South than did any other leader who had a chance in his own section. Mainly, what Douglas could offer was the prospect of further southward expansion, where the climate might have been more hospitable to the spread of slavery.[43] What eventually doomed Douglas's national appeal was the natural outgrowth of his opposition to Lecompton, which raised the question of whether popular sovereignty truly could be a neutral principle.

Neutrality, of course, is in the eyes of the beholder. Increasingly, South and North were unable to agree about what moves were truly neutral, and each insisted on tests of sincerity that the other region found anathema. As that happened, Douglas lost the vital zone of ambiguity within which his appeal must remain. The Lincoln-Douglas debates were a way station in that unraveling of popular sovereignty, but—despite the folklore surrounding the Freeport question—they were not the original cause. What happened to Douglas probably would have happened even had there been no Lincoln-Douglas debates.

As for Lincoln, little known at the outset, by holding his own with Douglas in the debates he gained immensely, both as the recognized leader of Illinois Republicans and as the object of attention in other states as well. In the immediate aftermath of the campaign, his supporters touted him as a presidential prospect, often in impassioned letters. Horace White, for example, wrote Lincoln that "your popular majority in the State will give *us* the privilege of naming our man for the national ticket in 1860—either President or Vice President. *Then*, let me assure you, Abe Lincoln shall be an honored name before the American people."[44] Although Ward Hill Lamon recalls that Lincoln carried one such prediction in his pocket, there is little indication that Lincoln or others took this prospect seriously.[45] Neither the *Illinois State Journal* nor the *Chicago Press and Tribune*, probably the two papers closest to Lincoln, mentioned the possibility, and Lincoln's name did not appear among twenty-one sketches of presidential candidates published in 1859 or among thirty-four memoirs of "Our Living Representative Men" published in 1860.[46]

Lincoln disclaimed candidacy for the office, writing in the spring of 1859, "I must, in candor, say I do not think myself fit for the Presidency," and declining speaking engagements that fall in Illinois, Wisconsin, and Minnesota. His only speaking tour would be in Ohio.[47] He devoted his political energies to securing Trumbull's reelection in 1860, denying rumors of any rift between Trumbull and himself, and urging prompt redistricting of the legislature in order to improve Trumbull's chances. When Judd reportedly suggested that Lincoln contest for Trumbull's seat, Lincoln rebuked Judd and reminded him that he was pledged to support Trumbull.[48]

Nevertheless, during the spring of 1859 Lincoln's Illinois friends continued to think of him as presidential material; when the state Republican convention met that May, many were convinced that he had a good chance. Lincoln's first indication of possible interest came in a letter on November 1, 1859, in which the erstwhile candidate pledged to "labor faithfully in the ranks, unless as I think not probable, the judgment of the party shall assign me a different position."[49] By 1860, he was being considered as a practical alternative to Seward. The party needed a moderate, though with strong free-soil principles, and Seward was hurt by the seeming belligerence of his irrepressible-conflict doctrine. Lincoln, whose antislavery commitment was at least as firm as Seward's, was perceived as more moderate when it came to relations between the sections.

But, from the perspective of 1858, the 1860 presidential election appeared to be in the distant future. One of Lincoln's more immediate needs was to prevent a realignment of parties in which Republicans would endorse Douglas. In a letter to Trumbull, Lincoln predicted that Democrats would drive Douglas from the national party, not by outvoting him at the convention but by insisting on a new litmus test—perhaps a slave code for the territories—that Douglas could not support. Then, he foresaw, the Little Giant "will bolt at once, turn upon us, as in the case of Lecompton, and claim that all Northern men shall make common cause in electing him President as the best means of breaking down the Slave power." Such a position would not be in the Republican interest; it would dissipate Republican strength by yoking the party to a platform that denied the moral significance of the slavery question. As Lincoln summarized his position with respect to fusion, "I am for it, if it can be had on republican grounds; and I am not for it on any other terms. A fusion on any other terms, would be as foolish as unprincipled. It would lose the whole North, while the common enemy would still carry the whole South."[50]

Several events during 1859 and 1960 were both the natural outgrowth of the debates and the opening skirmishes in the coming presidential contest. In the fall of 1859, Douglas published an article in *Harper's* in which he maintained that popular sovereignty had been seen by the Founding Fathers as the principle dividing between federal and local authority. This article was his response to the inconclusive nature of the historical argument in the Lincoln-Douglas debates. It was mainly an attempt to refute Lincoln for a Northern audience, among whom subscriptions to *Harper's* were concentrated.

Johannsen reports that Douglas spent the months following the debates in a search for precedents in early American history for the popular sovereignty principle. He "withdrew from the Library of Congress such standard works as "The Federalist, Jonathan Elliot's *Debates*, and the first six volumes of George Bancroft's *History of the United States*." The result was a long, somewhat ponderous essay arguing that the Revolution had been fought for the principle of popular sovereignty, that territories were virtually the same as states, and that Congress could confer to the territorial legislatures powers that it could not itself exercise. Johannsen characterizes the article as "long and tedious, written in a dull, turgid style, . . . repetitious to the point of annoyance. . . . The arguments were often contrived and involved, and the tone suggested the air of a man pushed to desperation by the attacks of his critics."[51]

Several of the arguments could be criticized easily. The discussion of the intent of the Founders was selective; Douglas omitted any reference to the Northwest Ordinance, which Lincoln often cited as proof that the Founders claimed for the Congress authority over slavery in the territories. And the analysis of the *Dred Scott* case was somewhat misleading. It assumed that the Supreme Court had acknowledged the ability of the territorial legislature to regulate slavery, whereas the Court had not ruled on that question and might well subject the territorial legislatures to the same strictures as the Congress. Nevertheless, the article's publication was a significant political event. Nevins concludes that "it was hard reading for most politicians; yet no other article of the decade was so widely discussed," and Fehrenbacher gave it second place only to the Harper's Ferry raid in the major events of 1859. It produced, he writes, "an astonishing increase in the volume and intensity of the argument."[52] Interestingly, as the debate intensified, Douglas referred to his program less as *popular sovereignty*, a term that no longer expressed a universal democratic value but had become quite controversial. Instead, he began using *the doctrine of nonintervention* or *adherence to the Cincinnati platform* as more euphemistic characterizations.[53]

If Douglas found his extension of the debates in the *Harper's* article, Lincoln's came in speaking tours in Ohio and New England during the fall of 1859–60. The Ohio canvass was a virtual replay of the debates since Douglas spoke there as well. The Little Giant spoke in Columbus, Cincinnati, and Wooster on behalf of Democratic candidates, and, just like the year before, Lincoln followed him around the state. The Little Giant attributed to the Republicans an activist intention to abolish slavery, drawing his inferences from Lincoln's "house divided" doctrine and Seward's prediction of an "irrepressible conflict." He then argued, as in the *Harper's* essay, that this view put the Republicans at odds with the Founding Fathers, who had waged the Revolution in order to establish popular sovereignty. Indeed, the Republicans, by denying the authority of territorial inhabitants to govern themselves in all respects, were akin to the Tories, who had defended taxation without representation. Douglas also began to argue that the Republicans and Southern fire-eaters were essentially similar, differing only as to when they would have the federal government intervene in what properly ought to be a local matter.

Lincoln attacked these doctrines, as he had in Illinois, and he specifically refuted the *Harper's* article, which he described as an attempt by

Douglas to arrogate to himself the ethos of the revolutionary generation. For his part, Lincoln developed three major themes. First, slavery was fundamentally a moral issue. To view it otherwise, or to regard it as a trifling matter, was to break down public opinion, which stood in the way of its expansion. Second, Douglas's popular sovereignty would lead to the nationalization of slavery, not because of any conspiracy, but because of its own internal logic. The Freeport doctrine was inconsistent and would lead to Supreme Court approval for a federal slave code under the guise of friendly legislation. In his notes for the Ohio speeches, Lincoln noted that Douglas's "plan" for nationalizing slavery differed from that of his imagined enemies, the Southern fire-eaters, only in that his was practicable while theirs was not. (Both Lincoln and Douglas were trying to liken the other to the fire-eaters.) Third, in adhering to these principles, Lincoln maintained, it was the Republican party that was truly conservative, preserving the vision of the Founders.[54]

Lincoln spoke not only in Ohio but also in Indiana, Wisconsin, Iowa, Missouri, and Kansas. His growing prominence led to an invitation to visit New England during the winter of 1860. That trip, which also enabled him to visit his son Robert, at Harvard, culminated with a speech at the Cooper Institute in New York. The Cooper Union speech, as it is commonly called, was his fullest elaboration of the historical argument—the match for Douglas's essay in *Harper's*. Herndon contends that it was he who persuaded Lincoln to make the Cooper Institute the site for a political speech rather than the unexciting "Discoveries and Inventions," which he had been using on the lecture circuit for over a year.[55]

The speech had three basic parts. The longest was historical: Lincoln outlined the views of the thirty-nine signers of the Constitution regarding the extension of slavery to the territories, concluding that they believed that the federal government had the power to regulate slavery in the territories and that the peculiar institution must eventually disappear. He also examined the twelve amendments to the Constitution and concluded that none of them set aside the force of what he had said. In the second section, Lincoln ostensibly made an appeal to southerners, assuring them of his moderation but stressing his devotion to republican principles and his unwillingness to see the Union dissolved. It is quite possible that the Southern audience was a foil and that Lincoln's true audience was the Northern Republicans to whom he also addressed the final portion, urging them to persevere but to consider matters in a calm and mature fashion.[56]

The message of the speech was potentially radical, but the tone was conservative. The speech was presented as a lawyer's brief. As Wright has observed, there was "a lack of bitterness and vindictiveness which gave his speech an overall effect that was more conservative than the implications of his main arguments warranted. There was none of the name calling, the irritating tone of moral superiority, the preaching quality of the abolitionists and many of the radical politicians."[57] Lincoln was pleased with the speech; he wrote his wife that it "went off passably well, and gave me no trouble whatever." Most historians have seen it as more significant than that; King, for example, maintains that when Lincoln went east he had some thought of the vice presidency but that the Cooper Union speech made him a plausible candidate for president.[58] He had held his own with Seward on the New Yorker's own ground.

Douglas, meanwhile, was caught on the horns of a Democratic dilemma. His 1858 campaign demonstrated the power of an anti-Lecompton appeal for Northern Democrats but further alienated the Buchanan administration and its Southern allies. The Illinois senator was finding it increasingly difficult to receive support from both camps. Already he had been stripped of his chairmanship of the Senate Committee on Territories. Now the fire-eaters launched a campaign for a federal slave code for the territories, both as a rallying cry to mobilize their own forces and prevent calls for secession and as a device to thwart Douglas from taking over leadership of the party and giving it a distinctly Northern cast.

According to Collins, the proposal never had the support of a majority of the legislators in any state of the Deep South.[59] But it put Douglas on the spot. In the Jonesboro debate the year before, he had answered Lincoln's fifth interrogatory by suggesting that a slave code would violate the principle of congressional nonintervention. To maintain that position would cause him to fail the litmus test and widen the growing breach in his party. Some thought that he would bend. Herndon wrote Trumbull, "Is not Douglas in a 'tickleish' fix? I am aware of his inexhaustible falsity and the grand immensity of his aspiring hypocracy [sic], and ready to hear of anything from him." Palmer even suggested to Trumbull that Douglas would acquiesce in the reopening of the slave trade by having the laws against it "annihilated by the action of the federal Judiciary."[60] Instead, Douglas stood his ground, only to find his unwillingness to endorse a slave code cited by the Southern "ultras" as an indirect cause of John Brown's raid at Harper's Ferry.[61]

Lincoln made another major decision in the fall of 1859: to seek publication of the texts of his debates with Douglas. Reporters had taken down the texts in shorthand, and the speeches had appeared in the *Chicago Times* and the *Chicago Press and Tribune*. Each paper usually published its own candidate's speeches in full and abbreviated those of the other, so by combining Douglas's speeches from the *Times* and Lincoln's from the *Press and Tribune* one would have a reasonably complete record. Lincoln did that, collecting the texts in a scrapbook that he forwarded to George M. Parsons, Ohio Republican chairman, following the Republican victories in that state in 1859. Parsons passed the text along to the publishing firm of Follett, Foster, and Company, who brought out the first edition of the debates in the spring of 1860, just in time for the presidential campaign.[62] The 1860 Follett, Foster edition became "a best seller—an unusual distinction for a political discussion of constitutional law"; it went through four printings in the year 1860 alone.[63]

Douglas originally dismissed publication as an insignificant event but began to think otherwise as the wide distribution of his 1858 statements coincided with his 1860 need to seek Southern votes in order to prevent a deadlock in the Democratic convention. In June, he wrote the publishing company, protesting "against the unfairness of this publication, and especially against the alterations and mutilations in the Reports of my speeches." Lincoln's speeches, Douglas alleged, "have been revised, corrected, and improved . . . while mine have been mutilated."[64] The publication was fortuitous for Lincoln's 1860 presidential campaign as it "gave the great multitude the first opportunity to learn somewhat of the man who had been chosen in preference to Seward and Chase and others who, like them, had long been distinguished in public affairs."[65] The debates have remained significant texts in American politics. A 1943 essay counted ten separate editions and thirty-eight printings to date, and the texts were made easily accessible through their republication on the occasion of the debates' centennial.[66]

Lincoln used the publication of the debates, as well as of his 1859 Ohio speeches and the Cooper Union speech, as a reason for his failure to campaign actively in 1860. His positions were well known, he insisted, and easily available in the public record; anything else he might say would only trigger a new round of misrepresentations by his opponents. He faced the delicate problem, in key Northern states, of maintaining the Republican base while wooing enough Fillmore supporters to carry the state. Without abandoning principle, Lincoln had to appear moderate and conservative; that goal could be achieved through silence in the campaign and a suggestion to inquirers that they read the ambiguous text of the 1858 debates.

Douglas, on the other hand, became the first candidate to campaign actively throughout the country for the office. He appealed always for compromise and moderation and noted the common interest of Republicans and fire-eaters in conspiring against the will of the people.

The Little Giant did not neglect the South, even though he clearly had no chance to win there. His Southern campaign was probably intended less to block Lincoln's election than to urge a Unionist vote, and in this goal he succeeded: the combination of Lincoln, Douglas, and John Bell outpolled John C. Breckinridge. Yet the Southern tour profoundly alarmed Douglas. He had heard rumors of a Southern conspiracy to stage a coup d'état and install Breckinridge in the president's chair by force. In a Chicago speech, he exclaimed that he thought that the country was in greater danger than ever before and that only a strong appeal to union would enable it to surmount the deadly combination of Northern and Southern sectionalism.[67]

The results of the 1860 election are well known, as is the aftermath. The South saw the election of Lincoln not necessarily as obnoxious in itself but as a portent of the destruction of constitutional rights. Once deny the right to property in the territories, and what constitutional right was safe? Secession, as Holt explains, was prompted "less to save black slavery than to escape white slavery by avoiding Republican tyranny." No means remained within the Union to resist this usurpation since the South had lost the balance of power, personal liberty laws were eloquent testimony to the absence of Northern good will, and constitutional guarantees were inadequate since they were precisely what was at issue.[68] So the South moved to dissolve the Union of 1861 in order to preserve the Constitution of 1787.

Like most Republicans, Lincoln did not take the secession threat seriously. Talk of disunion had become so common in the midcentury rhetorical culture that it was regarded as "rhetorical bluster to coerce the North into accepting Southern demands."[69] It was a campaign device, and if ignored it would go away. Not just for that reason, though, were Republicans unwilling to compromise in 1860–61. Having won an election victory, they would have squandered the objective for which it was obtained. They would not have been able to change public opinion or shift discussion to a new level. As Nevins explains, Republican acceptance of any of the compromise measures discussed in 1861 would revitalize those committed to the expansion of slavery: "They would *toil* to make New Mexico a slave state; they would redouble their filibustering efforts; they would dream, however hopelessly, of Cuba, Lower California, Sonora, and Central America."[70] In the face of intransigence from both sides, the outcome was what Lincoln described in his Second Inaugural Address: "Both parties deprecated war; but one of them would *make* war rather than let the nation survive; and the other would *accept* war rather than let it perish. And the war came."[71]

IV

Although no one could know the uses to which an abstract right to transport slaves into a territory might be put, most of the specific issues that prompted the debates were settled soon after 1858. Symbolic considerations loomed so large, however, that sectional conflicts were not resolved even though the underlying issues ceased to be controversial. Instead, as Morison describes the 1860 election, "the sense of differences was sharper than ever, while the apparent cause for division was becoming less and less real."[72]

To start with, few slaves were taken to the new territories. The 1860 census showed a total of only forty-six slaves in all the territories— twenty-nine in Utah, fifteen in Nebraska, and two in Kansas. Six years after Kansas and Nebraska had been opened to slavery, it was clear that slavery in those territories was not a practical option. Of course, no one could be sure that slavery would be infeasible under other economic or technological conditions. New Mexico adopted a slave code in 1859; for many Republicans, that action proved "that slavery knew no natural limits. It mattered little," Sewell explains, that by 1861 there were only two dozen slaves in New Mexico, "most of them female domestics in the service of federal officials." Popular sovereignty had been shown not to be an antislavery device; the institution would go where it was not contained, and it could be adapted to uses other than agriculture. In similar fashion, Jaffa suggests that the relative absence of slaves in Kansas between 1858 and 1861 proves only that "under existing conditions owners did not take them. Owners were awaiting the outcome of the struggle."[73]

At the same time, events in Kansas seemed to demonstrate the ability of a territory to prevent slavery, if it so chose. As settlement increased, Kansas came under antislavery, Republican control. Shortly after the 1858 election, *Chicago Tribune* reporter Horace White wrote Trumbull, proposing that Douglas's view about the need for "friendly local legislation" be put to the test. Why not induce the Kansas territorial legislature to pass "unfriendly legislation" and claim that it was only exercising its rights under popular sovereignty, which Douglas after all had reconciled with the *Dred Scott* decision? So White proposed that Kansas abolish slavery and nullify the fugitive slave law in the territory, "both of the measures to be argued from texts in Douglas' Freeport speech and his still later one at Memphis."[74] Early in 1859, the territorial legislature did vote to abolish slavery. The bill was killed by the territorial governor's pocket veto, but there was enough antislavery sentiment to override the veto in 1860.[75] Jefferson Davis, in a fall 1858 speech in Maine, had endorsed Douglas's view on the need for friendly local legislation, but he considered the Congress obligated to pass such legislation. For Douglas it was the other way around: popular sovereignty could be used to block slavery in the territories, notwithstanding *Dred Scott.* In the long run, this discrepancy would heighten the Little Giant's dilemma of how to appeal to both North and South at the same time. But in the immediate context it suggested that Douglas's means could be used to achieve Lincoln's ends, in which case not all that much was in dispute in the Lincoln-Douglas debates.

For their part, Republicans appeared if anything to abandon the principles for which they contended in the debates and the 1860 campaign. In February and March 1861, Republicans in Congress passed bills to organize new territories in Colorado, Nevada, and Dakota. The bills to create these new territories said nothing about excluding slavery; Randall aptly notes that "they went not a step farther in stopping slavery in these new areas than Douglas had done in providing for Kansas and Nebraska."[76] Nor was that all. In the closing days of the congressional session in March 1861, both houses—with Republican support—passed and sent to the states a proposed thirteenth amendment to the Constitution that would have barred the federal government in perpetuity from interfering with slavery in those states where it already existed. Lincoln acquiesced in this amendment, which Ohio, Maryland, and Illinois ratified "before events crowded it into oblivion."[77]

To be sure, mitigating circumstances explained each of these moves. The failure to prohibit slavery in the new territories could be seen as a matter of tactics rather than principle. Republicans knew that they would control the patronage in the three territories; they could assume confidently that slavery did not have a chance, so they did not need to inflame tensions further with a legal prohibition.[78] Moreover, in June 1862, Congress abolished slavery in all the territories, despite the fact that the *Dred Scott* decision was still on the books. As for the amendment perpetually guaranteeing slavery where it already existed, this was regarded as a final effort to reassure the South, particularly since Lincoln never believed that he had the power to interfere anyway. This amendment seemed in 1861 to be a low-cost way of making a "final offer" to the South and inducing the border states to remain in the Union. Viewing 1858 from the perspective of 1861, though, these matters seemed to suggest that the debates had not made much difference to the political landscape.

Does it follow, then, that the debates ultimately lacked substance and significance and that the performance of neither candidate is to be commended? Some have made just that argument. In his biography of Lincoln, Brogan laments that "both Lincoln and Douglas had earlier reached greater heights of eloquence, of courage, of candor, of cogency of argument than they did in the joint debates. . . . There was no Socratic deliverance of the truth; too often that delicate child was stifled by sophistries, and, when needs must, both debaters were admirable sophists."[79] But others have regarded the contests as influencing American culture and society profoundly. Reflecting back on the debates after studying the moral argument, Rietveld concluded, "No episode in American history raised in a more fundamental way the question of what it was that Americans agreed upon, what they disagreed upon, and whether or not a common platform existed upon which Northerners and Southerners could live in peace forever under a common constitution."[80]

However much the debates affected the issues, they surely affected the candidates, although it is not clear how much or in what direction. With respect to Douglas, some early biographers took for granted that he had bested Lincoln by the end of the series. Some gave Lincoln the contest but admitted "that no one then living could have made a more brilliant or masterful defense than did Senator Douglas under the peculiar circumstances in which he stood."[81] Still others believed that Douglas was the villain of the piece. The ambiguities of his Freeport doctrine had been broadcast to a wider audience, and the debates seemed to transform Lincoln from a relative unknown into a high-credibility alternative to Douglas. Yet another writer concludes that the debates did not have an unusual effect on Douglas' career; their influence, according to Milton, "was no greater than the Compromise of 1850 or the repeal of the Missouri Compromise. Certainly they were not so determinative as Douglas's break with Buchanan."[82] Douglas's debate skills likewise came in for mixed reviews. Some praised him for statesmanship and eloquence; others, such as the humorist Petroleum V. Nasby, found Douglas to be "the demagogue all the way through. There was no trick of presentation that he did not use. He suppressed facts, twisted conclusions, and perverted history. He wriggled and turned and dodged; he appealed to prejudices."[83]

Lincoln's performance in the debates, too, has been evaluated differently, but by far most assessments are positive. Regardless of the election outcome, the debates made Lincoln rather than Trumbull the state's most popular Republican. His ability to deal with Douglas on an equal basis attracted national attention to him. He managed to take a moderate position without antagonizing the more radical members of his party. His language was simple and clear, his illustrations powerful yet homely. He was sensitive to parallel structure, to repetition, and especially to antithesis. One writer summarized all these considerations in the pithy statement, "It was Douglas most Illinoisians came to hear that summer of 1858; it was Lincoln they remembered."[84]

Beyond assessing the issues and the men, the debates also spoke to the culture and indexed a rapidly growing polarization between North and South in virtually all areas of American life. Some have argued that the polarization was unnecessary, that it was the needless preliminary to a needless war. Wells, for example, finds both candidates tilting at windmills: "Lincoln attacked not a reality but a legal tendency of slavery to expand into some hypothetical future territory; Douglas defended his popular sovereignty against an onslaught from a free-soil Congress which was nowhere to be found." Even at the time, Buchanan condemned the "sectional hatred and bigotry which these debates were regenerating at the very moment when the storm seemed at last to be receding."[85] Polarization might be undesirable, but few could deny that it was taking place or that it was reflected in these debates. By the late 1850s, Donald has noted, "the reservoir of goodwill and compassion that Americans had hitherto shared was being drained. Slowly and usually reluctantly, more and more came to think of themselves as forming not one but two distinct peoples."[86]

In such an atmosphere, the significance of Kansas was magnified. It was important not so much in its own right, or even as a representative of other territories, but as a concrete embodiment of the choices facing the nation's future, a surrogate for the larger questions of time and destiny. Although Republicans disclaimed any intention to interfere with slavery where it already existed, it was widely believed that over the long run the institution must either spread or die.[87] If the Kansas question had little immediate effect, it certainly enabled discussion of what would be the nature of the Union generations hence.

What made the choice seem even starker was the widespread belief that the plantation economy, a prerequisite for slavery, and the society of small farmers characteristic of the Old Northwest could not coexist. The question, then, was whether the territories would be settled by slaveholders or by free whites. Referring to Kansas, Illinois Republican congressman John F. Farnsworth stated, "You might as well prohibit by an act of Congress the emigration of the free laboring man of the North to that State, as to permit slavery to exist there."[88] In the fate of Kansas lay the fate of future territories as well. The country would become all slave or all free because the economic conditions needed for the expansion of freedom and for the expansion of slavery were seen as incompatible.

V

Very shortly after Lincoln's death, the process of deification began. To support a judgment that the assassination was the ultimate evil, Lincoln in life was seen as embodying ultimate good. His life was a grand struggle in which a man of such lowly beginnings came to such a noble end. Herndon delivered lectures on Lincoln's greatness, although his lecture on "Lincoln and Ann Rutledge" aroused the ire of Robert Todd Lincoln, who wrote that his father's law partner was "making an ass of himself in his lectures. . . . His reflections, which make up a large portion, would be very ludicrous if I did not feel strongly that he speaks with a certain amount of authority from having known my father so long." When Ward Hill Lamon, a Lincoln aide during the war, published an even more critical biography, Herndon was quick to deny that he had written "a page—paragraph—sentence or word" of it, although he had sold his own unfinished manuscript to Lamon and contended in the same letter that most of the content of the book actually came from his material.[89]

The glorification of Lincoln affected memories of Douglas and of the debates of 1858. In his own day among the most prominent senators, the most persistent advocate of territorial expansion, and a constant defender of local self-government, he was remembered as a stepping-stone in Lincoln's career or, worse yet, as an apologist for slavery. Douglas's demagogy contrasted with Lincoln's statesmanship, his moral obtuseness with Lincoln's moral elevation.[90] From this mind-set followed the belief that Lincoln scored a decisive victory in the debates but somehow managed to lose a rigged election. From it too came the popular belief that Lincoln's loss was a strategic feint, that he asked the second Freeport question against the advice of his aides, and knowing that it would probably cost him the election, because he realized that in the long run it would undercut Douglas's national base, and he was "after bigger game." From it continues to follow the belief that the 1858 encounters were the paradigm case of what political debate ought to be and that the quality of contemporary American politics would be enhanced if we could raise ourselves to the level of debate in which Lincoln and Douglas conducted themselves.

These beliefs, generally implausible and not supported by the record, blind us to what was the true genius of the Lincoln-Douglas debates. Conducted for a divided electorate, in a close election, amid a political culture in great flux, they imposed constraints on what each speaker could say. Some issues could not be discussed at all; some differences had to be magnified; some embarrassments had to be smoothed over; some audiences had to be placated; some unusual coalitions had to be built. In the face of these constraints, the debates reveal two accomplished politicians jockeying for advantage by carefully selecting and effectively using the weapons in their rhetorical arsenal. All things considered, both candidates made excellent use of the materials they had. And those materials came from the political culture of the place and time, with its fund of beliefs and values, concerns and fears. To discuss the slavery question meaningfully, the candidates had to address it in terms of that fund of social knowledge. In the process, it became transformed from an abstract and global proposition to specific issues of motive, law, history, and morality. The Lincoln-Douglas debates deserve their exalted historical position not for the reasons often given but because they so clearly demonstrate the possibilities for discussion when a fundamental issue is transformed in the crucible of public debate. If we find contemporary debate thwarted by the seeming incommensurability between opposed economic, military, diplomatic, or moral values, we might appropriately look once again to the tactical genius of the Lincoln-Douglas debates to see if they display rhetorical principles applicable to our own time.

8

The Debates and Public Argument

Why, more than 130 years later, do the Lincoln-Douglas debates remain the model for American political debate, the standard against which contemporary campaign debates are measured? To confront that question, one must return to the paradoxes of the 1858 encounters themselves. Puzzling through those anomalies may lead to a deeper understanding of what in the debates is worthy of celebration.

Conventional wisdom has it that the debates were valuable as a stepping-stone in Lincoln's career, propelling him toward the presidency. Certainly the debates made him better known. The national attention drawn to the debates worked especially to Lincoln's benefit, since he was less known, and resulted in invitations to speak outside the state during 1859 and 1860. Yet it must be remembered that it was *Douglas* who won the Senate race. He won it not because of quirks in the legislative apportionment, certainly not because Lincoln deliberately threw the race while setting his sights on the White House. The Little Giant triumphed mainly because, during the debates and in other campaign speeches, he convinced the swing voters of central Illinois that Lincoln was really a radical, an abolitionist in disguise, who certainly would not have received the endorsement of the beloved Henry Clay had the sage of Ashland still been alive. Since we remember Lincoln as the Great Emancipator, we might think that he would delight in Douglas's portrayal. But he sought throughout the campaign to deny it, both because abolition was a greater evil than slavery in the minds of the swing voters and because he was no abolitionist himself. Memory plays tricks on the unsuspecting. Not until the fall of 1862 did Lincoln proclaim emancipation, and he was careful to limit the scope of the proclamation to the rebel states, precisely the area where he lacked power to put it into effect. If the substance of the debates worked to Lincoln's benefit, the way in which it did so must be considerably more subtle.

A second virtue often claimed for the debates is that, because of the number, length, and format of the encounters, they permitted extensive discussion of the issues. This call is sounded especially by those disillusioned with political debate during the 1980s, when candidates were asked questions by journalists and then given very short time to reply or to comment on the opponent's answer. Certainly, the Lincoln-Douglas debates were long. Each candidate controlled ten and a half hours of speaking time, which was divided into units no shorter than thirty minutes. But it is questionable whether this length resulted in intensive consideration of issues. The debates were often repetitive; they are characterized by the trading of charges, often without evidence; the arguments were incompletely developed; and the candidates' remarks often veered down the byways of local politics. Something important was happening as the audiences endured sweltering August afternoons or the cold rain of an October day, but extensive discussion is probably not what it was.

Then, too, the debates are celebrated for their ability to bring together opposing views on the leading moral issue of the day, exploring the issue in spirited but respectful argument, thereby establishing the value of speech in a free society. Those who decry evasion of the moral dimension of contemporary political issues often point to the Lincoln-Douglas debates as an object lesson. In fact, however, the moral question received scant attention in the debates, having been foreshadowed at the end of the first debate but not really developed until the sixth. With rare exceptions, moreover, the candidates set out their own beliefs but did not grapple with the opponent's conception—hardly a strong debate on slavery and morality. Yet here, too, something significant is indeed happening through the way the moral issue is treated. In fact, unpacking this last paradox may be the place to begin, if the goal is to understand what accounts for the enduring significance of the Lincoln-Douglas debates.

I

Of all the argument patterns in the debates, clearly the moral argument was primary. It furnished the template for viewing the prospect of slavery's expansion into new territories. But the moral battle lines were not clearly drawn. It was not that one candidate favored and the other opposed slavery. Rather, two very different conceptions of the locus of morality were at issue, and neither could encompass the other. For Lincoln, the key issue was the immorality of slavery itself, and the basis for belief was an individualistic philosophy that stressed equal opportunity to rise economically.[1] For Douglas, on the other hand, slavery per se was not the moral question; the issue was who had the right to decide for or against the institution. Douglas answered his question by reference to the power of local communities and the value of self-determination. He assigned a much lower value to the question of slavery itself, asserting in Alton that self-government was a more important value than "all the negroes in Christendom."[2]

These two moral positions did not directly engage each other, and each candidate could dismiss the other's challenges as beside the point. If Lincoln insisted that slavery was evil, Douglas could reply that the views of those present did not really matter; the real question was who had the power to decide whether to admit the institution into a community. If it really were an evil system, then let the people who choose it suffer the evil. On the other hand, if it were a positive good, let them enjoy the good. Whether slavery was good or evil really did not affect Douglas's position since it was grounded in a concept of morality as procedure. Lincoln had no alternative but to lambaste Douglas for professing indifference for the very issue most on everyone's mind. This attack, of course, was somewhat misleading. Douglas was maintaining not that he had no views about whether slavery was right but that, whatever anyone's views were on that issue, the approach to deciding whether slavery could be extended into the territories was the same.

In like fashion, Lincoln's moral position made much of Douglas's argument irrelevant. The incumbent could insist that his challenger was bent on obliterating the distinctions among states and imposing national uniformity, violating the principles of federalism and local self-determination on which the nation was founded. Lincoln's reply, in effect, was that he generally supported such principles, particularly when exemplified by reference to such topics as the liquor laws of Maine or the cranberry laws of Indiana. But slavery was different, the Republican insisted, because it involved a fundamental human right that derived from natural law. There were limits to which Lincoln was willing to press his case. Because of his respect for the Constitution, he did not wish to uproot the peculiar institution where it already existed. But he certainly wished for it not to grow, and one way to assure that result was to keep it out of the virgin territories. So, when Douglas appealed to the value of local self-determination, Lincoln replied that he generally endorsed that value but that it was simply inapplicable to the case at hand.

The two moral positions were not just different; they were incommensurable. As a result, extended development and repetition of the competing views would have served no purpose other than to restate assertions: 'tis and 'taint. It is fitting, therefore, that the moral claims received their fullest development in the last debate, when Lincoln proclaimed the evil of slavery to be the real issue and Douglas maintained that local self-government was more important than all the blacks on earth. If these statements had been made at Ottawa, it is hard to imagine where the debates could have gone from there.

When confronted with incommensurable arguments, one might attempt to dislodge one or the other position by showing it to be self-contradictory.[3] Douglas very briefly attempted to do so when he asserted that starvation of the slaves would be the means by which Lincoln would set the institution on the course of ultimate extinction and that this was hardly a moral approach for someone concerned with individual rights. The Little Giant did not develop this claim, and, if he had, it could have been answered easily. Lincoln believed that the absence of new slave lands in the West would create the conditions under which the institution would cease to be profitable, and then it would be ended voluntarily—just as Douglas said had been the case in Illinois. Although they were quite different, each of the moral positions was sufficiently cogent to avoid the charge of internal inconsistency. If it was unlikely that either view could be refuted, and if the clash of the debate could not develop either position further, then there seems little more to say.

Does it follow, then, that all the rest of the debate—the conspiracy claims, the constitutional and historical arguments—was filler, time-wasting maneuvers so that the competing moral claims could be introduced at the very end, when no extension or refutation was possible? It might seem so at first glance, but closer examination suggests that the four argument patterns were linked. The constitutional and historical arguments functioned as surrogates for the moral argument, and the conspiracy claims highlighted the difference between the candidates and thereby prepared the audience for the competing moral visions.

What made the moral arguments incommensurable was the absence of common ground. Rather than withdrawing from the dispute in the face of this condition, the debaters sought other argument patterns on which common ground was available and used these as surrogates for the issue that could not be fully discussed.[4] Both candidates reached not for the appeals that divided but for those that united their listeners.

In the mid-nineteenth century, reverence for the Constitution provided such a basis for appeal. To be sure, there were fundamental differences as to whether the people or the states were the ultimate basis of sovereignty, and there were differences between those favoring strict and those favoring loose interpretation. These differences make the

Constitution an "essentially contested concept" whose meaning cannot be known precisely.[5] But they in no sense deny the underlying reverence that Americans had for their founding document. That being so, great benefit could be had by aligning one's own position with the Constitution and being able to dismiss the opponent's view as extra- or even unconstitutional. Rather than probe the basic values of local self-government and individual rights, the debaters could argue about which notion of morality was privileged in the Constitution, a document that commanded the loyalty of both. If invoking this document could avert too searching a probe on incommensurable positions, then the identity of the society can be preserved. Even if there is no clear answer to the question of which moral system is preferred, the discussion takes place with the anchor of a consensual value, so the conversation can proceed. Both sides must relate their arguments to the common theme of what the Constitution permits or enjoins, so there is an available standard for evaluation. The extended discussion of the Constitution can thus substitute for the clash of competing moral systems.

The historical argument furnishes an even clearer case of how one pattern may function as a surrogate for another. The 1850s, as has been noted, were characterized by a sentimental worship of the Founding Fathers so intense that one writer has labeled it "filiopiety."[6] Lincoln and Douglas both espoused the view that the Founders understood all aspects of the slavery question at least as well as, if not better than, those present on the scene in 1858. Since the authority of the Founders was a shared warrant for arguments, the choice between moral systems could be transformed into the question, What would the men of the Revolution have done had they been here? Reviewing the speeches or writings of Jefferson and Washington was not an idle exercise or a way for the candidates to score what are derided as "debating points." Rather, it was a way to settle a dispute that could not be settled, by referring to the judgment of others whose authority both sides accepted. Again, the fact that the Founders did not speak univocally was not a deterrent. It meant that divining their views was not just an empirical matter but a process of extended argument. Yet the commonly accepted warrant permitted lengthy dispute in a way that the clash of moral systems did not.

What was true of the Founding Fathers was even more true in the case of Henry Clay. The last of the Founders had died over twenty years before the debates, but Clay's name was still very much on the tongue. The Kentuckian was not just the patron saint of the Old Line Whigs of central Illinois; he was regarded by Whigs and Democrats alike as the political descendant of the Founders and as a spiritual link to them. For this reason, both candidates sought to align their positions with Clay.

Lincoln quoted Clay, insisted that he had been a Clay Whig for all his adult life, and assured his audiences that Clay would sanction the position he was taking in the debates. Douglas, on the other hand, maintained that Lincoln had abandoned Clay politically in 1848 and philosophically in the "House Divided" speech. Clay's views on the particular issue of 1858 are unknown, but, if either candidate could successfully claim Clay's mantle, he would have a powerful substitute for the unprovable claim that his view of morality was superior to that of his opponent. The closest modern parallel to this bipartisan appropriation of a partisan figure is Ronald Reagan's invocation of Franklin Delano Roosevelt to support the claim that the values of the Republican right are more consistent with the New Deal than are those of the Democratic left.[7]

Both the constitutional and the historical arguments served as surrogates for the main issue. What, then, of the conspiracy claims? These arguments prepared the way for the moral polarity by heightening the contrast between the candidates and the parties. At the beginning of the campaign, matters were in a state of flux. There was even talk of the Republicans' acceptance of Douglas as a fusion candidate because of his opposition to Lecompton. The practical differences between the two candidates were also hard to discern since it appeared that both the Republican doctrine of nonextension and Douglas's view of popular sovereignty would have resulted in freedom for the territories. And Douglas had the advantage of incumbency.

Lincoln needed to sharpen the difference between himself and the incumbent, and what better way to do that than to proclaim that the Little Giant was part of a secret conspiracy to spread slavery across the land? As for Douglas, the best way to answer a conspiracy charge was to respond in kind. Since both men were competing for the middle-of-the-road central Illinois Whigs, each wanted to portray his opponent as extreme. The response to Lincoln's conspiracy charge therefore was to insist that the Republican was part of a secret abolitionist cabal. These and the other conspiracy charges were not altogether fanciful. There was enough circumstantial evidence to support them, and there is no reason to doubt that each candidate viewed them sincerely. But, interestingly, they virtually disappeared by the middle of the debates. It is as though the candidates both recognized that they would not be winning arguments in their own right. Their strength came as they enabled Lincoln and Douglas to anticipate other positions.

The conspiracy arguments sensitized listeners to the fact that the differences between candidates mattered. They were also useful to make later arguments seem more credible. For example, the charge that

Douglas was an active participant in a cabal to spread slavery across the land could be dismissed as preposterous. But this charge made it easier to take seriously the later claim that Douglas was an unwitting dupe, the "instrument" of a conspiratorial design who behaved as effectively as if he had been in on the plot all along. He was anesthetizing the public mind for a move in the direction away from that of the Founding Fathers and hence away from true morality. In this example, the conspiracy claim sets the stage for the historical argument, which in turn is the surrogate for a moral claim that can be neither proved nor tested directly.

Likewise, Douglas's assertion that Lincoln, Trumbull, and others had schemed to abolitionize the two major parties was difficult to sustain. But even raising the possibility that Lincoln was an avowed abolitionist made it easier to take seriously the proposition that his platform tended toward abolitionism as the only way to overcome the condition of the "house divided." That proposition, in turn, could be used to set the Republican challenger at odds with both the Constitution and the Founding Fathers. Again, the conspiracy claim served to anticipate and to increase the credibility of the constitutional and historical claims that substituted for incommensurable moral positions.

On this reading, the four argument patterns in the debates are clearly related. Paradoxically, the moral issue of slavery does receive extended discussion, but it does so through the substitute forms that were available to American rhetors of the 1850s. It is important to stress that the surrogate arguments really were arguments, not just ideological labels that could be applied to the opponent's proposals. Michael McGee has referred to such labels as *ideographs,* the incipient propositions by which ideological content is developed in rhetorical discourse.[8] Among the clearest examples of ideographs are labeling a proposal as "communist" or even "liberal"; less obvious examples might include a reference to "making government work," which presumes a pragmatic, technocratic ideology of politics. Instead of such labels, the Lincoln-Douglas debates feature well-developed arguments, but they are arguments for one claim in terms of something else. A close modern parallel might be the use of a "family" metaphor to characterize relations between the American people and the national government. Where liberal and conservative philosophies might prove incommensurable, the common value of protecting and providing for the family permits the argument to proceed. The metaphor not only permits the argument to proceed but suggests a standard for judgment.

Describing the role of symbolism in politics, Michael Walzer speaks of the importance of applying familiar symbols to new circumstances, enabling discourse to proceed yet simultaneously transforming the symbols themselves. "The creative genius in political thought," Walzer writes, "is not a man who invents new symbols. . . . He is rather a man . . . who elaborates old symbols with a new fullness and eloquence, or . . . who explores the meaning of symbols just emerging in the thought and activity of his immediate predecessors and contemporaries."[9] The recognition that arguments are incommensurable is what calls forth the creative genius to find older, mutually accepted symbols that enable the discourse to continue. At the same time, of course, these more established, consensual symbols are subtly altered as they are drawn on in the new conflict.

The response to incommensurability that is evident in the Lincoln-Douglas debates is atypical. Certainly in contemporary public discourse it is more common for opposing advocates to proclaim their rival moral positions, repeating the same key phrases and symbols without extending the argument. In an essay on the new Christian Right of the 1980s, Pearce, Littlejohn, and Alexander refer to the pattern of discussion as "reciprocated diatribe." Neither the Christian Right nor the "secular humanists," they explain, can understand the others' premises within a common framework of moral norms. Neither can comprehend "the very way of thinking and talking adopted by the other." Rather, each places the other's arguments within its own worldview and concludes that the opponents are inept. The consequence is a pattern of public discourse marked by judgmental statements and personal attacks, which in each case are "taken by the other side as evidence that its own statements are valid."[10] Each side is reduced to self-persuasion. Even when advocates of opposing views appear on the same platform, as when Senator Edward Kennedy spoke at Liberty Baptist College in 1983, the proceedings are ritualistic rather than substantive. Nothing happens to advance the argument, to modify the views of any of the participants, or to permit substantive debate.

This standoff characterizes many moral disputes, whether the issue is abortion, gay rights, creation science, or medical ethics. Nor is it limited to moral conflicts. In an incisive study of "argument fields," Charles Arthur Willard has suggested that, whenever an issue crosses or overlaps fields, advocates working from within a particular field's worldview have difficulty in coming to terms or developing a common understanding.[11] If an issue engages, say, both ecology and economics as fields of discourse, advocates often discover that they cannot proceed very far because their very ways of thinking about and characterizing the issue are incommensurable.

The Lincoln-Douglas debates dealt with this problem by invoking common constitutional and historical values to serve as the premises for surrogate arguments. Interestingly, these values had potent symbolic status just as the Founders were receding into history and as sectionalism threatened the Constitution. In somewhat the same way, just when the family as an institution seemed threatened during the 1980s, appeals to the metaphor of "family" were employed in an attempt to find surrogate arguments. Conservatives invoked "family" to justify traditional values, liberals to emphasize the interdependence of society and to justify public measures to aid the unfortunate. Few political figures of the 1980s were as disparate ideologically as President Ronald Reagan and New York governor Mario Cuomo. Yet each man, Reagan in his acceptance speech at the 1980 Republican convention and Cuomo in his keynote speech at the 1984 Democratic convention, invoked the same value.

But there is a difference. The Lincoln-Douglas debates were marked by substantial discussion about what the Constitution really meant or what the Founders really would have done. Indeed, as has been suggested, these topics consumed much of the debates. In a real sense, they were surrogate *arguments*. In contrast, the 1980s invocation of family values is far more like McGee's description of an ideograph. Each side tries to attach the positive connotations of "family" to its own proposals, but the discourse is devoid of real argument about what a family is, what family values are paramount, or why one or another political position is most conducive to the protection of the family. The telescoping of contemporary discourse, the gradual shortening of messages, makes it more likely that common values will be sought in ideographs rather than arguments.

In the absence of surrogate arguments, how can a basic moral conflict be resolved? Not by discourse, surely, for the pattern of reciprocated diatribe only intensifies positions and hardens the conflict. Only two alternatives seem available. One is a kind of vicious relativism, in which disputants conclude that, since no good reason can be adduced for one position over another, the proper stance is indifference to the outcome; the participants merely agree to disagree. Wayne Booth has described this stance as "scientism."[12] It not only fails to resolve moral conflicts but denies in principle that they can be resolved and thereby trivializes the disputes themselves. This approach is the philosophical descendant of the logical positivism of the Vienna circle in the early twentieth century. Applied to practical situations in which choice is required, this view would hold that one choice is as good as another. It seems far more likely even than Douglas's "don't care" position to anesthetize the public mind and induce political quiescence.

The other alternative is to acknowledge that the choice between moral views cannot be made on argumentative grounds and hence to seek other bases for making it. Booth calls this stance "irrationalism" and identifies it with the existential actions characterizing radical protest in the late 1960s. Pearce, Littlejohn, and Alexander make a similar argument about the reciprocal diatribe of the 1980s. They suggest that, in the absence of mutually satisfying "good reasons," disputes will be resolved on the basis of "which side is best able to 'get out the vote' on a particular day or which is most able to link its agenda to a photogenic, charismatic political figure."[13] Sometimes, as in the case of bombing abortion clinics or shouting down speakers on the Right, real or symbolic violence may be the method of resolution.

Argumentation is often described as a "middle way" between scientism and irrationalism, a way out of the dilemma posed by diatribe on the one hand and vicious relativism on the other. The effectiveness of argumentation as a means for addressing moral disputes, however, depends on a common currency—shared values and premises that may be drawn on by otherwise opposed advocates. The Lincoln-Douglas debates offer a powerful example of how surrogate arguments permit the discussion to advance in the face of incommensurable moral positions. Ironically, then, the great moral issue of slavery does find extensive discussion, even though a first reading of the debates would suggest otherwise.

It might be objected that this discussion was to no avail since the moral issue of slavery was not resolved by discourse and was finally settled only by the Civil War. But this assertion betrays oversimplification. The Civil War was not about slavery—at least not until the Emancipation Proclamation, and that applied only in geographic areas where it could not be enforced. Not until the Thirteenth Amendment, *after* the war, was slavery finally abolished. Rather, the war was about the nature of the federal system and the conditions—if any—under which a state might secede. As for the issue of extending slavery to new territories, the late 1850s had arrived at a sort of rhetorical compromise that could be extracted from the very inconclusiveness of the Lincoln-Douglas debates. The country was not prepared explicitly to prohibit the spread of slavery, but it would do so implicitly. No existing territory was hospitable to the introduction of slavery—the chances were greatest in Kansas, and there the peculiar institution had been decisively rejected. Only if the nation expanded to the south would slavery be a live issue. And, unlike the situation in the early 1850s, the votes in Congress were there to block further territorial expansion, largely as a way to keep the slavery question effectively settled.

What upset this de facto equilibrium in 1860 was the Southern belief that Lincoln was an abolitionist who would interfere with slavery where it already existed, denying states rights that were protected by the Constitution. In 1858, this specter led doubtful Whig voters to vote for Douglas; in 1860 and 1861, it led disaffected southerners to withdraw from the Union. The Civil War established that no state could leave the Union, and then after the war the Constitution was amended to do what many mistakenly thought Lincoln would have done in 1858: abolish slavery all across the land.

II

For many, the debates are also nostalgically celebrated because they permitted extended discussion. The relevant unit of time was three hours, rather than the thirty-second spot characteristic of political messages in the 1970s and 1980s. When presidential debates reemerged in 1960, even with a different format including panels of questioners and very brief responses to the candidates, a total length of sixty to ninety minutes appeared to strain the attention span of the audience. The contemporary audience, of course, viewed debates in the comfort of their living rooms, not assembled in crowds on the prairie under the August sun or the October rain. Presented with alternatives for television viewing, many today choose not to watch debates at all. Surely, it might be reasoned, this comparison suggests the decline of American political discourse. It gives us reason to exalt the political competence of Illinois farmers in the 1850s and cause to lament how far we have fallen since that time.

As with the conventional belief that the candidates discussed a great moral issue, this popular view of the debates is also true, although probably not in the sense generally supposed. Serious questions can be raised about how actively audiences followed the arguments. To start with, it is not likely that many in the audience heard much of the discourse. Anecdotes to the contrary notwithstanding, it is hard to imagine how those in the far reaches of a crowd of twenty thousand at Galesburg—or even two thousand at Jonesboro, the smallest audience—could hear all that the candidates had to say, no matter how silent and attentive they were. Moreover, even with larger attention spans than are now customary, audiences of the debates must have suffered from fatigue. After all, crowds often assembled in midmorning for a debate that would not occur until midafternoon. There had been picnics and parades and hours of exposure to the elements. The audiences themselves were composed of a mixture of the politically involved, the interested and curious, and the neutral or even apathetic. Some came because they were attracted by the substance of the debates, others because they were drawn to the drama of the debates and the campaign, and others because they were in search of recreation and entertainment, which in antebellum America was often provided through political oratory.

But the audience for political argument can be looked at in different ways. One is empirical, focusing on the characteristics of the people actually present. Another, however, is conceptual, focusing on the audience as a construct of the speaker. Any speaker, consciously or otherwise, fashions a speech with some notion of the audience in mind. This mental picture reveals the audience that the speaker aims to address. It is not necessarily the same as the audience actually present, although—for the speech to be effective—the speaker's mental construct and the actual audience characteristics must be congruent. This means both that the speaker's arguments must be adapted to the audience and that the speaker's image of the audience should be a standard that the actual audience strives to reach. And the speaker's construct of audience can be inferred from clues in the text.

Certainly, the arguments were well adapted to the audience. The appeal to the Founding Fathers and the spirit of Henry Clay struck responsive chords among the Old Line Whigs. Douglas's doctrine of self-government and Lincoln's of basic human rights were appealing to the descendants of the pioneers. Both candidates' denial of Negro equality reflected the fact that the audience was more strongly antiabolition than antislavery. Each side even pandered to nativist prejudice, one raising the specter of the Irish and the other of the Germans.

Still, a reading of the texts suggests that both men must have had a high opinion of their audience. They developed their claims elliptically, expecting the audience to fill in missing links and details. They presumed much of what in the 1850s was "common knowledge" and counted on listeners to supply the missing premises from their own knowledge. They assumed familiarity with the founding documents and with the Bible, offering brief allusions rather than full discussion. They presumed the audience's ability to follow the intricacies of conspiracy arguments. They expected the audience to be attentive to nuances of law and political philosophy. To the degree that the Illinois audiences rose to these standards, the Lincoln-Douglas debates elevated American public discourse. With good reason Frank concludes "that the level of discussion was extraordinarily high for political debate. The real heroes of the occasion were the common people of Illinois who demonstrated by their prodigiously patient attendance their capacity to digest this heavy political fare."[14]

It was the extended nature of the discussion, both within a given debate and across the series as a whole, that made it possible for listeners to participate in the unfolding of argument rather than merely enduring the show as spectators. In one sense, the extended discussion accomplished little. Rawley notes that virtually all the arguments in the debates were present in the two Springfield speeches delivered by Lincoln and Douglas in June 1857. What the debates added was a sense of clash, as positions were extended and modified in the heat of controversy. Although intending to be derogatory, Cole captured the essence of the debates by noting, "No debate was in itself a unit, there were charges and countercharges, sturdy defense was followed by bitter attack, the opening of one debate was the rebuttal of the concluding speech of the preceding."[15] In other words, the debates gave the arguments a diachronic character. They were not fully developed in advance but evolved over time and in the heat of controversy.

To be sure, the content of the debates can be laid out as formal arguments and diagrammed analytically.[16] Such a procedure complements the method of this book, but it misses the interactive and evolving nature of the arguments, and it slights the rhetorical processes of adapting arguments to audiences. The genius of the Lincoln-Douglas debates resides, in part, in the fact that they are both dialectical contests and pragmatic struggles; they were encounters that were both timely and timeless.

Compared to an argument that can be presented formally as a structure of premises and conclusion, arguments that develop in time have a less obviously argumentative character. Bauer concludes, for example, "that the speakers did not place emphasis on argument as a persuasive method. The proportion of argumentative means to other methods of persuasion is small."[17] High on the list of "other methods" is narrative, casting argument in the form of a story. Extended public argument is situated not only in chronological time but in symbolic, narrative time as well. Each of the major argument patterns has a narrative dimension, with a plot, heroes and villains, and movement through past, present, and future. The conspiracy argument is self-evidently a tale with a plot, as is the historical argument predicting decline and fall unless the promise of restoration is grasped and achieved. The moral argument gained greatest force from its temporal dimension, projecting the imagined consequences of each choice into the far distant future and making a claim about how the story would end. Even the legal argument had an important narrative dimension, offering links to the Revolutionary past as well as dire warnings about the inevitable future consequences of each candidate's legal positions. The argumentative positions are both embedded in and bolstered by narrative; the most credible public argument often is a good story.

Prompted in part by the writing of Alasdair MacIntyre, some rhetorical theorists have argued for the primacy of narrative in understanding public communication. Foremost among them is Walter R. Fisher, who has defined man as a storytelling creature, opposed narrative to what he calls the "rational world paradigm" of formal and informal argument, and posed coherence and fidelity as tests for the soundness of narrative claims.[18] Fisher's work has been somewhat controversial, particularly with respect to whether narrative constitutes a "paradigm." But whether paradigm or perspective, narrative theory facilitates understanding of arguments that develop across time and reflect the persuasive power of telling a story.

Probably the greatest consequence of extended discussion was the transformation of the audience into a *public,* a community in which common interests—transcending the individual self-interest of the members—can be discovered and given form through discourse. A public is composed of people who see their interests implicated in larger issues that may not seem to affect them directly and who through discourse attempt to choose among courses of action that likewise cannot be confined to specialized fields or to the realm of the personal.[19]

The chronology of the debates illustrates the evolution of a public state of mind. The early debates are marked by farfetched conspiracy claims and then by arguments that are meaningful only within the specialized field of congressional politics. But those do not take either candidate very far, so by the fifth debate both were speaking far more of large "public" questions in which the Illinois voters were implicated.

The very fact that the debates focused on slavery in the territories indicates their public character. Few Illinoisians would be directly affected by the outcome of this dispute since Illinois had been a state rather than a territory for forty years and since its revised constitution of 1847 unequivocally ended slavery in the state. By one line of reasoning, the whole issue of the debates was irrelevant to Illinois voters. Yet there is no question that it aroused their attention and concern. What linked them to the issue of slavery in Kansas was the recognition that they were "really" addressing an issue about the future of the country. If slavery went into Kansas, that would change a view of what the country was about and where it was headed—and that was a matter of vital importance to them.

At different times, writers have lamented that "the public" has been eclipsed, lost in a flurry of concern for personal self-interest and apathy in the face of larger issues. Such laments were sounded especially after World War I and again during the late 1970s and the 1980s. There have been repeated calls for the rediscovery or reinvigoration of public consciousness, and the Lincoln-Douglas debates suggest that extended discussion of an issue under conditions that foster elaboration and development of the controversy is conducive to such a revival.

Nurturing what Walter Lippmann called a "public philosophy" is important because public issues do not go away even when the public is in a state of decline.[20] Either decision making is abdicated to experts, to those with a vested interest in the matter at hand, or else nothing is done, and the problems remain, waiting to be solved by other people in another time. In the former case, such a distance develops between rulers and ruled that democratic governance is called into question. The trappings of political participation remain, but they serve the purposes of ritual and spectacle rather than deliberation. In the latter case, the inability of a people to address its common needs also calls into question the legitimacy of the social order.

A public does not just "emerge," however. It is called into being by advocates, even as they respond to the very public they evoke. Writing about the 1850s, Holt observed, "Some one has to politicize events, to define their political relevance in terms of a choice between or among parties, before popular grievances can have political impact. It was not events alone that caused Northerners and Southerners to view each other as enemies of the basic rights they both cherished."[21] Likewise, it was not events alone that made the activity in Kansas of interest to voters in Illinois or defined that activity as emblematic of larger questions of time and national destiny. These perspectives were given by political leaders who created symbolic systems as "overlays" for events. Such systems, Walzer explains, represent worldviews and "set (rough) limits to thought, supporting certain ideas, making others almost inconceivable."[22] Symbolic systems gave the events of the 1850s a public character, made them seem relevant to those not directly involved, and led to their discussion in terms of social choice rather than individual or group self-interest.

At the same time, advocates cannot call up a public from nothing. There must be an audience receptive to being summoned, and, more important, political leaders must evince a genuine respect for the decisions of that audience. That the first condition existed can be inferred from the texts of the debates themselves. References to events and trends of the time—political, economic, and social—as Heckman has noted, seem confusing and misleading to one not familiar with the events.[23] They are also incomplete. These observations suggest not that Lincoln and Douglas were poor rhetors but that the audience was familiar enough with public events that brief references and allusions would suffice. To be sure, nineteenth-century Americans often regarded both politics and public speaking as means of entertainment, but they took their politics seriously enough to be familiar with events and to understand the allusions.

That the candidates had great respect for the judgment of the audience is also evident. It is most obvious in Lincoln's statement at Ottawa, "In this and like communities, public sentiment is everything. With public sentiment, nothing can fail; without it nothing can succeed." It was public sentiment that "makes statutes and decisions possible or impossible to be executed."[24] Lincoln spoke these words trying to establish Douglas's role in a conspiracy to nationalize slavery because of the incumbent's failure to mold public opinion to the contrary. But his remarks have a far more general application. They recognize that the bounds of permissible action are set by a public, that citizens are not pawns to be manipulated by leaders but active participants in a civic dialogue and people to whose beliefs leaders must pay heed. Douglas showed the same regard for the competence of his audience, most obviously by the fact that the central tenet of his position was their right as a community to regulate their own affairs.

The quality that Lincoln and Douglas prized in their audiences was judgment, the capacity to make reasoned choices among beliefs and actions under conditions of uncertainty, when no conclusive proof is possible. Judgment is the exercise of practical wisdom; it is a middle ground between the certitude of deductive proof and the irrationality of unreasoned choice.[25] Just as speakers must find a way to continue the dialogue in the face of incommensurable positions, so audiences must find a way to make sound choices when matters are not certain. This capacity is in evidence when there is a strong public consciousness; it fades when the public is in decline.

The Lincoln-Douglas debates illustrate the ability of political debate to "coach" public judgment. Audiences hear opposing candidates address the issues of the day and challenge each other. Inevitably, the results are not conclusive, yet the voter must make a decision. Attending to the arguments in the debates helps make that decision a reasoned and intelligent one. Those who champion political debates in the 1970s and 1980s have many of the same values in mind, but it is often not clear that the values are achieved. When the press reaction to debates is more important than the debates themselves, when the search for a "winner" focuses on matters of image and appearance rather than substance, and when the format encourages superficial comments and the repetition of set speeches rather than the development of positions through sustained argument, the cause of public judgment is not well served. The nation is still better off with debates than without them, if only because debates focus attention on the campaign, but the standards of argument and judgment would be improved if there were more emphasis on encounters like those between Lincoln and Douglas.

III

What, finally, of the most common judgment about the debates, that they were milestones in Lincoln's rise to the presidency and that they sealed Douglas's fate by demonstrating that, after all, he was not acceptable to the South? There is a trivial sense in which this perception is clearly correct. As the underdog in the contest, Lincoln reaped a great advantage in publicity just by appearing on the same platform with Douglas; he benefited disproportionately from the drama of the debates and the newspaper coverage that they received. As a result of this coverage, he became a sought-after speaker for the Republicans and gave speeches outside his own state on a significant scale during 1859 and 1860. In this respect, the debates clearly helped Lincoln. Likewise, Douglas was hurt after 1858 by southerners who did not believe that popular sovereignty could favor slavery, although this development probably owes more to Douglas's opposition to the Lecompton constitution than to the Lincoln-Douglas debates themselves.

But if anyone gained in the fall of 1858 from the debates, it was Douglas. Of the two, Lincoln may have spoken more to the ages, but Douglas was more effective at responding to the anxieties of the voters. He turned the "house divided" doctrine against Lincoln and forced the Republican on the defensive, raised the specter of abolitionism, and convinced enough old Whigs in the central counties that he rather than Lincoln was the true ideological descendant of Henry Clay. Popular sovereignty seemed to many to be an acceptable way to settle the slavery question, particularly once it was clear that it would make Kansas free just as would Lincoln's "no-extension" approach.

Nevertheless, the conventional belief that the debates helped Lincoln is well founded, and not just in the trivial sense that he went on to win the presidency and that the Civil War settled the issues. The kernel of his philosophical position was more in keeping with the times and harder to refute than was Douglas's. He gave voice to the still latent moral concerns of the North and was yet able to reconcile them with prevailing views of history, legality, and race. He anticipated emergent views and gave them voice, espousing the unspoken claims toward which the moderates were gradually tending. In this sense, his were the arguments constitutive of American character and culture.

If Lincoln was a man "ahead of his time" in this respect, Douglas was one who, without realizing it, was behind. His beliefs were those of the late 1840s, when it was widely thought that the slavery question—and any other domestic issue, for that matter—was a minor problem that would be subsumed by territorial expansion, which was, after all, the nation's manifest destiny. Popular sovereignty was above everything else a formula for removing a sticky question from the national forum so the country could get on with its more important business. What Douglas failed to recognize was that the status of the slavery issue had changed. It had become, as Lincoln said at Alton, "the very thing that every body does care the most about."[26] That being so, it had become a preemptive issue, and Douglas's argument for the primacy of a procedural morality proved less and less compelling. Douglas's fate was not unlike that which befell Lyndon Johnson more than a century later. Having labored throughout his career under one set of assumptions and values, he reached the pinnacle of power just when, unbeknownst to him, all the assumptions and values were changing. The attitude that one could be indifferent to whether slavery was voted down or up soon became, as Angle has noted, "as anachronistic as belief in the right to practice polygamy."[27]

Part of Douglas's difficulty, then, was that he was "out of synch" with the times. But there was more to it than that. Any moral position can be refuted only by showing that it is internally inconsistent or that it leads to outcomes that its own proponents would disclaim. In this respect, Douglas's position was more vulnerable than Lincoln's.

Popular sovereignty regarded the *community* as the unit of analysis, but the scope of that term was never completely clear. Douglas thought of the state as the relevant community, and he regarded a territory as an incipient state. He argued that the national government should not determine the purely domestic institutions of a state; that was a matter for the people who actually lived there. But his argument was subject to a slippery slope. If what he said were true of the state, why not of the town? Why should the proslavery town of Lecompton, for example, be able to regulate the domestic institutions of the antislavery town of Lawrence—or vice versa? If the principle applied at the level of the town, then why not at the level of the neighborhood, or the family, or the individual? The very logic of "local self-government," which popular sovereignty was all about, was strongest when applied to smaller and smaller groups.

But if the popular sovereignty principle were applied to the individual, it would produce one of two results, either of which would be fatal to Douglas. First, the very existence of slavery would be seen as a denial of popular sovereignty since there clearly was no local self-government for the slave. Or, second, no one opposed to slavery could presume to regulate the domestic institutions of his slaveholding neighbor. Douglas could uphold the first of these positions only by maintaining that slaves were subhuman and that therefore rights of local self-government did not apply to them. He was not prepared to go that far since that view would make the presence of free blacks in the North indefensible. It would entail national slavery, the very result that Lincoln charged that Douglas was helping to produce. Instead, Douglas waffled, granting the humanity of the Negro even while regarding him as inferior to the white. He claimed that justice and Christianity required that Negroes be given all the privileges that were consistent with public safety and welfare and then left it up to each state to decide just what those privileges were. That only brought him back to the same starting point, however. Why should the decision be made by the state? Why not the town, or why not the individual?

The second outcome of applying popular sovereignty to the individual was that no man had a right to regulate the domestic institutions of his neighbor. That, however, would have granted the extreme Southern view that there was an absolute federal obligation to support the spread of slavery. There would be no way that a territory could prevent the introduction of slavery, and that would be in direct contradiction to the whole idea of popular sovereignty. Moreover, while the candidates were discussing the territories during the 1858 campaign, the same principle logically would apply to the states as well. If so applied, it too would lead to national slavery. Any reasoning according to which popular sovereignty justified national slavery would bear out Lincoln's conspiracy allegations and lose Douglas all credibility in the North.

To refute a slippery-slope argument, an advocate usually tries to find some distinction between the position actually defended and the extensions of that position that lead down the slope. In Douglas's case, that would have meant asserting that there was something about the nature of states and territories that made them the logical resting place for popular sovereignty and therefore that the same grounds on which he opposed Lincoln's federal solution and favored state or territorial action would not be used against him as well. But it is hard to imagine what that distinction might be. If the claim were that the unit of government needed to be large enough to encompass divergent views, that would seem to argue for federal action and to be inconsistent with the priority of local self-government. If the claim were that those affected by the laws should be the ones to make them, that principle would apply to lower levels of government as well. In short, the incumbent's fundamental argumentative position appears to have been inherently unstable.

Revisionist historians of the Civil War, such as Milton and Craven, treated popular sovereignty as usefully ambiguous, capable of speaking in different ways to the needs of both North and South.[28] They regard the Civil War as unnecessary and the result of Northern Republicans and Southern fire-eaters closing in on Douglas and forcing him to choose sides. But this criticism misses the point. As the analysis here suggests, popular sovereignty was an inherently weak rhetorical position in that its logic could not be matched to a single level of government. In the crucible of public debate, virtually any sustained challenge would cause the argument to unravel. Lincoln was indirect in his attack on the principle; after all, popular sovereignty still enjoyed wide support. His most fundamental attacks were developed in quite other contexts. But, when he predicted, as at Ottawa, that the outcome of Douglas's program would be nationwide slavery, and when he closed his remarks at Alton by facetiously labeling Douglas an abolitionist, he was indicating the two extremes to which popular sovereignty might lead. A formula designed to hold on to the middle ground could easily have the opposite effect instead.

If Douglas's view was susceptible to uncomfortable logical extension, so too was Lincoln's. The Republican's argument was premised on a notion of individual human rights. If slavery was evil, then how could Lincoln condone slavery where it already existed? And if it was evil because it denied the right to rise, then how could Lincoln countenance racial discrimination and inequality, which also denied that right? One might surmise that Lincoln's views led down the slippery slope to abolitionism and racial equality, outcomes that Lincoln was quick to disclaim in 1858.

There were two significant differences, however, between the rhetorical positions of Lincoln and Douglas. First, unlike his opponent, Lincoln *was* able to formulate distinctions that spoke to the needs of the 1850s. What distinguished his position from abolition was his respect for the Constitution—which itself was characteristic of the age. To be sure, he undoubtedly would have preferred to see the South without slavery. But he was obligated to abide by the fundamental charter of the nation, which recognized slavery, left it there, and safeguarded the property rights of slaveowners. Nor was Lincoln's acquiescence in Southern slavery hypocritical. He reconciled his dissonant beliefs—against slavery and for the Constitution—through the importance of public opinion. If the "public mind" regarded slavery as being on the "course of ultimate extinction," then eventually the institution would collapse of its own weight, without violating any constitutional protections. And nothing would put the public mind in such a state better than prohibiting the extension of slavery into new territories.

As for the slippery slope by which freedom led to racial equality, Lincoln was also ready with a distinction. The right to rise was essentially an economic right, secured, in the parlance of the time, by being able to eat the bread earned by the sweat of one's own brow. Economic rights were one thing; social and political equality was another. This compartmentalization of equality enabled Lincoln to uphold his own position while dismissing Douglas's attempts to draw him down the slippery slope. Most explicitly, at Charleston he insisted, "I am not, nor ever have been in favor of bringing about in any way the social and political equality of the white and black races,—that I am not nor ever have been in favor of making voters or jurors of negroes, nor of qualifying them to hold office, nor to intermarry with white people." This distinction between economic and social or political rights enabled Lincoln to ridicule his opponent's attacks. He went on to draw the middle ground between having a Negro woman for a slave or for a wife. Moreover, since Douglas was so concerned that the social relations between the races would be altered, and since that could be done only by the state legislature and not by the U.S. Congress, "I propose as the best means to prevent it that the Judge be kept at home and placed in the state legislature to fight the measure."[29] If the Charleston debate found Lincoln denying social and political equality, the Ottawa debate saw him clearly separate those outcomes from the economic principle that he defended: "I agree with Judge Douglas [that the Negro] is not my equal in many respects—certainly not in color, perhaps not in moral or intellectual endowment. But in the right to eat the bread, without leave of anybody else, which his own hand earns, *he is my equal and the equal of Judge Douglas, and the equal of every living man.*"[30]

Unlike Douglas, Lincoln was able to prevent his position from being taken down the slippery slope. But there was a second significant difference between them. When times changed and the distinctions were no longer relevant, they could be effectively excised, without detracting from the main point of Lincoln's argument. When, near the end of the Civil War, the Constitution was amended to outlaw slavery—a move that Lincoln supported but did not initiate—then reverence for the Constitution and opposition to slavery no longer were at cross-purposes. What would be recalled through the ages was not Lincoln's legalistic deference to a historical document but his forthright defense of individual human rights.

Similarly, in the twentieth century the distinction between the right to economic advancement and social and political equality seems less compelling. If anything, the great civil rights struggles of recent years have been more about the latter than the former. But Lincoln's arguments are still relevant. His remarks at Charleston are conveniently "forgotten," excused as a necessary adaptation to local politics or disparaged by those wishing to argue that by today's standards the Great Emancipator was actually a racist. What is collectively remembered from the debates is instead Lincoln's masterful statement at Alton: "The real issue in this controversy—the one pressing upon every mind—is the sentiment on the part of one class that looks upon the institution of slavery *as a wrong*, and of another class that *does not* look upon it as a wrong."[31] Gone are the elaborations about why it is a wrong; the unqualified statement of Lincoln's principles is what endures.

Each candidate defended a position that his opponent tried to coax down a slippery slope. Douglas was particularly vulnerable to this problem, whereas Lincoln was able to draw crucial distinctions. Moreover, Douglas spoke the language and values of a time that had already passed. Lincoln's argument had multiple levels; he was able to speak to his own time and to anticipate the future as well. It is in this sense, in the light of history, that Lincoln "won" the debates.

IV

Each of the conventional beliefs about the debates has been found to be true, though not in the sense often supposed. There was a great moral issue at stake, but it was discussed in the terms of surrogate arguments because the opposing views were incommensurable. The extended discussion that marked the debates was valuable less because of anything that was said than because of what it revealed about the audience as a public. Lincoln ultimately "won" the debates, not because he triumphed on any one argument, and certainly not because he was later elected president, but because his arguments met the needs of his own time yet spoke to the ages as well.

The distinguished historian David Potter has written that we remember the Lincoln-Douglas debates for the wrong reasons, and this discussion suggests that he is probably right.[32] Certainly, the debates reveal a richer texture and a subtler argument than we often suppose. To be sure, as Johannsen correctly notes, they were not "a timeless and epic struggle between good and evil."[33] But they should be appreciated for what they were. They provide a valuable lesson in the "micromanagement" of value conflicts and of the conditions under which public argument is meaningful and successful. They illustrate successful patterns of argument and refutation. They elucidate the public concerns of the mid-nineteenth century and bring the lost cause back as a live option so that the nature of the choices confronting the voters of Illinois can be recognized and appreciated.

Moreover, the debates reveal a quest for common values, language, and appeals at the very time that sectional pressures were driving North and South further apart. "Politics," Michael Walzer has written, "is an art of unification; from many, it makes one. And symbolic activity is perhaps our most important means of bringing things together." It is so not only because it "provide[s] the units of thought and feeling; it also connects those units with other structures. . . . It unifies the universe, provides politics with a series of references, links it closely with other realms of human experience."[34] How this quest for unity is achieved becomes evident in a text like the Lincoln-Douglas debates. Common terms and values, the sanction of venerated heroes such as the Founding Fathers and Henry Clay, the authority of sacred documents, the claim to a golden mean between the extremes, the values of honor and honesty—all these become symbols to be fought over by advocates who wish to reconstitute community even as they identify their own beliefs and proposals with the community's store of practical wisdom.

The world of the debates was one in which the familiar terms of political discourse had reached an impasse. For some, the presence of slavery belied claims to liberty and freedom. For others, slavery was actually viewed as a precondition for freedom. For still others, the conflict was not between slavery and freedom but between morality and legality or between support for a radical end and insistence on moderate means. The impasse reflected the profound cultural dislocation of the time, but it seemed as if—to borrow James Boyd White's phrase—words had lost their meaning.[35] Unless the political community is to be torn apart, it must be made coherent again, and that is done through discourse. Old symbols are given new meanings as a result of the creative genius of the rhetor. Exercises such as the reinterpretation of the Founding Fathers, the invocation of the "public mind" as a moral construct, and the appeal to the consistency of one's principles are not diversions from the main argument. On the contrary, they are the new channels through which the conversation can proceed. Public argument revitalizes a political community by coaching public judgment. Engaging in the argument changes the participants and the listeners. They engage in the act of shaping their world as they shape their language—even though, paradoxically, they are constrained by the very culture they create.

It is just such processes of constituting and reconstituting culture that are made clear by treating the debates as rhetorical phenomena and that are missed by viewing them only as a historical event. To see Lincoln and Douglas as rhetors facing specific problems is to gain a heightened sense of how rhetors work. They seek to recover a rhetorically usable tradition. They make distinctions in order to appeal to the values of the audience while simultaneously redefining them. They identify and invoke common values in an attempt to align their positions with those values. They look for comparisons, resemblances, and compelling narratives in which to frame their appeals. They try to locate their opponents outside the bounds of the community that their discourse creates. They make strategic use of time, finding remnants of the past in the present and also projecting forward into the future. In these and countless other ways, persuaders build the world of words in which they live and in which they try to forge agreement. The rhetorical study of the Lincoln-Douglas debates yields insights into how these processes work at the hands of gifted advocates contesting for public support through a long and difficult election campaign.

Beyond all that, however, the debates should be appreciated for the mastery that they reflect of the strategy and tactics of argumentation. Both candidates were masters at selecting effective arguments from the realm of possibilities, making the most of the arguments they picked, minimizing their own burdens of proof while adding to those of the opponent, employing humor and ridicule gracefully, asking questions that got to the heart of the matter and put the opponent on the spot, drawing on available sources of evidence and using the opponent's own words and acts as evidence, and involving the audience in the evolution of the argument. Often dismissed as only matters of technique, these are skills that bespeak the art of public argumentation. Without them, no debate could proceed beyond the statement of opposing positions; there would be no way to test those positions or to resolve the conflict. If not the epitome of eloquence and statesmanship, the Lincoln-Douglas debates were an outstanding case of argumentative artistry. The skills they reflect are not always present in contemporary public debate. They are valuable skills about which we may be both enlightened and inspired by the great forensic clash on the Illinois prairies in the fall of 1858.

Notes

Preface

1. Norman Corwin, "Lincoln and Douglas: The Tangled Weave," in *Lincoln: A Contemporary Portrait,* ed. Allan Nevins and Irving Stone (Garden City, N.Y.: Doubleday, 1962), 78.

2. Reinhard Luthin, *The Real Abraham Lincoln* (Englewood Cliffs, N.J.: Prentice-Hall, 1960), 197.

3. *Louisville Democrat,* September 5, 1858, quoted in William Baringer, *Lincoln's Rise to Power* (Boston: Little, Brown, 1937), 44; *Chicago Times,* October 2, 1858.

4. Damon Wells, *Stephen Douglas: The Last Years, 1857–1861* (Austin: University of Texas Press, 1971), 134; Don E. Fehrenbacher, "The Historical Significance of the Lincoln-Douglas Debates," *Wisconsin Magazine of History* 42 (Spring 1959): 193.

5. On this point, see J. G. Randall, *Lincoln the President: Springfield to Gettysburg* (New York: Dodd, Mead, 1945), 1:121.

Chapter One

1. In the two preceding paragraphs, the reference to "circuses and menageries" appeared in the *Chicago Times* on July 30, 1858; the first quotation from Lincoln is from a letter to Stephen A. Douglas, July 24, 1858, *The Collected Works of Abraham Lincoln,* ed. Roy P. Basler, Marion Dolores Pratt, and Lloyd A. Dunlap (New Brunswick, N.J.: Rutgers University Press, 1953), 2:522; the statement accepting the terms is from Lincoln to Stephen A. Douglas, July 31, 1858, ibid., 531. Harry V. Jaffa, *Crisis of the House Divided: An Interpretation of the Issues in the Lincoln-Douglas Debates* (1959; reprint, Chicago: University of Chicago Press, 1982), 433.

2. Douglas to J. H. Crane, D. M. Johnson, and L. J. Eastin, December 17,

1853, *The Letters of Stephen A. Douglas*, ed. Robert W. Johannsen (Urbana: University of Illinois Press, 1961), 270.

3. Jaffa, *Crisis of the House Divided*, 52.

4. See, e.g., Frank Heywood Hodder, "The Railroad Background of the Kansas-Nebraska Act," *Mississippi Valley Historical Review* 12 (June 1925): 6.

5. William J. Cooper, Jr., *The South and the Politics of Slavery, 1828–1856* (Baton Rouge: Louisiana State University Press, 1978), 346.

6. See Michael F. Holt, "The Democratic Party, 1828–1860," *History of U.S. Political Parties*, ed. Arthur M. Schlesinger, Jr. (New York: Chelsea, 1973), 1:526.

7. See Robert W. Johannsen, *Stephen A. Douglas* (New York: Oxford University Press, 1973), 397; Jaffa, *Crisis of the House Divided*, 90. There is a November 30, 1852 letter from Douglas to Parmenas Taylor Turnley in which the senator announced his intention "to bring forward a Bill to repeal altogether that compromise" (see Johannsen, ed., *The Letters of Stephen A. Douglas*, 255). There are serious questions about the authenticity of the letter, however, and as late as December 1853 Douglas was not openly proposing repeal of the Missouri Compromise.

8. Richard H. Sewell, *Ballots for Freedom: Antislavery Politics in the United States, 1837–1860* (New York: Oxford University Press, 1976), 254.

9. Gerald W. Wolff, "Party and Section: The Senate and the Kansas-Nebraska Bill," *Civil War History* 18 (December 1972): 301.

10. See Michael F. Holt, *The Political Crisis of the 1850s* (New York: Wiley, 1978), 146; Cooper, *The South and the Politics of Slavery*, 350.

11. Holman Hamilton, *Prologue to Conflict: The Crisis and Compromise of 1850* (Lexington: University Press of Kentucky, 1964), 182.

12. Quoted in Philip Shriver Klein, *President James Buchanan: A Biography* (University Park: Pennsylvania State University Press, 1962), 289.

13. See Avery Craven, *The Coming of the Civil War* (1942; reprint, Chicago: University of Chicago Press, 1966), 337; Gerald M. Capers, *Stephen A. Douglas: Defender of the Union* (Boston: Little, Brown, 1959), 115.

14. See James MacGregor Burns, *The Vineyard of Liberty* (New York: Knopf, 1982), 546.

15. Douglas to the editor of the *Concord, N.H., State Capitol Reporter*, February 16, 1854, Johannsen, ed., *The Letters of Stephen A. Douglas*, 288.

16. Capers, *Stephen A. Douglas*, 109.

17. On this point, see G. S. Boritt, *Lincoln and the Economics of the American Dream* (Memphis: Memphis State University Press, 1978), 155, and "The Right to Rise," in *The Public and the Private Lincoln: Contemporary Perspectives*, ed. Cullom Davis, Charles G. Strozier, Rebecca Monroe Veach, and Geoffrey C. Ward (Carbondale: Southern Illinois University Press, 1979), 64.

18. Speech at Peoria, Ill., October 16, 1854, *The Collected Works of Abraham Lincoln*, 2:259.

19. On these matters, see Douglas to Twenty-five Chicago Clergymen, April 6, 1854, Johannsen, ed., *The Letters of Stephen A. Douglas*, 300–321; Allen Johnson, *Stephen A. Douglas: A Study in American Politics* (New York: Macmillan,

1908), 255; Stephen B. Oates, *With Malice toward None: The Life of Abraham Lincoln* (New York: Harper and Row, 1977), 114. Douglas knew that he would face a hostile audience in Chicago. He wrote Charles H. Lanphier, editor of the *Illinois State Register*, "I speak to the people of Chicago on Friday next Sept 1st on Nebraska. They threaten a mob but I have no fears" (August 25, 1854, Charles H. Lanphier MSS, Illinois State Historical Library).

20. Don E. Fehrenbacher, *The South and Three Sectional Crises* (Baton Rouge: Louisiana State University Press, 1980), 49; Capers, *Stephen A. Douglas*, 113.

21. Roy F. Nichols and Philip S. Klein, "Election of 1856," in *The Coming to Power: Critical Presidential Elections in American History*, ed. Arthur M. Schlesinger, Jr. (New York: Chelsea, 1971), 98–99; Fehrenbacher, *The South and Three Sectional Crises*, 49.

22. Michael F. Holt, "The Politics of Impatience: The Origins of Know Nothingism," *Journal of American History* 60 (September 1973): 310.

23. Eugene H. Berwanger, *The Frontier against Slavery: Western Anti-Negro Prejudice and the Slavery Extension Controversy* (Urbana: University of Illinois Press, 1967), 3.

24. See Holt, *The Political Crisis of the 1850s*, 147; Saul Sigelschiffer, *The American Conscience: The Drama of the Lincoln-Douglas Debates* (New York: Horizon, 1973), 79.

25. On these points, see Charles W. Ramsdell, "The Natural Limits of Slavery Expansion," *Mississippi Valley Historical Review* 16 (September 1929): 162; Allan Nevins, *Ordeal of the Union*, vol. 1, *Fruits of Manifest Destiny, 1847–1852*, vol. 2, *A House Dividing, 1852–1857* (New York: Scribner's, 1947), 2:382; Berwanger, *The Frontier against Slavery*, 98, 101.

26. See Robert W. Johannsen, ed., *The Lincoln-Douglas Debates of 1858* (New York: Oxford University Press, 1965), 5; Fehrenbacher, *The South and Three Sectional Crises*, 27; Eric Foner, *Free Soil, Free Labor, Free Men: The Ideology of the Republican Party before the Civil War* (New York: Oxford University Press, 1970), 57.

27. Allan Nevins, *The Emergence of Lincoln*, vol. 1, *Douglas, Buchanan, and Party Chaos, 1857–1859*, vol. 2, *Prologue to Civil War, 1859–1861* (New York: Scribner's, 1950), 1:303.

28. The actual events of the "sack" of Lawrence were minimal. One person was killed and some dwellings pillaged or burned, a level of violence not unusual for the frontier. But the events were exaggerated in the Eastern press and portrayed as the result of a proslavery conspiracy. See James A. Rawley, *Race and Politics: "Bleeding Kansas" and the Coming of the Civil War* (Philadelphia: Lippincott, 1969), 132; Sigelschiffer, *The American Conscience*, 42. Similar patterns of exaggerated reporting were characteristic of both sides in the Kansas dispute.

29. For an excellent summary of the case and its antecedents and consequences, see Don E. Fehrenbacher, *The Dred Scott Case: Its Significance in American Law and Politics* (New York: Oxford University Press, 1978).

30. Craven, *The Coming of the Civil War*, 385.

31. Fehrenbacher, *The Dred Scott Case*, 195.

32. On the principle of interstate comity, see esp. Paul Finkelman, *An Imperfect Union: Slavery, Federalism, and Comity* (Chapel Hill: University of North Carolina Press, 1981).

33. Fehrenbacher has analyzed the need for all elements of the decision, in terms of the politics of the court and the process of coalition building (see *The Dred Scott Case*, passim).

34. Jaffa, *Crisis of the House Divided*, 284.

35. The election of the territorial legislature itself had been questionable. In the March 30, 1855 election, 5,427 proslavery and 791 free-soil votes were cast. Much of the proslavery vote came from Missourians who crossed into Kansas on election day in order to vote. An investigation showed that only a total of 1,410 ballots had been legally cast; 4,908 were illegal. The proslavery legislature flaunted its power, passing among other measures a law that made it a felony to claim that persons in the territory had no right to hold slaves. It also issued land charters and franchises, sometimes denying these benefits to free-state settlers. From this perspective, the calling of the Lecompton convention seemed to fit a pattern, and the results of the convention were quite predictable. On these points, see Nevins, *Ordeal of the Union*, 2:385; Herndon-Weik Collection of Lincolniana, reel 1, group I.B., Library of Congress; Roy Franklin Nichols, *The Disruption of American Democracy* (New York: Macmillan, 1948), 94–95.

36. For explanations of some of these problems, see Fehrenbacher, *The South and Three Sectional Crises*, 54, and *The Dred Scott Case*, 464; Klein, *President James Buchanan*, 302.

37. Klein, *President James Buchanan*, 292; Mark E. Neely, Jr., *The Abraham Lincoln Encyclopedia* (New York: McGraw-Hill, 1982), 44.

38. For accounts of the sequence of events, see Don E. Fehrenbacher, *Prelude to Greatness: Lincoln in the 1850's* (Stanford: Stanford University Press, 1962), passim; Klein, *President James Buchanan*, 302.

39. Klein, *President James Buchanan*, 302, 307.

40. Graham Fitch, Speech in the Senate, December 22, 1857, *Congressional Globe*, 35th Cong., 1st sess., 27, pt. 1:138; Thomas L. Anderson, Speech in the House, January 26, 1858, ibid., 419; Trusten Polk, Speech in the Senate, March 11, 1858, ibid., pt. 2:1064.

41. Stephen R. Mallory, Speech in the Senate, March 16, 1858, ibid., 1138. Buchanan's biographer points out that Lincoln adopted a similar stance in 1863 in the case of West Virginia (see Klein, *President James Buchanan*, 302).

42. For example, Lucius Q. C. Lamar, Speech in the House, January 13, 1858, *Congressional Globe*, 35th Cong., 1st sess., 27, pt. 1:281. Republican representative Schuyler Colfax of Indiana, however, sought to give the lie to this theory, pointing out that it would require the admission of Utah with a constitution sanctioning polygamy, a prospect few wished to endorse (Speech in the House, March 20, 1858, ibid., pt. 2:1222).

43. James Buchanan, Message to Congress, February 2, 1858, ibid., pt. 1:535. There were contrary precedents, however. Indiana was admitted with a constitution that forbade amendments for twelve years, and the Topeka rival to

the Lecompton constitution would have disallowed changes until 1865. These cases were pointed out by James S. Green, Speech in the Senate, March 1, 1858, ibid., 905.

44. Klein, *President James Buchanan*, 303.

45. Douglas, Speech in the Senate, December 21, 1857, *Congressional Globe*, 35th Cong., 1st sess., 27, pt. 1:120; Lyman Trumbull to Lincoln, December 5, 1857, Lyman Trumbull MSS, Illinois State Historical Library; Fehrenbacher, *Prelude to Greatness*, 55. There was good reason for Douglas's political fears since fifty-five of fifty-six Democratic newspapers in Illinois had opposed Lecompton (see Richard Allen Heckman, "The Douglas-Lincoln Campaign of 1858," [Ph.D. diss., Indiana University, 1960], 38n).

46. Douglas to John A. McClernand, November 23, 1857, John A. McClernand MSS, Illinois State Historical Library; Douglas, Speech in the Senate, February 4, 1858, *Congressional Globe*, 35th Cong., 1st sess., 27, pt. 1:570.

47. Douglas, Speech in the Senate, December 9, 1857, *Congressional Globe*, 35th Cong., 1st sess., 27, pt. 1:16.

48. See Nevins, *The Emergence of Lincoln*, 1:278.

49. Fehrenbacher, *The Dred Scott Case*, 466. The reference is to Douglas's June 12, 1857 speech at Springfield.

50. Klein, *President James Buchanan*, 305; Wells, *Stephen Douglas*, 25; Johnson, *Stephen A. Douglas*, 340.

51. J. C. D. Atkins, Speech in the House, February 17, 1858, *Congressional Globe*, 35th Cong., 1st sess., 27, pt. 1:748.

52. Holt, "The Democratic Party," 533. See also Klein, *President James Buchanan*, 303.

53. William Pitt Fessenden, Speech in the Senate, February 8, 1858, *Congressional Globe*, 35th Cong., 1st sess., 27, pt. 1:614; Calvin C. Chaffee, Speech in the House, February 24, 1858, ibid., 855; Lyman Trumbull, Speech in the Senate, December 8, 1857, ibid., 7. Illustrative of the conspiracy allegations are John P. Hale, Speech in the Senate, January 18, 1858, ibid., 316; James Harlan, Speech in the Senate, January 25, 1858, ibid., 384; Henry Wilson, Speech in the Senate, January 25, 1858, ibid., 387.

54. Lyman Trumbull to Lincoln, December 25, 1857, Lyman Trumbull MSS, Illinois State Historical Library.

55. Albert J. Beveridge, *Abraham Lincoln, 1809–1858* (Boston: Houghton Mifflin, 1928), 2:637; Lyman Trumbull to John M. Palmer, December 14, 1857, John M. Palmer MSS, Illinois State Historical Library.

56. Jno. P. Heiss to Douglas, July 15, 1858, Stephen A. Douglas MSS, box 19, folder 6, University of Chicago Library.

57. Klein, *President James Buchanan*, 329; George W. Saunders to Douglas, July 1, 1858, Stephen A. Douglas MSS, box 18, folder 44, University of Chicago Library.

58. On this point, see Bruce W. Collins, "The Democrats' Electoral Fortunes during the Lecompton Crisis," *Civil War History* 24 (December 1978): 322.

59. Benjamin P. Thomas, *Abraham Lincoln: A Biography* (New York: Knopf, 1952), 178; Burns, *The Vineyard of Liberty*, 581.

60. Frank Heywood Hodder, "Some Aspects of the English Bill for the Admission of Kansas," in *Annual Report of the American Historical Association for the Year 1906* (Washington, D.C.: U.S. Government Printing Office, 1908), 1:207.

61. This theory is advanced by Nichols, *The Disruption of American Democracy*, 174.

62. For information on the Lecompton votes, see Nevins, *The Emergence of Lincoln*, 1:301; Rawley, *Race and Politics*, 250; *Chicago Press and Tribune*, August 10, 1858.

63. Rawley, *Race and Politics*, 253.

64. Berwanger, *The Frontier against Slavery*, 115.

65. Nichols, *The Disruption of American Democracy*, 23.

66. George B. Forgie, *Patricide in the House Divided: A Psychological Interpretation of Lincoln and His Age* (New York: Norton, 1979), 4.

67. For an elaboration of these themes, see Rush Welter, *The Mind of America, 1820–1860* (New York: Columbia University Press, 1975), 371.

68. Carl Bode, *The Anatomy of American Popular Culture, 1840–1861* (Berkeley: University of California Press, 1959), 141, 128.

69. Jean H. Baker, *Affairs of Party: The Political Culture of Northern Democrats in the Mid-Nineteenth Century* (Ithaca, N.Y.: Cornell University Press, 1983), 24.

70. George H. Mayer, *The Republican Party, 1854–1964* (New York: Oxford University Press, 1964), 4.

71. Holt, *The Political Crisis of the 1850s*, 4.

72. Leon F. Litwack, *North of Slavery: The Negro in the Free States, 1790–1860* (Chicago: University of Chicago Press, 1961), vii, 91. The five were Massachusetts, Rhode Island, Maine, New Hampshire, and Vermont. Together they represented only 6 percent of the Northern Negro population.

73. On these points, see Foner, *Free Soil, Free Labor, Free Men*, 265; Nevins, *Ordeal of the Union*, 2:383. Stampp indicates, however, that some Republican leaders espoused racist sentiments not out of genuine conviction but as a matter of adaptation to their audience. For some, he writes, it was "a matter of political tactics—as an expedient appeal to the undecided and to those who constituted the least common denominator in their party" (Kenneth M. Stampp, *The Imperiled Union: Essays on the Background of the Civil War* [New York: Oxford University Press, 1980], 120).

74. George M. Fredrickson, "A Man but Not a Brother: Abraham Lincoln and Racial Equality," *Journal of Southern History* 41 (February 1975): 51.

75. For a list of officers of the American Colonization Society, see Litwack, *North of Slavery*, 24. Lincoln continued to support colonization during the late 1850s and even into his presidency (see, e.g., Berwanger, *The Frontier against Slavery*, 4).

76. This argument is developed in Cooper, *The South and the Politics of Slavery*, 371.

77. Dwight G. Anderson, *Abraham Lincoln: The Quest for Immortality* (New York: Knopf, 1982), 149.

78. William E. Gienapp, "'Politics Seem to Enter into Everything': Political Culture in the North, 1840–1860," *Essays in American Antebellum Politics, 1840–1860,* ed. Stephen E. Maizlish and John J. Kushma (College Station: Texas A&M University Press, 1982), 40.

79. Capers, *Stephen A. Douglas,* 15; Mayer, *The Republican Party,* 11.

80. Bode, *The Anatomy of American Popular Culture,* 250; Neely, *The Abraham Lincoln Encyclopedia,* 223; Mayer, *The Republican Party,* 7.

81. See Benson, *Toward the Scientific Study of History* (Philadelphia: Lippincott, 1972), 317; Cooper, *The South and the Politics of Slavery,* 242.

82. See, e.g., Milo Milton Quaife, *The Doctrine of Non-Intervention with Slavery in the Territories* (Chicago: Mac C. Chamberlin, 1910), 59. Polk's vice president, George M. Dallas, is sometimes credited with authorship of "popular sovereignty" (see Eric Foner, "Politics, Ideology, and the Origins of the American Civil War," in *A Nation Divided: Problems and Issues of the Civil War and Reconstruction,* ed. George M. Fredrickson [Minneapolis: Burgess, 1975], 24).

83. Fehrenbacher, *Prelude to Greatness,* 132.

84. Oates, *With Malice toward None,* 84–85.

85. See Nevins, *Ordeal of the Union,* 1:349; Fehrenbacher, *The South and Three Sectional Crises,* 51.

86. David M. Potter, *The Impending Crisis, 1848–1861* (New York: Harper & Row, 1976), 251. On the relation between nativism and Republicanism, see esp. William E. Gienapp, "Nativism and the Creation of a Republican Majority in the North before the Civil War," *Journal of American History* 72 (December 1985): 529–59, esp. 539–47.

87. Holt, *The Political Crisis of the 1850s,* 163, and "The Politics of Impatience," 323–24. Holt has suggested that the Know-Nothing movement was the cause, not the result, of the Whig party's demise: "Put briefly, in the early 1850s an intensified anti-Catholicism emerged simultaneously with a hostility to politicians and an impatience with established parties that resulted in huge numbers of voters deserting the Whigs on the grassroots level" ("The Politics of Impatience," 313). Thus, there was no infrastructure to fall back on when the slavery issue divided national Whig leaders.

88. Foner, *Free Soil, Free Labor, Free Men,* 233; Holt, "The Politics of Impatience," 320.

89. See Foner, *Free Soil, Free Labor, Free Men,* 310.

90. Neely, *The Abraham Lincoln Encyclopedia,* 264.

91. Malcolm Moos, *The Republicans: A History of Their Party* (New York: Random House, 1956), 22.

92. Reinhard H. Luthin, "Abraham Lincoln Becomes a Republican," *Political Science Quarterly* 59 (September 1944): 427–28; George F. Brown to Lyman Trumbull, January 9, 1856, Lyman Trumbull MSS, Illinois State Historical Library; Oates, *With Malice toward None,* 118.

93. Douglas to Charles H. Lanphier and George Walker, October 15, 1855, Johannsen, ed., *Letters of Stephen A. Douglas,* 344; Lyman Trumbull to Lincoln, July 5, 1856, Lyman Trumbull MSS, Illinois State Historical Library.

94. Douglas to James Buchanan, September 29, 1856, Johannsen, ed., *Letters of Stephen A. Douglas*, 368.

95. Speech at Springfield, Ill., June 26, 1857, *The Collected Works of Abraham Lincoln*, 2:405.

96. See Klein, *President James Buchanan*, 290; Nevins, *Ordeal of the Union*, 2:504–5.

97. The origins of the "Egypt" designation are unclear. Among the explanations are these: the junction of the Ohio and Mississippi rivers resembled the Nile Delta; the name was suggested by the town of Cairo; the Indian mounds were reminiscent of the Pyramids; settlers from northern and central Illinois who came to Cairo to purchase grain during the bleak winter of 1830–31 were reminiscent of Jacob's sons going down to Egypt; and the region was marked by "mental darkness" (see Richard Allen Heckman, *Lincoln vs. Douglas: The Great Debates Campaign* [Washington, D.C.: Public Affairs Press, 1967], 101, 173n; Sigelschiffer, *The American Conscience*, 94; Henry Parker Willis, *Stephen A. Douglas* [Philadelphia: George W. Jacobs, 1910], 276). Similarly, the appellation of Illinois as the "Sucker State" is of uncertain origin. Suckers were lead miners who went home for the winter, but the phrase might also derive from an anecdote that Douglas told about George Rogers Clark, who called out, "Surrender, you suckers, you," to Frenchmen at Kaskaskia who were sipping mint juleps as the militia arrived (see Alexander Davidson and Bernard Stuve, *A Complete History of Illinois from 1673 to 1873* [Springfield: Illinois Journal Co., 1876], 347n).

98. Davidson and Stuve, *A Complete History of Illinois*, 357.

99. Fehrenbacher, *Prelude to Greatness*, 14.

100. Ibid., 15.

101. Heckman, *Lincoln vs. Douglas*, 59–60.

102. Ibid., 39. Compare N. Dwight Harris, *The History of Negro Servitude in Illinois and of the Slavery Agitation in That State, 1719–1864* (Chicago: A. C. McClurg, 1904), 67, describing the 1830s.

103. On the ambiguity in the Northwest Ordinance, see Paul Finkelman, "Slavery and the Northwest Ordinance: A Study in Ambiguity," *Journal of the Early Republic* 6 (Winter 1986): 343–70. On the course of slavery in early Illinois, see Finkelman, *An Imperfect Union*, 96; George W. Smith, *History of Illinois and Her People* (Chicago and New York: American Historical Society, 1927), 2:16; Paul Simon, *Lincoln's Preparation for Greatness: The Illinois Legislative Years* (Norman: University of Oklahoma Press, 1965), 125; Davidson and Stuve, *A Complete History of Illinois*, 317.

104. Harris, *History of Negro Servitude*, 51.

105. Davidson and Stuve, *A Complete History of Illinois*, 311; Finkelman, *An Imperfect Union*, 150.

106. Harris, *The History of Negro Servitude*, 62.

107. Ibid., 226.

108. Henry H. Simms, *A Decade of Sectional Controversy, 1851–1861* (1942; reprint, Westport, Conn.: Greenwood, 1978), 128.

109. Ibid., 128; Charles H. Coleman, *Abraham Lincoln and Coles County, Illinois* (New Brunswick, N.J.: Scarecrow, 1955), 110.

110. Harris, *The History of Negro Servitude*, 238.

111. Ibid., 62, 123, 125; Smith, *History of Illinois and Her People*, 2:364.

112. Allan Nevins, "Stephen A. Douglas: His Weaknesses and His Greatness," *Journal of the Illinois State Historical Society* 42 (December 1949): 395; Baker, *Affairs of Party*, 195. The Baker book is a particularly good explanation of the ideological and racial foundations of Douglas's thinking.

113. Johannsen, *Stephen A. Douglas*, vii.

114. Nevins, "Stephen A. Douglas," 396; Lincoln to John T. Stuart, March 1, 1840, *The Collected Works of Abraham Lincoln*, 1:206.

115. Johannsen, *Stephen A. Douglas*, 66. There is some disagreement as to when the Little Giant nickname originated. Beveridge traces it to an 1834 speech at a Democratic meeting in Jacksonville, when Douglas rallied a disheartened crowd. Milton found the origin in the acclaim that Douglas received for his denunciation of Nicholas Biddle and the Whigs during a rally in 1835. Sigelschiffer finds the first *written* mention of the nickname in November 1839. Compare Albert J. Beveridge, quoted in Paul M. Angle, ed., *The Lincoln Reader* (New Brunswick, N.J.: Rutgers University Press, 1947), 82; George Fort Milton, *The Eve of Conflict: Stephen A. Douglas and the Needless War* (Boston: Houghton Mifflin, 1934), 19; Sigelschiffer, *The American Conscience*, 142.

116. Milton, *The Eve of Conflict*, 3.

117. Capers, *Stephen A. Douglas*, 16.

118. Douglas Autobiographical Sketch, September 1, 1838, Johannsen, ed., *Letters of Stephen A. Douglas*, 67.

119. Capers, *Stephen A. Douglas*, 15.

120. Fragment on Stephen A. Douglas, December 1856 (?), *The Collected Works of Abraham Lincoln*, 2:382.

121. Statement of Nat Grigsby, September 12, 1865, W. H. Herndon, "Life of Lincoln," 1:91, MS LN 2408, Henry E. Huntington Library; David Turnham to William H. Herndon, October 19, 1866, ibid., 205; Dennis F. Hanks to William H. Herndon, March 12, 1866, ibid., 265.

122. The text of this speech is in *The Collected Works of Abraham Lincoln*, 1:108–15. Excellent detailed analyses may be found in Jaffa, *Crisis of the House Divided;* and Anderson, *Abraham Lincoln*.

123. Speech on Annexation of Texas, May 22, 1844, *The Collected Works of Abraham Lincoln*, 1:337; Lincoln to Williamson Durley, October 3, 1845, ibid., 347.

124. Charles B. Strozier, *Lincoln's Quest for Union: Public and Private Meanings* (New York: Basic, 1982), 149, 152.

125. Paul M. Angle, *"Here I Have Lived": A History of Lincoln's Springfield, 1821–1865* (Springfield, Ill.: Abraham Lincoln Assoc., 1935), 136.

126. Randall, *Lincoln the President*, 1:36.

127. On Lincoln's study program, see Lord Charnwood, *Abraham Lincoln* (New York: Holt, 1916), 103.

128. For texts of the Winchester, Springfield, and Peoria speeches, see *The Collected Works of Abraham Lincoln*, 2:226–27, 240–47, 247–83. On the other speeches, see Paul M. Angle, *Lincoln, 1854–1861* (Springfield, Ill.: Abraham Lincoln Assoc., 1933), x.

129. Douglas to Charles H. Lanphier, December 18, 1854, Johannsen, ed., *Letters of Stephen A. Douglas*, 331.

130. Elwell Crissey, *Lincoln's Lost Speech* (New York: Hawthorn, 1967), 148; Oscar Handlin and Lilian Handlin, *Abraham Lincoln and the Union* (Boston: Little, Brown, 1980), 103; Luther Emerson Robinson, *Abraham Lincoln as a Man of Letters* (New York: Putnam's, 1923), 54.

131. Vernon L. Parrington, *Main Currents in American Thought* (1927; reprint, New York: Harcourt, Brace, & World, 1954), 149.

132. On these elements of Lincoln's political thought, see T. Harry Williams, "Abraham Lincoln—Principle and Pragmatism in Politics: A Review Article," *Mississippi Valley Historical Review* 40 (June 1953): 96–97; J. G. Randall, *Lincoln, the Liberal Statesman* (New York: Dodd, Mead, 1947), 175; Glen E. Thurow, *Abraham Lincoln and American Political Religion* (Albany: State University of New York Press, 1976), 35; T. Harry Williams, "Abraham Lincoln: Pragmatic Democrat," in *The Enduring Lincoln*, ed. Norman A. Graebner (Urbana: University of Illinois Press, 1959), 33; Anderson, *Abraham Lincoln*, 161; Leonard Swett to William H. Herndon, January 17, 1866, Herndon, "Life of Lincoln," 2:90; T. Harry Williams, ed., *Abraham Lincoln: Selected Speeches, Messages, and Letters* (New York: Holt, Rinehart, & Winston, 1966), ix.

133. Simon, *Lincoln's Preparation for Greatness*, 129; Statement of John Hanks, n.d., Herndon, "Life of Lincoln," 1:121. Compare Hanks's statement with Richard N. Current, *The Lincoln Nobody Knows* (New York: McGraw-Hill, 1958), 217; Neely, *The Abraham Lincoln Encyclopedia*, 221.

134. Protest in Illinois Legislature on Slavery, March 3, 1837, *The Collected Works of Abraham Lincoln*, 1:75; Sigelschiffer, *The American Conscience*, 108; Neely, *The Abraham Lincoln Encyclopedia*, 207.

135. Speech at Kalamazoo, Mich., August 27, 1856, *The Collected Works of Abraham Lincoln*, 2:364.

136. On these points, see Benjamin Quarles, *Lincoln and the Negro* (New York: Oxford University Press, 1962), 35.

137. Don E. Fehrenbacher, "Only His Stepchildren: Lincoln and the Negro," in *A Nation Divided*, ed. Fredrickson, 49.

138. Speech at Peoria, Ill., October 16 1854, *The Collected Works of Abraham Lincoln*, 2:255. See also Speech at Bloomington, Ill., September 12, 1854, ibid., 230.

139. Statement of Nat Grigsby, September 12, 1865, Herndon, "Life of Lincoln," 1:93.

140. Handlin and Handlin, *Abraham Lincoln and the Union*, 22.

141. Ibid., 16; Daniel Kilham Dodge, "Abraham Lincoln: The Evolution of His Literary Style," *University of Illinois Studies* 1 (May 1900): 10.

142. William Henry Herndon, "Analysis of the Character & Mind of Abraham Lincoln," 23, enclosed with Herndon to Ward Hill Lamon, December 18, 1869, Henry E. Huntington Library.

143. On Lincoln's knowledge of the Bible, see Dodge, "Abraham Lincoln," 18; Davidson and Stuve, *A Complete History of Illinois*, 706.

144. Theodore C. Blegen, *Lincoln's Imagery: A Study in Word Power*

(LaCrosse, Wis.: Emerson G. Wulling, Sumac Press, 1954), 8–9; Roy P. Basler, *A Touchstone for Greatness: Essays, Addresses, and Occasional Pieces about Abraham Lincoln* (Westport, Conn.: Greenwood, 1973), 96.

145. Mildred Freburg Berry, "Abraham Lincoln: His Development in the Skills of the Platform," in *A History and Criticism of American Public Address*, ed. William Norwood Brigance (1943; reprint, New York: Russell & Russell, 1960), 2:847, 850.

146. Simon, *Lincoln's Preparation for Greatness*, 112; Johannsen, *Stephen A. Douglas*, 66.

147. Johannsen, *Stephen A. Douglas*, 76; Thomas, *Abraham Lincoln*, 74–75; Speech at Springfield, Ill., December 18, 1839, *The Collected Works of Abraham Lincoln*, 1:157–58; J. Gillespie to William H. Herndon, January 31, 1866, Herndon, "Life of Lincoln," 2:22.

148. "From Old Hickory," May 15, 1840, Johannsen, ed., *Letters of Stephen A. Douglas*, 79.

149. Willard L. King, *Lincoln's Manager, David Davis* (Cambridge, Mass.: Harvard University Press, 1960), 38. See also Statement of James H. Matheny, n.d., Herndon, "Life of Lincoln," 2:213.

150. The details of this case are in Johannsen, *Stephen A. Douglas*, 91.

151. Willis, *Stephen A. Douglas*, 47.

152. Neely, *The Abraham Lincoln Encyclopedia*, 235. The text of the speech is in *The Collected Works of Abraham Lincoln*, 2:247–83.

153. These details about the Douglas speech are taken from Johannsen, *Stephen A. Douglas*, 1; Rawley, *Race and Politics*, 199; and Fehrenbacher, *Prelude to Greatness*, 134.

154. Speech at Springfield, Ill., June 26, 1857, *The Collected Works of Abraham Lincoln*, 2:399, 405. The complete text of the speech is found on 398–410. See also Beveridge, *Abraham Lincoln*, 2:519; Angle, *Lincoln, 1854–1861*, xviii.

Chapter Two

1. On the origin of the term *Danite*, see Angle, *"Here I Have Lived,"* 227n; Sigelschiffer, *The American Conscience*, 66–67. The name was derived from the biblical prophecy of the dying Jacob concerning one of his sons: "Dan shall be a serpent in the way" (Gen. 49:17).

2. See, e.g., Thomas M. Hope to Douglas, September 12, 1858, Stephen A. Douglas MSS, box 19, folder 39, University of Chicago Library. Hope interrupted Douglas as he prepared to open the Alton debate, asking the embarrassing question, "Do you believe that the territorial legislatures ought to pass laws to protect slavery in the territories?"

3. *Chicago Times*, September 7, 23, 1858.

4. Beveridge, *Abraham Lincoln*, 2:551; Fehrenbacher, *Prelude to Greatness*, 114; *Chicago Press and Tribune*, October 7, 1858.

5. *Illinois State Register*, July 5, 1958; S. S. Marshall to Charles H. Lanphier, October 9, 1858, Charles H. Lanphier MSS, Illinois State Historical Library; Johannsen, *Stephen A. Douglas*, 652; Horace White, *The Life of Lyman Trumbull* (Boston: Houghton Mifflin, 1913), 91.

6. Rawley, *Race and Politics*, 249; Thomas L. Harris to Charles H. Lanphier, March 11, 1858, Charles H. Lanphier MSS, Illinois State Historical Library.

7. M. Knapp to Ozias M. Hatch, March 31, 1858, Ozias M. Hatch MSS, Illinois State Historical Library; Benjamin Kirk to Douglas, June 4, 1858, Stephen A. Douglas MSS, box 18, folder 9, University of Chicago Library; Lincoln to Ward Hill Lamon, June 11, 1858, *The Collected Works of Abraham Lincoln*, 2:459.

8. Lyman Trumbull to Lincoln, January 3, 1858, Robert Todd Lincoln Collection of the Papers of Abraham Lincoln, reel 2, frames 731–34, Library of Congress; *Illinois State Journal*, June 29, 1858; N. B. Judd to Lyman Trumbull, 16 (?) July 1858, Lyman Trumbull MSS, reel 4, Library of Congress.

9. A. Jonas to Lyman Trumbull, April 11, 1858, Lyman Trumbull MSS, reel 4, Library of Congress; Trumbull to Lincoln, January 3, 1858, Robert Todd Lincoln Collection of the Papers of Abraham Lincoln, reel 2, frames 731–34, Library of Congress; Trumbull to John M. Palmer, June 19, 1858, John M. Palmer MSS, Illinois State Historical Library; King, *Lincoln's Manager, David Davis*, 117; Heckman, *Lincoln vs. Douglas*, 26; Jesse K. Dubois to Trumbull, April 8, 1858, Lyman Trumbull MSS, reel 4, Library of Congress.

10. An example of the allegation that Douglas and Seward made a corrupt bargain is C. H. Ray to Ozias M. Hatch, December 7, 1858, Ozias M. Hatch MSS, Illinois State Historical Library. For Ray there is no doubt. Like others, however, he denied that Douglas's national activities would hurt Republicans at the state level. See C. H. Ray to Lyman Trumbull, March 9, 1858, Lyman Trumbull MSS, reel 4, Library of Congress; William H. Herndon to Trumbull, April 24, 1858, ibid.; J. Grimshaw to Ozias M. Hatch, April 5, 1858, Ozias M. Hatch MSS, Illinois State Historical Library; N. B. Judd to Lincoln, June 1, 1858, Robert Todd Lincoln Collection of the Papers of Abraham Lincoln, reel 2, frames 832–33, Library of Congress.

11. Paul M. Angle, *Stephen Arnold Douglas: Chicagoan and Patriot* (Chicago: Chicago Historical Society, 1961), 10; C. H. Ray to Lyman Trumbull, March 9, 1858, Lyman Trumbull MSS, reel 4, Library of Congress; D. L. Phillips to Lincoln, June 9, 1858, Robert Todd Lincoln Collection of the Papers of Abraham Lincoln, reel 2, frames 864–65, Library of Congress; George W. Rives to Lincoln, June 4, 1858, ibid., frames 849–50; Josiah M. Lucas to Lincoln, May 3, 1858, ibid., frames 769–71; Thomas, *Abraham Lincoln*, 179.

12. These reasons are outlined in Don E. Fehrenbacher, "The Nomination of Lincoln in 1858," *Abraham Lincoln Quarterly* 6 (March 1950): 30.

13. Neely, *The Abraham Lincoln Encyclopedia*, 79; Fehrenbacher, *Prelude to Greatness*, 48.

14. Don E. Fehrenbacher, "The Origins and Purpose of Lincoln's 'House Divided' Speech," *Mississippi Valley Historical Review* 46 (March 1960): 631.

15. On the details of speech preparation, see C. D. Hay to Lyman Trumbull, May 29, 1858, Lyman Trumbull MSS, reel 4, Library of Congress; William Henry Herndon, "Facts Illustrative of Mr. Lincoln's Patriotism and Statesmanship," January 23 1866, MS LN 1949, Henry E. Huntington Library; Richard Nelson

Current, *Speaking of Abraham Lincoln: The Man and His Meaning for Our Times* (Urbana: University of Illinois Press, 1983), 11; Mildred Freburg Berry, "Lincoln—the Speaker (Part I)," *Quarterly Journal of Speech* 17 (February 1931): 34; Arthur Charles Cole, *The Centennial History of Illinois* (Springfield, Ill.: Illinois Centennial Commission, 1919), 3:164; Sigelschiffer, *The American Conscience,* 177.

16. The later comparison between a "living dog" and a "dead lion" is also biblical (see Eccles. 9:4).

17. Strozier, *Lincoln's Quest for Union,* 180; Lincoln to George Robertson, August 13, 1855, *The Collected Works of Abraham Lincoln* 2:318; Albert A. Woldman, *Lawyer Lincoln* (Boston: Houghton Mifflin, 1936), 241.

18. Russel B. Nye, *Fettered Freedom: Civil Liberties and the Slavery Controversy, 1830–1860* (East Lansing: Michigan State University Press, 1963), 287; Nevins, *Ordeal of the Union,* 2:78; C. Vann Woodward, *American Counterpoint: Slavery and Racism in the North-South Dialogue* (Boston: Little, Brown, 1971), 130.

19. See Fehrenbacher, *Prelude to Greatness,* 70–95; Michael C. Leff, "Rhetorical Timing in Lincoln's 'House Divided' Speech" (the Van Zelst Lecture in Communication, delivered at Northwestern University, 1983). The text of the speech is in *The Collected Works of Abraham Lincoln,* 2:461–69.

20. W. H. Herndon to Ward Hill Lamon, February 19, 1870, Ward Hill Lamon MSS, MSS LN 347, LN 368, Henry E. Huntington Library; Herndon, "Facts Illustrative of Mr. Lincoln's Patriotism and Statesmanship," 9.

21. See, e.g., *Illinois State Register,* June 17, 1858.

22. Fredrickson, "A Man but Not a Brother," 50; Lincoln to John L. Scripps, June 23, 1858, *The Collected Works of Abraham Lincoln,* 2:471.

23. *Chicago Times,* July 27, 1858; *Illinois State Register,* August 7, 1858.

24. Both sides had identified this region as crucial, assuming that Lincoln would carry the northern end of the state and Douglas the southern. See, e.g., N. B. Judd to Lyman Trumbull, April 19, 1858, Lyman Trumbull MSS, reel 4, Library of Congress; Thomas L. Harris to Douglas, July 7, 1858, quoted in Forest L. Whan, "Stephen A. Douglas," in *A History and Criticism of American Public Address,* ed. Brigance, 794.

25. Paul M. Angle, ed., *Created Equal? The Complete Lincoln-Douglas Debates of 1858* (Chicago: University of Chicago Press, 1958), xxiv; Johnson, *Stephen A. Douglas,* 363.

26. Wells, *Stephen Douglas,* 88.

27. *Chicago Times,* September 19, 1858; T. J. Pickett to Lincoln, August 3, 1858, Robert Todd Lincoln Collection of the Papers of Abraham Lincoln, reel 3, frames 1138–40, Library of Congress.

28. *Chicago Times,* June 27, 1858; Henry C. Whitney to Lincoln, June 23, 1858, Robert Todd Lincoln Collection of the Papers of Abraham Lincoln, reel 2, frames 914–17, Library of Congress.

29. Thomas L. Harris to Douglas, July 6, 1858, Stephen A. Douglas MSS, box 18, folder 49, University of Chicago Library; John Mathers to Lincoln, July 19,

1858, Robert Todd Lincoln Collection of the Papers of Abraham Lincoln, reel 3, frames 984–86, Library of Congress; Lyman Trumbull to John M. Palmer, June 19, 1858, John M. Palmer MSS, Illinois State Historical Library.

30. J. Grimshaw to Ozias M. Hatch, July 11, 1858, Ozias M. Hatch MSS, Illinois State Historical Society.

31. The text of the speech is in *The Collected Works of Abraham Lincoln*, 2:484–502. Texts of both Lincoln's and Douglas's speeches can also be found in Angle, ed., *Created Equal?* 9–42.

32. The text of Lincoln's Springfield speech is in *The Collected Works of Abraham Lincoln*, 2:504–21. Both texts also are included in Angle, ed., *Created Equal?* 43–82.

33. *Illinois State Journal*, July 20, 1858.

34. On the details of the Trumbull invitation, see C. H. Ray to Lyman Trumbull, July 17, 1858, Lyman Trumbull MSS, reel 4, Library of Congress; Trumbull to John M. Palmer, June 19, 1858, John M. Palmer MSS, Illinois State Historical Library; Mark M. Krug, "Lyman Trumbull and the Real Issues in the Lincoln-Douglas Debates," *Journal of the Illinois State Historical Society* 57 (Winter 1964): 390.

35. Beveridge, *Abraham Lincoln* 2:626; Heckman, *Lincoln vs. Douglas*, 75; Thomas S. Halbach to Douglas, July 16, 1858, Stephen A. Douglas MSS, box 19, folder 8, University of Chicago Library; Lincoln to Gustave P. Koerner, July 15, 1858, *The Collected Works of Abraham Lincoln*, 2:502.

36. David Davis to Lincoln, August 9, 1858, Robert Todd Lincoln Collection of the Papers of Abraham Lincoln, reel 3, frames 1186–87, Library of Congress; Lincoln to William Fithian, September 3, 1858, *The Collected Works of Abraham Lincoln*, 3:84; *Chicago Times*, July 30, 1858.

37. N. B. Judd to Lyman Trumbull, July 16 (?), 1858, Lyman Trumbull MSS, reel 4, Library of Congress; John Mathers to Lincoln, July 19, 1858, Robert Todd Lincoln Collection of the Papers of Abraham Lincoln, reel 3, frames 984–86, Library of Congress; Lincoln to John Mathers, July 20, 1858, *The Collected Works of Abraham Lincoln* 2:522; J. H. Jordan to Lincoln, July 25, 1858, Robert Todd Lincoln Collection of the Papers of Abraham Lincoln, reel 3, frames 1048–52, Library of Congress.

38. Beveridge, *Abraham Lincoln*, 2:628–29; Johannsen, ed., *The Lincoln-Douglas Debates of 1858*, 11; W. J. Usrey to Lincoln, July 19, 1858, Robert Todd Lincoln Collection of the Papers of Abraham Lincoln, reel 3, frames 995–96, Library of Congress; J. H. Jordan to Lincoln, July 25, 1858, ibid., frames 1048–52.

39. For examples of these two motives, see Milton, *The Eve of Conflict*, 329; Heckman, *Lincoln vs. Douglas*, 77.

40. Richard Allen Heckman, "The Lincoln-Douglas Debates: A Case Study in 'Stump Speaking,' " *Civil War History* 12 (March 1966):54; Nevins, *The Emergence of Lincoln*, 1:74; *Chicago Press and Tribune*, July 26, 1858. The *Press and Tribune*, however, noted that Douglas had declined a debate challenge by Trumbull in 1854. Unlike Lincoln, though, Trumbull had not been officially identified as the candidate of his political party.

41. Douglas to Lincoln, July 24, 1858, Johannsen, ed., *The Letters of Stephen A. Douglas*, 423–24.

42. For example, *Chicago Press and Tribune*, July 28, 1858; *Chicago Times*, July 29, 1858.

43. N. B. Judd to Lincoln, July 27, 1858, Robert Todd Lincoln Collection of the Papers of Abraham Lincoln, reel 3, frame 1079, Library of Congress.

44. Lincoln to Douglas, July 29, 1858, *The Collected Works of Abraham Lincoln*, 2:528–30.

45. Douglas to Lincoln, July 30, 1858, Johannsen, ed., *The Letters of Stephen A. Douglas*, 424–25; Lincoln to Douglas, July 31, 1858, *The Collected Works of Abraham Lincoln*, 2:531.

46. Mayer, *The Republican Party*, 11. Fehrenbacher argues that such an extensive campaign was made possible only by the development of railroads in Illinois during the 1850s (*Prelude to Greatness*, 8).

47. Prominent Democratic outsiders included Kentucky congressman James B. Clay (Henry Clay's son), Virginia governor Henry A. Wise, Ohio senator George E. Pugh and congressman Clement L. Vallandigham, the pro-Lecompton Missouri senator James S. Green, and Reverdy Johnson of Maryland. Republicans were represented by Senator James R. Doolittle of Wisconsin, Governor Salmon P. Chase of Ohio, Congressmen Schuyler Colfax of Indiana and Francis P. Blair of Missouri, former governor William F. Johnston of Pennsylvania, Frederick Douglass, and Theodore Parker. (Heckman, *Lincoln vs. Douglas*, 61–62.)

48. Wells, *Stephen Douglas*, 91.

49. Capers, *Stephen A. Douglas*, 184. See also Christopher N. Breiseth, "Lincoln, Douglas, and Springfield in the 1858 Campaign," in *The Public and the Private Lincoln*, ed. Davis et al., 119; Johannsen, *Stephen A. Douglas*, 666. For a general discussion of strategy in the debates, see Robert T. Oliver, *History of Public Speaking in America* (Boston: Allyn & Bacon, 1965), 308–14.

50. J. H. Jordan to Lincoln, July 25, 1858, Robert Todd Lincoln Collection of the Papers of Abraham Lincoln, reel 3, frames 1048–52, Library of Congress.

51. Angle, ed., *Created Equal?* xxviii.

52. The clipping book is in the Herndon-Weik Collection of Lincolniana, reel 1, group I.B, Library of Congress.

53. Fehrenbacher, *Prelude to Greatness*, 104.

54. Harris, *The History of Negro Servitude*, 212.

55. James C. Y. Chu, "Horace White: His Association with Abraham Lincoln, 1854–1860," *Journalism Quarterly* 49 (Spring 1972): 55–56. White later wrote to Herndon that he "accompanied Mr. Lincoln almost constantly during the memorable campaign of 1858" (Horace White to William H. Herndon, May 17, 1865, Herndon-Weik Collection of Lincolniana, reel 7, group IV, Library of Congress).

56. *Chicago Times*, November 2, 1858.

57. Fehrenbacher, *Prelude to Greatness*, 97.

58. Milton, *The Eve of Conflict*, 337.

59. Douglas to Charles H. Lanphier, August 15, 1858, Johannsen, ed., *The Letters of Stephen A. Douglas*, 426–27.

60. *Illinois State Register*, August 24, 1858; *Chicago Times*, August 22, 1858.

61. *Chicago Press and Tribune*, August 23, 1858; *Chicago Times*, August 25, 1858.

62. Richard Yates to Lincoln, August 26 (?), 1858, Robert Todd Lincoln Collection of the Papers of Abraham Lincoln, reel 3, frame 1303, Library of Congress; King, *Lincoln's Manager, David Davis*, 122; R. R. Hitt to Horace White, December 10, 1892, Horace White MSS, Illinois State Historical Library; Lincoln to Joseph O. Cunningham, August 22, 1858, *The Collected Works of Abraham Lincoln*, 3:37.

63. J. H. Jordan to Lincoln, August 24, 1858, Robert Todd Lincoln Collection of the Papers of Abraham Lincoln, reel 3, frames 1282–83, Library of Congress; H. C. Whitney to Lincoln, August 26, 1858, ibid., frames 1301–2; L. D. Whiting to Lincoln, August 23, 1858, frames 1279–81.

64. *Chicago Times*, August 25, 1858; *Illinois State Register*, August 24, 1858.

65. Lincoln to Ebenezer Peck, August 23, 1858, *The Collected Works of Abraham Lincoln: Supplement, 1832–1865*, ed. Roy P. Basler (Westport, Conn.: Greenwood, 1974), 32–33; Joseph Medill to Lincoln, August 26 (?), 1858, Robert Todd Lincoln Collection of the Papers of Abraham Lincoln, reel 3, frames 1333–36, Library of Congress. Henry Clay Whitney offered Lincoln differing advice, suggesting that he *not* allude to the Douglas "catechism" in his opening speech and urging that Lincoln ought "to ring in the Trumbull argument as to him as to striking out the submission clause" (Whitney to Lincoln, August 26, 1858, ibid., frames 1301–2. Lincoln would follow this advice later, in the Charleston debate.

66. Lincoln to Henry Asbury, July 31, 1858, *The Collected Works of Abraham Lincoln*, 2:530.

67. Potter, *The Impending Crisis*, 338.

68. *Chicago Times*, August 29, 1858; *Illinois State Register*, September 1, 1858.

69. *Chicago Press and Tribune*, August 30, 1858; *Illinois State Journal*, August 30, 1858.

70. Alonzo Rothschild, *Lincoln, Master of Men: A Study in Character* (Boston: Houghton Mifflin, 1906), 106; Willis, *Stephen A. Douglas*, 276; Elihu B. Washburne, quoted in Allen Thorndike Rice, ed., *Reminiscences of Abraham Lincoln by Distinguished Men of His Time* (New York: North American Review, 1888), 27; Joseph Medill to John A. Gurley, August 28, 1858, Joseph Medill MSS, Chicago Historical Society Library.

71. On the political complexion of the region, see John Y. Simon, "Union County in 1858 and the Lincoln-Douglas Debate," *Journal of the Illinois State Historical Society* 62 (Autumn 1969): 271–73; Neely, *The Abraham Lincoln Encyclopedia*, 167.

72. Heckman, *Lincoln vs. Douglas*, 101.

73. Ibid., 106.

74. *Chicago Press and Tribune*, September 4, 1858.

75. Douglas to Usher F. Linder, August 1858, Johannsen, ed., *The Letters of*

Stephen A. Douglas, 427; A. Compton to Lincoln, September 7, 1858, Robert Todd Lincoln Collection of the Papers of Abraham Lincoln, reel 3, frame 1374, Library of Congress.

76. *Chicago Press and Tribune,* September 17, 20, 1858; *Illinois State Journal,* September 20, 1858; *Chicago Times,* September 17, 1858; *Illinois State Register,* September 20, 1858.

77. On these points, see Simon, "Union County in 1858," 287, 291.

78. N. B. Judd to Lincoln, September (?), 1858, Robert Todd Lincoln Collection of the Papers of Abraham Lincoln, reel 3, frames 1422–23, Library of Congress.

79. Angle, ed., *Created Equal?* 235.

80. Potter, *The Impending Crisis,* 346; *Illinois State Journal,* September 28, 1858.

81. Ronald Deane Rietveld, "The Moral Issue of Slavery in American Politics, 1854–1860" (Ph.D. diss. University of Illinois, 1967), 146–47.

82. *Chicago Times,* October 1, 1858; *Illinois State Register,* October 8, 1958.

83. Speech at Chicago, July 10, 1858, *The Collected Works of Abraham Lincoln,* 2:502. The quoted section is the peroration.

84. See Coleman, *Abraham Lincoln and Coles County,* 182; Angle, ed., *Created Equal?* 271–72.

85. *Chicago Times,* September 21, 1858; *Chicago Press and Tribune,* September 21, 1858; *Illinois State Journal,* September 23, 1858.

86. For this speculation, see Neely, *The Abraham Lincoln Encyclopedia,* 123.

87. *Chicago Times,* October 9, 1858; *Illinois State Register,* October 13, 1858.

88. *Chicago Press and Tribune,* October 9, 11, 1858; *Illinois State Journal,* October 12, 1858.

89. Neely, *The Abraham Lincoln Encyclopedia,* 249.

90. *Chicago Press and Tribune,* October 15, 1858; *Illinois State Journal,* October 18, 1858.

91. Herndon, "Life of Lincoln," 2:357.

92. Neely, *The Abraham Lincoln Encyclopedia,* 250.

93. Ibid., 250.

94. *Illinois State Journal,* October 16, 18, 1858; *Chicago Press and Tribune,* October 15, 1858; *Illinois State Register,* October 18, 1858.

95. Heckman, *Lincoln vs. Douglas,* 126.

96. Neely, *The Abraham Lincoln Encyclopedia,* 4.

97. Sigelschiffer, *The American Conscience,* 335.

98. James W. Anderson, "'The Real Issue': An Analysis of the Final Lincoln-Douglas Debate," *Lincoln Herald* 69 (Spring 1967): 28.

99. Angle, ed., *Created Equal?* 393.

100. Ibid., 396.

101. *Chicago Times,* October 17, 1858; *Illinois State Journal,* October 18, 1858; *Chicago Press and Tribune,* October 18, 1858.

Chapter Three

1. For an excellent collection of specimens of conspiracy argument, see David Brion Davis, ed., *The Fear of Conspiracy: Images of Un-American Subversion from the Revolution to the Present* (Ithaca, N.Y.: Cornell University Press, 1971).

2. For a discussion of how conspiracy arguments mix the pragmatic and the fantastic as frames of reference, see G. Thomas Goodnight and John Poulakos, "Conspiracy Rhetoric: From Pragmatism to Fantasy in Public Discourse," *Western Journal of Speech Communication* 45 (Fall 1981): 299–316.

3. Angle, ed., *Created Equal?* 105, 108–9. Very similar charges were made in the Freeport, Jonesboro, and Charleston debates (see ibid., 161–63, 192–94, 197, 260–61, 263). They were also current in the Douglas papers (see, e.g., *Illinois State Register*, August 17 and 26, 1858).

4. On these points, see Krug, "Lyman Trumbull and the Real Issues," 385.

5. Douglas to Charles H. Lanphier, December 18, 1854, Charles H. Lanphier MSS, Illinois State Historical Library.

6. James W. Sheahan to Charles H. Lanphier, January 17, 1855, James A. Shields to Lanphier, January 14, 1855, and Shields to Lanphier, January 19, 1855, ibid.

7. White, *The Life of Lyman Trumbull*, 46.

8. Angle, ed., *Created Equal?* 105; *The Collected Works of Abraham Lincoln: Supplement*, 28.

9. Angle, ed., *Created Equal?* 115.

10. Ibid., 206–7. Lincoln also cast doubt on the authenticity of the document that Douglas read. In another conspiracy charge, Lincoln was maintaining that a document that Douglas purported to be the 1854 Republican platform was fraudulent. If Douglas could read from *one* forged document, then perhaps this one was a fake as well.

11. Ibid., 196.

12. Krug, "Lyman Trumbull and the Real Issues," 386.

13. Angle, ed., *Created Equal?* 106.

14. Ibid., 115, 131–32. See also King, *Lincoln's Manager, David Davis*, 104. Lincoln went to Pekin, where Judge David Davis was holding court. His name was placed on the State Central Committee in his absence, but he did not serve.

15. Angle, ed., *Created Equal?* 144–45.

16. Ibid., 157–59, 164–66.

17. Ibid., 171–72.

18. Milton, *The Eve of Conflict*, 335.

19. Douglas to Charles H. Lanphier, August 15, 1858, Charles H. Lanphier MSS, Illinois State Historical Library.

20. *Illinois State Register*, August 26, 1858.

21. Charles L. Wilson to Lincoln, August 1858 (date uncertain), Robert Todd Lincoln Collection of the Papers of Abraham Lincoln, reel 3, frames 1337–40, Library of Congress.

22. Johannsen, ed., *The Letters of Stephen A. Douglas*, 427n. Lanphier's

Illinois State Register struck the same theme, noting on August 26, "The question before the people of Illinois is not whether a certain resolution was adopted by republicanism at Aurora or Springfield, but does that party—does Mr. Lincoln—indorse the dogmas laid down above as part of their political creed?"

23. Whan, "Stephen A. Douglas," 799n.

24. David Davis to Lincoln, August 25, 1858, Robert Todd Lincoln Collection of the Papers of Abraham Lincoln, reel 3, frames 1288–89, Library of Congress; Joseph Medill to Lincoln, August 26 (?), 1858, ibid., frames 1333–36; *Illinois State Journal*, September 2, 1858; *Chicago Press and Tribune*, August 23, 1858.

25. For the unfolding of this argument, see Angle, ed., *Created Equal?* 305–7.

26. Heckman, *Lincoln vs. Douglas*, 87.

27. Angle, ed., *Created Equal?* 307.

28. Ibid., 316–17, 338.

29. *Illinois State Register*, August 28, 30, 1858.

30. Angle, ed., *Created Equal?* 359.

31. See, e.g., a speech by Democrat J. C. D. Atkins of Tennessee, House of Representatives, February 17, 1858, *Congressional Globe*, 35th Cong., 1st sess., 27, pt. 1:750; Speech by Clement C. Clay, Jr., Senate, March 19, 1858, ibid., app.:148.

32. Brieseth, "Lincoln, Douglas, and Springfield," 116; Stampp, *The Imperiled Union*, 116.

33. On this point, see Harry V. Jaffa, *Equality and Liberty: Theory and Practice in American Politics* (New York: Oxford University Press, 1965), 48; Boritt, *Lincoln and the Economics of the American Dream*, 172.

34. J. G. Randall, *Lincoln and the South* (Baton Rouge: Louisiana State University Press, 1946), 33.

35. Speech at Springfield, Ill., June 26, 1857, *The Collected Works of Abraham Lincoln*, 2:405.

36. Ibid.; Angle, ed., *Created Equal?* 117, 235.

37. Speech at Springfield, Ill., June 26, 1857, *The Collected Works of Abraham Lincoln*, 2:408; Breiseth, "Lincoln, Douglas, and Springfield," 114.

38. Foner, "Politics, Ideology, and the Origins," 30.

39. Rawley, *Race and Politics*, 266; Foner, *Free Soil, Free Labor, Free Men*, 90; Bruce Collins, *The Origins of America's Civil War* (New York: Holmes & Meier, 1981), 62; William R. Brock, *Parties and Political Conscience: American Dilemmas, 1840–1850* (Millwood, N.Y.: KTO, 1979), 197; Capers, *Stephen A. Douglas*, 104; Beveridge, *Abraham Lincoln*, 2:563–64; Speech by Henry Wilson, Senate, February 4, 1858, *Congressional Globe*, 35th Cong., 1st sess., 27, pt. 1:576; Speech by Henry Waldron, House, March 20, 1858, ibid., pt. 2:1210; Speech by Mason W. Tappan, House, March 31, 1858, ibid., app.: 326; Finkelman, *An Imperfect Union*, 320.

40. Speech by Benjamin F. Wade, Senate, March 13, 1858, *Congressional Globe*, 35th Cong., 1st sess., 27, 2:1111; Speech by Elihu B. Washburne, House, March 25, 1858, ibid., 1346; Speech by William Pitt Fessenden, Senate, February 8, 1858, ibid., pt. 1:614; Speech at Peoria, Illinois, October 16, 1854, *The Collected Works of Abraham Lincoln*, 2:273; Speech by William H. Seward, Senate, March 3, 1858, *Congressional Globe*, 35th Cong., 1st sess., 27, pt.

1:941; Speech by Owen Lovejoy, House, February 17, 1858, ibid., pt. 1:752.

41. Bernard Bailyn, *The Ideological Origins of the American Revolution* (Cambridge Mass.: Harvard University Press, 1967), 233. See also David Brion Davis, *The Slave Power Conspiracy and the Paranoid Style* (Baton Rouge: Louisiana State University Press, 1969), 52.

42. William E. Gienapp, "The Republican Party and the Slave Power," in *New Perspectives on Race and Slavery in America: Essays in Honor of Kenneth M. Stampp,* ed. Robert H. Abzug and Stephen E. Maizlish (Lexington: University Press of Kentucky, 1986), 62.

43. See Nye, *Fettered Freedom,* 314.

44. Russel B. Nye, "The Slave Power Conspiracy: 1830–1860," *Science and Society* 10 (Summer 1946): 272.

45. Neely, *The Abraham Lincoln Encyclopedia,* 80–81; Simms, *A Decade of Sectional Controversy,* 133; Speech at Carlinville, Ill., August 31, 1858, *The Collected Works of Abraham Lincoln,* 3:80.

46. Nye, *Fettered Freedom,* 291; Foner, *Free Soil, Free Labor, Free Men,* 91, and "Politics, Ideology, and the Origins," 29; Sewell, *Ballots for Freedom,* 314.

47. Nye, "The Slave Power Conspiracy," 264–65, 269. Nye credits James G. Birney of the Liberty party and William Goodell as being the first to recognize the importance of the argument that slavery degraded the freedom of Northern whites (see Nye, *Fettered Freedom,* 286).

48. Speech at Peoria, Ill., October 16, 1854, *The Collected Works of Abraham Lincoln,* 2:255. A quite similar argument was advanced by John F. Kennedy during the 1960 presidential campaign with respect to racial segregation.

49. Fehrenbacher, *Prelude to Greatness,* 92–93. The editors of *The Collected Works of Abraham Lincoln* date the speech fragment ca. May 18, 1858 (see 2:448), but Fehrenbacher argues persuasively that the draft was written several months earlier than that date (Fehrenbacher, *Prelude to Greatness,* 89–92).

50. "A House Divided," in *The Collected Works of Abraham Lincoln,* 2:466. The four men, of course, were Senator Douglas, Chief Justice Taney, and Presidents Pierce and Buchanan. For the Ottawa debate, see Angle, ed., *Created Equal?* 121.

51. Holt, *The Political Crisis of the 1850s,* 191.

52. Wm. C. Phillips to Lincoln, July 24, 1858, Robert Todd Lincoln Collection of the Papers of Abraham Lincoln, reel 3, frames 1040–44, Library of Congress. Phillips also urged Lincoln to make Douglas "tell us definitely what is meant by popular sovereignty and other clap trap."

53. *Chicago Press and Tribune,* August 3, 1858.

54. Angle, ed., *Created Equal?* 128–29.

55. Forgie, *Patricide in the House Divided,* 258.

56. A copy of the editorial has been preserved with the Lyman Trumbull MSS, Illinois State Historical Library.

57. Fehrenbacher, *Prelude to Greatness,* 80n; Speech of James Harlan, Senate, January 25, 1858, *Congressional Globe,* 35th Cong., 1st sess., 27, pt. 1:385; Speech of William Pitt Fessenden, Senate, February 8, 1858, ibid., 617; Speech of Zachariah Chandler, Senate, March 12, 1858, ibid., pt. 2:1089.

58. Finkelman, *An Imperfect Union*, 239; Jaffa, *Crisis of the House Divided*, 292.

59. Foner, *Free Soil, Free Labor, Free Men*, 98. For example, Henry Wilson of Massachusetts, in a February 1858 Senate speech, had cited this case as the vehicle for "*Dred Scott* II" (see *Congressional Globe*, 35th Cong., 1st sess., 27, pt. 1:547).

60. Fehrenbacher, *The Dred Scott Case*, 444.

61. Speech at Springfield, Ill., June 26, 1857, *The Collected Works of Abraham Lincoln*, 2:399. Republicans had long argued that popular sovereignty was not neutral because, once slavery had established a toehold in a territory, it "would be devilishly hard to dislodge": "Men would find the practical difficulties of liquidating an already established form of property to be virtually insurmountable" (Sewell, *Ballots for Freedom*, 296).

62. John Mathers to Lincoln, July 19, 1858, Robert Todd Lincoln Collection of the Papers of Abraham Lincoln, reel 3, frames 984–86, Library of Congress; J. H. Jordan to Lincoln, July 25, 1858, ibid., frames 1048–52; Joseph Medill to Lincoln, August 26 (?), 1858, ibid., frames 1333–36.

63. Fragment, Notes for Speeches, ca. August 21, 1858, *The Collected Works of Abraham Lincoln*, 2:548–49. For judgment of others, cf. Capers, *Stephen A. Douglas*, which dismisses the possibility that Lincoln believed the charge, with Neely, *The Abraham Lincoln Encyclopedia*, 171, which supports it.

64. Angle, ed., *Created Equal?* 123–24.

65. Ibid., 50; Speech at Springfield, Ill., July 17, 1858, *The Collected Works of Abraham Lincoln*, 2:521.

66. *Chicago Times*, July 23, 31, 1858; Milton, *The Eve of Conflict*, 333.

67. Angle, ed., *Created Equal?* 135.

68. Ibid., 136.

69. Ibid., 148–49.

70. Ibid., 153.

71. Ibid., 136–37.

72. Ibid., 169–70, 175–76.

73. See, e.g., Sewell, *Ballots for Freedom*, 298; George M. Fredrickson, *The Black Image in the White Mind: The Debate on Afro-American Character and Destiny, 1817–1914* (New York: Harper & Row, 1971), 139. These arguments contrast with Ramsdell, "The Natural Limits of Slavery Expansion."

74. Douglas to the Editor of the *Concord, N.H., State Capitol Reporter*, February 16, 1854, Johannsen, ed., *The Letters of Stephen A. Douglas*, 289; George Fort Milton, "Douglas' Place in American History," *Journal of the Illinois State Historical Society* 26 (January 1934): 338.

75. Speech at Peoria, Ill., October 16, 1854, *The Collected Works of Abraham Lincoln*, 2:262; King, *Lincoln's Manager, David Davis*, 103; Boritt, *Lincoln and the Economics of the American Dream*, 166; Sewell, *Ballots for Freedom*, 193. Boritt theorizes that Lincoln's imputation of hypocrisy to Douglas and the accusation that the incumbent had "covert real zeal" for the spread of slavery reflected Lincoln's concern that Douglas accepted the natural limits theory regarding slavery extension when his strong interest in economic development

should have caused him to know better (*Lincoln and the Economics of the American Dream,* 168).

76. *Chicago Press and Tribune,* October 23, 1858.

77. See, e.g., Wells, *Stephen Douglas,* 27.

78. Willis, *Stephen A. Douglas,* 259; Heckman, *Lincoln vs. Douglas,* 23; David Davis to John F. Henry, July 29, 1858, David Davis MSS, Chicago Historical Society Library; Nichols, *The Disruption of American Democracy,* 212.

79. Thomas L. Harris to Charles H. Lanphier, May 7, 1858, Charles H. Lanphier MSS, Illinois State Historical Library; Lyman Trumbull to John M. Palmer, May 20, 1858, John M. Palmer MSS, Illinois State Historical Library; James Madison Cutts to Douglas, June 26, 1858, Stephen A. Douglas MSS, box 18, folder 38, University of Chicago Library; W. W. Churchwell to Douglas, July 11, 1858, ibid., box 19, folder 2.

80. Nichols, *The Disruption of American Democracy,* 214.

81. Quoted in Angle, ed., *Created Equal?* 12.

82. Daniel McCook to Thomas L. Harris, September 15, 1858, Charles H. Lanphier MSS, Illinois State Historical Library. Douglas was getting conflicting reports, however. In August, Blanton Duncan of Louisville wrote, "In some portions of Illinois, the professed administration men are beginning warmly to support you, & that gives color to the impression, that you intend to reconcile all your previous differences & stand by the President" (Duncan to Douglas, August 18, 1858, Stephen A. Douglas MSS, box 19, folder 29, University of Chicago Library).

83. Lyman Trumbull to John M. Palmer, June 19, 1858, John M. Palmer MSS, Illinois State Historical Library; *Chicago Times,* August 14, 26, 29, 1858; Johannsen, *Stephen A. Douglas,* 628.

84. Angle, ed., *Created Equal?* 169–70.

85. Ibid., 289–90.

86. These various incidents are described in Johannsen, *Stephen A. Douglas,* 649; Robert W. Johannsen, "The Lincoln-Douglas Campaign of 1858: Background and Perspective," *Journal of the Illinois State Historical Society* 73 (Winter 1980): 261; D. L. Phillips to Lincoln, July 24, 1858, Robert Todd Lincoln Collection of the Papers of Abraham Lincoln, reel 3, frames 1038–39, Library of Congress; A. Sherman to Ozias M. Hatch, September 27, 1858, Ozias M. Hatch MSS, Illinois State Historical Library; Fehrenbacher, *Prelude to Greatness,* 113; John Wentworth to Lincoln, June 6, 1858, Robert Todd Lincoln Collection of the Papers of Abraham Lincoln, reel 2, frames 856–58, Library of Congress; N. B. Judd to Lyman Trumbull, March 19, 1858, Lyman Trumbull MSS, reel 4, Library of Congress; Joseph Medill to Lyman Trumbull, April 22, 1858, ibid.; Milton, *The Eve of Conflict,* 289.

87. Angle, ed., *Created Equal?* 304–5.

88. Lincoln to Samuel Wilkinson, June 10, 1858, *The Collected Works of Abraham Lincoln,* 2:458; Lincoln to Lyman Trumbull, June 23, 1858, ibid., 471–72. Milton, however, theorizes that Lincoln may have been kept in the dark about the extent of collusion with the Buchaneers. He quotes Herndon as having

written to Trumbull, "Lincoln does not know the details of how we get along. I do, but he does not" (*The Eve of Conflict*, 303).

89. *Illinois State Journal*, June 21, 1858; W. H. Herndon to Lyman Trumbull, June 24, 1858, Lyman Trumbull MSS, reel 4, Library of Congress; Charles Leib to Trumbull, July 20, 1858, ibid.

90. Angle, *Lincoln, 1854–1861*, 236. See also Fehrenbacher, *Prelude to Greatness*, 113, which makes reference to the July 8, 1858 letter from Herndon to Trumbull (Lyman Trumbull MSS, reel 4, Library of Congress).

91. On these points, see Fehrenbacher, *Prelude to Greatness*, 114.

92. Sewell, *Ballots for Freedom*, 345; Milton, *The Eve of Conflict*, 301; George W. Jones to Sidney Breese, September 17, 1858, Sidney Breese MSS, Illinois State Historical Library; Douglas to John A. McClernand, December 8, 1859, John A. McClernand MSS, Illinois State Historical Library.

93. Speech of William Bigler, Senate, December 21, 1857, *Congressional Globe*, 35th Cong., 1st sess., 27, pt. 1:114; Speech of John P. Hale, Senate, January 18, 1858, ibid., 319; Speech of William Bigler, Senate, March 13, 1858, ibid., pt. 2:1117–18; Milton, *The Eve of Conflict*, 334; Angle, ed., *Created Equal?* 236–37. Douglas had asked why Trumbull was making the charge now rather than at the time of the Toombs Bill dispute. Sigelschiffer theorizes that Trumbull wanted to avoid antagonizing Douglas during the time when the Little Giant joined the Republicans in opposing the Lecompton constitution (*The American Conscience*, 263).

94. On these details, see esp. Nichols and Klein, "Election of 1856," 111; Rawley, *Race and Politics*, 153–55; Johannsen, *Stephen A. Douglas*, 525. Rawley also notes a paradox in the Toombs Bill: "The bill, in implementing popular sovereignty, paradoxically repudiated in part the doctrine of Congressional nonintervention. Congress would intervene to guard the integrity of the ballot box and to repeal certain laws of the Shawnee legislature" (*Race and Politics*, 155). Trumbull had explained the paradox himself in an 1856 letter to Lincoln (Lyman Trumbull to Lincoln, July 5, 1856, Lyman Trumbull MSS, Illinois State Historical Library). This paradox, however, did not figure prominently in the dispute.

95. Crissey, *Lincoln's Lost Speech*, 286. See also Rawley, *Race and Politics*, 156.

96. For example, Buchanan's Lecompton Message of February 2, 1858, *Congressional Globe*, 35th Cong., 1st sess., 27, pt. 1:534; Speech by John R. Thomson, Senate, March 3, 1858, ibid., 947; Speech by William D. Bishop, House, March 22, 1858, ibid., pt. 2, 1248.

97. Speech by John Hickman, House, January 28, 1858, *Congressional Globe*, 35th Cong., 1st sess., 27, pt. 1:475.

98. Whan, "Stephen A. Douglas," 804n.

99. M. W. Delahay to Lincoln, August 13, 1858, Robert Todd Lincoln Collection of the Papers of Abraham Lincoln, reel 3, frames 1223–25, Library of Congress; Ozias M. Hatch to Lincoln, August 17, 1858, ibid., frames 1252–53; J. H. Jordan to Lincoln, August 24, 1858, ibid., frames 1282–83.

100. Angle, ed., *Created Equal?* 238–39.

101. Ibid., 239–40.

102. Ibid., 241.

103. Ibid., 242.

104. Ibid., 243–46.

105. Ibid., 249.

106. Ibid., 250.

107. Ibid., 272.

108. Ibid., 273.

109. *Illinois State Register*, September 23, 1858; Johnson, *Stephen A. Douglas*, 380.

110. Earl G. Creps III, "The Conspiracy Argument as Rhetorical Genre" (Ph.D. diss., Northwestern University, 1980), esp. 96–97.

111. Speech by Clark B. Cochrane, House, January 26, 1858, *Congressional Globe*, 35th Cong., 1st sess., 27, pt. 1:426.

112. Hayden White, "The Value of Narrativity in the Representation of Reality," in *On Narrative*, ed. W. J. T. Mitchell (Chicago: University of Chicago Press, 1981), 23.

113. Forgie, *Patricide in the House Divided*, 268.

114. Richard M. Merelman, "The Dramaturgy of Politics," in *Drama in Life: The Uses of Communication in Society*, ed. James E. Combs and Michael W. Mansfield (New York: Hastings, 1976), 292; David Brion Davis, "Some Ideological Functions of Prejudice in Ante-Bellum America," *American Quarterly* 15 (Summer 1963): 121.

115. David Brion Davis, "Some Themes of Counter-Subversion: An Analysis of Anti-Masonic, Anti-Catholic, and Anti-Mormon Literature," *Mississippi Valley Historical Review* 47 (September 1960): 215, and *The Slave Power Conspiracy*, 51.

116. Strozier, *Lincoln's Quest for Union*, 185; Baker, *Affairs of Party*, 168.

117. Whan, "Stephen A. Douglas," 795.

118. E. Culpepper Clark, "Argument in Historical Analysis," in *Advances in Argumentation Theory and Research*, ed. J. Robert Cox and Charles Arthur Willard (Carbondale: Southern Illinois University Press, 1982), 300.

119. Fragment on Sectionalism, July 23, 1856, *The Collected Works of Abraham Lincoln*, 2:350.

120. *Chicago Times*, August 26, 1858.

121. Rawley, *Race and Politics*, 255.

122. B. Lewis to Lincoln, August 25, 1858, Robert Todd Lincoln Collection of the Papers of Abraham Lincoln, reel 3, frames 1292–94, Library of Congress.

Chapter Four

1. This is the list of issues offered in William H. Pease and Jane H. Pease, ed., *The Antislavery Argument* (Indianapolis: Bobbs-Merrill, 1965), lvii.

2. Jaffa, *Crisis of the House Divided*, 285.

3. On this point, see Quaife, *The Doctrine of Non-Intervention*, 144.

4. Buchanan's Lecompton message, February 2, 1858, *Congressional Globe*, 35th Cong., 1st sess., 27, pt. 1:534.

5. Carl Sandburg, in Angle, ed., *The Lincoln Reader*, 222; Breiseth, "Lincoln, Douglas, and Springfield," 111; Angle, ed., *Created Equal?* 319–20, 344.

6. *Illinois State Register*, September 2, 1858.

7. Hugh Gordon Seymour to Lincoln, August 11, 1858, Robert Todd Lincoln Collection of the Papers of Abraham Lincoln, reel 3, frames 1215–17, Library of Congress; Schuyler Colfax to Lincoln, August 25, 1858, ibid., frames 1286–87.

8. Speech at Springfield, Ill., June 26, 1857, *The Collected Works of Abraham Lincoln*, 2:402.

9. Welter, *The Mind of America*, 237.

10. Fragments: Notes for Speeches, ca. August 21, 1858, *The Collected Works of Abraham Lincoln*, 2:552.

11. Angle, ed., *Created Equal?* 309–10, 320.

12. This episode is described in King, *Lincoln's Manager, David Davis*, 41; Capers, *Stephen A. Douglas*, 12; Johannsen, *Stephen A. Douglas*, 84.

13. Wm. S. Frinke to Lincoln, July 30, 1858, Robert Todd Lincoln Collection of the Papers of Abraham Lincoln, reel 3, frames 1103–4, Library of Congress.

14. Angle, ed., *Created Equal?* 129, 310.

15. Ibid., 128–29, 310.

16. Speech at Springfield, Ill., June 26, 1857, *The Collected Works of Abraham Lincoln*, 2:401; Don E. Fehrenbacher, "Lincoln and the Constitution," in *The Public and the Private Lincoln*, ed. Davis et al., 133.

17. John S. Wright, *Lincoln and the Politics of Slavery* (Reno: University of Nevada Press, 1970), 118. See also Fehrenbacher, *The Dred Scott Case*, 419; Holt, *The Political Crisis of the 1850s*, 202.

18. Speech at Galena, Ill., July 23, 1856, *The Collected Works of Abraham Lincoln*, 2:355.

19. See, e.g., the Senate Speech of John P. Hale, January 18, 1858, *Congressional Globe*, 35th Cong., 1st sess., 27, pt. 1:320. The Supreme Court itself had made little use of the "political question" doctrine at this time.

20. Lyman Trumbull, Speech in the Senate, February 2, 1858, ibid., 524. On the other hand, since the Circuit Court had considered all aspects of the case on their substantive merits, one might argue that it was appropriate for the Supreme Court to go beyond the question of jurisdiction. On this view, "whatever else Taney's ruling was, it was not *obiter dictum*" (James M. McPherson, *Battle Cry of Freedom: The Civil War Era* [New York: Oxford University Press, 1988], 175).

21. J. F. Alexander to Lincoln, August 5, 1858, Robert Todd Lincoln Collection of the Papers of Abraham Lincoln, reel 3, frames 1160–62, Library of Congress; Heckman, *Lincoln vs. Douglas*, 17.

22. *Illinois State Register*, September 18, 1858.

23. The best single source on the details of the case is Fehrenbacher, *The Dred Scott Case*.

24. John W. Allen, *It Happened in Southern Illinois* (Carbondale: Southern Illinois University, Central Publications, 1959), 290.

25. Samuel Eliot Morison, Henry Steele Commager, and William E. Leuchtenburg, *The Growth of the American Republic*, 7th ed. (New York: Oxford

University Press, 1980), 1:594. See also F. H. Hodder, "Some Phases of the Dred Scott Case," *Mississippi Valley Historical Review* 16 (June 1929): 4; Nevins, *Ordeal of the Union,* 1:26.

26. *Illinois State Register,* September 2, 1858. This argument is also made by Capers, *Stephen A. Douglas,* 199.

27. Lincoln continued to develop this argument well after the debates. See, e.g., Speech at Leavenworth, Kans., December 3, 1859, *The Collected Works of Abraham Lincoln,* 3:500.

28. *Congressional Globe,* June 9, 1856, 34th Cong., 1st sess., 26, pt. 2:1371–74, cited in Heckman, "The Douglas-Lincoln Campaign of 1858," 167n; Fehrenbacher, *Prelude to Greatness,* 131.

29. The history of this argument is drawn from Don E. Fehrenbacher, "Lincoln, Douglas, and the 'Freeport Question,'" *American Historical Review* 66 (April 1961): 607; Johannsen, *Stephen A. Douglas,* 103, 656; Hodder, "Some Phases of the Dred Scott Case," 21; Fehrenbacher, *Prelude to Greatness,* 135–36; Johnson, *Stephen A. Douglas,* 359.

30. Angle, ed., *Created Equal?* 231, 296, 152.

31. Robert R. Russel, "What Was the Compromise of 1850?" *Journal of Southern History* 22 (August 1956): 300; Berwanger, *The Frontier against Slavery,* 121; Whan, "Stephen A. Douglas," 801; Fehrenbacher, "Lincoln, Douglas, and the 'Freeport Question,'" 610.

32. Schuyler Colfax to Lincoln, August 25, 1858, Robert Todd Lincoln Collection of the Papers of Abraham Lincoln, reel 3, frames 1286–87, Library of Congress.

33. Speech at Peoria, Ill., October 16, 1854, *The Collected Works of Abraham Lincoln,* 2:262; Fehrenbacher, *The South and Three Sectional Crises* 12; Angle, ed, *Created Equal?* 218.

34. Fragment: Notes for Speeches, September 15, 1858 (?), *The Collected Works of Abraham Lincoln,* 3:98; Speech at Cincinnati, Ohio, September 17, 1859, ibid., 450; Speech at Columbus, Ohio, September 16, 1859, ibid., 417.

35. Angle, ed., *Created Equal?* 218–19. A similar theory was advanced by proslavery writers who denied any distinction between direct and indirect action. As Bestor characterizes that view, the essential criterion for constitutionality was purpose. Weakening slavery was therefore an unconstitutional goal in and of itself, regardless of the means employed. (See Arthur Bestor, "State Sovereignty and Slavery: A Reinterpretation of Proslavery Constitutional Doctrine, 1846–1860," *Journal of the Illinois State Historical Society* 54 [Summer 1961]: 127, 163.)

36. Angle, ed., *Created Equal?* 220, 229; *Chicago Press and Tribune,* September 13, October 25, 1858; Lyman Trumbull to Lincoln, September 14, 1858, Robert Todd Lincoln Collection of the Papers of Abraham Lincoln, reel 3, frames 1401–3, Library of Congress.

37. Speech at Peoria, Ill., October 16, 1854, *The Collected Works of Abraham Lincoln,* 2:267; Lyman Trumbull, Speech in the Senate, March 17, 1858, *Congressional Globe,* 35th Cong., 1st sess., 27, pt. 2:1161; Speech at Bloomington, Ill., September 4, 1858, *The Collected Works of Abraham Lincoln,* 3:88.

38. Ronald N. Satz, "The African Slave Trade and Lincoln's Campaign of 1858," *Journal of the Illinois State Historical Society* 65 (Autumn 1972): 274, 276–77, 278.

39. Hamilton, *Prologue to Conflict*, 22.

40. Angle, ed., *Created Equal?* 395–96.

41. Finkelman, *An Imperfect Union*, 4; see also 127, 182, 235.

42. Jaffa, *Equality and Liberty*, 133.

43. Johannsen, *Stephen A. Douglas*, 218.

44. Bestor, "State Sovereignty and Slavery," 164.

45. Douglas to Twenty-five Chicago Clergymen, April 6, 1854, Johannsen, ed., *The Letters of Stephen A. Douglas*, 320; Douglas to James W. Stone et al., September 15, 1855, ibid., 341.

46. See Robert W. Johannsen, "Stephen A. Douglas, *Harper's Magazine*, and Popular Sovereignty," *Mississippi Valley Historical Review* 45 (March 1959): 618.

47. Milton, *The Eve of Conflict*, 37; Jesse T. Carpenter, *The South as a Conscious Minority, 1789–1861: A Study in Political Thought* (New York: New York University Press, 1930), 151.

48. Douglas to the Editor of the *Concord, N.H., State Capitol Reporter*, February 16, 1854, Johannsen, ed., *The Letters of Stephen A. Douglas*, 284. Welter also explains the popularity of the doctrine by noting that it set a decision by the people against a decision by the government, consistent with the thinking of "American liberal democrats [who] so far identified democracy with freedom as to call government itself into question" (*The Mind of America*, 165).

49. Forgie, *Patricide in the House Divided*, 137.

50. Speech at Peoria, Ill., October 16, 1854, *The Collected Works of Abraham Lincoln*, 2:263.

51. Johannsen, "The Lincoln-Douglas Campaign of 1858," 246; Capers, *Stephen A. Douglas*, 148. Quaife concluded that "non-intervention was essentially an opportunist doctrine. As such the applications made of it varied to accord with the political bias of every politician who wielded it" (*The Doctrine of Non-Intervention*, 143).

52. Johannsen, *Stephen A. Douglas*, 255; Wells, *Stephen Douglas*, 62.

53. Johannsen, *Stephen A. Douglas*, 568.

54. Speech at Bloomington, Ill., September 26, 1854, *The Collected Works of Abraham Lincoln*, 2:239.

55. Speech at Peoria, Ill., October 16, 1854, ibid., 267; Fragment of a Speech, May 15, 1858, ibid., 451–52.

56. Lyman Trumbull, Speech in the Senate, March 17, 1858, *Congressional Globe*, 35th Cong., 1st sess., 27, pt. 2:1162; Nevins, *Ordeal of the Union*, 1:26.

57. Speech at Jacksonville, Ill., September 6, 1856, *The Collected Works of Abraham Lincoln*, 2:370; *Illinois Sentinel*, September 12, 1856.

58. Angle, ed., *Created Equal?* 401.

59. Ibid., 110.

60. Ibid., 297; see also 365.

61. Ibid., 387.

62. Ibid., 308.

63. Lyman Trumbull to Lincoln, June 12, 1858, Robert Todd Lincoln Collection of the Papers of Abraham Lincoln, reel 2, frames 874–75, Library of Congress. See also H. E. Drummer to Lincoln, July 10, 1858, ibid., reel 3, frames 951–53.

64. Angle, ed., *Created Equal?* 106. The question immediately following was functionally equivalent, and Lincoln later combined them: "I want to know whether he stands pledged against the admission of a new state into the Union with such a constitution as the people of that state may fit to make."

65. Ibid., 142.

66. Ibid., 339, 366.

67. John P. Frank, *Lincoln as a Lawyer* (Urbana: University of Illinois Press, 1961), 131.

68. Angle, ed., *Created Equal?* 106–7.

69. Herndon, "Facts Illustrative of Mr. Lincoln's Patriotism and Statesmanship."

70. Angle, ed., *Created Equal?* 141.

71. Charles L. Wilson to Lincoln, August 1858 (date uncertain), Robert Todd Lincoln Collection of the Papers of Abraham Lincoln, reel 3, frames 1337–40, Library of Congress; Joseph Medill to Lincoln, August 26 (?), 1858, ibid., frames 1333–36.

72. Angle, ed., *Created Equal?* 140, 143–45, 220.

73. Ibid., 150; Joseph Medill to John A. Gurley, August 28, 1858, Joseph Medill MSS, Chicago Historical Society Library.

74. For an illustrative example of the "Freeport myth," see Charnwood, *Abraham Lincoln*, 147.

75. Milton, *The Eve of Conflict*, 342; W. H. Herndon to Horace White, August 26, 1890, Horace White MSS, Illinois State Historical Library.

76. Fehrenbacher, *Prelude to Greatness*, 121–42. See also Joseph Medill, quoted in Angle, ed., *The Lincoln Reader*, 242; Cole, *The Centennial History of Illinois*, 3:272. Fehrenbacher also suggests that the Freeport question did not really fit into Lincoln's overall plan, which was to stress *affinities* between Douglas and the slaveholding South (*The Dred Scott Case*, 488).

77. Henry Asbury to Lincoln, July 28, 1858, Robert Todd Lincoln Collection of the Papers of Abraham Lincoln, reel 3, frames 1087–88, Library of Congress; Joseph Medill to Lincoln, August 26 (?), 1858, ibid., frames 1333–36; Fehrenbacher, *Prelude to Greatness*, 126.

78. Lincoln at Chicago, July 10, 1858, Angle, ed., *Created Equal?* 29; Lincoln at Springfield, Ill., July 17, 1858, ibid., 70.

79. James W. Sheahan, *The Life of Stephen A. Douglas* (New York: Harper & Bros., 1860), 417; Beveridge, *Abraham Lincoln*, 2:656; *Chicago Times*, September 9, 1858; Douglas to the Editors of the *San Francisco National*, August 16, 1859, Johannsen, ed., *The Letters of Stephen A. Douglas*, 455–56.

80. Thomas, *Abraham Lincoln*, 189; Frank, *Lincoln as a Lawyer*, 134.

81. Nevins, *The Emergence of Lincoln*, 1:392; Nichols, *The Disruption of American Democracy*, 217.

82. For these points of view, see Heckman, *Lincoln vs. Douglas*, 94; Cole,

The Centennial History of Illinois, 3:171; Lincoln-Douglas Society of Freeport, Ill., *Freeport's Lincoln* (Freeport, Ill.: W. T. Rawleigh, 1930), vii.

83. Cole, *The Centennial History of Illinois,* 3:172; Joseph Medill, in Angle, ed., *The Lincoln Reader,* 242; *Illinois State Register,* September 1, 1858.

84. Wells, *Stephen Douglas,* 123; Elbert B. Smith, *The Death of Slavery: The United States, 1837–1865* (Chicago: University of Chicago Press, 1967), 151; Douglas to the Editors of the *San Francisco National,* August 16, 1859, Johannsen, ed., *The Letters of Stephen A. Douglas,* 460.

85. Jno. L. Peyton to Douglas, September 5, 1858, Stephen A. Douglas MSS, box 19, folder 37, University of Chicago Library; Fehrenbacher, *Prelude to Greatness,* 135n. Not all the favorable reaction was based on the merits of Douglas's case, however. For example, Vice President Breckinridge wrote in October, "I have often, in conversation expressed the wish that Mr. Douglas may succeed over his Republican Competitor. But it is due to candor to say that this preference is not founded on his course at the late session of Congress . . . or of all the positions he has taken in the present canvass." Breckinridge then rationalized his preference for Douglas despite some offensive positions taken by the candidate. He pointed out that "the Kansas question is practically ended." (John C. Breckinridge to John Moore, October 4, 1858, Charles H. Lanphier MSS, Illinois State Historical Library.)

86. See Wells, *Stephen Douglas,* 123; Fehrenbacher, "Lincoln, Douglas, and the 'Freeport Question,'" 611.

87. Baringer, *Lincoln's Rise to Power,* 50.

88. Angle, ed., *Created Equal?* 154.

89. Ibid., 107; for a similar statement of this position, see also 195.

90. Heckman, *Lincoln vs. Douglas,* 33; John W. Beveridge, "Lincoln's Views on Slavery and Blacks as Expressed in the Debates with Stephen A. Douglas," *Lincoln Herald* 83 (Winter 1981): 796; Frank, *Lincoln as a Lawyer,* 125.

91. David Herbert Donald, *Liberty and Union* (Boston: Little, Brown, 1978), 27; Speech in United States House of Representatives on Internal Improvements, June 20, 1848, *The Collected Works of Abraham Lincoln,* 1:488.

92. Fehrenbacher, *The Dred Scott Case,* 104.

93. Daniel Walker Howe, *The Political Culture of the American Whigs* (Chicago: University of Chicago Press, 1979), 23; Fehrenbacher, *The Dred Scott Case,* 126, 140. See also Baker, *Affairs of Party,* 153; Donald, *Liberty and Union,* 27; Fehrenbacher, *The South and Three Sectional Crises,* 16.

94. Bestor, "State Sovereignty and Slavery," 121; Jaffa, *Equality and Liberty,* 134; Robert R. Russel, "Constitutional Doctrines with Regard to Slavery in Territories," *Journal of Southern History* 32 (November 1966): 466.

95. E. L. Doctorow, "A Citizen Reads the Constitution," *Nation,* February 21, 1987, 214; Harold M. Hyman, *A More Perfect Union: The Impact of the Civil War and Reconstruction on the Constitution* (New York: Knopf, 1973), 4; Brock, *Parties and Political Conscience,* xv.

96. Hyman, *A More Perfect Union,* 5.

97. Arthur Bestor, "The American Civil War as a Constitutional Crisis," *American Historical Review* 69 (January 1964): 328; Howe, *The Political Culture of the American Whigs,* 23.

Chapter Five

1. John Locke Scripps to Abraham Lincoln, June 22, 1858, Robert Todd Lincoln Collection of the Papers of Abraham Lincoln, reel 2, frames 906–8, Library of Congress.

2. Abraham Lincoln to John L. Scripps, June 23, 1858, Herndon-Weik Collection of Lincolniana, reel 1, group II, Library of Congress.

3. Some of these historical antecedents are traced in Corwin, "Lincoln and Douglas," 575.

4. Fehrenbacher, *Prelude to Greatness,* 71.

5. Harlan Hoyt Horner, "The Substance of the Lincoln-Douglas Debates: Part 1," *Lincoln Herald* 63 (Summer 1961): 89–98; Milton, *The Eve of Conflict,* 332.

6. *Illinois State Register,* July 26, 1858.

7. Strozier, *Lincoln's Quest for Union,* 55; Edmund Wilson, *Patriotic Gore: Studies in the Literature of the American Civil War* (New York: Oxford University Press, 1962), 102.

8. Welter, *The Mind of America,* 26.

9. Paul C. Nagel, *One Nation Indivisible: The Union in American Thought, 1776–1861* (New York: Oxford University Press, 1964), 182.

10. Angle, ed., *Created Equal?* 109–10, 113.

11. Ibid., 110, 113, 114.

12. Ibid., 167–68.

13. Ibid., 199–200.

14. Ibid., 267.

15. Ibid., 364.

16. This theme is developed at length in Nagel, *One Nation Indivisible.*

17. Bestor, "State Sovereignty and Slavery," 147; Forgie, *Patricide in the House Divided,* 126.

18. Martin Duberman, "The Northern Response to Slavery," in *The Antislavery Vanguard: New Essays on the Abolitionists,* ed. Martin Duberman (Princeton, N.J.: Princeton University Press, 1965), 399.

19. On the comparison between Lincoln and Chase, see Oates, *With Malice toward None,* 112.

20. Speech at Peoria, Ill., October 16, 1854, *The Collected Works of Abraham Lincoln,* 2:249; Speech at Springfield, Ill., October 4, 1854, ibid., 241.

21. Speech at Chicago, Ill., July 10, 1858, ibid., 492.

22. Neely, *The Abraham Lincoln Encyclopedia,* 324–25.

23. John Hope Franklin, *From Slavery to Freedom: A History of Negro Americans,* 3d ed. (New York: Random House, 1967), 129; Winthrop D. Jordan, *White over Black: American Attitudes toward the Negro, 1550–1812* (Chapel Hill: University of North Carolina Press, 1968), 291; Bailyn, *The Ideological Origins of the American Revolution,* 235.

24. Abraham Lincoln to George Robertson, August 15, 1855, *The Collected Works of Abraham Lincoln,* 2:318.

25. Welter, *The Mind of America,* 365.

26. Angle, ed., *Created Equal?* 353.

27. Speech at Peoria, Ill., October 16, 1854, *The Collected Works of Abraham Lincoln*, 2:276; Lincoln to George Robertson, August 15, 1855, ibid., 318. For an analysis of the Lyceum speech, see Jaffa, *Crisis of the House Divided*, 183–232. The theme of degeneration from the Founders was common in free-soil rhetoric. See a discussion of this topic in Major L. Wilson, *Space, Time, and Freedom: The Quest for Nationality and the Irrepressible Conflict, 1815–1861* (Westport, Conn.: Greenwood, 1974), 194.

28. *Illinois State Journal*, June 25, 1858.

29. Wilson, *Space, Time, and Freedom*, 8.

30. Speech at Springfield, Ill., October 4, 1854, *The Collected Works of Abraham Lincoln*, 2:245.

31. Lincoln alluded to this argument at Alton, alleging that Douglas had changed the status of slavery from a dying institution by "*putting it upon Brooks' cotton gin basis,*—placing it where he openly confesses he has no desire there shall ever be an end of it" (Angle, ed., *Created Equal?* 394). The assertion that the cotton gin had arrested the otherwise certain demise of slavery had been made earlier by South Carolina congressman Preston S. Brooks.

32. Nevins, *The Emergence of Lincoln*, 1:392.

33. Finkelman, *An Imperfect Union*, 84; Capers, *Stephen A. Douglas*, 59; Angle, ed., *Created Equal?* 59–60 (Douglas speech at Springfield, Ill., July 17, 1858); Douglas to Edward Coles, February 18, 1854, Johannsen, ed., *The Letters of Stephen A. Douglas*, 293–98.

34. Harris, *The History of Negro Servitude*, 10, 15.

35. See Neely, *The Abraham Lincoln Encyclopedia*, 164.

36. Stampp, *The Imperiled Union*, 20–30. Even later the term *experiment* was used to describe the Union, but in the older sense of making a known principle manifest, rather than in the sense of an uncertain trial (see Welter, *The Mind of America*, 23).

37. Some writers have suggested that Jefferson, as the author of the Declaration, was the inspiration for Lincoln's political philosophy. See, e.g., Richard Hofstadter, *The American Political Tradition and the Men Who Made It*, 25th anniversary ed. (New York: Knopf, 1973), 101; Neely, *The Abraham Lincoln Encyclopedia*, 163.

38. Anderson, *Abraham Lincoln*, 123. Indeed, "there is no evidence that Lincoln ever read the *Federalist* papers, the classic commentary on the Constitution" (Neely, *The Abraham Lincoln Encyclopedia*, 70–71).

39. See, e.g., Wilson, *Space, Time, and Freedom*, 37–38; Nagel, *One Nation Indivisible*, 190.

40. Speech at Lewistown, Ill., August 17, 1858, *The Collected Works of Abraham Lincoln*, 2:546–47.

41. Angle, ed., *Created Equal?* 298. In this respect, there is strong support for Lincoln's position. Jaffa, e.g., writes, "That Washington, Jefferson, Adams, Madison, Hamilton, Franklin, Patrick Henry, and all others of their general philosophic persuasion understood the Declaration in its universalistic sense, and as including the Negro, is beyond doubt or cavil" (*Crisis of the House Divided*, 314).

42. Angle, ed., *Created Equal?* 206.

43. Ibid., 294; see also 201.

44. Douglas to Twenty-five Chicago Clergymen, April 6, 1854, Johannsen, ed., *The Letters of Stephen A. Douglas*, 320.

45. Angle, ed., *Created Equal?* 201. In some formulations of this argument, Douglas had limited the Declaration's applicability to *Englishmen*, enabling Lincoln to bid for the immigrant vote by pointing out that Douglas read out of the American covenant not just blacks but also whites of European descent. An early example of this rejoinder is found in Lincoln's June 26, 1857 Springfield speech, where he alleges that "the French, Germans, and other white people of the world are all gone to pot along with the Judge's inferior races" (*The Collected Works of Abraham Lincoln*, 2:407).

46. *Illinois State Register*, July 28, 1858.

47. Harry V. Jaffa, "'Value Consensus' in Democracy: The Issue in the Lincoln-Douglas Debates," *American Political Science Review* 52 (September 1958): 752.

48. *Illinois State Journal*, October 11, 1858.

49. Anderson, *Abraham Lincoln*, 116.

50. See Chaim Perelman and L. Olbrechts-Tyteca, *The New Rhetoric*, trans. John Wilkinson and Purcell Weaver (Notre Dame, Ind.: University of Notre Dame Press, 1969), 411–59.

51. Angle, ed., *Created Equal?* 117, 327.

52. *Illinois State Journal*, October 11, 1858.

53. Angle, ed., *Created Equal?* 379.

54. Jaffa, *Crisis of the House Divided*, 195.

55. Speech at Springfield, Ill., June 26, 1857, *The Collected Works of Abraham Lincoln*, 2:406. Anderson has disputed this claim, noting that "the assertion of equality provided proof that monarchy was itself illegitimate, and therefore was of considerable use in justifying independence" (*Abraham Lincoln*, 116).

56. Roy P. Basler, "Abraham Lincoln: An Immortal Sign," in *The Enduring Lincoln*, ed. Graebner, 14.

57. Angle, ed., *Created Equal?* 379.

58. The quotation is from the Alton debate (ibid., 384; for similar statements, see 119, 205, 353).

59. Ibid., 394.

60. Foner, *Free Soil, Free Labor, Free Men*, 86.

61. Johannsen, "Stephen A. Douglas, *Harper's Magazine*, and Popular Sovereignty," 613.

62. Douglas to George Bancroft, April 11, 1859, Johannsen, ed., *The Letters of Stephen A. Douglas*, 442; Johannsen, "Stephen A. Douglas, *Harper's Magazine*, and Popular Sovereignty," 613; William J. Wolf, *The Almost Chosen People: A Study of the Religion of Abraham Lincoln* (Garden City, N.Y.: Doubleday, 1959), 111. See also Earl W. Wiley, "Abraham Lincoln: His Emergence as the Voice of the People," in *A History and Criticism of American Public Address*, ed. Brigance, 865.

63. *Chicago Times*, September 29, 1858; Louis Didies to Douglas, August (?) 1858, Stephen A. Douglas MSS, box 19, folder 21, University of Chicago Library.

For a discussion of the significance of the Old Line Whigs, see Milton, *The Eve of Conflict*, 317; Foner, *Free Soil, Free Labor, Free Men*, 196.

64. Lincoln to Trumbull, June 7, 1856, *The Collected Works of Abraham Lincoln*, 2:343; Wright, *Lincoln and the Politics of Slavery*, 109; Mayer, *The Republican Party*, 55.

65. A. G. Henry to Douglas, June 2, 1858, Stephen A. Douglas MSS, box 19, folder 3, University of Chicago Library.

66. The passages from the Clay eulogy can be found in *The Collected Works of Abraham Lincoln*, 2:126, 130. On Lincoln's regard for Clay in general, see Luthin, *The Real Abraham Lincoln*, 39; Fredrickson, "A Man but Not a Brother," 41.

67. Luthin, *The Real Abraham Lincoln*, 195; Speech at Rushville, Ill., October 20, 1858, *The Collected Works of Abraham Lincoln*, 3:329; Fredrickson, "A Man but Not a Brother," 41.

68. Compare *Illinois State Journal*, July 16, 1858, and *Chicago Press and Tribune*, October 26, 1858, with *Chicago Times*, October 17, 1858.

69. Edgar Dewitt Jones, *The Influence of Henry Clay upon Abraham Lincoln* (Lexington, Ky.: Henry Clay Memorial Foundation, 1952), 21.

70. Angle, ed., *Created Equal?* 130, 311. Compare Eulogy on Henry Clay, July 6, 1852, *The Collected Works of Abraham Lincoln*, 2:131.

71. Angle, ed., *Created Equal?* 358.

72. Ibid., 380–82.

73. Beveridge, *Abraham Lincoln*, 2:673.

74. Speech at Tremont, Ill., August 30, 1858, *The Collected Works of Abraham Lincoln*, 3:76–77. See also Speech at Edwardsville, Ill., September 11, 1858, ibid., 93; Speech at Petersburg, Ill., October 29, 1858, ibid., 333.

75. Speech at Jacksonville, Ill., September 6, 1856, ibid., 2:370.

76. *Chicago Times*, September 29, 1858.

77. Herndon, "Life of Lincoln," 2:50. Strozier claims that Lincoln later regretted this action (*Lincoln's Quest for Union*, 162). For the newspaper reaction, see *Chicago Times*, September 29, 1858.

78. *Illinois State Register*, September 17, 21, November 1, 1858.

79. Neely, *The Abraham Lincoln Encyclopedia*, 327; Richard N. Current, "Lincoln and Daniel Webster," *Journal of the Illinois State Historical Society* 48 (Autumn 1955): 315.

80. Angle, ed., *Created Equal?* 161, 260, 371–72.

81. Speech at Lewistown, Ill., August 17, 1858, *The Collected Works of Abraham Lincoln*, 2:545; Speech at Bloomington, Ill., September 4, 1858, ibid., 3:89; Speech at Monmouth, Ill., October 11, 1858, ibid., 244. Lincoln had made the same protest as early as 1854 (see Speech at Peoria, Ill., October 16, 1854, ibid., 2:282).

82. *Chicago Press and Tribune*, August 5, 1858; *Illinois State Journal*, September 24, 1858. See also Cole, *The Centennial History of Illinois*, 3:176.

83. Clement Eaton, *Henry Clay and the Art of American Politics* (Boston: Little, Brown, 1957), 118.

84. Herndon-Weik Collection of Lincolniana, reel 1, group I.B., Library of

Congress; Eaton, *Henry Clay*, 13, 118, 131, 189; Sigelschiffer, *The American Conscience*, 97; Fredrickson, "A Man but Not a Brother," 43; Cooper, *The South and the Politics of Slavery*, 124.

85. Dickey to Isaac N. Arnold, February 7, 1883, Theophilus Lyle Dickey MSS, Chicago Historical Society Library. For an account of this episode, see also King, *Lincoln's Manager, David Davis*, 115.

86. Edward Magdol, *Owen Lovejoy: Abolitionist in Congress* (New Brunswick, N.J.: Rutgers University Press, 1967), 206.

87. Davis to Lincoln, August 2, 1858, David Davis MSS, Chicago Historical Society Library; *Chicago Times*, August 7, 1858. Earlier, however, Davis had also tried to block the nomination of Lovejoy and to secure it for himself (Magdol, *Owen Lovejoy*, 189–97).

88. *Illinois State Register*, August 9, 1858; *Illinois State Journal*, August 10, 1858; David Davis to Lincoln, August 9, 1858, Robert Todd Lincoln Collection of the Papers of Abraham Lincoln, reel 3, frames 1186–87, Library of Congress.

89. For Stuart's endorsement, see *Illinois State Register*, October 8, 1858. The other endorsements by Old Line Whigs are described in Ronald Dean Rietveld, "The Moral Issue of Slavery," 165; Milton, *The Eve of Conflict*, 296.

90. Lyman Trumbull to John M. Palmer, June 19, 1858, John M. Palmer MSS, Illinois State Historical Library; Lincoln to John J. Crittenden, July 7, 1858, *The Collected Works of Abraham Lincoln*, 2:483–84; Crittenden to Lincoln, July 29, 1858, Robert Todd Lincoln Collection of the Papers of Abraham Lincoln, reel 3, frames 1094–96, Library of Congress. The next week, Owen Lovejoy wrote Lincoln to ask if it was true "that Crittenden is exerting his influence for Douglas" (August 4, 1858, ibid., frames 1150–52).

91. Thomas L. Harris to Douglas, July 6, 1858, Stephen A. Douglas MSS, box 18, folder 49, University of Chicago Library; *Illinois State Register*, September 3, 1858.

92. Rietveld, "The Moral Issue of Slavery," 190.

93. See, e.g., *Illinois State Journal*, October 25, 29, 1858.

94. *Illinois State Journal*, September 28, 1858.

95. *Illinois State Register*, October 26, 30, 1858; Fehrenbacher, *Prelude to Greatness*, 118. See also Rothschild, *Lincoln, Master of Men*, 110; Crittenden to Lincoln, October 27, 1858, Robert Todd Lincoln Collection of the Papers of Abraham Lincoln, reel 4, frames 1446–47, Library of Congress.

96. Glassberg has examined the change in historical writing that led professional historians to divorce past from present; he attributes this change to the historians in the Progressive era (see David Glassberg, "History and the Public: Legacies of the Progressive Era," *Journal of American History* 73 [March 1987]: 957–80).

97. On the notion of irreversible choices, see J. Robert Cox, "The Die Is Cast: Topical and Ontological Dimensions of the *Locus* of the Irreparable," *Quarterly Journal of Speech* 68 (August 1982): 227–39. The nature of the choice was forecast in a March Senate speech by Republican Daniel Clark of New Hampshire. He said, "Gentlemen of the South complain that if slavery is excluded from Kansas they cannot go and carry their slaves there. Very true. Let me state the other

side. If they go and carry their slaves there, free labor cannot go there to any great extent. You have got to exclude one or the other *in toto*" (*Congressional Globe*, 35th Cong., 1st sess., 27, app:108).

98. This view of the effect of narrative form is consistent with the theory of Alasdair MacIntyre (*After Virtue: A Study in Moral Theory*, 2d ed. [Notre Dame, Ind.: University of Notre Dame Press, 1984]).

99. Fehrenbacher, *Prelude to Greatness*, 94–95.

100. Major L. Wilson, "Of Time and the Union: Kansas-Nebraska and the Appeal from Prescription to Principle," *Midwest Quarterly* 10 (Autumn 1968): 74.

101. See White, "The Value of Narrativity," 13, 20.

102. See Ernest R. May, *"Lessons" of the Past: The Use and Misuse of History in American Foreign Policy* (New York: Oxford University Press, 1973); Richard E. Neustadt and Ernest R. May, *Thinking in Time: The Uses of History for Decision Makers* (New York: Free Press, 1986).

Chapter Six

1. Collins, *The Origins of America's Civil War*, 135; Avery Craven, "The 1840's and the Democratic Process," *Journal of Southern History* 16 (May 1950): 176; Wright, *Lincoln and the Politics of Slavery*, 12–13.

2. Wright, *Lincoln and the Politics of Slavery*, vii.

3. Robert W. Johannsen, "Stephen A. Douglas and the South," *Journal of Southern History* 33 (February 1967): 32.

4. Johannsen, ed., *The Letters of Stephen A. Douglas*, xxvi.

5. Angle, ed., *Created Equal?* 375.

6. Neely, *The Abraham Lincoln Encyclopedia*, 278.

7. Wells, *Stephen Douglas*, 129. See also Johnson, *Stephen A. Douglas*, 272; Nevins, *Ordeal of the Union*, 2:107.

8. Douglas to Twenty-five Chicago Clergymen, April 6, 1854, Johannsen, ed., *The Letters of Stephen A. Douglas*, 314.

9. Capers, *Stephen A. Douglas*, 120.

10. Jaffa, *Crisis of the House Divided*, 145.

11. On Douglas's use of the Creation story, see Rietveld, "The Moral Issue of Slavery," 65. As Lincoln would point out during the Senate campaign, however, man was not given a free choice but was commanded not to eat of the forbidden fruit (Gen. 2:17). Similarly, in Deuteronomy, the Israelites were told, "I have put before you life and death, blessing and curse," but then were commanded, "Choose life" (Deut. 29:19).

12. Jaffa, *Equality and Liberty*, 95; Douglas to Twenty-five Chicago Clergymen, April 6, 1854, Johannsen, ed., *The Letters of Stephen A. Douglas*, 318.

13. Jaffa, *Crisis of the House Divided*, 103.

14. Brock, *Parties and Political Conscience*, 268.

15. Angle, ed., *Created Equal?* 110, 111–12.

16. Ibid., 200.

17. Ibid., 400.

18. Milton, "Douglas' Place in American History," 339.

19. On this point, see Russel, "What Was the Compromise of 1850?" 306.

20. Jaffa, *Crisis of the House Divided*, 63.

21. Speech of James Harlan, January 25, 1858, *Congressional Globe*, 35th Cong., 1st sess., 27, pt. 1:385.

22. Anderson, *Abraham Lincoln*, 117.

23. Douglas, Senate Speech, December 9, 1857, *Congressional Globe*, 35th Cong., 1st sess., 27, pt. 1:18.

24. Fehrenbacher, *Prelude to Greatness*, 181.

25. Owen Lovejoy to Lincoln, August 4, 1858, Robert Todd Lincoln Collection of the Papers of Abraham Lincoln, reel 3, frames 1150–52, Library of Congress.

26. Angle, ed., *Created Equal?* 35.

27. Jaffa, *Crisis of the House Divided*, 151; Angle, ed., *Created Equal?* 389.

28. Angle, ed., *Created Equal?* 392.

29. Richard M. Weaver, *The Ethics of Rhetoric* (Chicago: Henry Regnery, 1953), 94; Speech to Chicago Republicans, March 1, 1859, *The Collected Works of Abraham Lincoln*, 3:368–69.

30. Speech at a Republican Banquet, December 10, 1856, *The Collected Works of Abraham Lincoln*, 2:385. A year earlier, Lincoln had noted the same declension, writing in a letter to Judge George Robertson of Lexington, Ky., "On the question of liberty, as a principle, we are not what we have been" (August 15, 1855, ibid., 318).

31. Angle, ed., *Created Equal?* 311.

32. Notes for Speeches at Columbus and Cincinnati, September 16–17, 1859, *The Collected Works of Abraham Lincoln*, 3:429–30.

33. Johannsen, ed., *The Lincoln-Douglas Debates of 1858*, 7. In an early biography of Douglas, Allen Johnson attributes Douglas's apparent fatigue during the Quincy debate to the fact that "the consciousness that he was made to seem morally obtuse, cut Douglas to the quick. . . . When he rose to reply to Lincoln, his manner was offensively combative" (*Stephen A. Douglas*, 386).

34. Notes for Speeches at Columbus and Cincinnati, September 16–17, 1859, *The Collected Works of Abraham Lincoln*, 3:427. On the general effect of the debates, see also Frank L. Dennis, *The Lincoln-Douglas Debates* (New York: Mason & Lipscomb, 1974), 74.

35. Speech at Peoria, Ill., October 16, 1854, *The Collected Works of Abraham Lincoln*, 2:274; Speech at Edwardsville, Ill., September 11, 1858, ibid., 3:92.

36. Eric Foner, *Politics and Ideology in the Age of the Civil War* (New York: Oxford University Press, 1980), 47.

37. Lincoln to Joshua F. Speed, August 24, 1855, *The Collected Works of Abraham Lincoln*, 2:320.

38. Jaffa, *Crisis of the House Divided*, 305; Thurow, *Abraham Lincoln and American Political Religion*, 116.

39. Speech at Springfield, Ill., October 4, 1854, *The Collected Works of Abraham Lincoln*, 2:245; Speech at Peoria, Ill., October 16, 1854, ibid., 264; Fehrenbacher, *The Dred Scott Case*, 16.

40. Speech at Peoria, Ill., October 16, 1854, *The Collected Works of Abraham*

Lincoln, 2:266; Speech at Cincinnati, Ohio, September 17, 1859, *The Collected Works of Abraham Lincoln: Supplement*, 44.

41. Speech at Kalamazoo, Mich., August 27, 1856, *The Collected Works of Abraham Lincoln*, 2:364; Boritt, *Lincoln and the Economics of the American Dream*, 159, and "The Right to Rise," 64.

42. Speech at Cincinnati, Ohio, September 17, 1859, *The Collected Works of Abraham Lincoln: Supplement*, 43–44.

43. Speech at Edwardsville, Ill., September 11, 1858, *The Collected Works of Abraham Lincoln*, 3:95; Lincoln to Henry L. Pierce and Others, April 6, 1859, ibid., 376.

44. Fragment on Pro-Slavery Theology, October 1, 1858 (?), ibid., 204–5; Speech at Chicago, Ill., July 10, 1858, ibid., 2:501; Abraham Smith to Lincoln, July 20, 1858, Robert Todd Lincoln Collection of the Papers of Abraham Lincoln, reel 3, frames 1002–4, Library of Congress. On the prophetic character of the antislavery argument, see Davis, *The Slave Power Conspiracy*, 76. Jaffa argues that it is "impossible to grasp fully what Lincoln believed he was doing in his debates with Douglas throughout the period of 1854–60 without seeing it as a performance of a prophetic role in the Old Testament sense" (*Crisis of the House Divided*, 226).

45. Angle, ed., *Created Equal?* 130.

46. Rietveld, "The Moral Issue of Slavery," 161–62.

47. Angle, ed., *Created Equal?* 303–4.

48. Ibid., 333–35.

49. Ibid., 352, 353.

50. Ibid., 390, 392.

51. Ibid., 393.

52. Thomas, *Abraham Lincoln*, 192.

53. Fehrenbacher, *Prelude to Greatness*, 78. See also Jaffa, *Crisis of the House Divided*, 276.

54. Fehrenbacher, *Prelude to Greatness*, 108.

55. Mayer, *The Republican Party*, 56.

56. Speech at Peoria, Ill., October 16, 1854, *The Collected Works of Abraham Lincoln*, 2:268.

57. *Illinois State Register*, July 28, 1858; *Chicago Times*, October 3, 1858.

58. Randall, *Lincoln, the Liberal Statesman*, 26.

59. Strozier, *Lincoln's Quest for Union*, 156 (the text of this protest may be found in *The Collected Works of Abraham Lincoln*, 1:74–75); Jaffa, *Crisis of the House Divided*, 236–72; Speech in United States House of Representatives on Internal Improvement, June 20, 1848, *The Collected Works of Abraham Lincoln*, 1:484.

60. *Illinois State Journal*, July 16, 1858.

61. David Davis to Lincoln, August 3, 1858, Robert Todd Lincoln Collection of the Papers of Abraham Lincoln, reel 3, frames 1130–32, Library of Congress; Owen Lovejoy to Lincoln, August 4, 1858, ibid., frames 1150–52; D. G. Hay to Lincoln, September 1, 1858, ibid., frames 1348–50.

62. Speech at Augusta, Ill., August 25, 1858, *The Collected Works of Abra-*

ham Lincoln, 3:38; Speech at Macomb, Ill., August 25, 1858, ibid., 38; Speech at Greenville, Ill., September 13, 1858, ibid., 96; Angle, ed., *Created Equal?* 235.

63. Wells, *Stephen Douglas*, 99. See also Burns, *The Vineyard of Liberty*, 587.

64. William H. Herndon to John A. McClernand, December 8, 1859, John A. McClernand MSS, Illinois State Historical Library.

65. Stampp, *The Imperiled Union*, 125. See also Hofstadter, *The American Political Tradition*, 113. For examples of speeches in which Lincoln does develop this appeal, see Speech at Carlinville, Ill., August 31, 1858, *The Collected Works of Abraham Lincoln*, 3:79; Speech at Cincinnati, Ohio, September 17, 1859, *The Collected Works of Abraham Lincoln: Supplement*, 45.

66. Angle, ed., *Created Equal?* 304, 391.

67. Ibid., 128.

68. The quotation is from the "House Divided" speech (see ibid., 2).

69. Jaffa, *Crisis of the House Divided*, 393.

70. Smith, *The Death of Slavery*, 152.

71. Angle, ed., *Created Equal?* 207.

72. Ibid., 393.

73. Jaffa, *Crisis of the House Divided*, 287. Lincoln made this claim during the Galesburg debate (see Angle, ed., *Created Equal?* 309).

74. Speech at Peoria, Ill., October 16, 1854, *The Collected Works of Abraham Lincoln*, 2:255; Speech at Chicago, Ill., July 10, 1858, Angle, ed., *Created Equal?* 42; Speech at Edwardsville, Ill., September 11, 1858, *The Collected Works of Abraham Lincoln*, 3:92.

75. On these points, see Foner, *Free Soil, Free Labor, Free Men*, 262.

76. Speech at Peoria, Ill., October 16, 1854, *The Collected Works of Abraham Lincoln*, 2:256; Fredrickson, "A Man but not a Brother," 44; J. Gillespie to Herndon, January 31, 1866, Herndon, "Life of Lincoln," 2:23.

77. Angle, ed., *Created Equal?* 235.

78. Ibid., 343–44.

79. Ibid., 400–401; see also 343, where Douglas attacks this argument during the Quincy debate.

80. See Henry W. Johnstone, Jr., *Philosophy and Argument* (University Park: Pennsylvania State University Press, 1959), chap. 6.

81. Fredrickson, "A Man but Not a Brother," 49.

82. Benson, *Toward the Scientific Study of History*, 297.

83. Angle, ed., *Created Equal?* 107, 194–95.

84. Ibid., 209–15.

85. Ibid., 227–28.

86. Ibid., 264–65, 268.

87. Ibid., 299.

88. For Lincoln's argument, see ibid., 299–302; For Douglas's reply, see ibid., 316.

89. Ibid., 299–300, 315–16.

90. Ibid., 326–28, 340, 357.

91. Johnson, *Stephen A. Douglas*, 385.

92. Smith, *The Death of Slavery*, 9. See also Wells, *Stephen Douglas*, 110.

93. W. Barnett Pearce, Stephen W. Littlejohn, and Alison Alexander, "The New Christian Right and the Humanist Response: Reciprocated Diatribe," *Communication Quarterly* 35 (Spring 1987): 187.

94. Sigelschiffer, *The American Conscience*, 124.

95. Rawley, *Race and Politics*, 269.

96. This position is articulated in a speech, "Religious Belief and Public Morality: A Catholic Governor's Perspective," delivered by Cuomo to the Department of Theology at the University of Notre Dame, September 13, 1984. The text is available from the Office of the Governor of the State of New York. Interestingly, Cuomo refers—albeit obliquely—to the comparison with the slavery controversy, suggesting that the reluctance of Catholic bishops to advocate abolition was not necessarily a sign of moral weakness.

97. Angle, ed., *Created Equal?* 351.

Chapter Seven

1. *Illinois State Journal*, October 26, 1858.

2. Speech at Springfield, Ill., October 30, 1858, *The Collected Works of Abraham Lincoln*, 3:334.

3. *Illinois State Journal*, October 28, 1858. Perhaps because he understood popular sovereignty in this way, DeBow had pledged his support to Douglas. On October 23, 1858, he wrote the Little Giant, "In common with most of the States rights men of the South my sympathies are with you cordially in this struggle, whatever differences of opinion may exist between us on minor points" (J. D. B. DeBow to Douglas, October 23, 1858, Stephen A. Douglas MSS, box 19, folder 48, University of Chicago Library).

4. *Chicago Press and Tribune*, October 23, 1858.

5. George W. Jones to Sidney Breese, September 17, 1858, Jones to Breese, October 17, 1858, Sidney Breese MSS, Illinois State Historical Library.

6. J. Burdick to Douglas, July 25, 1858, Stephen A. Douglas MSS, box 19, folder 16, University of Chicago Library.

7. *Illinois State Journal*, October 14, 1858.

8. *Chicago Press and Tribune*, October 30, 1858. Another reference to the alleged mistreatment of Douglas's slaves appeared in the *Press and Tribune* on November 1, the day before the election.

9. *Chicago Press and Tribune*, October 30, 1858.

10. Daniel McCook to Thomas L. Harris, September 15, 1858, Charles H. Lanphier MSS, Illinois State Historical Library.

11. C. R. Parke to P. D. Vroom, October 26, 1858, C. R. Parke MSS, Illinois State Historical Library.

12. *Chicago Times*, October 27, 1858.

13. *Chicago Times*, November 2, 1858.

14. *Illinois State Register*, September 2, 1858.

15. Alex Sympson to John C. Bagby, October 15, 1858, William T. Ramsey to John C. Bagby, October 21, 1858, John C. Bagby MSS, Illinois State Historical

Library. (The letter from Ramsey bears both the 1858 and the 1856 debates, but was probably written in 1858.)

16. *Chicago Press and Tribune,* October 12, 22, 1858.

17. Angle, *Lincoln, 1854–1861,* 251; Speech at Meredosia, Ill., October 18, 1858, *The Collected Works of Abraham Lincoln,* 3:328; Lincoln to Norman B. Judd, October 20, 1858, ibid., 329–30.

18. *Chicago Times,* October 8, 28, 1858.

19. See the account of this speech in *The Collected Works of Abraham Lincoln,* 3:328–29.

20. Thomas H. Hollback to Douglas, June 8, 1858, Stephen A. Douglas MSS, box 18, folder 15, University of Chicago Library, Blanton Duncan to Douglas, August 18, 1858, Stephen A. Douglas MSS, box 19, folder 29, University of Chicago Library; Rietveld, "The Moral Issue of Slavery," 186.

21. Whan, "Stephen A. Douglas," 790.

22. *Illinois State Register,* September 25, 1858, October 14, 1858; *Chicago Times,* October 28, 1858; S. S. Marshall to Charles H. Lanphier, October 24, 1858, Charles H. Lanphier MSS, Illinois State Historical Library.

23. Rothschild, *Lincoln, Master of Men,* 109; Randall, *Lincoln the President,* 127; Johannsen, "The Lincoln-Douglas Campaign of 1858," 259.

24. For examples of this interpretation, see Nevins, *The Emergence of Lincoln,* 1:403; Johannsen, *Stephen A. Douglas,* 677; Milton, *The Eve of Conflict,* 354. It was also the judgment of contemporaries. For example, William Elliott of Indianapolis wrote Douglas, "We *now* feel confident that the Lecompton 'fraud' has received its death stroke, and that the true democratic doctrine of 'Popular Sovereignty' has received another unqualified sanction from the people" (November 5, 1858, Stephen A. Douglas MSS, box 20, folder 1, University of Chicago Library). Collins, however, maintains that Republican losses in 1858 were primarily the result of the crisis posed by the Panic of 1857 (see Bruce W. Collins, "The Lincoln-Douglas Contest of 1858 and Illinois' Electorate," *Journal of American Studies* 20 [Fall 1986]: 418–19 [which emphasizes the role of railroad issues], and "The Democrats' Electoral Fortunes," 328).

25. See Beveridge, *Abraham Lincoln,* 2:697n; King, *Lincoln's Manager, David Davis,* 126. Interestingly, each man carried the other's home county: Sangamon County went for Douglas and Cook County for Lincoln.

26. Breiseth, "Lincoln, Douglas, and Springfield," 118; Whan, "Stephen A. Douglas," 823.

27. G. W. Rives to Ozias M. Hatch, November 10, 1858, John Tillson to Ozias M. Hatch, November 15, 1858, Ozias M. Hatch MSS, Illinois State Historical Library; David Davis to Lincoln, November 7, 1858, Robert Todd Lincoln Collection of the Papers of Abraham Lincoln, reel 4, frames 1463–65, Library of Congress.

28. David Davis to Lincoln, June 14, November 7, 1858, David Davis MSS, Chicago Historical Society Library. Tillson also expressed surprise at the result, writing Hatch, "We are beaten not badly but what is equal to that in moral effect *unexpectedly* beaten" (John Tillson to Ozias M. Hatch, November 15, 1858, Ozias M. Hatch MSS, Illinois State Historical Library).

29. G. W. Rives to Ozias M. Hatch November 5, 1858, Ozias M. Hatch MSS, Illinois State Historical Library.

30. Norman B. Judd to Ozias M. Hatch, November 9, 1858, ibid.; W. H. Herndon to Lyman Trumbull, November 30, 1858, Lyman Trumbull MSS, Library of Congress.

31. L. H. Waters to Ozias M. Hatch, November 3, 1858, Ozias M. Hatch MSS, Illinois State Historical Library; David Davis to George Davis, November 7, 1858, David Davis MSS, Chicago Historical Society Library. Another operative wrote Hatch that there had been at least one hundred illegal votes cast in his county but admitted that, even without them, the result would have been the same: the election of a Douglas Democrat (Alex. B. Morean to Ozias M. Hatch, November 5, 1858, Ozias M. Hatch MSS, Illinois State Historical Library).

32. Rietveld, "The Moral Issue of Slavery," 205; John Tillson to Ozias M. Hatch, November 15, 1858, J. Grimshaw to Ozias M. Hatch, November 11, 1858, G. W. Rives to Ozias M. Hatch, November 10, 1858, Ben L. Wiley to Ozias M. Hatch, December 7, 1858, Ozias M. Hatch MSS, Illinois State Historical Library.

33. John Tillson to Ozias M. Hatch, November 15, 1858, Ozias M. Hatch MSS, Illinois State Historical Library.

34. Cole, *The Centennial History of Illinois,* 3:179; Thomas C. Sharpe to John C. Bagby, November 4, 1858, John C. Bagby MSS, Illinois State Historical Library.

35. This analysis relies heavily on Fehrenbacher, *Prelude to Greatness,* 118–20. Fehrenbacher notes further that, even had the Republicans' redistricting bill passed, their party would have held only fifty-three seats out of a new total of 105—the barest of majorities. See also Milton, *The Eve of Conflict,* 351.

36. Lincoln to Charles H. Ray, November 20, 1858, *The Collected Works of Abraham Lincoln,* 3:342. See also Lincoln to Henry Asbury, November 19, 1858, ibid., 339; Lincoln to Anson S. Miller, November 19, 1858, ibid., 340; Lincoln to B. Clarke Lundy, November 26, 1858, ibid., 342.

37. Lincoln to Anson G. Henry, November 19, 1858, ibid., 339; Lincoln to Norman B. Judd, November 15, 1858, ibid., 337; Lincoln to Alexander Sympson, December 12, 1858, ibid., 346.

38. Sheahan, *The Life of Stephen A. Douglas,* 433; Lyman Trumbull to John M. Palmer, December 19, 1858, John M. Palmer MSS, Illinois State Historical Library; *Chicago Times,* October 7, 1858.

39. Actually, Douglas retained substantial Southern support, whether because his positions were not yet clearly understood or because of the greater imperative of party unity (Johannsen, *Stephen A. Douglas,* 650–51).

40. The text of the Dorr letter is in Johannsen, ed., *The Letters of Stephen A. Douglas,* 446–47.

41. See David E. Meerse, "The Northern Democratic Party and the Congressional Elections of 1858," in *Beyond the Civil War Synthesis: Political Essays of the Civil War Era,* ed. Robert P. Swierenga (Westport, Conn.: Greenwood, 1975), 96–97; Johannsen, *Stephen A. Douglas,* 681.

42. Capers, *Stephen A. Douglas,* 190.

43. Ibid., 194–95.

44. Horace White to Lincoln, November 5, 1858, Robert Todd Lincoln Collection of the Papers of Abraham Lincoln, reel 4, frames 1457–58, Library of Congress.

45. Ward Hill Lamon, *Recollections of Abraham Lincoln, 1847–1865,* ed. Dorothy Lamon (Chicago: A. C. McClurg, 1895), 27.

46. Chu, "Horace White," 57; William H. Lambert, "Abraham Lincoln: Commander-in-Chief of the Army and Navy of the United States" (annual oration delivered before the Society of the Army of the Potomac, Pittsburgh, October 11, 1899, Henry E. Huntington Library).

47. Lincoln to Thomas J. Pickett, April 16, 1859, *The Collected Works of Abraham Lincoln,* 3:377; Lincoln to D. J. Powers, August 18, 1859, ibid., 397; Lincoln to Daniel Rohrer, August 19, 1859, ibid., 397.

48. Lincoln to Lyman Trumbull, February 3, 1859, ibid., 355; Lincoln to Norman B. Judd, November 15, 1858, *The Collected Works of Abraham Lincoln: Supplement,* 34; Lincoln to Norman B. Judd, December 9, 1859, *The Collected Works of Abraham Lincoln,* 3:505.

49. Don C. Sietz, *Lincoln the Politician* (New York: Coward-McCann, 1931), 144; Lincoln to William E. Frazer, November 1, 1859, *The Collected Works of Abraham Lincoln,* 3:491.

50. Lincoln to Lyman Trumbull, December 11, 1858, *The Collected Works of Abraham Lincoln,* 3:345; Lincoln to Salmon P. Chase, April 30, 1859, ibid., 378; Lincoln to Theodore Canisius, May 17, 1859, ibid., 380. Throughout this period, Lincoln often expressed similar sentiments. See, e.g., Lincoln to W. H. Wells, January 8, 1859, ibid., 349; Fragments: Notes for Speeches, ca. September 1859, ibid., 398. Not all Republican leaders were so wary. For example, Norman B. Judd thought that Douglas could become a Republican yet be forced to "take a back seat" within the party (Norman B. Judd to David Davis, December 26, 1858, David Davis MSS, Chicago Historical Society Library).

51. Johannsen, "Stephen A. Douglas, *Harper's Magazine,* and Popular Sovereignty," 613, 616.

52. Nevins, *The Emergence of Lincoln,* 2:48; Fehrenbacher, *The Dred Scott Case,* 515.

53. Wells, *Stephen Douglas,* 76.

54. On Lincoln's Ohio tour, see Speech at Columbus, Ohio, September 16, 1859, *The Collected Works of Abraham Lincoln,* 3:421; Notes for Speeches at Columbus and Cincinnati, September 16–17, 1859, ibid., 426–29; Sewell, *Ballots for Freedom,* 359; Nevins, *The Emergence of Lincoln,* 2:55.

55. W. H. Herndon to Ward Hill Lamon, March 6, 1870, Ward Hill Lamon MSS, MS LN 366, Henry E. Huntington Library.

56. The text of the speech is in *The Collected Works of Abraham Lincoln,* 3:522–50. An excellent analysis of this speech is in Michael C. Leff and G. P. Mohrmann, "Lincoln at Cooper Union: A Rhetorical Analysis of the Text," *Quarterly Journal of Speech* 60 (October 1974): 346–58.

57. Wright, *Lincoln and the Politics of Slavery,* 165.

58. Lincoln to Mary Todd Lincoln, March 4, 1860, *The Collected Works of Abraham Lincoln: Supplement,* 49; King, *Lincoln's Manager, David Davis,* 131.

59. Collins, *The Origins of America's Civil War*, 122.

60. W. H. Herndon to Lyman Trumbull, November 30, 1858, J. M. Palmer to Lyman Trumbull, December 9, 1858, Lyman Trumbull MSS, Library of Congress.

61. Capers, *Stephen A. Douglas*, 193.

62. On these details, see Johannsen, ed., *The Lincoln-Douglas Debates of 1858*, v. In late November 1858, Lincoln had written Charles H. Ray of the *Press and Tribune* requesting copies of the debates so that he might make a scrapbook (November 20, 1858, *The Collected Works of Abraham Lincoln*, 3:341). In March 1859, he suggested that each candidate's speeches be taken from his respective paper since "this would represent each of us, as reported by his own friends, and thus be mutual, and fair" (Lincoln to William A. Ross, March 26, 1859, ibid., 372–73). This concern for fairness was also evident in a letter that Lincoln wrote in December 1859, as the publication was being prepared: "Of course I wish the whole to be accurately done, but especially let there be no color of complaint, that a word, or letter in Douglas's speeches has been changed" (Lincoln to Samuel Galloway, December 19, 1859, *The Collected Works of Abraham Lincoln: Supplement*, 47).

63. Jay Monaghan, "The Lincoln-Douglas Debates," *Lincoln Herald* 45 (June 1943): 2.

64. Douglas to Follett & Foster Co., June 9, 1860, Johannsen, ed., *The Letters of Stephen A. Douglas*, 489.

65. Lambert, "Abraham Lincoln: Commander in Chief."

66. The figures are from Monaghan, "The Lincoln-Douglas Debates," 2. The centennial edition is Angle, ed., *Created Equal?*

67. This speech is in the *Illinois State Register*, October 9, 1860.

68. Holt, *The Political Crisis of the 1850s*, 243; Michael Davis, *The Image of Lincoln in the South* (Knoxville: University of Tennessee Press, 1971), 11.

69. Davis, *The Image of Lincoln in the South*, 19.

70. Nevins, *The Emergence of Lincoln*, 2:404.

71. Second Inaugural Address, March 4, 1865, *The Collected Works of Abraham Lincoln*, 8:332.

72. Elting Morison, "Election of 1860," in *The Coming to Power*, ed. Schlesinger, 143. See also Don E. Fehrenbacher, "Disunion and Reunion," in *The Reconstruction of American History*, ed. John Higham (New York: Harper & Row, 1962), 101.

73. Sewell, *Ballots for Freedom*, 297; Jaffa, *Crisis of the House Divided*, 299.

74. Horace White to Lyman Trumbull, December 8, 1858, Lyman Trumbull MSS, Library of Congress.

75. See Fehrenbacher, *The Dred Scott Case*, 526.

76. Randall, *Lincoln, the Liberal Statesman*, 19.

77. Bestor, "State Sovereignty and Slavery," 125n.

78. Wright, *Lincoln and the Politics of Slavery*, 197; Wells, *Stephen Douglas*, 78; Jaffa, *Crisis of the House Divided*, 403–4.

79. D. W. Brogan, *Abraham Lincoln* (London: Duckworth, 1974), 75.

80. Rietveld, "The Moral Issue of Slavery," 201.

81. Harris, *The History of Negro Servitude*, 221. For an early judgment in favor of Douglas, see Willis, *Stephen A. Douglas*, 287.

82. Milton, *The Eve of Conflict*, 315.

83. David R. Locke [Petroleum V. Nasby], quoted in Rice, ed., *Reminiscences of Abraham Lincoln*, 444–45.

84. Wells, *Stephen Douglas*, 83. For other examples of favorable assessments of Lincoln's performance, see Fehrenbacher, *Prelude to Greatness*, 152; Thomas, *Abraham Lincoln*, 192–93; Woldman, *Lawyer Lincoln*, 244; Roy P. Basler, "Abraham Lincoln's Rhetoric," *American Literature* 11 (May 1939): 167, 169.

85. Wells, *Stephen Douglas*, 108; Klein, *President James Buchanan*, 329.

86. Donald, *Liberty and Union*, 81.

87. See, e.g., ibid., 72. However, Randall and Donald noted that expansion of the institution might be possible *within* the South, where "there were vast areas of unexploited land . . . [so] there is no good reason to believe that self-strangulation was approaching" (J. G. Randall and David Donald, *The Civil War and Reconstruction*, 2d ed. [Boston: Heath, 1961], 75).

88. John F. Farnsworth, Speech in the House of Representatives, March 20, 1858, *Congressional Globe*, 35th Cong., 1st sess., 27, pt. 2:1205.

89. Robert Todd Lincoln to David Davis, November 19, 1866, David Davis MSS, Illinois State Historical Library; W. H. Herndon to Horace White, April 28, 1890, Horace White MSS, Illinois State Historical Library.

90. For these contrasts, see Allan Nevins, "Stephen A. Douglas," 385.

Chapter Eight

1. Indeed, according to Boritt, Lincoln gave new meaning to the Jacksonian idea of equality, extending it "to equality of opportunity to get ahead in life. This was his '*central idea*'" (*Lincoln and the Economics of the American Dream*, 158).

2. Angle, ed., *Created Equal?* 400.

3. On this method for refuting a philosophical argument, see Johnstone, *Philosophy and Argument*, esp. chap. 6.

4. This view contrasts with Heckman's belief that there were no basic disagreements. He writes, "Had the candidates been in more serious disagreement, their speeches would surely have been devoted more extensively to an elaboration of their positions on these points of difference, but instead, the addresses reveal an abundance of taunts, repetitions, charges, and counter charges" (*Lincoln vs. Douglas*, 128). The introduction of what Heckman regarded as "extraneous matter," though, was an attempt to continue the discussion in the face of *very* fundamental disagreements that could not be resolved.

5. On "essentially contested concepts," see John Kekes, "Essentially Contested Concepts: A Reconsideration," *Philosophy and Rhetoric* 10 (Spring 1977): 71–89.

6. See Forgie, *Patricide in the House Divided*.

7. See William E. Leuchtenburg, *In the Shadow of FDR: From Harry Truman to Ronald Reagan* (Ithaca, N.Y.: Cornell University Press, 1983), esp. chap. 7.

8. For an explanation of this concept, see Michael Calvin McGee, "The 'Ideograph': A Link between Rhetoric and Ideology," *Quarterly Journal of Speech* 66 (February 1980): 1–16.

9. Michael Walzer, "On the Role of Symbolism in Political Thought," *Political Science Quarterly* 82 (June 1967): 196.

10. Pearce, Littlejohn, and Alexander, "The New Christian Right," esp. 177, 187.

11. Charles Arthur Willard, *Argumentation and the Social Grounds of Knowledge* (University, Ala.: University of Alabama Press, 1983).

12. Wayne C. Booth, *Modern Dogma and the Rhetoric of Assent* (Notre Dame, Ind.: University of Notre Dame Press, 1974), 23.

13. Ibid., 23; Pearce, Littlejohn, and Alexander, "The New Christian Right," 177.

14. Frank, *Lincoln as a Lawyer,* 124.

15. Rawley, *Race and Politics,* 198; Cole, *The Centennial History of Illinois,* 3:172–73.

16. For a recent, excellent example of a rigorous formal analysis of the debates, see Erik A. Devereaux, "Processing Political Debate: A Methodology for Data Production with Special Application to the Lincoln-Douglas Debates of 1858" (B.A. honors thesis, Massachusetts Institute of Technology, 1985).

17. Marvin G. Bauer, "Persuasive Methods in the Lincoln-Douglas Debates," *Quarterly Journal of Speech* 13 (February 1927): 29.

18. MacIntyre, *After Virtue;* Walter R. Fisher, *Human Communication as Narration: Toward a Philosophy of Reason, Value, and Action* (Columbia: University of South Carolina Press, 1987).

19. This view of the public is heavily influenced by G. Thomas Goodnight, "The Personal, Technical, and Public Spheres of Argument: A Speculative Inquiry into the Art of Public Deliberation," *Journal of the American Forensic Association* 18 (Spring 1982): 214–27. See also Lloyd F. Bitzer, "Rhetoric and Public Knowledge," in *Rhetoric, Philosophy, and Literature: An Exploration,* ed. Don M. Burks (West Lafayette Ind.: Purdue University Press, 1978), 67–94.

20. Walter Lippmann, *Essays in the Public Philosophy* (Boston: Atlantic-Little, Brown, 1955).

21. Holt, *The Political Crisis of the 1850s,* 184.

22. Walzer, "On the Role of Symbolism," 196.

23. Heckman, *Lincoln vs. Douglas,* iv.

24. Angle, ed., *Created Equal?* 128.

25. For a thorough discussion of the concept of judgment and its relation both to rhetoric and to political choice, see Ronald Beiner, *Political Judgment* (Chicago: University of Chicago Press, 1983).

26. Angle, ed., *Created Equal?* 389.

27. Angle, *Stephen Arnold Douglas,* 18.

28. Milton, *The Eve of Conflict;* Craven, *The Coming of the Civil War.*

29. Angle, eds., *Created Equal?* 235–36.

30. Ibid., 117.

31. Ibid., 390.

32. Potter, *The Impending Crisis*, 332.

33. Johannsen, "The Lincoln-Douglas Campaign of 1858," 246.

34. Walzer, "On the Role of Symbolism," 194–95.

35. James Boyd White, *When Words Lose Their Meaning* (Chicago: University of Chicago Press, 1984), esp. 277. My debt to White is evident throughout this paragraph.

Bibliography

Primary Sources

Angle, Paul M., ed. *Created Equal? The Complete Lincoln-Douglas Debates of 1858.* Chicago: University of Chicago Press, 1958.

Bagby, John C. MSS. Illinois State Historical Library, Springfield.

Basler, Roy P., ed. *The Collected Works of Abraham Lincoln: Supplement, 1832–1865.* Westport, Conn.: Greenwood, 1974.

Basler, Roy P., ed., Marion Dolores Pratt and Lloyd A. Dunlap, asst. eds. *The Collected Works of Abraham Lincoln.* 9 vols. New Brunswick, N.J.: Rutgers University Press, 1953–55.

Breese, Sidney. MSS. Illinois State Historical Library, Springfield.

Browning, Orville H. MSS. Illinois State Historical Library, Springfield.

Congressional Globe. 46 vols. Washington, D.C., 1834–73.

Davis, David. MSS. Chicago Historical Society Library.

Davis, David. MSS. Illinois State Historical Library.

Dickey, Theophilus Lyle. MSS. Chicago Historical Society Library.

Douglas, Stephen A. MSS. University of Chicago Library.

Hatch, Ozias M. MSS. Chicago Historical Society Library.

Hatch, Ozias M. MSS. Illinois State Historical Library.

Herndon-Weik Collection of Lincolniana. Library of Congress, Washington, D.C.

Johannsen, Robert W., ed. *The Letters of Stephen A. Douglas.* Urbana: University of Illinois Press, 1961.

Lamon, Ward Hill. MSS. Henry E. Huntington Library, San Marino, Calif.

Lanphier, Charles H. MSS. Illinois State Historical Library, Springfield.

Lincoln, Abraham. MSS. Chicago Historical Society Library.

Lincoln, Robert Todd. Collection of the Papers of Abraham Lincoln. Library of Congress, Washington, D.C.

McClernand, John A. MSS. Illinois State Historical Library, Springfield.

Medill, Joseph. MSS. Chicago Historical Society Library.
Palmer, John M. MSS. Illinois State Historical Library, Springfield.
Parke, C. R. MSS. Illinois State Historical Library, Springfield.
Trumbull, Lyman. MSS. Illinois State Historical Library, Springfield.
Trumbull, Lyman. MSS. Library of Congress, Washington, D.C.
White, Horace. MSS. Illinois State Historical Library, Springfield.
Yates, Richard. MSS. Illinois State Historical Library, Springfield.

Books

Abzug, Robert H., and Stephen E. Maizlish, eds. *New Perspectives on Race and Slavery in America: Essays in Honor of Kenneth M. Stampp.* Lexington: University Press of Kentucky, 1986.
Allen, John W. *It Happened in Southern Illinois.* Carbondale: Southern Illinois University, Central Publications, 1959.
Anderson, Dwight G. *Abraham Lincoln: The Quest for Immortality.* New York: Knopf, 1982.
Angle, Paul M. *"Here I Have Lived": A History of Lincoln's Springfield, 1821–1865.* Springfield, Ill.: Abraham Lincoln Association, 1935.
———. *Lincoln, 1854–1861.* Springfield, Ill.: Abraham Lincoln Assn., 1933.
———, ed. *The Lincoln Reader.* New Brunswick, N.J.: Rutgers University Press, 1947.
Bailyn, Bernard. *The Ideological Origins of the American Revolution.* Cambridge, Mass.: Belknap Press, Harvard University Press, 1967.
Bailyn, Bernard, David Brion Davis, David Herbert Donald, John L. Thomas, Robert H. Wiebe, and Gordon S. Wood. *The Great Republic: A History of the American People.* Boston: Little, Brown, 1977.
Baker, Jean H. *Affairs of Party: The Political Culture of Northern Democrats in the Mid-Nineteenth Century.* Ithaca, N.Y.: Cornell University Press, 1983.
Baringer, William. *Lincoln's Rise to Power.* Boston: Little, Brown, 1937.
Beiner, Ronald. *Political Judgment.* Chicago: University of Chicago Press, 1983.
Benson, Lee. *Toward the Scientific Study of History.* Philadelphia: Lippincott, 1972.
Bernstein, Barton, ed. *Towards a New Past: Dissenting Essays in American History.* New York: Random House, 1967.
Berwanger, Eugene H. *The Frontier against Slavery: Western Anti-Negro Prejudice and the Slavery Extension Controversy.* Urbana: University of Illinois Press, 1967.
Beveridge, Albert J. *Abraham Lincoln, 1809–1858.* Boston: Houghton Mifflin, 1928.
Bitzer, Lloyd F. "Rhetoric and Public Knowledge." In *Rhetoric, Philosophy, and Literature: An Exploration,* edited by Don M. Burks. West Lafayette, Ind.: Purdue University Press, 1978.
Blegen, Theodore C. *Lincoln's Imagery: A Study in Word Power.* LaCrosse, Wis.: Emerson G. Wulling, Sumac Press, 1954.
Bode, Carl. *The Anatomy of American Popular Culture, 1840–1861.* Berkeley: University of California Press, 1959.

Booth, Wayne C. *Modern Dogma and the Rhetoric of Assent*. Notre Dame, Ind.: University of Notre Dame Press, 1974.

Boritt, G. S. *Lincoln and the Economics of the American Dream*. Memphis: Memphis State University Press, 1978.

Brigance, William Norwood, ed. *A History and Criticism of American Public Address*. 1943. Reprint. New York: Russell & Russell, 1960.

Brock, William R. *Parties and Political Conscience: American Dilemmas, 1840–1850*. Millwood, N.Y.: KTO, 1979.

Brogan, D. W. *Abraham Lincoln*. London: Duckworth, 1974.

Burns, James MacGregor. *The Vineyard of Liberty*. New York: Knopf, 1982.

Capers, Gerald M. *Stephen A. Douglas: Defender of the Union*. Boston: Little, Brown, 1959.

Carpenter, Jesse T. *The South as a Conscious Minority, 1789–1861: A Study in Political Thought*. New York: New York University Press, 1930.

Charnwood, Lord. *Abraham Lincoln*. New York: Henry Holt, 1916.

Clark, E. Culpepper. "Argument in Historical Analysis." In *Advances in Argumentation Theory and Research*, edited by J. Robert Cox and Charles A. Willard. Carbondale: Southern Illinois University Press, 1982.

Cole, Arthur Charles. *The Era of the Civil War, 1848–1870*. Vol. 3 of *The Centennial History of Illinois*. Springfield: Illinois Centennial Commission, 1919.

Coleman, Charles H. *Abraham Lincoln and Coles County, Illinois*. New Brunswick, N.J.: Scarecrow, 1955.

Collins, Bruce. *The Origins of America's Civil War*. New York: Holmes & Meier, 1981.

Combs, James E., and Michael W. Mansfield. *Drama in Life: The Uses of Communication in Society*. New York: Arlington, 1976.

Cooper, William J., Jr. *The South and the Politics of Slavery, 1828–1856*. Baton Rouge: Louisiana State University Press, 1978.

Cox, LaWanda. *Lincoln and Black Freedom: A Study in Presidential Leadership*. Columbia, S.C.: University of South Carolina Press, 1981.

Craven, Avery. *The Coming of the Civil War*. 1942. Reprint. Chicago: University of Chicago Press, 1966.

Crissey, Elwell. *Lincoln's Lost Speech*. New York: Hawthorn, 1967.

Current, Richard N. *The Lincoln Nobody Knows*. New York: McGraw-Hill, 1958.

————. *Speaking of Abraham Lincoln: The Man and His Meaning for Our Times*. Urbana: University of Illinois Press, 1983.

Davidson, Alexander, and Bernard Stuve. *A Complete History of Illinois from 1673 to 1873; Embracing the Physical Features of the Country; Its Early Explorations; Aboriginal Inhabitants; French and British Occupation; Conquest by Virginia; Territorial Condition and the Subsequent Civil, Military, and Political Events of the State*. Springfield: Illinois Journal Co., 1876.

Davis, Cullom, Charles B. Strozier, Rebecca Monroe Veach, and Geoffrey C. Ward, eds. *The Public and the Private Lincoln: Contemporary Perspectives*. Carbondale: Southern Illinois University Press, 1979.

Davis, David Brion, ed. *The Fear of Conspiracy: Images of Un-American Sub-version from the Revolution to the Present.* Ithaca, N.Y.: Cornell University Press, 1971.

———. *The Slave Power Conspiracy and the Paranoid Style.* Baton Rouge: Louisiana State University Press, 1969.

Davis, Michael. *The Image of Lincoln in the South.* Knoxville: University of Tennessee Press, 1971.

Dennis, Frank L. *The Lincoln-Douglas Debates.* New York: Mason & Lipscomb, 1974.

Dodge, Daniel Kilham. "Abraham Lincoln: The Evolution of His Literary Style," *University of Illinois Studies* 1 (May 1900): 1–58.

Donald, David. *Charles Sumner and the Coming of the Civil War.* New York: Knopf, 1960.

———. *Liberty and Union.* Boston: Little, Brown, 1978.

———. *Lincoln Reconsidered: Essays on the Civil War Era.* 2d ed. New York: Vintage, 1961.

Duberman, Martin, ed. *The Antislavery Vanguard: New Essays on the Abolitionists.* Princeton, N.J.: Princeton University Press, 1965.

Eaton, Clement. *Henry Clay and the Art of American Politics.* Boston: Little, Brown, 1957.

Fehrenbacher, Don E. *The Dred Scott Case: Its Significance in American Law and Politics.* New York: Oxford University Press, 1978.

———. *Prelude to Greatness: Lincoln in the 1850's.* Stanford: Stanford University Press, 1982.

———. *The South and Three Sectional Crises.* Baton Rouge: Louisiana State University Press, 1980.

Finkelman, Paul. *An Imperfect Union: Slavery, Federalism, and Comity.* Chapel Hill: University of North Carolina Press, 1981.

Fisher, Walter R. *Human Communication as Narration: Toward a Philosophy of Reason, Value, and Action.* Columbia, S.C.: University of South Carolina Press, 1987.

Foner, Eric. *Free Soil, Free Labor, Free Men: The Ideology of the Republican Party before the Civil War.* New York: Oxford University Press, 1970.

———. *Politics and Ideology in the Age of the Civil War.* New York: Oxford University Press, 1980.

Forgie, George B. *Patricide in the House Divided: A Psychological Interpretation of Lincoln and His Age.* New York: Norton, 1979.

Frank, John P. *Lincoln as a Lawyer.* Urbana: University of Illinois Press, 1961.

Franklin, John Hope. *From Slavery to Freedom: A History of Negro Americans.* 3d ed. New York: Random House, 1967.

Fredrickson, George M. *The Black Image in the White Mind: The Debate on Afro-American Character and Destiny, 1817–1914.* New York: Harper & Row, 1971.

———, ed. *Manifest Destiny.* Indianapolis: Bobbs-Merrill, 1968.

———, ed. *A Nation Divided: Problems and Issues of the Civil War and Reconstruction.* Minneapolis: Burgess, 1975.

Graebner, Norman A., ed. *The Enduring Lincoln.* Urbana: University of Illinois Press, 1959.

Hamilton, Holman. *Prologue to Conflict: The Crisis and Compromise of 1850.* Lexington: University of Kentucky Press, 1964.

Handlin, Oscar, and Lilian Handlin. *Abraham Lincoln and the Union.* Boston: Little, Brown, 1980.

Harris, N. Dwight. *The History of Negro Servitude in Illinois and of the Slavery Agitation in That State, 1719–1864.* Chicago: A. C. McClurg, 1904.

Heckman, Richard Allen. *Lincoln vs. Douglas: The Great Debates Campaign.* Washington, D.C.: Public Affairs Press, 1967.

Herndon, William H., and Jesse W. Weik. *Herndon's Lie of Lincoln.* New York: Albert & Charles Boni, 1936.

Higham, John, ed. *The Reconstruction of American History.* New York: Harper & Row, 1962.

Hofstadter, Richard. *The American Political Tradition and the Men Who Made It.* 25th anniversary ed. New York: Knopf, 1973.

Holt, Michael F. *The Political Crisis of the 1850s.* New York: Wiley, 1978.

Howe, Daniel Walker. *The Political Culture of the American Whigs.* Chicago: University of Chicago Press, 1979.

Hyman, Harold M. *A More Perfect Union: The Impact of the Civil War and Reconstruction on the Constitution.* New York: Knopf, 1973.

Jaffa, Harry V. *Crisis of the House Divided: An Interpretation of the Issues in the Lincoln-Douglas Debates.* 1959. Reprint. Chicago: University of Chicago Press, 1982.

———. *Equality and Liberty: Theory and Practice in American Politics.* New York: Oxford University Press, 1965.

Johannsen, Robert W. *Stephen A. Douglas.* New York: Oxford University Press, 1973.

———, ed. *The Lincoln-Douglas Debates of 1858.* New York: Oxford University Press, 1965.

———, ed. *The Union in Crisis, 1850–1877.* New York: Free Press, 1965.

Johnson, Allen. *Stephen A. Douglas: A Study in American Politics.* New York: Macmillan, 1908.

Johnstone, Henry W., Jr. *Philosophy and Argument.* University Park: Pennsylvania State University Press, 1959.

Jones, Edgar DeWitt. *The Influence of Henry Clay upon Abraham Lincoln.* Lexington, Ky.: Henry Clay Memorial Foundation, 1952.

Jordan, Winthrop D. *White over Black: American Attitudes toward the Negro, 1550–1812.* Chapel Hill: University of North Carolina Press, 1968.

King, Willard L. *Lincoln's Manager, David Davis.* Cambridge, Mass.: Harvard University Press, 1960.

Klein, Philip Shriver. *President James Buchanan: A Biography.* University Park: Pennsylvania State University Press, 1962.

Kraditor, Aileen S. *Means and Ends in American Abolitionism: Garrison and His Critics on Strategy and Tactics, 1834–1850.* New York: Random House, 1969.

Lamon, Ward Hill. *Recollections of Abraham Lincoln, 1847–1865.* Edited by Dorothy Lamon. Chicago: A. C. McClurg, 1895.

Leuchtenburg, William E. *In the Shadow of FDR: From Harry Truman to Ronald Reagan.* Ithaca, N.Y.: Cornell University Press, 1983.

Lincoln-Douglas Society, Freeport, Ill. *Freeport's Lincoln.* Freeport, Ill.: W. T. Rawleigh, 1930.

Lippmann, Walter. *Essays in the Public Philosophy.* Boston: Atlantic–Little, Brown, 1955.

Litwack, Leon F. *North of Slavery: The Negro in the Free States, 1790–1860.* Chicago: University of Chicago Press, 1961.

Luthin, Reinhard H. *The Real Abraham Lincoln.* Englewood Cliffs, N.J.: Prentice-Hall, 1960.

MacIntyre, Alasdair. *After Virtue: A Study in Moral Theory.* 2d ed. Notre Dame, Ind.: University of Notre Dame Press, 1984.

Maizlish, Stephen E., and John J. Kushma. *Essays on American Antebellum Politics, 1840–1860.* College Station: Texas A&M University Press, 1982.

May, Ernest R. *"Lessons" of the Past: The Use and Misuse of History in American Foreign Policy.* New York: Oxford University Press, 1973.

Mayer, George H. *The Republican Party, 1854–1964.* New York: Oxford University Press, 1964.

Merk, Frederick. *Manifest Destiny and Mission in American History.* New York: Random House, 1966.

Milton, George Fort. *The Eve of Conflict: Stephen A. Douglas and the Needless War.* Boston: Houghton Mifflin, 1934.

Mitchell, W. J. T., ed. *On Narrative.* Chicago: University of Chicago Press, 1981.

Moos, Malcolm. *The Republicans: A History of Their Party.* New York: Random House, 1956.

Morison, Samuel Eliot, Henry Steele Commager, and William E. Leuchtenburg. *The Growth of the American Republic.* 7th ed. New York: Oxford University Press, 1980.

Nagel, Paul C. *One Nation Indivisible: The Union in American Thought, 1776–1861.* New York: Oxford University Press, 1964.

Neely, Mark E., Jr. *The Abraham Lincoln Encyclopedia.* New York: McGraw-Hill, 1982.

Neustadt, Richard E., and Ernest R. May. *Thinking in Time: The Uses of History for Decision Makers.* New York: Free Press, 1986.

Nevins, Allan. *The Emergence of Lincoln.* Vol. 1, *Douglas, Buchanan, and Party Chaos, 1857–1859.* Vol. 2, *Prologue to Civil War, 1859–1861.* New York: Scribner's, 1950.

———. *Ordeal of the Union.* Vol. 1, *Fruits of Manifest Destiny, 1847–1852.* Vol. 2, *A House Dividing, 1852–1857.* New York: Scribner's, 1947.

Nevins, Allan, and Irving Stone, eds. *Lincoln: A Contemporary Portrait.* Garden City, N.Y.: Doubleday, 1962.

Nichols, Roy Franklin. *The Disruption of American Democracy.* New York: Macmillan, 1948.

————. *The Stakes of Power, 1845–1877.* New York: Hill & Wang, 1961.

Nye, Russel B. *Fettered Freedom: Civil Liberties and the Slavery Controversy, 1830–1860.* East Lansing: Michigan State University Press, 1963.

Oates, Stephen B. *Abraham Lincoln: The Man behind the Myths.* New York: Harper & Row, 1984.

————. *With Malice toward None: The Life of Abraham Lincoln.* New York: Harper & Row, 1977.

Parrington, Vernon L. *Main Currents in American Thought.* New York: Harcourt, Brace, & World, 1927.

Pease, William H., and Jane H. Pease, eds. *The Antislavery Argument.* Indianapolis: Bobbs-Merrill, 1965.

Perelman, Chaim, and L. Olbrechts-Tyteca. *The New Rhetoric.* Translated by John Wilkinson and Purcell Weaver. Notre Dame, Ind.: University of Notre Dame Press, 1969.

Potter, David M. *The Impending Crisis, 1848–1861.* New York: Harper & Row, 1976.

Quaife, Milo Milton. *The Doctrine of Non-Intervention with Slavery in the Territories.* Chicago: Mac C. Chamberlin, 1910.

Randall, James G. *Lincoln and the South.* Baton Rouge: Louisiana State University Press, 1946.

————. *Lincoln, the Liberal Statesman.* New York: Dodd, Mead, 1947.

————. *Lincoln the President: Springfield to Gettysburg.* New York: Dodd, Mead, 1945.

Randall, James G., and David Donald. *The Civil War and Reconstruction.* 2d ed. Boston: Heath, 1961.

Rawley, James A. *Race and Politics: "Bleeding Kansas" and the Coming of the Civil War.* Philadelphia: Lippincott, 1969.

Rice, Allen Thorndike, ed. *Reminiscences of Abraham Lincoln by Distringuished Men of His Time.* New York: North American Review, 1888.

Rothschild, Alonzo. *Lincoln, Master of Men: A Study in Character.* Boston: Houghton Mifflin, 1906.

Schlesinger, Arthur M., Jr., ed. *The Coming to Power: Critical Presidential Elections in American History.* New York: Chelsea, 1971.

————, ed. *History of U.S. Political Parties.* New York: Chelsea, 1973.

Seitz, Don C. *Lincoln the Politician.* New York: Coward-McCann, 1931.

Sewell, Richard H. *Ballots for Freedom: Antislavery Politics in the United States, 1837–1860.* New York: Oxford University Press, 1976.

Sheahan, James W. *The Life of Stephen A. Douglas.* New York: Harper & Bros., 1860.

Sigelschiffer, Saul. *The American Conscience: The Drama of the Lincoln-Douglas Debates.* New York: Horizon, 1973.

Simms, Henry H. *A Decade of Sectional Controversy, 1851–1861.* 1942. Reprint. Westport, Conn.: Greenwood, 1978.

Simon, Paul. *Lincoln's Preparation for Greatness: The Illinois Legislative Years.* Norman: University of Oklahoma Press, 1965.

Smith, Elbert B. *The Death of Slavery: The United States, 1837–1865.* Chicago: University of Chicago Press, 1967.

Smith, George W. *History of Illinois and Her People.* Chicago and New York: American Historical Society, 1927.

Stampp, Kenneth M. *The Imperiled Union: Essays on the Background of the Civil War.* New York: Oxford University Press, 1980.

Strozier, Charles B. *Lincoln's Quest for Union: Public and Private Meanings.* New York: Basic, 1982.

Swierenga, Robert P., ed. *Beyond the Civil War Synthesis: Political Essays of the Civil War Era.* Westport, Conn.: Greenwood, 1975.

Tarbell, Ida M. *The Life of Abraham Lincoln.* New York: Doubleday, Page & Co., 1909.

Thomas, Benjamin P. *Abraham Lincoln: A Biography.* New York: Knopf, 1952.

Thurow, Glen E. *Abraham Lincoln and American Political Religion.* Albany: State University of New York Press, 1976.

Weaver, Richard M. *The Ethics of Rhetoric.* Chicago: Henry Regnery, 1953.

Wells, Damon. *Stephen Douglas: The Last Years, 1857–1861.* Austin: University of Texas Press, 1971.

Welter, Rush. *The Mind of America, 1820–1860.* New York: Columbia University Press, 1975.

White, Horace. *The Life of Lyman Trumbull.* Boston: Houghton Mifflin, 1913.

White, James Boyd. *When Words Lose Their Meaning.* Chicago: University of Chicago Press, 1984.

Willard, Charles Arthur. *Argumentation and the Social Grounds of Knowledge.* University, Ala.: University of Alabama Press, 1983.

Willis, Henry Parker. *Stephen A. Douglas.* Philadelphia: George W. Jacobs, 1910.

Wilson, Edmund. *Patriotic Gore: Studies in the Literature of the American Civil War.* New York: Oxford University Press, 1962.

Wilson, Major L. *Space, Time, and Freedom: The Quest for Nationality and the Irrepressible Conflict, 1815–1861.* Westport, Conn.: Greenwood, 1974.

Woldman, Albert A. *Lawyer Lincoln.* Boston: Houghton Mifflin, 1936.

Woodward, C. Vann. *American Counterpoint: Slavery and Racism in the North-South Dialogue.* Boston: Little, Brown, 1971.

Wright, John S. *Lincoln and the Politics of Slavery.* Reno: University of Nevada Press, 1970.

Articles

Basler, Roy P. "Abraham Lincoln's Rhetoric," *American Literature* 11 (May 1939): 167–82.

Bauer, Marvin G. "Persuasive Methods in the Lincoln-Douglas Debates," *Quarterly Journal of Speech* 13 (February 1927): 29–39.

Berry, Mildred Freburg. "Lincoln—the Speaker," *Quarterly Journal of Speech* 17 (February 1931): 25–40.

Bestor, Arthur. "The American Civil War as a Constitutional Crisis," *American Historical Review* 69 (January 1964): 327–52.

———. "State Sovereignty and Slavery: A Reinterpretation of Proslavery Constitutional Doctrine, 1846–1860," *Journal of the Illinois State Historical Society* 54 (Summer 1961): 117–80.

Beveridge, John W. "Lincoln's Views on Slavery and Blacks as Expressed in the Debates with Stephen A. Douglas," *Lincoln Herald* 83 (Winter 1981): 791–800.

Bradford, M. E. "Dividing the House: The Gnosticism of Lincoln's Political Rhetoric," *Modern Age* 23 (Winter 1979): 10–24.

Chu, James C. Y. "Horace White: His Association with Abraham Lincoln, 1854–1860," *Journalism Quarterly* 49 (Spring 1972): 51–60.

Collins, Bruce W. "The Democrats' Electoral Fortunes during the Lecompton Crisis," *Civil War History* 24 (December 1978): 314–31.

———. "The Lincoln-Douglas Contest of 1858 and Illinois Electorate," *Journal of American Studies* 20 (1986): 391–420.

Cox, J. Robert. "The Die Is Cast: Topical and Ontological Dimensions of the *Locus* of the Irreparable," *Quarterly Journal of Speech* 68 (August 1982): 227–39.

Craven, Avery. "The 1840's and the Democratic Process," *Journal of Southern History* 16 (May 1950): 161–76.

Current, Richard N. "Lincoln and Daniel Webster," *Journal of the Illinois State Historical Society* 48 (Autumn 1955): 307–21.

Davis, David Brion. "Some Ideological Functions of Prejudice in Ante-Bellum America," *American Quarterly* 15 (Summer 1963): 115–25.

Doctorow, E. L. "A Citizen Reads the Constitution," *Nation*, February 21, 1987, 208–17.

Fehrenbacher, Don E. "Lincoln, Douglas, and the 'Freeport Question,'" *American Historical Review* 66 (April 1961): 599–617.

———. "The Nomination of Lincoln in 1858," *Abraham Lincoln Quarterly* 6 (March 1950): 24–36.

———. "Only His Stepchildren: Lincoln and the Negro," *Civil War History* 20 (December 1974): 293–310.

———. "The Origins and Purpose of Lincoln's 'House Divided' Speech," *Mississippi Valley Historical Review* 46 (March 1960): 615–43.

Finkelman, Paul. "Slavery and the Northwest Ordinance: A Study in Ambiguity," *Journal of the Early Republic* 6 (Winter 1986): 343–70.

Foner, Eric. "The Wilmot Proviso Revisited," *Journal of American History* 56 (September 1969): 262–79.

Fredrickson, George M. "A Man but Not a Brother: Abraham Lincoln and Racial Equality," *Journal of Southern History* 41 (February 1975): 39–58.

Gienapp, William E. "The Crime against Sumner: The Caning of Charles Sumner and the Rise of the Republican Party," *Civil War History* 25 (September 1979): 218–45.

Glassberg, David. "History and the Public: Legacies of the Progressive Era," *Journal of American History* 73 (March 1987): 957–80.

Goodnight, G. Thomas. "The Personal, Technical, and Public Spheres of Argument: A Speculative Inquiry into the Art of Public Deliberation," *Journal of the American Forensic Association* 18 (Spring 1982): 214–27.

Goodnight, G. Thomas, and John Poulakos. "Conspiracy Rhetoric: From Pragmatism to Fantasy in Public Discourse," *Western Journal of Speech Communication* 45 (Fall 1981): 299–316.

Heckman, Richard Allen. "The Lincoln-Douglas Debates: A Case Study in 'Stump Speaking,'" *Civil War History* 12 (March 1966): 54–66.

Hodder, Frank Heywood. "The Railroad Background of the Kansas-Nebraska Act," *Mississippi Valley Historical Review* 12 (June 1925): 3–22.

———. "Some Phases of the Dred Scott Case," *Mississippi Valley Historical Review* 16 (June 1929): 3–22.

———. "Some Aspects of the English Bill for the Admission of Kansas." In *Annual Report of the American Historical Association for the Year 1906*, vol. 1. Washington, D.C.: U.S. Government Printing Office, 1908.

Holt, Michael F. "The Politics of Impatience: The Origins of Know Nothingism," *Journal of American History* 60 (September 1973): 309–31.

Horner, Harlan Hoyt. "The Substance of the Lincoln-Douglas Debates: Part 1," *Lincoln Herald* 63 (Summer 1961): 89–98.

———. "The Substance of the Lincoln-Douglas Debates: Part 2," *Lincoln Herald* 63 (Fall 1961): 139–49.

Jaffa, Harry V. "'Value Consensus' in Democracy: The Issue in the Lincoln-Douglas Debates," *American Political Science Review* 52 (September 1958): 745–53.

Johannsen, Robert W. "The Lincoln-Douglas Campaign of 1858: Background and Perspective," *Journal of the Illinois State Historical Society* 73 (Winter 1980): 242–62.

———. "Stephen A. Douglas and the South," *Journal of Southern History* 33 (February 1967): 26–50.

———. "Stephen A. Douglas, *Harper's Magazine*, and Popular Sovereignty," *Mississippi Valley Historical Review* 45 (March 1959): 606–31.

Kekes, John. "Essentially Contested Concepts: A Reconsideration," *Philosophy and Rhetoric* 10 (Spring 1977): 71–89.

Krug, Mark M. "Lyman Trumbull and the Real Issues in the Lincoln-Douglas Debate," *Journal of the Illinois State Historical Society* 57 (Winter 1964): 380–96.

Leff, Michael C., and G. P. Mohrmann. "Lincoln at Cooper Union: A Rhetorical Analysis of the Text," *Quarterly Journal of Speech* 60 (October 1974): 346–58.

McGee, Michael Calvin. "The 'Ideograph': A Link between Rhetoric and Ideology," *Quarterly Journal of Speech* 66 (February 1980): 1–16.

Milton, George Fort. "Douglas' Place in American History," *Journal of the Illinois State Historical Society* 26 (January 1934): 323–48.

Monaghan, Jay. "The Lincoln-Douglas Debates," *Lincoln Herald* 45 (June 1943): 2–11.

Nevins, Allan. "Stephen A. Douglas: His Weaknesses and His Greatness," *Journal of the Illinois State Historical Society* 42 (December 1949): 385–410.

Nye, Russel B. "The Slave Power Conspiracy: 1830–1860," *Science and Society* 10 (Summer 1946): 262–74.

Pearce, W. Barnett, Stephen W. Littlejohn, and Alison Alexander. "The New Christian Right and the Humanist Response: Reciprocated Diatribe," *Communication Quarterly* 35 (Spring 1987): 171–92.

Ramsdell, Charles W. "The Natural Limits of Slavery Expansion," *Mississippi Valley Historical Review* 16 (September 1929): 151–71.

Russel, Robert R. "Constitutional Doctrines with Regard to Slavery in Territories," *Journal of Southern History* 32 (November 1966): 466–86.

———. "What Was the Compromise of 1850?" *Journal of Southern History* 22 (August 1956): 292–309.

Satz, Ronald N. "The African Slave Trade and Lincoln's Campaign of 1858," *Journal of the Illinois State Historical Society* 65 (Autumn 1972): 269–79.

Simon, John Y. "Union County in 1858 and the Lincoln-Douglas Debates," *Journal of the Illinois State Historical Society* 62 (Autumn 1969): 267–92.

Walzer, Michael. "On the Role of Symbolism in Political Thought," *Political Science Quarterly* 82 (June 1967): 191–204.

Wiley, Earl W. "Lincoln the Speaker, 1830–1837," *Quarterly Journal of Speech* 21 (June 1935): 305–22.

Wilson, Major L. "Of Time and the Union: Kansas-Nebraska and the Appeal from Prescription to Principle," *Midwest Quarterly* 10 (Autumn 1968): 73–87.

Wolff, Gerald W. "Party and Section: The Senate and the Kansas-Nebraska Bill," *Civil War History* 18 (December 1972): 293–311.

Other Sources

Angle, Paul M. "Stephen Arnold Douglas: Chicagoan and Patriot." Address delivered at the Chicago Historical Society, June 2, 1961.

Chicago Daily Times, June–November 1858.

Chicago Press and Tribune, June–November 1858.

Creps, Earl G., III. "The Conspiracy Argument as Rhetorical Genre." Ph.D. dissertation, Northwestern University, 1980.

Heckman, Richard Allen. "The Douglas-Lincoln Campaign of 1858." Ph.D. dissertation, Indiana University, 1960.

Herndon, William Henry. "Analysis of the Character & Mind of Abraham Lincoln." MS LN 1947. Henry E. Huntington Library, San Marino, Calif.

———. "Facts Illustrative of Mr. Lincoln's Patriotism and Statesmanship." January 23, 1866. MS LN 1949 Henry E. Huntington Library, San Marino, Calif.

———. "Life of Lincoln." MS LN 2408. Henry E. Huntington Library, San Marino, Calif.

Illinois State Journal, June–November 1858.

Illinois State Register, June–November 1858.

Lambert, William H. "Abraham Lincoln: Commander-in-Chief of the Army and Navy of the United States." Annual oration delivered before the Society of the

Army of the Potomac, October 11, 1899. MS Rare Book 35755. Henry E. Huntington Library, San Marino, Calif.

Leff, Michael C. "Rhetorical Timing in Lincoln's 'House Divided' Speech." The Van Zelst Lecture in Communication delivered at Northwestern University, May 19, 1983.

Rietveld, Ronald Deane. "The Moral Issue of Slavery in American Politics, 1854–1860." Ph.D. dissertation, University of Illinois, 1967.

Index